SSSP

Springer
Series in
Social
Psychology

SSSP

Hans-Werner Bierhoff

Person Perception and Attribution

With Contributions by R. Klein

90-1967

Springer-Verlag Berlin Heidelberg New York
London Paris Tokyo Hong Kong

Hans-Werner Bierhoff
Department of Psychology
University of Marburg
Gutenbergstr. 18
3550 Marburg/Lahn, FRG

With 33 Figures

ISBN 3-540-50356-0 Springer-Verlag Berlin Heidelberg New York
ISBN 0-387-50356-0 Springer-Verlag New York Berlin Heidelberg

Library of Congress Cataloging-in-Publication Data. Bierhoff, Hans Werner, 1948– Person perception and attribution / H.-W. Bierhoff. p. cm. – (Springer series in social psychology) Bibliography: p. Includes indexes. ISBN 0-387-50356-0 (U.S.: alk. paper) 1. Social perception. 2. Attribution (Social psychology) 3. Impression formation (Psychology) 4. Stereotype (Psychology) I. Title. II. Series. HM132.B54 1989 302′.12–dc20 89-11389

Typeset by K+V Fotosatz GmbH, 6124 Beerfelden, FRG.
Printed and bound by Edwards Brothers, Ann Arbor, Michigan.
2126/3130-543210 – Printed on acid-free paper

Preface

Person perception is of great importance in everyday life and human science. Judgment of other people's characteristics and intentions is important for successfully planning actions within a social environment. Questions about the formation of impressions and causal attributions are central to social psychology and the study of diagnostic judgment formation. The field of person perception deals with questions of how impression formation proceeds, what characteristics and intentions are attributed to other people, and how preformed schemata and stereotypes influence people's first impressions.

Research on person perception developed rapidly after the Second World War. In the 1950s the precision and accuracy of person perception received special interest, but the problems concerning whether an individual's assessment of another personality is exact or not could not be solved. Another approach, which began in the 1940s and was derived from the Gestalt psychological tradition, dealt with impression formation based on selected social cues. This approach, which proved to be very useful, had considerable influence on both the research methods and the theoretical orientation of the research work. On the one hand, by using a combination of individual cues (like physical characteristics) researchers tried to ascertain how an impression of a person was formed. On the other hand, the Gestalt psychological orientation led to an interest in the process of person perception, which in the last 10 years has concentrated on questions concerning information reception and processing.

In the 1960s a new field, attribution research, began to apply itself to the perceived causality of behavior. The distinction between internal and external causes led to a series of informative studies based on an average person's "naive" theory about social situations and people who act in these situations. Later analyses led to more refined multidimensional models of attributions.

This preface was written during a transatlantic flight. Waiting for the jet to land, I had the opportunity to devote some time to the perception of people. For example, I made comparisons related to possible sex differences. The man who was sitting in front of me read a physics journal while the woman on my left read a fashion magazine. These types of observations feed gender-related stereotypes, which are widespread in many societies. Is there a kernel of truth in gender stereotypes? If so, how can it be accounted for? These are some of the questions which are addressed in Chapters 3 and 5.

In this book four issues are given special emphasis: first impression formation, expectancy confirmation versus individuating processes, stereotypes, and attributions. The work on impression formation by Asch (1946) is taken as a starting point for a discussion of social cognition research. In this opening chapter − as in the whole text − a balance is sought between recent research and theory and basic studies and approaches which have contributed to the continuity of research on the perception of people over several decades.

Person perception as an inference process is discussed in Chapter 2. Issues pertaining to "going beyond the information given" were already emphasized by Bruner (1957a, b). We discuss selection of relevant data, strategies for sampling and classifying the data gathered, and subjective estimates of relationships between two variables. In addition, two inference models of social perception, one based on the diagnostic ratio derived from the Bayes theorem and the other on the anchor heuristic, are described in some detail.

Stereotypes are understood as cognitive schemata or prototypes. Gender stereotypes, ethnic stereotypes, and stereotypes which refer to physical appearance are discussed. The importance of the social structure as a determinant of the content of stereotypes is mentioned. Furthermore, motivational influences on derogation of the outgroup are discussed with reference to Sherif's realistic conflict theory and Tajfel's social identity theory.

Attributional phenomena are considered from a broad perspective. The pioneering ideas of Heider, Bem, Jones and Davis, and Kelley are discussed in some detail. The clarification of the covariation principle by the logical model of Jaspars and Hewstone and the analysis of commonsense attributions by Hansen are presented as examples of how knowledge and research in this area have advanced. Finally, the issue of attributions of responsibility is discussed in some detail. Responsibility attributions occupy an intermediate position between causal attributions and blaming. Although an understanding of responsibility attributions is crucial to an understanding of mechanisms of social sanctioning, it is unfortunately often not the case that researchers working on the latter have a genuine understanding of the former − especially when complex causal chains are involved.

In Chapters 3 and 5 expectancies which generalize over situations or people are contrasted with individuating processes and processes of self-verification. Issues of vividness of impressions, accuracy of social perception, and diagnostic information from single cases are related to this contrast between global schemata and individual evidence. Depending on their personal preferences, researchers have emphasized one or other end pole. More integration of theory and research in this respect would be desirable, although the work of Snyder and Swann and of Taylor and Fiske is promising. In this connection, different values are attached to individual cases. While from the perspective of the representativeness heuristic (Tversky and Kahneman, 1974) single cases are regarded as possible sources of distortion of the relevance of base-rate information used in forming rational judgments, from the perspective of stereotypes attention paid to single cases serves as a protection against overgeneralization and irrational distortions in person perception.

In this book I have emphasized the positive. In other words, I have tried to focus on promising lines of research without criticizing other approaches extensively. Another factor which contributed to my selectiveness is related to my personal biases and preferences. A second book, which might be titled *Critical Issues in Person Perception Research*, would certainly supplement this one very well. I am painfully aware of many methodological problems in the research reports. In fact, after reading the relevant literature I have become to some extent more skeptical on this point than I was before. I will mention here only replicability of results (especially of significant statistical interactions), the questionable reliability of many popular dependent measures, which neglect the processes which are supposed to be being studied, and demand characteristics caused by leading questions and a tendency to emphasize confirmation more than disconfirmation. Another problem relates to the small samples of subjects studied, which are also frequently not representative of people in general. I have tried to take these problems into account implicitly, but I am aware that I was only partially successful in this respect. Space limitations and the goal of providing a general overview of theories and research on person perception did not allow me to discuss this critical aspect more extensively in the text.

It is a truism that every study has its strengths and weaknesses. For example, naturalistic studies which promise a high ecological validity usually do not allow strict control of independent variables. In contrast, laboratory studies lack ecological validity. Therefore, different approaches complement each other, each one compensating for deficiencies which are inherent in another. Unfortunately, a tendency to concentrate on judgmental studies which allow easy and quick procedures for collecting data can be seen. Be this as it may, considerable efforts are being made to bring the study of person perception into the course of social interactions (see Chapter 5).

I want to thank a number of people who helped me during the preparation and writing of this book. These include Jörg Albers, Christiane Block, Michael Herner, Peter Kramp, Helmut Lamm, Angela Ludwig, Bernd Schäfer, Franziska Schneider, and Wolfgang Stroebe. My special thanks go to two people. Nicola Preese helped me with the translation into English and improved my English in parts which were originally written in English. Renate Klein, who is my co-author in the second chapter on inference processes in impression formation, read the whole manuscript and improved it in many ways.

In order to improve the readability of the text I have placed the more detailed reports on particular investigations and the details of some theoretical models in boxes (numbered I1 – I26 for investigations and T1 – T13 for theoretical models).

Hans-Werner Bierhoff

Contents

Chapter 1

The First Impression

The basic issues of person perception are forming a first impression about another person and drawing conclusions from this impression. These two topics are therefore treated in Chaps. 1 and 2. The first chapter emphasizes the processes involved in impression formation, whereas in Chap. 2 stress is laid upon the conclusions that are drawn from the first impression.

Consider the following example: in the 1970s "the godfathers of heavy metal" (*Rolling Stone*, July 1985), Jimmy Page and Robert Plant – better known as Led Zeppelin –, were famous for their characteristic stage shows. One of the topics discussed in this chapter deals with the question of whether there are certain central cues that influence the first impression of a person more than other peripheral cues. The loudness of Led Zeppelin's music was probably one such central cue that strongly determined how the band was perceived. In addition, I shall discuss the influence of overall evaluations of a stimulus person on ratings of specific aspects of that person. In terms of the above example, when an observer holds a positive opinion about Jimmy Page or Robert Plant, he or she will tend to attribute positively evaluated characteristics to them (e.g., sincere, dynamic, exciting, attractive). Given a negative overall evaluation, an observer will tend to attribute less favorable characteristics (e.g., not sincere) to the stimulus person. Thus an implicit personality theory about the "godfathers" emerges that is inferred from initial cues.

Central Characteristics and Gestalt Perception

Each of us meets a wide variety of people in everyday life. Even during short encounters a first impression emerges and subsequently influences social behavior (Kelley, 1950; Widmeyer & Loy, 1988).

Well-known public figures are good examples to illustrate how person perception functions. They may be politicians or actors and also heroes from fiction and comics. Consider Hagar the Horrible, by Dik Browne; Hagar is a mighty man but often expresses childish inclinations. His strength and vitality are manifested in his outer appearance, but the "born leader" often pursues infantile goals. For instance, Hagar gets extremely upset when he finds a leak in the wine cask, whereas he hardly takes any notice of a leak in the Viking ship. Another time he is eager to secure the largest piece of cake for himself.

In spite of the seemingly contradictory characteristics attributed to Hagar, his stories are very popular and fascinate many readers in a way only rarely reported of students reading a psychology textbook. In fact, everyday sayings provide schemata for categorizing Hagar's behavior. Hagar reminds one of the German proverb which says that there is a child in every man, which means that even sincere and maybe frightening men exhibit childlike wishes or behavior. Using this notion, Hagar's contradictory characteristics are integrated into a familiar overall impression that transcends the single traits.

How Contradictions May Form a Unity

First impressions do not emerge slowly over a long period of time but are formed almost immediately during the first encounter with the target person. Once an impression has been formed it is maintained over a long time, even if no further contact with the stimulus person takes place. From the very beginning an impression represents a homogeneous unity that develops quickly and usually lasts for a long time (Asch, 1946, p. 258; Hamilton, 1981).

Impression formation is best considered as a process by which an organized overall impression emerges in which single traits receive specific meanings. Every single trait can have a variety of meanings when seen in isolation. For instance, *daring* may be interpreted as *courageous* on the one hand and as *reckless* on the other hand. Connotative meanings of *crafty* may range from *clever* to *sly* (see Hamilton & Zanna, 1974). It is only in context that the range of meanings narrows and a trait receives a specific interpretation.

In the tradition of Gestalt psychology, Asch (1946) formulated the hypothesis that the impression of a person is more than the sum of his/her single characteristics. In "Forming Impressions of Personality" he contrasted three models of impression formation (see Box T 1) which since then have influenced research on person perception.

Box T1. Models of impression formation
Several models describe the process by which different information may be integrated to give an overall impression.

1. *Summation model:* The overall impression is the sum of the independent impressions based on single items of information: overall impression $= a+b+c+d+e$ (single items of information are represented by $a-e$).

2. *Generalized halo effect:* Rating scale judgments as measures of various traits and characteristics of a person tend to be strongly correlated. To the extent that these correlations are spurious and do not correspond to actual relationships between the rated traits, the overall impression is in-

fluenced by an (illusory) halo effect. Such a judgmental error was first discussed by Wells in 1907 and termed a halo effect by Thorndike in 1920 (see Cooper, 1981).

Two different processes may lead to halo effects. On the one hand an overall impression — transmitting positive or negative evaluations — may influence single judgments. On the other hand a single but salient characteristic may influence the judgment of the other characteristics. In this latter sense the *warm — cold* variable (see p. 7) produces a halo effect.

The consequences of the halo effect for impression formation may be described using an algebraic model:

$$R_c = W_c S_c + (1 - W_c) I \ .$$

R_c represents the rating of item c which has scale value S. I represents the overall impression. As the weights (W_c and $1 - W_c$) sum to unity, an averaging rule is applied. Weight represents an item's importance for impression formation.

The overall impression itself may be described in terms of an averaging model (Ostrom, 1977):

$$I = \frac{W_0 S_0}{\sum W_i + W_0} + \frac{\sum W_i S_i}{\sum W_i + W_0} \ .$$

S_0 marks an initial neutral impression and S_i represents the scale values of the different items of information. Weights W_0 and W_i again sum to unity. Note that the scale value of the target information c is represented in R_c as well as in I (among the different single items).

Halo effects threaten the validity of judgments (Cooper, 1981). The judgment of single items of information may be distorted when the overall impression dominates or influences the rating of this information. A halo effect may explain why a single trait is interpreted in different ways depending on the context. Given negative context information, the rating of the target trait tends to become more negative. Positive context information on the other hand should lead to a more positive evaluation of the target trait.

3. *Gestalt perception:* The notion of an entity being more than the sum of its parts and the idea that the specific interpretation of a single piece of information is modified by the overall impression is illustrated in Figure 1 (Asch, 1946). The relationships between the single items of information mediate their interpretation. The actual meanings of the traits interact in such a way that the overall impression reflects the relationship between the specific traits.

Psychological theorizing as well as common sense say that impression formation is characterized by a process of cognitive organization which leads to a coherent impression of the target person (Asch, 1946, p. 284). The observer intuitively tends to perceive the target person as an entity. This does not

IMPRESSION:

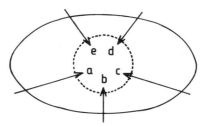

Figure 1. Forming an impression of the entire person. (From Asch, 1946, p. 259)

preclude complex or even contradictory impressions. Conflicting or contradictory information will be combined into a coherent impression using integration techniques like construction of a depth dimension, discovery of a common source of characteristics, or a means-end analysis (Asch & Zukier, 1984).

The Gestalt-theoretical explanation of impression formation has often been challenged. Watkins and Peynircioğlu (1984) describe the long history of research (see Box T 1 for a discussion of the competing approaches). For a long time inappropriate research designs prevented precise answers being found to the question of whether single ratings are context dependent. It was not until the "direct" approach of Hamilton and Zanna (1974) and its further elaboration by Watkins and Peynircioğlu (1984) that conclusive results emerged (see "Daring: Courage or recklessness?").

Many arguments concerning impression formation are influenced by general principles which are borrowed from research on memory and perception. As noted above, the perception of a person as an entity greater than the sum of its specific characteristic traits is derived from Gestalt-theoretic principles. Research on perception shows that the phenomenal (perceived) identity of single parts is determined by the system as a whole. The studies by Wertheimer and his colleagues are early demonstrations of this phenomenon. Ternus (1926) used luminous points to test the following hypothesis:

> Phenomenal identity depends on Gestalt identity, on the identity association of gestalt homologous parts; phenomenal identity emerges primarily from the whole, not from the parts (p. 110).

For instance, two appropriately timed expositions of five points create the impression of a cross moving from the left to the right (see Figure 2). Therefore, phenomenal identity is attributed to those points which have the same "function" within a figure (i.e., which are gestalt homologous), an example being the midpoint of a figure. Points as part of the whole appear to move between the first and second presentations.

In Ternus's studies a specific point was regarded as a central point at one time and as a peripheral point at another time (e.g., points b and c). That is to say, subjects perceived a specific point as having different meanings or func-

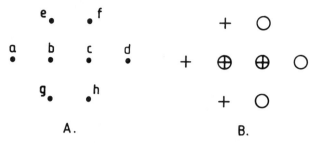

Figure 2. Identity interchange of luminous points. +, first presentation; ○, second presentation. Where both signs occur together, their coordinates are identical. (From Ternus, 1926, p. 88)

tions. Only the configuration of all luminous points shown at one time led to a restriction of the possible interpretations of a specific stimulus.

Asch describes the role of a single item of information correspondingly: the single item of information is assigned a specific meaning depending on the overall impression. For instance, *outspoken* tends to be interpreted as *tactless* in the context of *chatty* and *conceited*, but as *frank* in the context of *modest* and *deliberate*. Asch (1946) used a simple research paradigm to investigate impression formation. Subjects read lists of trait adjectives characterizing a target person and were asked to form an impression of the target person.

This procedure was modified in a series of later studies. Pepitone and Hayden (1955) presented subjects with a list of the memberships of a target person. Five memberships typical of upper middle class associations were: member of a country club, vestryman, member of the stock exchange, official of the National Association of Manufacturers, member of a property owners association. The sixth was membership of the Socialist Party. Subjects were asked to describe the personality of the target person, considering his preferences, values, and characteristic traits. The following examples illustrate the impressions elicited by the target person (p. 304):

> He is a shrewd businessman with a keen interest in public utilities. This can be inferred from his connection with the New York Stock Exchange and some of the basic underlying doctrine of the Socialist Party.
>
> He is a man of principle and firm conviction. This must be so, otherwise he would not belong to both the National Association of Manufacturers and the Socialist Party. There is good in both and he stands by the principles of both despite recognizable conflicting differences.

These examples demonstrate how some of the judges integrate conflicting memberships into a coherent impression of the target person's personality by pointing to underlying principles. Other subjects obtain a coherent personality impression by interpreting one of the memberships as a means of reaching specific ends, whereas others avoid contradictions by ignoring conflicting interactions or simply stated the contradiction as such (Pepitone & Hayden, 1955).

Asch and Zukier (1984) categorized the techniques used to resolve conflicts between contradictory characteristic traits of a target person. They distinguished between six techniques empirically — on the basis of descriptions of people formed when two discordant traits were present:

1. *Segregation:* The dispositions (e.g., *brilliant-foolish*) are each assigned to a different sphere of the person (e.g., to the intellectual and practical sphere).
2. *Inner versus outer (depth dimension):* One of the conflicting dispositions (e.g., *sociable*) is assigned to a surface manifestation of the person and the other (e.g., *lonely*) to a deep, inner layer.
3. *Cause and effect:* Two dispositions (e.g., *dependent-hostile*) are seen in a causal relationship (e.g., a person acts in a hostile way because of his futile efforts to break off his dependence on another person).
4. *Common source:* Two dispositions (e.g., *cheerful-gloomy*) are judged as resulting from the same basic disposition (e.g., *moody*).
5. *Means-end:* One disposition is interpreted as a means to achieve another disposition or end (e.g., with the pair *strict-kind*, strictness is regarded as a manifestation of kindness).
6. *Interpolation:* The disparity between *intelligent* and *unambitious* is bridged by inferring from disappointing former experiences that a person has now lost interest. Interpolating a unifying explanation smoothes the contrast between conflicting dispositions.

In an empirical investigation Asch and Zukier (1984) found that these techniques were selected according to the specific kind of contradiction to be solved. Depending on the conflicting traits, one technique was preferred to another. For instance, segregation was used when the contradiction of *brilliant* and *foolish* had to be explained, whereas the cause-effect technique was preferred with the pair *dependent-hostile*. In addition, it was shown that a specific contradiction could be solved using more than one technique. The pair *dependent-hostile* may be interpreted in terms other than a cause-effect relationship. Consider a person's different spheres of life: in one sphere he/she acts in a hostile way, in the other he/she acts dependently. Explaining this disparity in terms of a common source, one might argue that the person acts within a despotic system in which he/she behaves compliantly and dependently with his/her superior and is hostile towards his/her subordinates.

In general, subjects preferred techniques which allowed a hierarchical ordering of dispositions so that the dominant disposition determined the interpretation of the subordinate disposition. Structural dispositions such as *intelligent* and *brilliant* were often regarded as dominant. The same status was held by causal and internal dispositions.

Central and Peripheral Dispositions

Impression formation tends to result in an integrated, coherent picture of a target person. Thus it is reasonable to assume that distinctive and salient dispositions constitute the center of personality impression. Around this center associative relations of subordinate dispositions emerge. The central dispositions dominate the impression, whereas the peripheral dispositions carry less weight in impression formation.

For instance, the information coming first about a person may be the central information (see "Order of presentation of information") and serve as an anchor for later information. In addition, structural, causal, and internal attributes, as noted above, may gain central importance when forming an impression of a person. In particular, researchers' interests in impression formation concentrated on the dispositional pair *warm-cold*.

Asch (1946, exp. 1) asked his subjects to evaluate a target person described by seven trait adjectives. In one experimental condition *warm* served as the fourth trait, whereas *cold* was the fourth trait in a second condition. The remaining traits (*intelligent, skillful, industrious, determined, practical,* and *cautious*) were identical for both adjective lists. Subjects read a list of 18 pairs of opposite traits and were asked to select the one trait of each pair that was most in accordance with the impression they had formed about the target person. Table 1 presents the trait pairs of the checklist.

Results showed that subjects assigned more positive ratings to a "warm" target person than to a "cold" target person. 91% of subjects considered a warm stimulus person to be generous (vs. 8% of the subjects in the condition with the cold stimulus person); 90% considered a warm target person to be happy (vs. 34%); 94% regarded *good-natured* as fitting a warm person (vs. 17%); and 69% saw him/her as altruistic (vs. 18%). For the remaining dispositions there were no clear-cut differences between the experimental conditions (e.g., *reliable* and *honest*).

In a second experiment Asch (1946) prepared identical stimulus lists, except that the critical terms *warm* and *cold* were omitted. Ratings of the checklist trait pairs showed that in this experiment subjects formed a neutral impression of the target person. Percentages of ratings of fitting qualities were between those that had emerged in the warm and cold conditions.

In addition, the second experiment also points indirectly to the centrality of the *warm-cold* variable for impression formation as characterized by the specific checklist. *Warm* and *cold* were added to the *checklist* as the last pair. This allowed the experimenter to split the whole group of subjects into two subgroups according to whether subjects themselves had described the stimulus person as *warm* or *cold*. Thus it was possible to compare the checklist ratings of both subgroups. Subgroup ratings replicated the results of experiment 1. Omission of the central disposition from the stimulus list caused subjects to infer the *warm-cold* qualities of the target person and to integrate the inferred disposition with their overall impression of the stimulus person. This

Table 1. Percentage of subjects who judged the trait to fit the impression of the target person. (Modified from Asch, 1946, p. 263)

	Warm	*Cold*
generous-ungenerous	91	8
shrewd-*wise*	65	25
unhappy-*happy*	90	34
irritable-*good-natured*	94	17
humorous-humorless	77	13
sociable-unsociable	91	38
popular-unpopular	84	28
unreliable-*reliable*	94	99
important-insignificant	88	99
ruthless-*humane*	86	31
good-looking-unattractive	77	69
persistent-unstable	100	97
frivolous-*serious*	100	99
restrained-talkative	77	89
self-centered-*altruistic*	69	18
imaginative-hard-headed	51	19
strong-weak	98	95
dishonest-*honest*	98	94

Percentages refer to the trait in *italics*

overall impression was similar to the one that resulted from stimulus lists explicitly containing the *warm-cold* variable.

The combined results of both experiments strongly support the view that an impression is "a perceiver's organized cognitive representation of another person" (Hamilton, Katz & Leirer, 1980a, p. 123). Blanks in the schematic representation of the stimulus person are filled on the basis of the perceiver's implicit personality theory (Taylor & Crocker, 1981).

Moreover, the importance of the initial frame of reference will probably increase when delayed personality ratings are made, for example, 1 week after the original presentation of the relevant information (see Higgins, Rholes & Jones, 1977; Srull & Wyer, 1980). One may hypothesize that with a temporal interval between initial presentation and final judgment it becomes increasingly difficult for raters to discriminate between actual information and inferred schema-related information. Thus, after an appropriate time interval, concrete facts and derived suppositions become mixed up and both are perceived as evidence.

Whereas the experiments reviewed so far demonstrated the significant impact of central traits on person perception, a third experiment shows that a peripheral adjective pair exerts only a moderate influence on impression formation (Asch, 1946, exp. 3). Subjects again received a stimulus list identical to the one in the preceding experiments save that *warm* and *cold* were replaced by *polite* and *blunt*. Thus, there were two experimental conditions with seven trait adjectives each, the only difference being the use of *polite* versus *blunt*.

Consistent with the hypothesis that the *polite-blunt* dimension is peripheral to impression formation, impressions of the target person varied less between conditions than in the *warm-cold* experiment. For example, the target person was rated as generous by 56% of the subjects when described as polite and was rated as generous by 58% of the subjects when described as blunt.

Implicit Personality Theories Complete the First Impression

The effects of the *warm-cold* variable on impression formation have proven to be stable and replicable (Mensh & Wishner, 1947). However, the question of why a disposition gains central significance in impression formation is not yet settled. Taking into account the notion of an implicit personality theory structuring the relationships between traits, the following suggestion may be considered (see Wishner, 1960): an implicit personality theory describes relationships between dispositions. For instance, a close relationship is perceived between *warm* and *generous* and between *cold* and *ungenerous*. The perceiver believes that warm persons tend to be generous whereas cold persons are perceived as being ungenerous. On the other hand, the implicit personality theory may prescribe a zero correlation between the *warm-cold* dimension and the *good-looking-unattractive* dimension.

Tendencies to infer one disposition from another were systematically investigated by Bruner, Shapiro and Tagiuri (1958). The authors demonstrated the existence in the minds of the judges of an implicit personality theory about which dispositions go together. This result suggests new interpretations of the effect of the *warm-cold* variable on impression formation. It is reasonable to presume that the *warm-cold* variable strongly influences impression formation when checklist dispositions that correlate strongly with the *warm-cold* dimension are given.

Wishner (1960) examined this possibility and asked students to rate their lecturer with regard to Asch's (1946) trait pairs. In particular, Wishner determined correlations of the stimulus list traits with the checklist traits (see Table 1). As was expected, there were high correlations (e.g., *happy-unhappy*, $r = 0.54$), medium-sized correlations (e.g., *generous-ungenerous*, $r = 0.33$), and zero correlations (e.g., *good-looking* − *unattractive*, $r = 0.10$; and *frivolous-sincere*, $r = 0.02$) with the *warm-cold* pair. These correlations demonstrate that a person regarded as warm will often be perceived as happy and sometimes as generous.

An analogous implicit personality theory seemed to influence subjects' ratings in Asch's (1946) first experiment because the differences between percentages (see Table 1) were especially pronounced where there was a high correlation between the rated trait adjective and the *warm-cold* variable. Wishner (1960) calculated a correlation coefficient of 0.62 for the relationship between the absolute magnitude of correlations between the *warm-cold* variable and the checklist traits on the one hand and the magnitude of the difference in those traits between the *warm* and the *cold* conditions on the other hand.

These findings permit predictions concerning the specific conditions under which a trait adjective gains central or peripheral status in impression formation: a disposition will be of central importance if it correlates with most or all of the checklist traits. The disposition will be peripheral if correlations with checklist adjectives are low or even approach zero.

In his experiments Wishner (1960) showed that dispositions considered peripheral by Asch (1946) may be transformed into central dispositions by using checklists that consist of trait adjectives highly correlated with the target disposition. Ratings of checklist traits that have a low correlation with the target trait should not be altered by the target traits.

Subjects read the description of a stimulus person characterized by seven traits (*clumsy, industrious, determined, practical, cautious,* and *intelligent* or *unintelligent,* respectively). They then rated the stimulus person according to a checklist that consisted of opposite-trait pairs that had a strong or a weak correlation with the *intelligent-unintelligent* variable. Results are shown in Table 2.

Strong effects emerge for the first and second dispositions in Table 2. They correlate strongly ($r < 0.60$) with the *intelligent-unintelligent* variable and rep-

Table 2. Percentage of subjects who judged the trait to fit the impression of the target person. (Modified from Wishner, 1960, p. 102)

	Correlation	*Unintelligent*	*Intelligent*
stupid-wise	+	60	2
foolish-shrewd	+	35	1
shallow-profound	+	87	17
important-insignificant	+	33	92
ambitious-unambitious	+	90	97
critical-tolerant	○	43	58
ungenerous-generous	○	23	34
inflexible-flexible	○	62	32
kind-cruel	○	85	83
irritable-good-natured	○	22	28
sociable-unsociable	○	74	86

Trait pairs are presented in the sequence of their correlations with the *intelligent-unintelligent* variable. +, trait-pair correlation of 0.35 or more with *intelligent-unintelligent*; ○, correlations of 0.10 and lower. Ratings refer to the trait in *italics*

resent concepts close to the intelligence dimension. Virtually no difference appears for the *ambitious-unambitious* variable. This may be due to the fact that the *ambitious-unambitious* variable correlated with three additional stimulus list traits (the correlations are $r = 0.45$ for *industrious-lazy*, $r = 0.47$ for *determined-indecisive*, and $r = 0.62$ for *practical-unpractical*). As these stimulus traits were constant across conditions they probably served to balance the rating of the *ambitious-unambitious* dimension.

Finally, it is interesting to point out that the *intelligent-unintelligent* variable correlates positively with the above-mentioned traits (e.g., *industrious-lazy*, *determined-indecisive*, and *practical-unpractical*). Hence the description of the stimulus person as clumsy, industrious, determined, practical, and *intelligent* may be more consistent than the description of the stimulus person as clumsy, industrious, practical, and unintelligent. A lack of intelligence contradicts the implicit personality theory that there is a positive relationship between intelligence and industriousness, determination, and practicality. The inconsistency due to the *unintelligent* pole of the trait dimension therefore weakens the effect of the experimental manipulation. Analogous reasoning holds for the *foolish-shrewd* dimension correlating significantly with *skillful*, *industrious*, *determined*, and *practical*.

Therefore, it is reasonable to say that the status of central dispositions depends on the implicit personality theories observers employ in impression formation. The complex relationships among the stimulus traits on the one hand and between the stimulus traits and the checklist traits on the other hand exert an influence on whether a certain disposition gains central or peripheral status in impression formation.

In a study by Rosenberg, Nelson and Vivekananthan (1968) the perceived interrelationships of dispositions were examined. The authors explored the basic dimensions of the dispositions used by Asch (1946) and Wishner (1960) and estimated the relative position of dispositions within a multidimensional structure. Rosenberg et al. found that the 64 dispositions that were analyzed were best represented within a two-dimensional space defined by two oblique dimensions *socially good-socially bad* and *intellectually good-intellectually bad*. Both dimensions represent evaluative aspects differing only in their respective emphasis on social and intellectual dispositions.

Near the *intellectually good* pole the authors found the following dispositions: *determined, skillful, industrious, intelligent, practical,* and *cautious*. Note that these dispositions are identical to the ones Asch presented to his subjects. On the opposite pole of the *intellectual* dimension there was *foolish, frivolous, unintelligent,* and *clumsy.*

Happy, sociable, good-natured, humorous, popular, and *warm* clustered around the *socially good* pole. That is, the *socially good* pole was characterized by the variable *warm* as well as by other dipositions correlated with the *warm-cold* dimension. *Cold, unsociable, humorless,* and *unpopular* represented the opposite, *socially bad* pole.

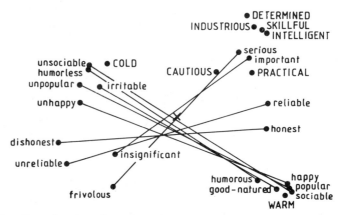

Figure 3. Two-dimensional configuration of stimulus list adjectives (*upper case letters*) and selected checklist adjectives (*lower case letters*) from the Asch experiment. Antonym trait pairs from the checklist are linked graphically. (From Rosenberg, Nelson & Vivekananthan, 1968, p. 292. Copyright 1968 by the American Psychological Association. Reprinted by permission)

The configuration of trait adjectives is represented in a two-dimensional space (see Figure 3): *warm* is located in a similar position to *happy, good-natured, humorous, sociable,* and *popular,* all of which were significantly related to the *warm-cold* variable. Trait adjectives that were not influenced by the *warm-cold* variable cluster around the *intellectually good* pole (*important, serious*) or between the *intellectually good* pole and the *warm* pole (*reliable, honest*). Trait adjectives held constant in the description of the stimulus person are located at the *intellectually good* pole (*determined, industrious, skillful, intelligent,* and, to a lesser degree, *practical* and *cautious*).

These findings convincingly demonstrate why the *warm-cold* variable had a central status in Asch's first experiment (1946). The *warm-cold* variable was highly correlated with the checklist adjectives, whereas the remaining stimulus list adjectives were relatively independent. Thus, the *warm-cold* variable and the checklist adjectives constituted the *socially good-socially bad* dimension.

This configuration helps to explain another of Asch's findings (1946, exp. 9). Stimulus persons characterized only by either *warm* or *cold* received more divergent ratings than those who were also described by the six remaining adjectives from the *intellectually good* pole. With *warm* or *cold* serving as the only cue to the *socially good-socially bad* dimension, the information relevant for impression formation was probably less mixed.

The interpretation given by Rosenberg et al. (1968) receives further support through the results of Asch's fourth experiment (1946). In this study *warm* and *cold* were presented together with context adjectives that were in part inconsistent with *warm* or *cold*. For example, the description of the stimulus person might read: "intelligent, skillful, sincere, cold, conscientious, helpful, modest."

The list contains the adjectives from the *socially good* pole (*sincere, helpful, modest*) that are inconsistent with the *socially bad* pole as represented by *cold*. Asch's (1946) comment on the results of the fourth experiment was that *cold* had lost its central status within the new context. One may add that *cold* is now a peripheral disposition because its impact is diminished or even neutralized by the presence of inconsistent information. Three socially good adjectives receive more weight than one socially bad adjective.

In another stimulus list *warm* was combined with *vain* and likewise lost its central status. *Distinctiveness* of information, therefore, was the important factor that caused the *warm-cold* variable to become a central disposition. In the original stimulus list *warm* or *cold* was the only disposition relating to the *socially good-socially bad* dimension. It is well known that distinctive information elicits increased attention (see Hamilton & Gifford, 1976; McArthur & Friedman, 1980). Distinctive information is salient and promotes better recall (Hamilton et al., 1980a).

Note that similar effects of distinctiveness on recall, known as the von Restorff effect, were demonstrated by Köhler and von Restorff (1937) in a series of experiments. The von Restorff effect describes the finding that a syllable is more easily recalled and more easily perceived in tachistoscopic presentations when the stimulus list contains no other syllables. Köhler and von Restorff (1937) showed that subjects were more able to recognize the word *brosk* during a short presentation when it had been presented in a pretest for 2 s and had been followed by a list of graphical figures than when it was followed by a list of nonsense syllables. In the same vein, recognition improved with the relative uniqueness of an element in a series (von Restorff, 1933).

We have already discussed two characteristics of Asch's (1946) investigation of the *warm-cold* variable that made this variable a central disposition: the correlation between *warm-cold* and several checklist adjectives, and the distinctiveness of the *warm-cold* variable in the stimulus list used. A third factor promoting centrality of a trait is the relative extremity or *polarization* of information with regard to a specific judgmental dimension. That is to say, *warm* and *cold* represent the extreme poles of the *socially good-socially bad* dimension (see Hays, 1958). The *warm-cold* variable is central because of its implications for other variables (Hays, 1958). In addition, Hays (1958) described a second dimension (opposite poles: *intelligent* and *stupid*) resembling the *intellectually good-intellectually bad* dimension from Rosenberg et al. (1968).

Hays' findings support a two-dimensional representation of trait ratings. Further evidence for the two-dimensional configuration stems from studies in which both dimensions were separated: information on social desirability influenced judgments of social desirability, whereas information on intellectual ability influenced judgments of intellectual ability (Hamilton & Fallot, 1974; Zanna & Hamilton, 1972).

In an extension of the Asch experiment, Zanna and Hamilton (1972) showed that the impact of the *warm-cold* variable is restricted to dispositions located on the social desirability dimension. On the other hand, the *industrious-lazy* variable only influenced dispositions related to the *intellectually good-intellectually bad* dimension. Therefore, the conclusion is justified that a disposition exerts an especially high influence on the judgmental dimension to which it is related.

This conclusion received further support in a second study (Hamilton & Fallot, 1974): social desirability ratings were influenced by information on social dispositions, whereas information on intellectual characteristics influenced judgments of intellectual ability. To measure social desirability, subjects indicated how much they liked the stimulus person; to measure intellectual ability subjects were asked to indicate how much they respected the stimulus person.

Consider two stimulus persons, for example: the first stimulus person was described as good-natured, unintelligent, helpful, and sociable, whereas the second stimulus person was described as intelligent, unsociable, imaginative, and practical. Given these stimulus persons, two different rating patterns emerged:

- Subjects indicated greater liking for the good-natured stimulus person than for the intelligent stimulus person;
- Subjects respected the intelligent person more than the good-natured person.

The experiments discussed above indicate another possible way of effectively integrating conflicting information. With differential weighting it is possible to neglect inconsistent information when it refers to a different judgmental dimension. The experiments presented deal with social and intellectual characteristics. Results indicated that subjects tend to distinguish between social competence and intellectual performance. Thus, *warm* implies being *generous* or *good-natured* but not being *intelligent* or *practical*.

Finally, some comments are necessary on the problem of whether the concept of central dispositions may be regarded as a substantial notion or whether it turns out to be nothing more than a methodological artifact without any substantial relevance for person perception. Asch's (1946) finding that the *warm-cold* variable was a central trait dimension was apparently caused by several factors. The *warm-cold* variable presented unique and distinct information in a context containing only intellectually relevant descriptions of the stimulus person; and most of the antonym trait pairs in the checklist represented the same judgment dimension as the *warm-cold* variable. However, social desirability ratings are probably especially important when a first impression about another person is formed. To this extent the original checklist probably possesses some ecological validity. Note, in addition, that the *warm-cold* variable represents the contrasting extreme poles of a social evaluation dimension (Hays, 1958).

Not surprisingly, therefore, the *warm-cold* variable not only influences impression formation, but it also influences social interaction. According to

Kelley (1950), subjects tended to engage in longer discussions with the speaker who was described as very warm than with a speaker who was presented as rather cold (the remaining adjectives in the description of the speaker were *industrious*, *critical*, *practical*, and *determined*). In addition, subjects perceived a "warm" speaker as more sociable, less irritable, more humane, less formal, and more humorous than a "cold" speaker. These results were replicated in a study by Widmeyer and Loy (1988).

In another study, Langer and Newman (1979) showed that the influence of the description of a speaker on speaker ratings was strongest when the audience did not listen to him carefully. The effect decreased when the audience paid attention to what the speaker was saying.

Talking about the effect of impression formation on social interaction, one may also note that the way the stimulus person interacts influences the application of implicit personality theories (Bierhoff & Bierhoff-Alfermann, 1976, 1977; Bierhoff-Alfermann, 1979). Judges do not apply implicit theories rigidly. Instead they take into account the given interaction contingencies the stimulus person has to deal with. Subjects applied different implicit personality theories depending on whether the stimulus person dominated another person in an asymmetrical contingency or whether the stimulus person acted within a mutual contingency where both partners influenced each other to the same extent. Findings indicate that observers use flexible attributional strategies and do not cling to a rigid use of strategies. For instance, observers distinguish between different prototypes that may be used to characterize male persons (see Chap. 3, "Sex stereotypes"). Members of a certain group will usually not be perceived using stereotypes in a global, general manner; it is possible to divide stereotypes of teachers, women, or blacks into a variety of prototypes.

Daring: Courage or Recklessness? Implicational Variety of Trait Adjectives

The meaning-change hypothesis states that the interpretation of a specific trait adjective depends on the context information that is presented together with the target adjective (see Box T 1). For instance, *daring* may be interpreted as *courageous* or *reckless* depending on context information. Asch (1946) himself favored the meaning-change hypothesis. His interpretation was challenged by Anderson (1966, 1971) and Kaplan (1971) who suggested an interpretation in terms of a generalized halo effect. This approach led to several interesting findings. However, the investigation of evaluative judgments largely neglected the meaning-change hypothesis and the impression formation processes that had been central to Asch's experiments (Hamilton et al., 1980a).

Therefore, in this section I will discuss those approaches which tried to measure the effects of trait adjectives on connotative meanings directly. Hamilton and Zanna (1974) successfully demonstrated meaning change pro-

Table 3. Test adjectives and corresponding rating scales to mea-
sure the connotative meaning of the test adjectives. (From
Hamilton & Zanna, 1974, p. 651. Copyright 1974 by the
American Psychological Association. Reprinted by permission)

Test attribute	Connotative meaning scale
M+ words	
proud	confident-conceited
daring	courageous-reckless
satirical	witty-cynical
persistent	diligent-uncompromising
N words	
excitable	lively-touchy
outspoken	frank-tactless
perfectionistic	conscientious-finicky
self-contented	poised-pompous
M− words	
undecided	open-minded-wishy-washy
conforming	cooperative-weak
clownish	humorous-silly
crafty	clever-sly

cesses in impression formation. They asked their subjects to rate three-adjec-
tive descriptions of stimulus persons, for example, "self-contented, fair, objective", or "persistent, rude, annoying."

The first adjective in both examples served as the test attribute. It contained
a mildly positive evaluative meaning (M+; e.g., *persistent*), a neutral meaning
(N; e.g., *self-contented*), or a mildly negative meaning (M−; e.g., *undecided*).
The remaining adjectives served as context information unrelated to the test
attributes. The context attributes were evaluated either positively (H; e.g., *happy, intelligent*), mildly positively (M+; e.g., *fair, efficient*), mildly negatively
(M−; e.g., *overcritical, ungraceful*), or negatively (L; e.g., *rude, annoying*).
Subjects had to rate the meaning of the test attribute on 8-point bipolar scales.
The end poles of the scales were marked with a positive or a negative trait adjective. For instance, subjects had to decide whether they considered a stimulus
person described as daring to be courageous or to be reckless. Test attributes
and corresponding rating scales are summarized in Table 3.

Inspection of Table 3 shows the widespread connotative meanings an adjective may assume. Human language appears to be highly differentiated and
manifold. Even words that seem to have a unique meaning (e.g., *satirical*) may
lead to almost opposite ratings on the desirability scale, depending on context.
Context strongly influences the connotative meaning of a given trait adjective,
even when it appears to represent a specific attribute.

The findings of Hamilton and Zanna (1974) illustrate the importance of context: for example the final interpretation of *daring* as *courageous* or *reckless* depended on the given context information. When positively evaluated context traits were given, the test attribute assumed a positive connotative meaning. On the other hand, negatively evaluated context traits fostered a negative interpretation of the test attribute.

In subsequent studies (Box I 1), Zanna and Hamilton (1977) demonstrated the robustness of context effects on connotative meaning scales and showed that context effects are especially pronounced when test-word synonyms were used as labels for the endpoints of the rating scale (high similarity in denotative meaning). To sum up, connotative variety of trait adjectives may be determined by context adjectives. Without this flexibility of connotative meanings, there would probably be no rich verbal communication.

Box I 1. Separated from context
Quotations separated from their context often lead to misunderstandings. Apparently, the connotative meaning of a statement depends on previous as well as subsequent statements. Kaplan (1975, exp. 1) replicated the experiment of Hamilton and Zanna (1974; see text). In addition to rating scales that were test-word synonyms he used rating scales that were not denotatively related to the test attributes. Kaplan reasoned that subjects tend to attribute characteristics to the stimulus person that are consistent with the social desirability of the context traits. As a matter of fact, the connotative meaning scales used by Hamilton and Zanna (1974; see Table 3) were marked with differently evaluated end poles. For example, *courageous* is more positive than *reckless*. According to Kaplan (1975), context effects on test attribute interpretations result from subjects' tendency to form a consistent judgment of the stimulus person.

Kaplan (1975) presented some support for his prediction in that he found context effects on those connotative meaning scales that were denotatively unrelated to the test attributes. Given positive context information, subjects chose ratings near the positively evaluated pole of the scales; negative context information led to ratings near the negative pole of the scale.

However, context effects were stronger on judgment scales that were denotatively related to the test attributes than on scales with no or only a minor relationship to the test attributes. This finding is consistent with the meaning-change hypothesis. Kaplan (1975) argued, however, that the rating scales denotatively related to the test attributes were not identical to the unrelated scales. Thus, there may have been different scale units.

Zanna and Hamilton (1977, exp. 1) disproved this rather farfetched argument. They used identical judgment scales in each experimental condition (i.e., related and unrelated). Therefore, the use of the rating scales cannot vary between conditions (see below). In the related condition the end poles of the rating scales corresponded in denotative meaning to the respective test attribute, as in the earlier Hamilton and Zanna (1974) study (e.g., *satirical* and *witty-cynical*); in the unrelated condition the same set of rating scales was used but they were no longer test-word synonyms as they were randomly assigned to the test attributes.

In a pretest subjects perceived a closer relationship between test attributes and rating scales when both were related with regard to their denotative meanings than when they were unrelated. However, subjects in general tended to assume some relationship between attribute and judgment scale, even when both were randomly assigned. This may be the reason why Kaplan (1975) observed context effects even when there was no relationship between test attribute and rating scale. Zanna and Hamilton (1977) again used test attributes of positive (M+), neutral (N), or negative (M−) connotative meaning. Test attributes were combined with four context traits each, the context traits all carrying either positive (H) or negative (L) meaning. Subjects rated six target persons on a related and on an unrelated rating scale. Thus, level of test attribute and level of context combined to give a 3×2 factorial design. Connotative meaning of the test attribute was rated on 9-point rating scales ranging from −4 (negative pole, e.g., *cynical*) to +4 (positive pole, e.g., *witty*), including 0 as the neutral point.

Table 4. Mean ratings on meaning scales depending on context, test adjective, and relatedness. (From Zanna & Hamilton, 1977, p. 229. Copyright 1977 by Academic Press. Reprinted by permission)

Test attribute	H context			L context		
	M+	N	M−	M+	N	M−
Related meaning	1.25	1.47	0.53	−1.97	−1.16	−1.59
Unrelated meaning	0.44	0.53	0.75	−0.62	−0.91	−0.84

The rating scales ranged from −4 (negative endpoint) to +4 (positive endpoint). See text for explanation of abbreviations

Results for both related and unrelated scales are presented in Table 4. They indicate that for the related denotative meaning scale and the unrelated denotative meaning scale the main effect for context reached significance. The desirability of the connotative meaning of the test attributes decreased when negatively evaluated context attributes were given. In addition, the effect of context on the related meaning scale (1.08 vs. −1.57) was greater than its effect on the unrelated meaning scale (0.57 vs. −0.79). This finding cannot be attributed to the use of different rating scales because identical scales − differing only in their assignment to the test attributes − were used in the related and in the unrelated condition.

In a second experiment, Zanna and Hamilton (1977) again presented evidence supporting the meaning-change hypothesis. The effect of a context attribute on the connotative meaning ratings of a test attribute was greater when test attribute and context attribute were denotatively related. The effect was weaker when the denotative similarity between test attribute and context attribute was low.

Zanna and Hamilton (1977) employed three levels of desirability of the test attribute (M+, N, M−) and two levels of context desirability (positive, negative). For each of the test attributes there was a related and an unrelated context word. In the *related context condition*, the stimulus person might, for example, be described as satirical, clever (positive context attribute) or as satirical, disrespectful (negative context attribute). For each of these descriptions, *witty* and *cynical* represented the respective end poles of the rating scale. The same scale was used in the *unrelated context condition* (which matches the respective condition of the previous studies). A stimulus person might then be described as satirical, helpful (positive context attribute) or as satirical, narrow-minded (negative context attribute).

In the examples above, *satirical*, an M+ test attribute, was combined with a positive or negative context attribute that was either related or unrelated to the test attribute. Results summarized over the levels of test attribute desirability (M+, N, M−) are presented in Table 5. The effect of context desirability was greater in the related context condition (difference = 1.46) than in the unrelated condition (difference = 0.57).

Table 5. Mean meaning ratings on meaning scales depending on desirability and relatedness of the context. (From Zanna & Hamilton, 1977, p. 235. Copyright 1977 by Academic Press. Reprinted by permission)

Related context		Unrelated context	
Positive	Negative	Positive	Negative
5.35	3.89	4.72	4.15

The rating scales ranged from 1 (negative endpoint) to 8 (positive endpoint)

Kaplan (1975, exp. 2) conducted a similar experiment, but did not collect data on the denotative meaning of the test attributes. Moreover, it is interesting to note that Zanna and Hamilton (1977) also obtained ratings of certainty of judgment when the connotative meaning of test attributes was rated. Certainty of judgment was greater when related context attributes had been present than when unrelated context attributes had been present. One might have expected this result since related context attributes contain additional information that furthers unequivocal interpretation of the test attribute.

The judgment of a trait adjective on an evaluative scale or on a connotative meaning scale, however, does not allow conclusive statements about how the trait adjective was integrated into the overall impression. Note that a lack of context effects may be attributed to the fact that the adjective rating was dissociated from context and simply represented the general meaning of the adjective. On the other hand, a successful demonstration of context effects does not necessarily imply that the meaning of an adjective was changed. This kind of judgmental effect may instead have been caused during collection of the dependent variable since subjects may be tempted to give their adjective ratings according to a consistent judgment scheme (Watkins & Peynircioğlu, 1984).

A cued recall test offers an attractive research alternative (Srull, 1984; Taylor & Fiske, 1981). Subjects are exposed to stimulus material that contains personal characteristics associated with people's names. Hamilton and Zanna's (1974) approach may be further developed by using stimulus material which contains trait adjectives that are presented either in a positive or in a negative context. A final memory test contains synonyms covering the connotative meanings of the stimulus attribute (see Table 3). For example, if the description of the stimulus person contained the adjective *self-contented*, *poised* or *pompous* could serve as a memory aid.

Using this experimental approach one may expect better recall when desirability of context is consistent with desirability of the cue word, (i.e., both are positive or both are negative) than when inconsistency between both items exists (one positive, one negative). This hypothesis may be derived from assumptions already formulated by Köhler and von Restorff (1937), who assumed that recall depends on "selective pairing according to relatedness". According to this assumption, recall rests on the formation of traces. In addition it is said (pp. 64/65):

> When the opening phase of recall processes is viewed from a gestalt-theoretical perspective, that is as a pairing of process and a related trace, it must be possible to show that recall occurs under conditions similar to these promoting pairing in perception.

Process refers to the required memory tasks. Pairing should be successful when similarity between trace and process exists. If context really influences the interpretation of a trait adjective, a cue word closely related to the specific meaning should be more effective than a cue word inconsistent with the context-induced meaning of the trait. In the former case the similarity between trace and process is greater than in the latter case.

The specific meaning assigned to an adjective changed when the adjective was preceded by a sentence in which the stimulus person was presented either in a positive or in a negative way. Subjects recalled more stimulus traits correctly (43%) when consistent cue words were present than when inconsistent cue words (27%) were present.

Consider the following stimulus person descriptions (from Watkins & Peynircioğlu, 1984, p. 1016):

Pamela wisely gives importance to detail, being aware that even a slight error can ruin a general impression: she is perfectionistic.

Pamela is very hard to please because of her excessive concern with trivial details: she is perfectionistic.

Taking two synonyms for *perfectionistic, meticulous* and *finicky*, results showed that the positive characteristic serves as a better cue for *perfectionistic* within the positive context (first example), whereas the negative trait adjective aided recall more within the negative context.

These findings support the hypothesis that the perceived meaning of a trait adjective is dependent on context information. The evidence, however, is limited to cases where context information and stimulus information were integrated into a coherent, overall impression. This is in accordance with Asch and Zukier's (1984) assumption that the person represents a coherent entity in person perception. If it is not possible to convey an impression of a coherent person, the specific meaning of single trait adjectives should not be determined by the context information.

Watkins and Peynircioğlu (1984) showed that context information consisting of positively or negatively evaluated single trait adjectives did not differentially influence the effectivity of positive or negative cue words. A loose sequence of trait adjectives does not produce such a coherent personality impression compared with stimulus traits embedded in a descriptive sentence. Although context effects as reported by Hamilton and Zanna (1974) were replicated, consistent cues did not improve recall in the cued recall tests in comparison with inconsistent cues.

Recent findings clearly demonstrate that the Asch (1946) paradigm − although extensively employed in research on impression formation − was not strictly speaking appropriate for testing the meaning-change hypothesis. That is to say, trait adjectives presented in a loose sequence probably evoke an analytical approach in the observer and therefore impede the formation of a coherent picture of the stimulus person. To the extent that separate traits are not integrated into a coherent whole, an analytical judgment of the individual attributes will emerge.

To sum up, intuition as well as cued recall experiments support the conclusion that the meaning of a trait is partly determined by the relevant context information. This idea is also expressed in a song by Pete Townshend ("It's hard"), part of which is quoted here to close this topic:

Any gang can scatter − few can form
Any kid can chatter − few can inform
Everyone complains − few can state
Anyone can stop − few can wait

Cognitive Representation of Persons

Impression formation is characterized by an integrated, homogeneous structure lending specific meaning to single traits (Asch, 1946). Thus it is reasonable to investigate the precise cognitive structure of the first impression. Describing the cognitive basis of impression formation constitutes an important extension and further development in the investigation of person perception.

Consistent with this approach, the first impression may be defined as "a perceiver's organized cognitive representation of another person" (Hamilton et al., 1980a, p. 123). Cognitive organization rests on schemata representing general knowledge structures. The perceiver uses such schemata (or cognitive categories) to select and code information about other persons. In addition, schemata are used to fill in information gaps and through this to complete the impression formed about another person (see Taylor & Crocker, 1981).

Suppose the perceiver forms an integrated impression of another person based on traits attributed to that person (see Asch, 1946). Then sequential information acquisition provides for new information to be integrated into the schematic representation of another person so that a meaningful overall impression emerges. The following has been suggested to tend to occur in this process of information acquisition (Hamilton et al., 1980a):

- Biases toward evaluative consistency among the relevant information lead to a halo effect, which in turn — starting from the overall impression — leads to strongly correlated judgments of the stimulus on different judgmental dimensions (see Box T1).
- Context effects emerge because the functional meaning of information depends on the surrounding context information.
- An interlocking network of associative relationships among the information about a stimulus person emerges.

The tendency to integrate information about another person in an associative network is shown in recall of this information. Recall of specific information should be facilitated by forming a coherent structure during impression formation. On the other hand, recall should be impeded when no impression formation took place.

To test this prediction, subjects in seven different experiments (for a comprehensive review see Hamilton, 1981) read 15 or 16 descriptions of behavioral episodes such as "Went to a movie with friends Saturday night", and "Tries to keep informed on a current event." In one of the groups subjects were told that the episodes described a person about whom they should form an impression. A second group of subjects thought the episodes were to be used in a memory test and no mention of person perception was made. Figure 4 depicts the results of the experiments. Each comparison shows that subjects given the instruction to form an impression remembered a higher percentage of episodes than those expecting a memory test. These findings provide strong support for the notion that the very process of impression formation itself creates a

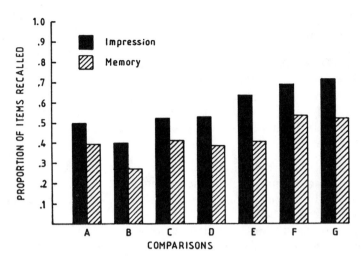

Figure 4. Items recalled by impression formation and memory test groups in seven different experiments. (From Hamilton, 1981, p. 142. Copyright 1981 by Lawrence Erlbaum Associates. Reprinted by permission)

coherent, associatively related structure that facilitates recall of the behavioral information presented.

We will now consider the question of how to describe this cognitive organization. In a series of experiments, Hamilton et al. (1980a) presented their subjects with 16 behavioral descriptions that belonged to four different categories:

- Social/interpersonal characteristics (e.g., "Helped a women fix her bicycle")
- Intellectual characteristics (e.g., "Checked some books out of the library")
- Interests in athletics (e.g., "Subscribes to sports magazines")
- Religious activities (e.g., "Volunteered to teach a Sunday school class at his church")

Subjects again had to recall as many ways of behaving as possible following a first (or second) presentation. Serial presentation of the single items served as a cue to a category-based organization of recall. Assuming a priori plausibility of the four categories, it was measured to what extent recalled items were clustered in accordance with these categories. Results showed that under conditions encouraging impression formation more clustering according to the a priori categories occurred than when the subjects expected a memory test. Thus, impression formation serves to organize given behavioral episodes according to schematic, personality-linked categories. Differences in the amount of clustering between the impression formation and the memory groups persisted for eight presentations of the behavioral episodes. Although there was an increase in clustering for both groups over all trials, category-based organization of recall was stronger for the impression formation group.

As recall measures were obtained for eight trials, it was possible to test whether there was any form of cognitive organization in the memory groups – independent of the a priori categories. Measures of the tendency to recall two items in immediate sequence were calculated. Consecutive recall may be regarded as evidence that both information items were stored together. No difference between the impression formation and the memory group emerged on this index. All in all, the amount of subjective organization increased over trials, with little difference between groups (Hamilton et al., 1980a).

To sum up:

- With impression formation about a stimulus person, information was organized according to schematic personality categories.
- Processing information for a memory task led to different cognitive organization (e.g., alphabetical order).
- Cognitive organization during impression formation yielded superior recall compared to cognitive organization during the memory task.

Ironically, those subjects that were instructed to remember the exact sentences were less able to recall the behavioral descriptions than subjects who were explicitly told not to concentrate on recall (see Hamilton, Katz & Leirer, 1980b) and therefore were surprised by the final memory test.

Finally, one may ask whether schematic organization into personality-relevant categories still occurs when the behavioral descriptions given relate to the self. Hamilton (1981) presents evidence that information related to the self will be organized according to specific domains of personality to the same extent as will information about another person. One may conclude that observers rely on schemata to structure domains of personality with regard to self-perception as well as with regard to perception of other persons and groups (Wyer, Bodenhausen & Srull, 1984; Wyer & Gordon, 1982, 1984).

Impression formation demonstrates that schemata play an important role in the perception and interpretation of social events. According to Taylor & Crocker (1981), schemata represent general knowledge of given domains specifying the interrelations of relevant attributes and providing typical examples of that domain. They continue (p. 91):

> As such, one of the chief functions of a schema is to provide an answer to the question "what is it?" The schema provides hypotheses about incoming stimuli, which include plans for interpreting and gathering schema-related information.... It may also provide a basis for activating actual behavior sequences or expectations of specific behavior sequences, i.e., scripts for how an individual behaves in a social situation.

The schema concept represents a family of similar concepts (Campbell, 1963; Taylor & Crocker, 1981) such as expectation, script, perceptual readiness, plan, hypothesis, prototype. Schemata are considered useful because they allow for fast identification of incoming stimuli, help to fill information gaps, and suggest further strategies for information gathering (Bruner, 1957a; Taylor & Crocker, 1981). Taylor and Crocker (1981) confine the applicability of a schema to a specific domain (for instance schemata for person description as they are described by Hamilton, 1981). When a schema is applied to its appropriate domain, the information items given will be organized in accordance with the structure of the schema. Impression formation in person perception was used as an example of how content-specific schemata organize the recall of person information.

Implications of the schema concept go far beyond the domain of impression formation in person perception. Schematic information processing plays an important role in the investigation and understanding of stereotypes. Stereotypes − for instance with regard to gender or physical attractiveness − facilitate information processing. In a sense, they may be compared to concepts that help to reduce the otherwise overwhelming complexity of our environment (Bruner, Goodnow & Austin, 1956). Note, however, that stereotypic information processing may lead to overgeneralization and arbitrary assessment of the information given (see Chap. 3). Self-fulfilling prophecies are used to confirm previously held expectations. They may be taken as an example of how schematic perception of social reality may bias social interaction, e.g., people negotiate more firmly with a women than with a man (Skrypnek & Snyder, 1982).

Schematic interpretations of social reality tend to resist contradictory information. Social stereotypes are known to be extremely difficult to change and many people abandoned any hope of successfully fighting stereotypes by means of explanation and clarification (see Sampson, 1971). With reference to statistical inference, Taylor and Crocker (1981) have termed the perseverance of stereotypes a type 1 error. Type 1 error in this context means that neutral or inconsistent information is interpreted as consistent with a given schema. For instance, consider a person known to be a typical extrovert. Many of this person's acts will be regarded as evidence for extroversion, even if they are not unequivocally related to extroversion.

In recent years the cognitive representation of people has often been analyzed with regard to general psychological findings (see Hastie, Ostrom, Ebbesen, Wyer, Hamilton & Carlston, 1980; Higgins, Herman & Zanna, 1981; Wyer & Srull, 1984). This research laid particular emphasis on how schemata, expectations, and attentional factors influence coding and recall of social information. Similar research was done by Bruner (1957a, b). Researchers revived nearly forgotten Gestalt psychological principles, for instance the figure-ground notion (see McArthur, 1981; see also Chap. 2, "Uncovering relationships") and the effect of recall cues given similarity of process and trace (see Wyer & Srull, 1981; see also "Daring: Courage or recklessness?").

The cognitive approach to the analysis of stereotypes has shown that a variety of general judgmental processes serves to sustain biased judgments of ingroup and outgroup (see Chap. 3, "Stereotype research − practical applications"). Cognitive explanations even tend to exaggerate the persistence of stereotypes since they predict more stability than actually occurs (Pettigrew, 1981). How the perception of a member of a stereotyped group may change at all remains unsolved.

Pettigrew (1981) analyzed demoscopic polls and found that stereotypes actually change in the long run. This was true regarding the perception of women or the perception of blacks in the United States. Changed perceptions depend closely on actual social change. At least three factors may produce attitude change:

- Concrete information from single cases – as may be obtained during face-to-face interaction – neutralizes contradictory category-based beliefs characteristically expressed as stereotypes (Deaux & Lewis, 1984; Hepburn & Locksley, 1983; Locksley, Borgida, Brekke & Hepburn, 1980; Locksley, Ortiz & Hepburn, 1982).
- Judgment of another person depends on the observer's perspective (see scale-end anchoring; Pettigrew, 1981; Sherif & Hovland, 1961).
- Stereotypes may be divided into several prototypes, allowing for more flexible impression formation than a global stereotype (Ashmore, 1981; Pettigrew, 1981).

Social Cognition

Research on social cognition addresses problems involved in the cognitive processes of perceiving and judging social stimuli, that is in the "knowing of people" (Higgins & Bargh, 1987). The very nature of social cognition research, as distinct from research on impression formation and social behavior, is difficult to define, but two important aspects may be mentioned briefly.

On the one hand, social cognition research emphasizes the investigation of *how* impressions are formed. It therefore focuses on the nature of the processes which lead to impressions of other persons. Research on impression formation used to focus on how accurate impressions are formed (Bruner & Tagiuri, 1954). Impressions and social judgments are often compared to normative judgmental models to determine the accuracy of human judgment (Kahneman, Slovic & Tversky, 1982).

On the other hand, social cognition research focuses on mental processes as determinants of social behavior (Strack, 1988). Within theoretical analyses and empirical investigations cognitive processes are regarded as the primary level of analysis for further understanding of social behavior. In contrast, research on social behavior emphasizes the investigation of interpersonal instead of intrapersonal processes and the influence of the social environment on human behavior (Graumann, 1988).

Research on social cognition has become increasingly popular within the last decade, building upon and integrating results and techniques concerning the investigation of memory and information processing in general.

Under the heading of social cognition, much attention is directed toward the functions of mental representations of external stimuli. A variety of different labels have been assigned to these representations, for instance, schemata, constructs, prototypes, plans, or categories (see Markus & Zajonc,

1985). However, the concept of mental representations already played an important role in the work of Bartlett (1932). Twenty-five years later Bruner (1957a) also noted that one central feature of perceptual processes is the connection of incoming external stimuli with internally stored categories.

Therefore, to a certain extent perception implies processes of categorization. The readiness with which the connection between incoming information and a stored category is made indicates the accessibility of that category. The accessibility of a category will increase if the category is activated by preceding information. This kind of activation is often referred to as priming (Higgins et al., 1977). A category being activated increases the likelihood that further information will be processed as if belonging in this category.

External information and internal categories may, therefore, exert an interrelated influence on the processing of information and the formation of a final judgment. Specifically, a single trait term may activate a related trait category, which will then prime further related categories. To the extent that the primed categories are applicable to the impression formation task at hand, they will influence the processing of subsequent information.

The results of Asch (1946) may be interpreted in terms of priming a relevant personality category. Describing the stimulus person as warm or cold activates the appropriate trait category. This trait category, in turn, influences the way in which further information about the stimulus person is processed.

Higgins et al. (1977) discriminate between direct and indirect effects of category activation. The direct effects are a function of the category itself being part of the memory, so that the denotative and evaluative implications of the category may form a basis for judgment as well as the effects of the external information. The indirect effects consist of biasing the incoming information towards the activated category with regard to interpretation, storage, and retrieval of the information.

The concept of category-guided information processing is immediately appealing for two reasons. First, categories help to process ambiguous stimuli, which would otherwise be difficult to interpret and to react upon. For the moment, there is no need to determine whether category-based interpretations are right or wrong. Secondly, categories may support rapid information processing under conditions of information overload.

The effects of category activation can be reliably separated from experimenter demand effects, since the unobtrusive presentation of seemingly unrelated words serves to activate an associated category. The effects of priming cannot, therefore, be attributed to public compliance with the experimenter's suggestions. It is not even necessary for participants to be aware of the words used for priming, as is demonstrated by the fact that they often cannot remember them.

Higgins et al. (1977) conducted a study with 60 undergraduate students in which they demonstrated the effects of category activation on impression formation. The procedure consisted of two "unrelated" studies, the first ostensibly on perception, the second ostensibly on reading comprehension. The perception study served to expose subjects to the priming words.

Subjects were shown ten different words on slides and were asked to name the color of the background of each slide as quickly as possible. Before each slide, subjects heard a "memory" word that they had to repeat after naming the color of the slide's background. Six of the memory words were object nouns (e.g., *furniture, corner*) and four were personality trait terms.

Depending upon the experimental condition the trait terms were

- Applicable to the impression formation task and positive (*adventurous, self-confident, independent, persistent*)
- Applicable and negative (*reckless, conceited, aloof, stubborn*)
- Not applicable and positive (*obedient, neat, satirical, grateful*)
- Not applicable and negative (*disrespectful, listless, clumsy, sly*)

The applicable trait terms were selected according to the results of a pilot study; they were those paired terms that were used by subjects with approximately equal frequency to characterize a stimulus person. The description of the stimulus person was designed to be as ambiguous as possible. The nonapplicable trait terms were intuitively selected. However, none of them were mentioned in the pilot study to characterize the stimulus person.

The stimulus person was described in a single paragraph which contained the four most ambiguous descriptions from the pilot study. The four descriptions were embedded in a very short report on the characteristics and behavior of the stimulus person. To illustrate the stimulus material, the descriptions are given below. In parentheses are the percentages of subjects in the pilot study who used the respective trait terms to characterize the stimulus person.

- (Donald) was thinking, perhaps, he would do some skydiving or maybe cross the Atlantic in a yacht (*adventurous* 43%/*reckless* 43%).
- By the way he acted one could readily guess that Donald was well aware of his ability to do many things well (*self-confident* 50%/*conceited* 40%).
- Other than business engagements, Donald's contacts with people were rather limited. He felt he didn't really need to rely on anyone (*independent* 43%/*aloof* 43%).
- Once Donald made up his mind to do something it was as good as done no matter how long it might take or how difficult the going might be. Only rarely did he change his mind even when it might well have been better if he had (*persistent* 53%/*stubborn* 43%).

When subjects had finished the perception study they were given the paragraph about the stimulus person in the seemingly unrelated reading comprehension study. Subjects read the paragraph and then worked on questionnaires. The first page of the questionnaire constituted another experimental condition in which the subject's public commitment to his/her evaluation of the stimulus person was varied. Subjects in the "overt" condition were asked to characterize the stimulus person on the basis of each of the descriptions. In the "no overt" condition subjects were not explicitly asked to characterize the stimulus person.

On the three remaining pages subjects answered factual questions on the text (to increase the credibility of the reading comprehension test), rated the stimulus person on a 10-point scale ranging from extremely undesirable to extremely desirable with no neutral point, and tried to rewrite the paragraph about the stimulus person word for word. Subjects were asked to evaluate the stimulus person and to reproduce the paragraph a second time 10–14 days later. Subjects did not notice that there was any relationship between the two tests of perception and reading comprehension.

To the extent that the "memory" words activate an associated trait category, which in turn will influence the impression formed about the stimulus person, it was predicted that subjects in the applicable, positive condition would form a more favorable impression about the stimulus person than subjects in the applicable, negative condition.

Results of subjects' characterizations in the overt condition confirmed this prediction. When positive, applicable memory words had been presented, seven out of ten subjects gave a positive characterization of the stimulus person. When negative, applicable words had been presented, seven out of ten subjects gave a negative characterization of the simulus person. The differences between the positive and the negative condition are significant at $p < 0.02$ using Fisher's exact test.

For the nonapplicable condition there were no significant differences, although there was a slight tendency for subjects to characterize the stimulus person in the opposite direction. Thus, it was not the desirability of trait terms which affected the characterization of the stimulus person but rather the activation of a relevant trait category.

For the desirability ratings in the applicable condition, a significant valence (positive vs. negative)×time (immediate vs. delayed measure) interaction emerged. This interaction can be attributed to the fact that the desirability ratings became more negative with time in the negative condition than in the positive condition.

Further analysis indicated that there were no significant differences between positive and negative conditions on the immediate measure. However, the differences on the delayed measure were significant. In a similar vein, more subjects rated the stimulus person as desirable in the positive than in the negative condition (13 vs. 6 subjects), and more subjects rated the stimulus person as undesirable in the negative than in the positive condition (14 vs. 7 subjects; $\chi^2 (40) = 3.61$, $p < 0.05$).

For all subjects in the applicable condition, 27 out of 40 rated the stimulus person in a manner consistent with the evaluative meaning of the respective memory words.

In the nonapplicable condition only nine out of 20 subjects rated the stimulus person in accordance with the evaluative meaning of the nonapplicable trait terms. Once more, it is obvious that verbal exposure to the memory words affected the evaluation of the stimulus person in an unrelated task only when the trait terms were applicable to the description of the stimulus person.

Therefore, the influence of the stimulus person on the final evaluation cannot be attributed to a generalized halo effect of the trait terms' positive or negative evaluative tone, since the nonapplicable trait terms did not influence the ratings of the stimulus person in the predicted direction.

The influence on the evaluations of the target, however, can be understood in terms of category accessibility. The data reported by Higgins et al. (1977) lend support to the notion that the final target ratings were affected by a process of category activation. Unrelated trait terms primed an associated category, which then influenced the processing of further information via the activation of related trait categories. Thus, the interpretation of further ambiguous stimulus information was influenced by related activated categories, whereas it was neither influenced by unrelated, activated categories nor by related but less accessible categories.

Higgins et al. (1977) demonstrated the effect of priming on the activation of related categories using single trait terms (the memory words). In addition, subsequent research showed that priming also occurs with other stimulus material. Specifically, Srull and Wyer (1979) reported that diagnostic behavioral descriptions, in contrast to trait adjectives, successfully activated related categories. The Higgins et al. (1977) study had already demonstrated that it is not necessary for the priming effect to occur for subjects to be aware of the exposure to critical features. This line of reasoning was extended by Bargh and Pietromonaco (1982), who showed that even subliminally presented trait terms primed relevant trait categories.

Relative category accessibility, therefore, seems to play an important role in social perception. This seems to be especially true with regard to ambiguous stimuli which increase the need to apply some interpretive guidelines. Moreover, there is evidence that internal sources may also result in increased accessibility of associated categories.

Frequent use of the same construct to account for environmental events or behavior of other persons may result in the construct becoming chronically accessible (Bargh & Thein, 1985). To the extent that they have chronically accessible constructs, people will be more sensitive to information consistent with that construct when forming an impression of another person.

The availability of chronically accessible categories will not only increase sensitivity to consistent information but also facilitate the processing of such information. This will be especially true when the information processing capacities of an individual are depleted due to information overload. Under such conditions chronically accessible constructs will allow the individual to process the incoming information more rapidly and to use it in forming an impression on-line. Without chronically accessible constructs impression formation will be primarily based on that part of the original information which can be retrieved from memory.

Empirical evidence suggests different impression formation processes depending on the amount of information an individual has to process at a given time. Under conditions of nonoverload, the individual is expected to form an impression on-line right from the start of the information presentation. This first impression will then serve as an expectancy with which further information can be compared.

As a result of this comparison process, subsequent information items may be regarded as consistent, inconsistent, or neutral with regard to the first impression. Research on memory and impression formation has shown that more elaborative processing is used for inconsistent information than for consistent information (see Hastie & Kumar, 1979).

The greater effort invested in the processing of inconsistent information results in superior recall of this information. Moreover, to the extent that an early impression about the target has been formed, final evaluation of the target will depend on the information presented and not on the information recalled. That is, to give the final evaluation of the target it will be merely necessary to recall the early impression, instead of recomputing the final evaluation from the information that was finally stored in memory (Bargh & Thein, 1985, pp. 1130–1131).

On the other hand, under conditions of information overload the individual is expected to lack the additional processing capacity required to form the early impression about the stimulus person. Therefore, when asked to give the final evaluation of the target the individual cannot retrieve an early impression but has instead to rely on the information items he/she can recall. The final evaluation will then correspond more closely to the items remembered than to the items actually presented.

Note, however, that the information load condition will interact with the existence of chronically accessible constructs. Specifically, under conditions of information overload subjects possessing chronically accessible constructs should be able to form an early impression about the target in spite of the large amount of information to be processed. An accessible construct will allow an individual to process related information with a minimal amount of attention. To the extent that a relevant accessible construct facilitates information processing, subjects under information overload conditions should again be able to form an early impression about the target and to give differential attention to subsequent impression-consistent and impression-inconsistent information and should base their final evaluation of the target more on the early impression than on the information remembered.

To investigate the effects suggested by the notion of chronically accessible constructs, Bargh and Thein (1985) conducted a study on impression formation under information overload and nonoverload conditions. Based on earlier work of Higgins, King and Mavin (1982), a free-response measure of accessible constructs was taken from 194 male and female psychology students.

This measure consists of listing up to 10 traits that best describe

- The type of person the individual seeks out
- The type of person the individual avoids
- The type of person the individual likes
- The type of person the individual dislikes
- The type of person the individual frequently encounters

Construct accessibility was operationalized in terms of output primacy; that is, chronically accessible constructs are those that are given first in response to the first four questions above, and first and second to the frequency question. This measure seems to differentiate reliably between persons with different chronically accessible constructs. The Bargh and Thein (1985) subjects were classified into a group of 90 chronics, who mentioned *honesty* (and the related terms *sincere* or *trustworthy*) but who did not mention *dishonesty*, and a second group of 92 nonchronics, who never mentioned *honesty, dishonesty,* or related terms in their answers to the five questions above.

Subjects then read a series of 24 behaviors describing a target person and were asked to form an impression about the target. Subjects received either 12 honest, 6 dishonest, and 6 neutral behaviors, or they read a sequence of 6 honest, 12 dishonest, and 6 neutral behaviors. The behavioral descriptions were presented on a screen one at a time.

To manipulate capacity load the presentation rate of the behavioral descriptions was varied. In the self-paced presentation (nonoverload), the subjects themselves controlled the presentation rate by pressing a button to read the next behavioral description. Thus it was also possible to measure reading time for each description.

In the rapid-paced presentation condition (overload), the behavior descriptions were presented automatically, with each description appearing for 1.5 s followed by a 0.5-s pause. When all descriptions had been read the dependent measures were obtained.

Dependent measures included a free recall test. Subjects were asked to list as many of the behaviors as possible. After the free recall test they were asked to name as many streets in the immediate area as they could. This task simply served to minimize the impact of the free recall test on a following surprise cued recall test. In the cued recall test subjects had to complete 24 questions which corresponded to the 24 behavioral descriptions given before. For instance, for the behavioral description "Gregory searched for the owner of the lost wristwatch" the cued recall question was "For whom did Gregory search?"

Finally, subjects rated the stimulus person on each of 12 traits on 11-point scales ranging from *not at all* to *extremely*. Half of the traits were positive or negative traits related to the dimension of *honesty-dishonesty* (e.g., *sincere, dependable, dishonest*) and half were positive or negative unrelated trait terms (e.g., *intelligent, stubborn, annoying*).

Two recall measures were included in the dependent variables because they are considered to measure different aspects of recall. Specifically, the cued recall test is regarded as more sensitive to what information was actually stored in memory even when it is not easily accessible. The free recall test, in contrast, measures the subset of encoded behaviors that are easily accessible and retrieved (Srull, 1984; Taylor & Fiske, 1981).

With regard to the impression formation process described above, it was hypothesized that under nonoverload conditions both chronics and nonchronics would form an initial impression of the target, would then perceive subsequent behaviors as either consistent or inconsistent with this initial impression, and would therefore spend more attention and processing time on the inconsistent behavior. Better recall of the inconsistent minority behavior should result.

Reading time was therefore analyzed as an indicator of processing activity. Consistent with the prediction, subjects gave more attention and processing time to minority behavior (mean 8.0 s) than to majority behavior (mean 7.0 s). Mean reading time for neutral behavior was 6.3 s. Moreover, similar results in the expected direction were obtained for the free recall test. The number of behavioral descriptions free recalled depended on behavior type. That is, minority behavior was better recalled than majority or neutral behavior. In addition, reading time and free recall correlated significantly for minority behavior ($r = 0.14$, t (95) $= 3.19$, $p < 0.01$), whereas this correlation did not differ significantly from zero for majority behavior ($r = 0.05$ n.s.).

The superior free recall of minority behavior may be attributed to it being more distinctive in the encoding context as well as in the retrieval context. Some support for this notion comes from the cued recall results. Since the cued recall is thought to circumvent the associative network, it is thought to be a better indicator of what was actually stored in memory. Results of the cued recall showed no differences between behavior types. That is, minority (mean 0.58), majority (mean 0.59), and neutral behavior (mean 0.60) were encoded with nearly identical frequency. Since, however, minority behavior was better *free* recalled, it must have been more accessible and distinctive in memory.

Chronicity did not influence recall or reading latency in the self-paced presentation condition. In contrast, for the rapid-paced presentation condition, important differences between chronics and nonchronics were expected. Specifically, for chronics, the same pattern of free recall as in the nonoverload condition was now expected, since their chronically accessible construct would allow them to process efficiently large amounts of information and to form an initial impression about the stimulus person. Nonchronics, on the other hand, should not be able to form an initial impression and should exhibit no differential recall of minority and majority behavior.

In fact, a significant interaction between chronicity, presentation mode, and behavior type emerged. Further analysis revealed reliable differences between recall of minority and majority behavior for chronics but not for nonchronics. That is, consistent with the hypothesis suggested by the impression formation model above, those individuals possessing relevant chronically accessible constructs were able to form an initial impression of the target person, even under conditions of information overload.

Results of the cued recall tests showed that fewer behavioral descriptions were recalled in the rapid-paced presentation condition than in the self-paced presentation condition, but this effect did not differentially affect minority, majority, or neutral behavior. In addition, there were no differences between chronics and nonchronics in cued recall under overload conditions. This finding suggests that nonchronics had a small amount of attentional capacity to encode the behavioral descriptions, although this was not enough for more elaborate processing and better free recall.

To test the assumption that subjects in the self-paced presentation condition and chronics in the rapid-paced presentation condition did indeed form impressions on-line, free recall was reanalyzed using six trial blocks as an additional within-subjects factor. Free recall of minority behavior was greater than that of majority behavior from block 2 onward for all groups except for nonchronics under overload conditions.

One final aspect concerning the impression formation process remains to be addressed. Given that individuals in the self-paced presentation condition and chronics in the rapid-paced presentation condition do form an initial impression of the target on which they may base directly their final target evaluation, there should be a close relationship between the ratio of honest to dishonest behavioral descriptions *presented* and their final evaluation of the target, whereas this evaluation should be unrelated to the ratio of behavioral descriptions freely recalled.

On the other hand, nonchronics under information overload should base their final evaluation of the target on the ratio of behavioral descriptions *free recalled*, since they are expected not to be able to form an initial impression of the target.

The hypothesized relationships between free recall and impressions under various conditions were supported by the results of path analyses. Under nonoverload conditions the same pattern of results emerged for both chronics and nonchronics, with substantial paths leading from the ratio of behavioral descriptions presented directly to the final impression, and negligible, nonsignificant paths leading from the free recall ratio to the final impression.

An identical pattern characterized chronics under overload conditions. However, opposite findings were obtained for nonchronics in this condition, with a significant path leading from the free recall ratio to the final impression. Final impressions, on the other hand, were virtually unrelated to the ratio of behaviors presented.

All in all, the results of the Bargh and Thein (1985) study lend support to the impression formation process depicted above. Additional results by Bargh, Bond, Lombardi and Tota (1986) indicate that chronic and situational sources of construct accessibility exert a joint influence on impression formation. Chronic accessibility and subliminal priming influenced impression ratings independently. Further results (Herr, 1986; Herr, Sherman & Fazio, 1983) show that priming with moderate exemplars elicits consistent impressions (an assimilation effect), while priming with extreme exemplars elicits divergent impressions (a contrast effect; see Eiser & Stroebe, 1972). Detailed analyses of the components of impression formation processes enable a more thorough understanding of person perception. The concept of chronically accessible constructs sheds some light on the general notion of attentional selectivity.

Attention may be diverted differentially to salient, distinctive stimuli under conditions of information overload to the extent that chronically accessible constructs exist which allow efficient processing of related stimuli. As long as people live in unchanging environments, chronically accessible constructs may even fulfill an adaptive function since they free the individual from the elaborate processing of repeatedly encountered "constant" information and thus preserve attentional and processing capacities which can then be directed toward the analysis of unknown, new, or potentially dangerous stimuli (Alloy & Tabachnik, 1984).

With regard to the relationship between impression formation and memory, it becomes obvious that recall and impressions will be related only when the impression was not formed during information acquisition. This may be the case when the individual did not intend to form an impression or did not have sufficient processing capacity to do so. Otherwise impressions will be related more closely to the actual input of information than to that part that can be free recalled afterwards. Thus, research on social cognition can give some detailed explanations of the processes underlying impression formation and the perception of people. General theoretical frameworks of social cognition which are based on theories of memory and search and retrieval processes have been described by Hastie, Park and Weber (1984), Wyer and Gordon (1984), and Wyer and Srull (1986).

Halo Effects: When Single Items of Information Are Dominated by the Overall Impression

Student teachers judged the behavior of stimulus teachers pursuing an asymmetrical or neutral style of interaction in class on the following rating scales: *open-minded, derogatory, restrictive, fair, tolerant, unsympathetic, humorless, likable, flexible, boring.*

Factor analysis of the trait descriptions revealed a general factor accounting for 62.4% of the variance (Bierhoff & Bierhoff-Alfermann, 1977). Although the trait descriptions had been deliberately selected to obtain a general evaluative measure, there were remarkably high intercorrelations between different trait adjectives (for instance *fair* and *boring*) so that a person considered to be fair was perceived as less boring (see Merz, 1962).

The overall impression, reflecting a general evaluative judgment of the stimulus person, is extremely important in person perception. This finding, which may sometimes be considered a judgmental bias, has been termed the halo effect. It is characterized by high intercorrelations of the given judgmental scales. I shall try to describe important causes of halo effects as well as processes leading to undue perseverance in the judgments of personality attributes. Finally, an alternative explanation of the meaning change hypothesis will be given (see Box 12).

Illusory Correlations Between Trait Characteristics

Halo effects are of practical importance with regard to diagnostic decision-making and scientific research as a whole as far as rating scales are considered. Discussions of the possibility of constant biases using rating scales may be found as early as 1907. Cooper (1981) reports that in that year Wells noted that judging persons on several attributes may produce a higher consistency among these attributes (illusory halo) than actually exists (true halo). This tendency should be especially pronounced with regard to ill-defined attributes because the meaning of ambiguous attributes may easily coincide with the overall impression of the stimulus person. This rating effect was termed the halo effect by Thorndike (1920). It is defined in terms of perceived correlations being higher than the true correlations. The effect is supposed to result from the fact that the judgment of single attributes is influenced by the overall impression of a person.

Subsequent analyses (see Cooper, 1981) showed that the halo effect may be regarded as a special example of implicit personality theories. Illusory assumptions concerning the interrelations of relevant attributes lead observers to perceive exaggerated dependency between the judgmental dimensions. To the extent that corresponding relationships do not exist in reality, person perception becomes biased.

The effect of the *warm-cold* variable (see "Central and peripheral dispositions") may be reinterpreted in terms of the halo-effect because this phenomenon reflects illusory correlations between trait characteristics. The *warm-cold* variable strongly influenced impression formation because it was closely related to the corresponding judgmental dimension (see Figure 3). It is reasonable to assume, therefore, that illusory correlations between the *warm-cold* variable and related test attributes determined impression formation.

For the halo-effect interpretation to be valid it is necessary for the actual correlations between the stimulus traits to be lower than ratings of the traits indicate. Only when the true correlations between traits are low does the halo effect occur (Murphy & Reynolds, 1988). In a sense, one can distinguish between a true halo effect based on actual interrelations between the judgmental dimensions and an illusory halo effect based on unwarranted assumptions concerning the correlations of traits (Cooper, 1981; Kenny & Berman, 1980; Murphy & Reynolds, 1988). Illusory halo effects may be attributed to five different sources (Cooper, 1981):

1. Observers lack information about the stimulus person and are therefore not able to give a sound judgment concerning the judgmental dimensions in

question. They rely on their overall impression to form a final judgment. For instance, stereotyped information processing occurs when there is insufficient information that does not allow for differentiated judgments (e.g., when there is only information about membership in a social group; see Chap. 3, "Areas of stereotype research").

2. Single judgments are influenced by the overall impression or by salient characteristics that are representative of the overall impression (e.g., *warm-cold*). Judgments are influenced by unwarranted assumptions concerning the interrelations of relevant trait characteristics. Such assumptions are made within implicit personality theories (see "Implicit personality theories complete the first impression").

3. Observers have to make their judgments on scales which are equivocal and lack concrete definition. Vaguely defined judgmental scales force observers to rely on global impressions because they cannot decide which item of the information presented is especially relevant for a specific judgment.

4. Raters do not devote enough time and effort to their task of differentiating between several trait dimensions. They employ a simple schema without exhausting the data base.

5. Observers incorrectly analyze the available information. Single observations may be simplified or supplemented when they are memorized so that they no longer represent the "true" information when they are used in impression formation. To the extent that information processing of stored data results in a loss of important details, storing of information in memory leads to illusory correlations. This source of error obviously may be used to explain stereotypes (see Chap. 3, "Stereotype research – practical applications").

The last source is important because in many cases judgments about another person are made after a considerable amount of time has elapsed from the moment information about this person was stored. With time memory traces lose their salience, and when a judgment finally has to be made only vague recollections are left. The resulting memory "gaps" are "refilled" using implicit personality theories (Cooper, 1981) and illusory halo effects result. Relying on schema-based recall becomes increasingly probable when little concrete and character-revealing information is present and only pale recollections of this information exist.

Weiss (1979) argued that given such a weak information base the observer is almost forced to rely on implicit personality theories. This sort of biased judgment should diminish when plenty of detailed information is provided. Weiss predicted that the greater the differentiation among assessees the more information about the assessees would be provided. Results supported this prediction: personality descriptions based on extensive interviews and behavioral assessments were more differentiated and less homogeneous than descriptions based on interview alone or behavioral assessment alone. Least variability resulted from personality descriptions made on the basis of stereotypes about race, age, profession, or place of birth of the assessees.

These findings indicate some of the conditions that instigate the use of stereotypes in person perception (see Chap. 3 "Areas of stereotype research"). It may be added that personality descriptions of assessees were least homogeneous when detailed information was provided (mean $r = 0.14 - 0.19$). On the other hand, homogeneity of descriptions was considerably higher when subjects had to rely on stereotypes (mean $r = 0.44$). Little information about the assessees leads to an increasing influence of implicit personality theories so that a homogeneous set of descriptions resulted.

This principle may be demonstrated with regard to the relationship between the kind of information provided and the variability of the ratings. For instance, when no information about personal values was provided, subjects had difficulties in making sophisticated judgments in this domain. On the other hand, subjects who had to rely exclusively on interview information showed little variability in descriptions concerning behavioral style.

Cooper (1981) mentions several processes than can lead to illusory halo effects:

— Errors in perceiver's covariation judgments, especially with regard to contingency tables (see Chap. 2, "Uncovering relationships")
— Undue emphasis on similarities between stimuli as opposed to differences
— Preference for verifying questions instead of falsifying questions (see Chap. 2, "Uncovering relationships")
— Assimilation of information to a preestablished anchor (see "The first impression: practical implications") and neglect of inconsistent evidence
— Use of prototypes serving as schematic expectations that organize perception (see Chap. 5, "Self-fulfilling prophecies and processes of expectation confirmation")
— Perseverance of discredited information (see "Order of presentation of information")

Finally, Cooper (1981) describes promising methods for reducing illusory halo effects. These methods are of special interest because halo effects call into question the validity of personality ratings and self-ratings of personality traits (see Shweder, 1975, 1980). To the extent that correlations within ratings or self-ratings indicate the subject's assumptions about general relationships between traits, their diagnostic value is limited.

Several methods for reducing illusory halo effects seem promising:

— Increasing the familiarity between observer and stimulus person, for instance, by providing sufficient time for observations, extensive interviews, and abundant information.
— Employing multiple observers, so that their ratings of the target person may be averaged. Averaging compensates for rater-specific biases.
— Inclusion of irrelevant judgmental dimensions known to influence the overall impression of a stimulus person (e.g., attractiveness).

– Providing for simultaneous exposure of information and impression formation.

The last factor gains central importance because memory-based judgments are especially prone to being distorted by illusory halo effects. Halo effects are very common. They are present when different judgmental dimensions are influenced by the overall impression. Halo effects may be regarded as evaluative effects, since the overall impression represents a general evaluation. That is, a positive or negative impression of the target person influences the judgments of his or her specific characteristics.

Halo effects may be controlled for by obtaining the overall impression and extracting the effect of the overall impression from ratings of single dimensions (Landy & Farr, 1980). In addition, correlational methods and confirmatory factor analysis permit an estimate of true halos which can be compared with estimates of illusory halos (Kenny & Berman, 1980). Besides statistical control, one should consider several rules of thumb concerning the construction of the rating scale. For instance, the number of scale categories should not exceed 9, and should not be lower than 5. End poles and judgmental dimensions should be well-defined and raters should be trained.

Halo Effect Versus Change of Meaning

It has been widely demonstrated that context influences the ratings of specific characteristics, such as with regard to person perception. In a typcial research design a test attribute is presented within a positive and within a negative context and ratings of the test attribute in both contexts are obtained. In contrast to studies on algebraic models of impression formation, which employ ratings of the stimulus person, rating of the test attribute is the main dependent variable for the measurement of context effects. Box I 2 reviews the most important findings on the controversy of halo effects versus the meaning-change hypothesis.

Box 12. Halo effect and change of meaning in trait combinations
Will a trait adjective be rated differently depending on the given context information? Cohen and Schümer (1972) asked their subjects to rate a test adjective according to different dimensions. As far as ratings of the dimension *friendly-aloof* (social evaluation dimension) are concerned a consistent pattern emerged:

> The rating of the specific test trait is assimilated to the context, almost independent of various rating instructions or the number of context attributes (Cohen & Schümer, 1972, p. 320).

Subjects were told that the adjectives described one person or that they described several different persons. This difference in instructions did not influence the context effect. Thus, the context effect may be easily triggered.

Analogous results were found by Balzer, Schümer-Kohrs and Schümer (1974). However, Anderson (1971), Wyer and Dermer (1968), and Wyer and Watson (1969) report a context effect only in conditions where the adjectives were attributed to a single person. Slight variations in the way the stimulus material is presented suffice to produce different amounts of assimilation.

In addition, Cohen and Schümer (1972) used different context conditions consisting of one or two (evaluatively consistent) adjectives. Assimilation of the test adjective to the context was observed, even within the one-adjective context. Again, a halo effect was elicited. A more recent study (Balzer et al., 1974) also found no difference in context effects depending on the number of context adjectives (two or four). This result is somewhat inconsistent with the findings of Anderson (1971) and Kaplan (1971), who observed set size effects, which were, however, of minor importance.

Balzer et al. (1974) used four levels of context likableness (very positive, positive, negative, and very negative). The interaction of context traits and test traits was significant for sympathy ratings of the test trait. Graphic representation of this result in Figure 5 shows the interaction to depend primarily on the influence of the negative context on the rating of the negative attribute.

Although context traits and test traits interacted significantly, context effects are present at all levels of the test attribute. At first glance, this context effect may be regarded as evidence in support of the meaning-change hypothesis (see Box T1). To the extent that the test trait likableness is

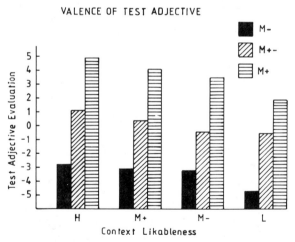

Figure 5. Mean ratings of likableness of test trait as a function of test trait likableness and context likableness. The rating scale ranged from −10 (very unlikable) to +10 (very likable). $M+$, Mildly positive; $M+−$, neutral; $M−$, mildly negative; H, very positive; L, very negative. (From Balzer, Schümer-Kohrs & Schümer, 1974, p. 33. Copyright 1974 by Verlag für Psychologie − C. J. Hogrefe. Reprinted by permission)

assimilated to the context, it is possible that the range of connotative meanings of the test attribute is narrowed. With a positive context there may be
a shift towards the positive direction, whereas a negative context could produce a shift towards the negative pole.

However, this interpretation is not conclusive. After all, evaluative
judgments do not genuinely indicate how the meaning of a characteristic
varies with the context. Test trait ratings may show assimilation of the evaluation to the context or they may show no such effect: the meaning-change
hypothesis is consistent with both results (see Watkins & Peynircioğlu,
1984; see also "Daring: Courage or recklessness?").

Anderson (1971) suggested an alternative hypothesis (see Box T 1)
assuming that a halo effect influences the attributes of the description of
a stimulus person. According to Anderson's suggestion, the final evaluation of a test trait represents a combination of a context-free rating of the
specific trait and the overall impression of the stimulus person. The halo
effect would then account for the assimilation of the test trait likableness
to the context.

To test this hypothesis, Anderson (1971) conducted two experiments in
which subjects had to rate a test attribute under two different conditions.
In one condition they first had to write a personality description of the
stimulus person and then rated the test attributes. In the second condition
they only rated the test attributes without previously thinking about the
personality of the stimulus person. Anderson hypothesized that subjects
would form a coherent picture of the stimulus person when they had to
describe the stimulus person, so that this condition would foster a change
of meaning of the test adjective. Hence, it was predicted that for the essay
condition the halo effect would be more pronounced than for the simple
rating condition.

Results, as displayed in Figure 6, did not support the prediction. There
is a strong assimilation to the context, so that the more positive the context,
the more positively a test attribute is rated. But there is no crossover of the
profiles. In the essay condition the test attribute was not rated more
negatively with a negative context and more positively with a positive context than in the simple rating condition.

Results show that the assimilation effect was not strengthened when
raters first formulated a description of the stimulus person. Another four
experiments replicated this finding (Simpson & Ostrom, 1975). However, it
is questionable whether these results argue against the meaning-change hypothesis. Anderson (1971) himself points to the possibility that even in the
simple rating condition subjects might have formed a coherent impression
of the stimulus person. On the other hand, subjects in the essay condition
were allowed only 2 min to write down their impression. Finally, one must
again point to the fact that evaluative judgments are not appropriate to settle the argument on the meaning-change hypothesis. All in all, it is important to keep in mind that strong halo effects emerge within trait combina-

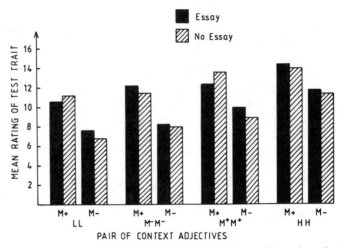

Figure 6. Mean ratings of likableness of test trait as a function of the value of test trait, the value of context likableness, and essay. The test adjective was selected to have a medium positive ($M+$) or medium negative ($M-$) scale value. Context consisted of two attributes, both being negative (NN), slightly negative ($M-M-$), slightly positive ($M+M+$), or positive (HH). Traits were selected from a list of normative trait ratings. Component trait ratings were made on numerical scales ranging from 1 to 20. Subjects had to indicate how much they liked the particular trait of the target person. 48 subjects took part in each of the two conditions. Results were replicated in a second experiment in which, again, 96 subjects took part. (From Anderson, 1971, p. 79. Copyright 1971 by Academic Press. Reprinted by permission)

tions describing a target person. Therefore, the "sign" of the individual trait depends on the context. The findings clearly demonstrate the wide range of halo effects in person perception.

The problem of a change of meaning as a function of context cannot be solved using the approach discussed above (see Ostrom, 1977). In addition, some results support the meaning-change hypothesis. Wyer (1974a) observed a weaker assimilation effect when the test trait had a very restricted range of meanings (see Figure 7). This finding supports the meaning-change hypothesis since stronger assimilation effects may be predicted given a large range of possible meanings.

However, with additional assumptions these results can also be interpreted as a halo effect (Ostrom, 1977). Suppose, for instance, that "wishy-washy" characteristics receive a lower weight in the overall judgment than salient characteristics. On the other hand, these results support the prediction that halo effects become more pronounced when equivocal information about the stimulus person is present. A wide range of possible meanings indicates that there are various possible ways to interpret the given trait. This interpretative range is characteristically found with unclear, equivocal information. Implicit personality theories probably exert a stronger

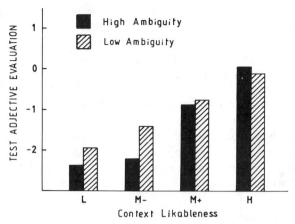

Figure 7. Mean ratings of likableness of test trait as a function of context likableness and test trait ambiguity. Test traits represent three levels of likableness, which were averaged in the graphical presentation. Context consisted of two adjectives that were negatively (*NN*), slightly negatively (*M−M−*), slightly positively (*M+M+*), or positively (*HH*) evaluated. Traits were selected from a list of normative trait ratings. Component trait ratings were made on a scale ranging from −10 (dislike very much) to +10 (like very much). Results are based on ratings of 36 subjects. (From Wyer, 1974, p. 831. Copyright 1974 by the American Psychological Association. Reprinted by permission)

influence on judgments when there is uncertainty concerning the specific information.

There is reason to suggest that halo effects result partly from a tendency of the raters not to judge a specific individual but to judge a person holding a social role (Merz, 1962). According to this view, inconsistent ratings of a target person by different perceivers − given close acquaintance − would be caused by inconsistent behavior of that person when interacting with the different perceivers. The more equivocal the given information is, the higher should be the probability of role-based judgments.

Order of Presentation of Information

A common notion is that the first information received exerts an enduring influence on the organization of knowledge. Following Asch (1946), the first information should dominate the impression of a person in comparison with subsequent information. The first information about the characteristics of another person serves as a reference point that may restrict the connotative range of subsequent trait attributions.

Information received at an early age is assumed to have more influence than that received at a later stage of development. A young child will be deeply influenced by his or her socialization agents, and the way they explain the world to him or her will structure the way the child interprets his or her experiences in later life. In contrast, later information has a lower weight. The anchor of childhood experience structures future incoming information, assimilates its meaning, and provides for a definition of personal viewpoints in society.

Freud (1976) was probably right when he emphasized the importance of childhood experiences for a person's biography. Order effects in daily life are also acknowledged in the form of proverbs and sayings like "First come, first served." Other proverbs, however, point to a recency effect: "He who laughs last laughs longest."

Order effects may gain importance in real life situations, for instance when a person applies for a new job at another company. Imagine an applicant characterized almost exclusively by positive aspects that prove to fit the new position, but – unfortunately – he/she is not fluent in a foreign language as was requested. Should one mention this flaw right at the beginning of the interview or would it be better to wait until a later moment in the conversation?

Another example: Try to imagine a car dealer who wants to sell cars as expensively as possible, knowing that most of his/her customers prefer cheap cars. Should the dealer start praising magnificent limousines without concealing what they cost or should he/she – trying the alternative strategy – concentrate on average cars equipped with some interesting specials. The dealer then waits until the customer has made up his/her mind to buy the car. At that moment the dealer points to the fact that everything has its price and that the wonderful car with all the extras will cost $ 14000.

As a matter of fact, the latter strategy, known as the low ball technique among car dealers, seems to be promising. In a series of experiments, Cialdini, Cacioppo, Bassett and Miller (1978) demonstrated that unpleasant information was more likely to be accepted when it was given at a later point in time than when it was presented earlier. In one of these studies students were asked to participate in an experiment which required them to arrive at 7 a.m. Students who learned that they had to arrive that early *after* they had already decided to participate showed more willingness to participate and more actual participation than students who were *first* informed about the time at which they had to arrive at the experimental laboratory. When the low ball technique was applied, 53% of the students contacted actually arrived at 7 a.m., whereas only 24% of the students who had been told straight away about the 7 a.m. time took part.

Obviously, a decision in favor of one alternative persisted even when the alternative was devalued by subsequent information. In contrast, early announcement of negative information led subjects to decide against the alternative. Commitment to a decision, the cognitive work preceding the decision, and an unfulfilled obligation to the requester seem to be sufficient to induce subjects to ignore later inconsistent information (Burger & Petty, 1981; Cialdini et al., 1978).

The findings discussed above suggest that prior information determines the way an alternative will be evaluated. Once a certain decision has been made, subsequent contradictory information tends to be ignored. To be sure, one will not stick rigidly to *any* decision no matter what happens. If subsequent information reveals that the decision was premature and will lead to very uncomfortable consequences the decision will, in most cases, be reversed. But, referring to the above example, a car dealer may be satisfied when he succeeds in pushing the price from \$ 12 200 to \$ 12 400 without causing the client to refuse the car.

First Come, First Served

The person who is the first to comment on something may structure the relevant issue. As an extreme example, consider the relationship between the small child and his or her parents. The way the parents interpret events, persons, and objects influences the cognitive organization of the child, suggesting specific expectations about how things go together. This influence of early information was termed the prior entry effect by Jones and Gerard (1967). Early information builds up expectations, so inconsistent later information is no longer considered in an unbiased manner.

When we want to convince somebody of a particular interpretation of an event, it obviously makes a difference whether he or she has not yet made up his or her mind about the issue or whether precise expectations based on a stable cognitive organization already exist. In the latter case new information will be assimilated in accordance with the existing expectations (see below), whereas in the first case the person will use the new information to develop categories from which expectations may be derived (Jones & Gerard, 1967).

Several examples illustrate the assimilation to existing expectations in the domain of social perception. In one study (Bruner & Minturn, 1955), capital letters and two-digit numbers were presented with short exposure times. Depending on the experimental condition, subjects had to recognize four numbers or four letters. Following this task, subjects saw a test figure that might be interpreted as *B* or as *13*, since the distance between the vertical line and the curved part was very small ("broken B").

Subjects were asked to draw what they had seen. With short exposures of the stimulus material, the interpretation of the test figure was influenced by context information. In the number condition, predominantly open test figures were drawn. 92% of the subjects drew an open test figure given the number context, whereas 67% drew closed or partly closed figures given the letter context. Even with longer exposure times, 33% of the subjects with the letter context drew closed figures. After a mixed series of two letters and two numbers, open drawings dominated regardless of short or long exposure times. Given short, medium, and long exposure times, 92%, 71%, and 58% of the subjects respectively identified the test figure as *B* in the letter context.

Bruner, Postman and Rodrigues (1951) reported an impressive example of the operation of expectation effects when they demonstrated that an initial hypothesis held by the subject influenced color perception. This effect emerged when the color was ambiguous but related to an unequivocal object shape.

The colors red, orange, and yellow were each represented by two objects definitely associated with the respective color:

- Tomato, boiled lobster claw
- Tangerine, carrot
- Lemon, banana

When a somewhat brownish-orange color was presented, red objects were judged to be "redder" and yellow objects to be "yellower" though the actual color presented remained constant. Subjects had to adjust a color-wheel, one time starting from the yellow pole, the other time starting from the red pole.

In fact, red and yellow objects were perceived to be particularly different when the color-wheel had to be adjusted relying on memory. However, expectation effects were also pronounced when the object was present while the color-wheel was adjusted. No expectation effects emerged when optimal conditions for perception were provided (except a minor effect in the recall test). This result points to the fact that the effects of a preestablished hypothesis may be eliminated when diagnostic information is available. The findings parallel research on the halo effect, where it was demonstrated that a stereotype or an evaluative overall impression exerted the strongest influence on judgments when the specific information regarding separate judgmental dimensions was ambiguous (Weiss, 1979).

More recent studies corroborated the finding that hypotheses about the color of an object influence color perception as described above (Hendrick, Wallace & Tappenbeck, 1968). As another effect of preestablished hypotheses, incongruent events may produce confusion (Bruner & Postman, 1949). Subjects took longer to identify playing cards correctly when playing cards inconsistent with expectations were presented for a short time, for instance a red two of spades and a black ace of diamonds.

Normal cards were correctly identified within an average of 28 ms, whereas identification took an average of 114 ms when the experimental cards were used. Average reaction time was 390 ms when the first experimental card was presented. When an experimental card had already been shown, reaction time decreased to 230 ms for the second experimental card. Recognition of subsequent experimental cards took an average of 84 ms.

The experiments indicate that, to a considerable extent, the cognitive organization is structured by expectations formed in the past (Bruner & Postman, 1949). Information acquired early exerts an influence on how subsequent information is processed and interpreted. Bruner (1957a) notes that perception may be regarded as generic to the extent that every event perceived gains its meaning through the categories according to which it is classified. "Thus, the meaning of a thing is the placement of an object in a network of hypothetical inference concerning its other observable properties, its effects, and so on" (Bruner, 1957a, p. 126).

Categories and concepts (equivalence classes) that are used to code perceptual input may be distinguished with regard to their accessibility. This accessibility determines the perceptual readiness of a person. It depends on two conditions (Bruner, 1957a):

1. Subjective probability estimates of the perceiver regarding the likelihood of given events in his or her environment
2. Specific search sets that are a consequence of a person's needs and wishes

According to this view, proper perception depends on a matching of the perceiver's perceptual readiness and the actual probabilities of events in his or her environment. Inappropriate expectations may be due to order effects, when the first item of information strongly influences the overall impression (see below). However, misperception due to a primacy effect will result only if the first item of information is biased and not representative (see Kruglanski & Ajzen, 1983). To the extent that subsequent information is biased and the preceding information has a higher validity, a primacy effect fosters precise perception because the expectations based on first information are comparatively valid, whereas subsequent contradictory evidence lacks validity.

Interference caused by blurred images is an example from visual perception that shows how erroneous hypotheses derived from blur delay correct identification of the object shown (Bruner & Potter, 1964). The interference effect of blurred images was striking because subjects who first viewed a very blurred image were impaired in their recognition of the picture when it was in focus compared with subjects who started viewing with light blurring. The blurred images probably caused the perceiver to establish erroneous hypotheses about the content of the images. As the image becomes clearer the erroneous hypotheses are not easily abandoned. When the initial presentations are slightly blurred, an appropriate hypothesis may be derived that leads to a fast identification of the object in question.

Self-fulfilling prophecies are examples of expectation effects in interpersonal perception (Merton, 1968). They involve processes of expectancy confirmation and are triggered by specific − sometimes arbitrary − definitions of the situation. Given certain conditions, the situation definition can elicit behavior patterns suitable for producing the expected events.

Chapter 5, "Self-fulfilling prophecies and processes of expectation confirmation," presents an extensive discussion of expectancy confirmation processes. For the moment, a brief review of the expectancy confirmation process may suffice to illustrate the conceptual parallels to order effects (see Box T 2).

Box T2. Expectancy confirmation in social interaction
Darley and Fazio (1980) distinguish between six stages of social interaction during which expectancies may be conveyed. As an example of this process, consider the situation of a teacher taking over a new class. His predecessor

tells him about some pupils that are gifted and promising, and about other pupils who are of average talent and from whom lower achievements may be expected. The sequence of interaction – in the present example that between teacher and pupil – may be divided into several stages, taking into account the perceiver (teacher) and the target person (pupil):

1. Based on observations or stereotypes, the perceiver forms an expectation concerning coming events in a given context.

2. The perceiver's expectations influence his/her behavior so that the behavior will be consistent with expectations.

3. The target person tries to make sense of the perceiver's behavior. The teacher, for example, conveys the impression that he considers the pupil's achievements to be somewhat below average. This impression may be attributed to the teacher (to the extent that other teachers convey a more positive impression) or it may be attributed to the pupil (to the extent that the teachers agree in their appreciation of the pupil's achievements). The probability that the target person changes his/her self-concept is lower if he/she makes an external attribution (to the teacher) than if an internal attribution (to the self) is made (see Snyder & Swann, 1978a).

4. The target person will act according to the attribution made. On the one hand, it is possible that he/she may try to compensate for the allegedly bad impression. On the other hand, he/she may act in accordance with the communication of the perceiver because he/she makes an internal attribution and accepts the perceiver's hypothesis. In addition, the behavior of the target person may be determined by the norm of reciprocity. For instance, this may happen when the perceiver acts in a hostile or friendly manner (Snyder & Swann, 1978a; Snyder, Tanke & Berscheid, 1977).

5. The perceiver interprets the target person's behavior and draws conclusions regarding the suitability of his/her expectations. If the expectations are confirmed, the original hypothesis will most likely be maintained and the perceiver will not recognize that he/she contributed to the confirmation process (Snyder & Swann, 1978a). Even if contradictory evidence is obtained, the wrong expectation may persevere to the extent that it serves as an anchor to which subsequent information is assimilated. The original expectation will also be maintained in the presence of ambiguous events that do not allow straightforward interpretation. Assimilation to the anchor is likely to take place with ambiguous feedback. In addition, one has to take into account that hypothesis-consistent events will be better remembered than hypothesis-inconsistent events (Snyder, 1981; Snyder & Uranowitz, 1978).

6. The target person changes his/her self-concept – in particular following internal attribution (see above) –, drawing self-concept-related conclusions from his/her behavior, which has been influenced by the biased behavior of the perceiver (Fazio, Effrein & Falender, 1981).

The way in which information is assimilated to an already existing viewpoint (anchor) will now be considered in more detail. Experimental results explicating the information processing sequence given communications in favor or against one's viewpoint are presented in Box 13.

Box 13. Biased assimilation to an anchor

In everyday life there are usually many persuasive arguments that contradict one's own viewpoint. Other communications support one's own position. How is information processed which is contained in persuasive communications?

Lord, Ross and Lepper (1979) handed two allegedly authentic research reports to their students that dealt with the pros and cons of capital punishment. Each report consisted of the presentation of the results and of a description of the methods in which technical details of the investigations were explained. Therefore, each subject read four messages. One report proved the deterrent effect of capital punishment, whereas the other questioned this effect. Reports were presented in varying order (pro-anti, anti-pro). Subjects were either convinced of the deterrent effect of capital punishment or they were against capital punishment. Subjects personal viewpoints served as an anchor representing a reference system for the interpretation of the communications (Deusinger, 1980).

Ratings of the quality and the convincingness of the respective investigations indicated a simple pattern of results: subjects advocating capital punishment attributed higher quality and more convincingness to the pro study, whereas opponents of capital punishment preferred the anti study, which they regarded as better conducted and more convincing. Some of the comments students gave illustrate the biased evaluations of the reports (from Lord et al., 1979, p. 2103).

Proponents on pro study and anti study:

> It does support capital punishment in that it presents facts showing that there is a deterrent effect and seems to have gathered data properly.
> The evidence given is relatively meaningless without data about how the overall crime rate went up in those years.

Opponents on pro study and anti study:

> The study was taken only 1 year before and 1 year after capital punishment was reinstated. To be a more effective study they should have taken data from at least 10 years before and as many years as possible after.
> There aren't as many uncontrolled variables in this experiment as in the other one, so I'm still willing to believe the conclusion made.

Following the presentation of results and technical details for both studies, subjects were asked to indicate whether their opinions about capital punishment had changed in the meantime (from -8 = more anti to $+8$ = more pro). The measure of attitude change showed that final opinions were more polarized. Proponents of capital punishment were even more convinced of their position and opponents of capital punishment more strongly rejected the matter in their final attitudes. To say it another way: proponents were more influenced by pro arguments than by anti arguments whereas the reverse relation held for opponents.

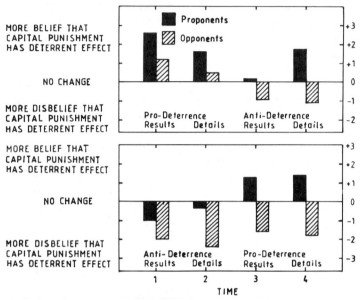

Figure 8. Perceived attitude changes after receiving supporting and contradictory information for proponents and opponents of capital punishment. Perceived attitude change is relative to the start of the experiment. The *top panel* depicts the four change measures in the order pro-anti. The *bottom panel* depicts the results in the order anti-pro. Results are based on the ratings of 24 proponents and opponents of capital punishment, respectively, who were selected from a larger sample. (From Lord, Ross & Lepper, 1979, p. 2107. Copyright 1979 by the American Psychological Association. Reprinted by permission)

Figure 8 shows the attitude changes of proponents and opponents concerning capital punishment following exposure to each of the four separate messages. Regardless of the order of presentation, one can appreciate how the anti position succeeded for opponents, and how proponents elaborated their pro attitudes.

Together with the findings that proponents and opponents merely considered those arguments to be convincing that were consistent with their own position, the results support the assumption that mixed persuasive communications were assimilated to the personal viewpoint. The polarization results were replicated in a similar study by Lord, Lepper and Preston (1984, study 1).

In a somewhat different context Deusinger (1980) noted that the self may serve as a reference system for evaluating the personality and capability of other persons. When no diagnostic information was provided, subjects inferred behavior sets of a stimulus person similar to their own behavior sets. Thus, self-concept may function as an important judgmental anchor.

Inspection of the attitude change sequence in Figure 8 suggests two additional aspects. Opponents of capital punishment were initially influenced by the pro arguments when reading the results of the pro study. But by the time they were presented with the technical details they reverted to their original position. Proponents of capital punishment were initially influenced by anti arguments, but returned to their original viewpoints when provided with pro arguments.

In short, preestablished beliefs and attitudes exert an influence on how new information is processed. In a similar vein, Lindsay and Norman (1975) suggest that theory-guided processes modify information processing on elementary levels — for instance with regard to letter identification (see Bruner & Minturn, 1955). The study of Lord et al. (1979) has already supported the notion that theory-guided processes induce existing expectations and beliefs to persevere in the presence of contradictory information. In the next section, I am going to analyze the meaning of perseverance in social judgment in more detail.

Perseverance and Confirmatory Attribution

Until recently social psychologists appeared to be rather careless concerning their treatment of human subjects for the sake of science. In one experiment (Bramel, 1963) participants were led to believe that they had homosexual inclinations. Although participants were informed later about the fictitious nature of the personality feedback, it was never thoroughly assessed whether debriefing had been successful.

Talking about primacy effects in person perception, the question may be raised of whether false feedback can be successfully reversed by denying its validity at a later point in time. The answer to this question must be "No" (see Box 14). At least very comprehensive and thorough explanations are necessary to correct false personality feedback that has been announced as highly credible.

Box 14. On successfully disclaiming false feedback
Walster, Berscheid, Abrahams and Aronson (1967) told their female subjects that the results of several personality tests suggested that the students were characterized by high or low social competence. A short time later, students learned that the personality feedback had been completely fic-

titious and bore no relation to their actual test scores. Subjects were then asked to rate their actual sociability. Students who had received the low social competence feedback indicated lower perceived social competence than students who had received the high social competence feedback.

In addition, students suffering from fear of social rejection and low self-esteem gave negative ratings of social competence concerning an interview in which they had to prove their competence. High self-esteem students, by contrast, gave especially high ratings of their interview performance and, thus, seemed to compensate for negative personality feedback (although they had already been debriefed). Results indicate the fictitious personality feedback was not completely compensated for, although careful and comprehensive debriefing took place.

This conclusion is corroborated by two further studies (Ross, Lepper & Hubbard, 1975). Subjects were led to believe that they were very able, of average ability, or not very able in discriminating between messages of suicidal persons and messages of other persons. Feedback was fictitious.

Following debriefing the induced performance information persevered as shown by self-ratings as well as by observer ratings. However, the effects of the false feedback were almost completely removed when additional information on the process of perseverance was presented. But minor indications that fictitious effects persisted were still present in observers even when additional explanations were given.

A more general question than those concerning deception in experiments emerges: Do wrong theories that are discredited in the end persevere if they have once been established as true? In a sense, the results presented in Box 14 hint at the existence of such a tendency; the experimental feedback may be regarded as the subjects' personality theory that is discredited through debriefing. Subsequent analyses (Anderson, 1983b; Anderson, Lepper & Ross, 1980; Anderson, New & Speer, 1985; Anderson & Sechler, 1986; Ross, Lepper, Strack & Steinmetz, 1977) did indeed show that theories about social factors persevere even when their validity is disproved.

In a series of experiments subjects were informed about a (fictitious) theory on the suitability of fire fighters. Employing two single case descriptions, it was either said that high-risk preference constituted the appropriate prerequisite or that low-risk preference constituted the appropriate prerequisite for a successful fire fighter. This information was partly resistant to debriefing which mentioned explicitly the fictitious nature of the theory (Anderson, 1983b; Anderson et al., 1980). Initial information about a positive or negative relationship between risk preference and performance as a fire fighter persevered on several dependent measures (assessment of the true relation between risk preference and performance, predictions of the success of several fire fighters, predictions of the risk test ratings of successful and unsuccessful fire fighters). Perseverance effects were smaller when statistical information instead of concrete examples was used. Statistical information referred to test scores from 20 fire fighters who had proved to be successful or unsuccessful (Anderson, 1983b). The perseverance effect had completely disappeared 1 week after the presentation of abstract information, whereas it was still present after 1 week when concrete case-study information was used.

Further results indicate that perseverance of a discredited theory increases when subjects are encouraged to engage in causal thinking (Anderson & Sechler, 1986). Persons who spend time thinking about the theory tend to show stronger perseverance. Moreover, abstract statistical information about a theory instigates less causal thinking than concrete single-case information (Anderson, 1983b).

It may be possible to avoid perseverance effects if judges consider both directions of the correlation between two attributes (positive and negative correlation) and generate plausible explanations for both directions of the relationship between two attributes (Anderson, 1982; Anderson & Sechler, 1986; Lord, Lepper & Preston, 1984). Students who had taken into consideration both a positive and a negative relationship between risk preference and fire fighter performance exhibited less perseverance than students who had considered only one direction of the relationship before they learned about the cases.

The judgmental pattern basic to perseverance is partly rational. The concept of perseverance does, of course, involve a negative judgmental tendency indicating erroneous and biased judgments (see Ross & Anderson, 1982). However, the resulting judgment is irrational only when the judge can be absolutely sure that the earlier information was wrong.

In general, however, the judge cannot be sure because he/she does not know whether an experimenter can be believed at the debriefing after the same experimenter has deceived the subject during the experiment. It is not reasonable for the experimenter to expect the subject to trust him/her and to take debriefing at face value after the subject has been misled. Actually, the debriefing experimenter has just demonstrated that he/she is the type of person who cheats and therefore has lost his/her trustworthiness. Given these circumstances a compromise between the information items available to the subject might result as the net effect: since the experimenter has lost his/her trustworthiness, the earlier information is taken into consideration to the same extent as the subsequent, contradictory information.

Compared to two conditions in which information about the fire fighter theory was not denied (see Figure 9), subjects beliefs that the theory was true decreased slightly when they were debriefed (Anderson et al., 1980). One may therefore suggest that the subjects do take into account contradictory information, but that they only partly revise their original judgment. Why should subjects blindly trust the experimenter who has staged and conceded a deception a few minutes ago?

To sum up, one has to keep in mind that judges do not necessarily behave in an irrational manner as far as perseverance is concerned. In fact, subjects

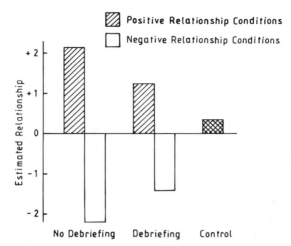

Figure 9. Generalization of an initial impression with and without debriefing. In the positive condition a positive correlation between risk preference and performance as a fire fighter was emphasized, whereas a negative correlation was proposed in the negative condition. The estimated relationship measure indicates the subjective assessments of the correlation between risk preference and fire fighter success. (From Anderson, Lepper & Ross, 1980, p. 1042. Copyright 1980 by the American Psychological Association. Reprinted by permission)

seem to take into account subsequent information that contradicts what they had first learned, but they do not totally ignore the original information in their final judgment. Hence, one may conclude that perseverance − that is, a discredited theory influencing the final judgment − does not necessarily lead to biased information processing. Whether the final judgment is biased or not depends on the quality of both the initial and subsequent information. It is only irrational to consider the initial information in the final judgment when one is absolutely sure that the original information was wrong.

Further considerations may be derived when one interprets the results (see Figure 9) in terms of integration models of social judgment. Without further information subjects have to rely on their personal beliefs, which are probably weak as far as theories about fire fighter performance are concerned. Actually, subjects who had not been provided with further information assumed that there was almost no relationship between risk preference and performance − only a slightly positive tendency was found (Anderson et al., 1980). This (probably weak) initial impression should then be integrated with the first information − and with subsequent contradictory information, if available:

1/2 (slightly positive relationship during the initial impression)
+1/2 (positive/negative relationship) − *without debriefing*
1/3 (slightly positive relationship during the initial impression)
+1/3 (positive/negative relation according to the theory)

+1/3 (no relation at all according to countercommunication) – *with debriefing*

On the basis of an averaging model (see Anderson, 1981) the weights were chosen so that they add up to 1 in each condition.

Anchor Heuristic

Perseverance of initial information may be interpreted as assimilation of subsequent information to an anchor (Tversky & Kahneman, 1974). Anchor effects in judgment formation can easily be demonstrated. A straightforward example will illustrate assimilation to an anchor: the product of eight consecutive numbers has to be estimated, not allowing sufficient time to calculate the result. The order in which the numbers are presented is varied between two conditions:

$$1\times2\times3\times4\times5\times6\times7\times8$$
$$8\times7\times6\times5\times4\times3\times2\times1$$

The anchor effect predicts that in the first condition the low product of the first numbers serves as an anchor. In the second condition, following this line of reasoning, the product of the first numbers results in a high anchor on which the final estimate is based. Thus, assimilation to an anchor predicts that estimates in the first condition will be lower than estimates in the second condition. In general, the correct result (40 320) is underestimated, but underestimation is higher in the first condition than in the second condition (Tversky & Kahneman, 1974).

Initial information serves to develop a reference system to which subsequent information is assimilated. The initial numbers in the estimation problem above induce an expectation about the likely magnitude of the final result; based on this expectation, the final result is estimated. In this sense, the concept of assimilation to an anchor is similar to the above-mentioned prior entry effect in impression formation.

The use of an anchor heuristic may lead to valid as well as to invalid conclusions depending on whether misleading information is presented at an early or at a later point in time (Kruglanski & Ajzen, 1983). Possible relations between primacy effects and psychoanalytic concepts are discussed in Box T3.

Box T3. Early acquired knowledge structures as the basis of person perception
The anchor heuristic is an example of the theory-based organization of cognitive information processing that influences perception, encoding, storing, and recall of information in the same way: while perceptual schemata exert an influence on perception (Lindsay & Norman, 1975), knowledge structures serve as reference systems according to which new information is categorized (Wyer & Srull, 1980). In each case, existing cogni-

tive structures influence how new information is perceived, interpreted, and recalled.

Particularly remarkable is the close parallel between these approaches of modern cognitive psychology and the psychoanalytic approach of Freud (Gaelick & Wyer, 1984). Freud emphasized the significance of early established knowledge structures for the perception and interpretation of subsequent life events. Consider, for instance, the transference reaction (Freud, 1976). A transference reaction takes place when early attachments to significant reference persons (in particular to the parents) are established anew in the present. The early prototypes are projected onto the new relationship (e.g., between client and therapist). The transference reaction implies that a new person is assimilated to the "anchor person". A former reference person serves as an anchor for emotional and cognitive reactions within a new relationship.

Freud's emphasis on the child's early reference persons (mostly the parents) concurs with the emphasis on primacy effects, which are important for the organization of knowledge structures. The early representations of the child's most important reference persons are likely to be the initial, formative prototypes that play an important interpretative role in person perception in later life (Gaelick & Wyer, 1984).

Another aspect emphasized by Freud was the separation of certain prototypes from the original contextual conditions that led to identification with significant reference persons. This process of increasing autonomy of knowledge structures may be interpreted as an interaction between episodic and semantic memory (Tulving, 1972). Episodic memory involves storage and recall of personally experienced episodes that are located in space and time. In contrast, semantic memory refers to the storage of knowledge about concepts and their characteristics. Thus, the semantic information is entirely independent of the focal or temporal conditions under which it originated (Tulving & Thomson, 1973, p. 354).

Impression Formation and Order of Information

Two experiments in a series of studies conducted by Asch (1946) explored order effects in impression formation. Both studies were conducted to demonstrate − as were the experiments on the *warm-cold* variable − that the meaning of an attribute is not fixed but that it is context dependent. Reciprocal influences of all attributes in an adjective list should lead to a Gestalt-like impression formation process (Asch & Zukier, 1984).

Asch (1946) used a simple version of an order paradigm, presenting six adjectives characterizing a person in two different sequences:

A. intelligent, industrious, impulsive, critical, stubborn, envious
B. envious, stubborn, critical, impulsive, industrious, intelligent

Subjects who were asked to form an impression based on the adjective lists described person A as competent whereas person B was considered a "problem". A typical description of person B was as follows:

> This individual is probably maladjusted because he is envious and impulsive.

Different impressions, although based on identical adjectives in both lists, were also revealed with regard to an adjective checklist from which subjects chose traits fitting the stimulus person. Although differences were not extreme, impressions diverged with regard to some traits. For instance, 52% of the subjects considered *humorous* a fitting quality for person A (vs. 21% for person B), and 32% of the subjects judged person A as *happy*, whereas only 5% attributed this quality to person B.

Asch (1946, pp. 271–272) commented:

> The accounts of the subjects suggest that the first terms set up in most subjects a *direction* [emphasis in the original] which then exerts a continuous effect on the later terms. When the subject hears the first term, a broad, uncrystallized but directed impression is born. The next characteristic comes not as a separate item, but is related to the established direction. Quickly the view formed acquires a certain stability, so that later characteristics are fitted – if conditions permit – to the given direction. Here we observe a factor of primacy guiding the development of an impression. This factor is not, however, to be understood in the sense of Ebbinghaus, but rather in a structural sense.

Summing up, one may state that the adjectives mentioned first which contradict subsequent attributes exert a dominant influence on the overall impression of the person. Asch and Zukier (1984) suggest that a conflict between two adjectives may frequently be resolved by assigning a dominant status to one adjective and discounting the importance of the second adjective. Thus, whether an adjective will dominate or not may depend on its temporal or spatial position.

Luchins (1957a) reviews a series of experiments where even more pronounced primacy effects were observed. The significance of these findings is enhanced because they are based on large samples. Moreover, he used remarkably lively stimulus material designed in an exemplary manner (see Luchins, 1948; Deusinger, 1980).

Subjects read the description of a pupil, Jim, who exhibited extroverted as well as introverted behavior (Luchins, 1957a, pp. 34, 35):

> Jim left the house to get some stationery. He walked out into the sun-filled street with two of his friends, basking in the sun as he walked. Jim entered the stationery store which was full of people. Jim talked with an acquaintance while he waited for the clerk to catch his eye. On his way out, he stopped to chat with a school friend who was just coming into the store. Leaving the store, he walked toward school. On his way out he met the girl to whom he had been introduced the night before. They talked for a short while, and then Jim left for school. After school Jim left the classroom alone. Leaving the school, he started on his long walk home. The street was brilliantly filled with sunshine. Jim walked down the street on the shady side. Coming down the street toward him, he saw the pretty girl whom he had met on the previous evening. Jim crossed the

street and entered a candy store. The store was crowded with students, and he noticed a few familiar faces. Jim waited quietly until the counterman caught his eye and then gave his order. Taking his drink, he sat down at a side table. When he had finished his drink he went home.

Obviously, prior to school Jim is described as extroverted, whereas he behaved in an introverted manner after school. Subjects read the description in the order presented above (EI sequence) or in reversed order (IE sequence). Additional groups of subjects were presented with only the first part of the description of Jim's behavior or only the second part (I or E).

Table 6. Attribution of friendliness as a function of sequence

	E	EI	IE	I
Friendly (%)	95	78	18	3
Unfriendly/shy (%)	3	11	63	86

E, Extroverted description only; I, introverted description only; EI, extroverted-introverted sequence; IE, introverted-extroverted sequence. Percentages do not sum to 100% because of missing or undecided answers. Opposite pairs presented were friendly/unfriendly or friendly/shy.

In an initial study, 437 judges chose between *friendly* and *unfriendly* or *shy* to characterize the stimulus person (other subjects chose no description at all). The distribution of choices on both alternatives is presented in Table 6. Ratings of friendliness/unfriendliness were obtained to measure the impressions subjects had formed about Jim's extroversion. It is questionable whether this dependent variable is an optimal measure. In subsequent studies Luchins used a greater variety of dependent measures. For instance, subjects were asked to judge whether Jim would spontaneously act out some idea in front of his class.

The percentage of friendly ratings in Table 6 decreases from left to right. It is especially interesting to compare the EI and IE conditions, because this comparison reveals a strong primacy effect. Two other studies with 350 and 264 subjects, respectively, corroborated and extended this general pattern of results. In these experiments subjects chose from lists containing more adjectives. Moreover, free descriptions and sentence completions were analyzed. Across all dependent measures Jim was rated as more extroverted in the EI condition than in the IE condition. Thus, it is reasonable to argue that a generalized primacy effect was observed.

According to Luchins' (1957a) interpretation of the results, the first part of the description finds the reader still receptive, whereas the second part of the description interferes with an already established picture and is unable to compete successfully with the initial information. Further causes were mentioned: more attention paid to the first part of the description; more readiness to accept the information coming first.

In another experiment with 300 subjects (Luchins, 1957b), several strategies were employed to reduce the primacy effect. In a control condition the primacy effect again emerged. However, when subjects were cautioned in advance that they would tend to over-emphasize the initial information the primacy effect was almost completely eliminated. In another condition where subjects were cautioned against premature judgments after they had read the first part of the description, a slight recency effect emerged. The recency effect was even more pronounced when arithmetic problems instead of a warning were interpolated between the two parts of the description (see Miller & Campbell, 1959).

In an additional experiment the effect of a temporal delay between the two parts of the EI sequence and the IE sequence was investigated by interpolating 5 or 17 min of a history lesson. The recency effect was more pronounced with the long interpolation than with the short interpolation. These results support the hypothesis that recency is fostered by forgetting.

Primacy effects were comprehensively documented in a study by Anderson (1965), who obtained a precise primacy curve by systematically varying the position of positive or negative traits within an adjective list. Two experimental designs were employed in which three negatively evaluated or three positively evaluated adjectives (3 L vs. 3 H) were interpolated into a series of six or nine adjectives. When the interpolated adjectives were negatively evaluated, they were combined with positively evaluated context adjectives and vice versa. For instance, the (3L)3H design consisted of four experimental conditions: LLLHHH, HLLLHH, HHLLLH, HHHLLL. The (3L)6H design consisted of the following seven conditions: LLLHHHHHH, HLLLHHHHH, HHLLLHHHH, HHHLLLHHH, HHHHLLLHH, HHHHHLLLH, HHHHHHLLL. In each experimental design every possible combination of interpolated and context adjectives was used.

Subjects read a series of six or nine adjectives, both describing a hypothetical person. In addition, subjects had to imagine that each adjective had been mentioned by an acquaintance of the stimulus person. The evaluation of the stimulus person was obtained on 8-point rating scales with end poles of 1 (very negative) and 8 (very positive). The results, presented in Figure 10, are clear: the effect of the interpolated adjective triplets on the final judgment decreased the later they were presented within the sequence of the context adjectives.

The profiles in Figure 10, ascending given negative interpolation and descending given positive interpolation, can be predicted using an averaging model. Assuming that the weight of an adjective decreases linearly as a function of position, the weights of the respective six positions of the (3L) 3H design may be described as a, $a-b$, $a-2b$, $a-3b$, $a-4b$, $a-5b$ (Anderson, 1965). In addition, the averaging model holds that all positive and negative attributes receive the same scale value. Thus, according to this interpretation the primacy effect is solely due to differences between weights that depend on position.

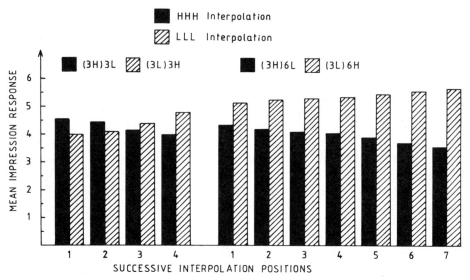

Figure 10. Primacy in impression formation. (From Anderson, 1965, p. 4. Copyright 1965 by the American Psychological Association. Reprinted by permission)

The analysis seems to be valid as long as dependent variables of the evaluative type are employed (in the above study the end poles of the scale were marked with *highly favorable* and *highly unfavorable*). Another condition seems to be fast presentation of stimulus persons, which keeps subjects from considering reciprocal implications and relationships between the traits describing each hypothetical person. Given this experimental design, a subject who does not want to fail in the presence of the experimenter is almost forced to assume fixed scale values of isolated traits to be able to form the requested overall judgment.

In additional experiments (Anderson, 1973) the notion of weights differing as a function of position was further pursued by estimating the weight parameters. The experimental design used is presented in Box T4.

Box T4. Obtaining position curves in impression formation

Table 7 presents an experimental design that permits position weights of stimuli presented in serial order to be measured. High (H) and Low (L) adjectives may be combined in $2^4 = 16$ different sequences in four positions (see Table 7). Now, considering only those conditions with a positive adjective in the first position, there are $2^3 = 8$ different sequences. In addition, eight analogous sequences are obtained in those conditions with a negative adjective in the first position (compare H1−H8 with L1−L8). Averaging across the ratings in the eight H conditions and across the ratings in the eight L conditions and determining the difference D_1, the result is theoretically proportional to the weight of the first position (Anderson & Farkas, 1973).

Table 7. Design used to obtain position weight curves

Experimental conditions		Positions			
		1	2	3	4
H1	HH1	H	H	H	H
H2	HH2	H	H	H	L
H3	HH3	H	H	L	H
H4	HH4	H	H	L	L
H5	HL1	H	L	H	H
H6	HL2	H	L	H	L
H7	HL3	H	L	L	H
H8	HL4	H	L	L	L
L1	LH1	L	H	H	H
L2	LH2	L	H	H	L
L3	LH3	L	H	L	H
L4	LH4	L	H	L	L
L5	LL1	L	L	H	H
L6	LL2	L	L	H	L
L7	LL3	L	L	L	H
L8	LL4	L	L	L	L

L and H represent adjectives of low and high scale values, respectively. H conditions have a positive adjective in the first position. L conditions have a negative adjective in the first position. HH conditions have positive adjectives in the first two positions. HL, LH, and LL are to be interpreted in a similar manner.

A difference D_2 proportional to the weight of the second position can also be obtained. To calculate this difference one has to compare HH and LH sequences with HL and LL sequences (see Table 7). In the same vein, differences D_3 and D_4 relating to the last two positions may be calculated.

That D_1 is proportional to the weight of the first position may be derived by representing the overall judgment (R) across four attributes by an algebraic averaging model, where $W_1 - W_4$ are the weights and $S_1 - S_4$ are the scale values:

$$R = W_1 S_1 + W_2 S_2 + W_3 S_3 + W_4 S_4 \ .$$

It is assumed that the weights sum up to unity. Assuming equal scale values for H adjectives and L adjectives, the difference D_1 may be derived:

$$D_1 = W_1 S_{H1} - W_1 S_{L1} = W_1 (S_{H1} - S_{L1})$$

since the eight H sequences and the eight L sequences are identical (except for the first position). Hence, it follows that the difference between H and

L sequences is proportional to the first position weight. Note that it must be assumed that the weights of positions 2, 3, and 4 are identical for H sequences and L sequences.

The following differences were obtained in a 2^5 design in which each hypothetical person was described by five adjectives: $D_1 = 1.75$, $D_2 = 1.63$, $D_3 = 1.66$, $D_4 = 1.47$, $D_5 = 1.28$.

Obviously, the position weights for the overall judgment decrease with increasing position number − a primacy effect. It may be concluded that the two last positions exert less influence on the overall judgment than the preceding positions.

The approach presented in Box T4 leads to the result that the weight of an adjective decreases almost linearly across positions, as was hypothesized by Anderson (1965). The results corroborate the assumption that the primacy effect is due to the different position weights of adjectives presented in serial order. Riskey (1979) reports results consistent with this reasoning (see Box I5).

Box I5. Position effect, attention decrement, and interference with short-term memory

Riskey (1979) used the method presented in Box T4 to obtain serial position curves. He employed sets of eight adjectives in a factorial design in which the four factors were serial positions. Two adjectives of equal value (either both very positive or both very negative) occupied each serial position. The stimulus persons were rated on a scale ranging from 1 (very, very unlikable) to 10 (very, very likable).

One possible way to account for position effects lies in the U-shaped recall function described by Murdoch (1962) and others. If verbal memory influences serial position effects, this interference should affect the impression serial position curve. Postman and Phillips (1965) had found that recall of 10, 20, or 30 words did not follow the well-known U-shaped function when subjects had to work on an interfering task − successive subtraction of 3 from a three-digit number − following presentation of the stimulus material. Given these conditions, recall of the later words was as poor as recall of the middle words, so that a primacy effect in recall resulted.

Can a comparable effect of interference be observed with regard to impression serial position curves? To answer this question, Riskey (1979) included in his design two interference conditions to minimize any recent effect on verbal recall. For 15 s or for 30 s subjects had to work on the subtraction problems described above. The subtraction immediately followed presentation of the sets of adjectives. Another group of subjects rated the target person immediately after the presentation of the sets of adjectives.

Figure 11 A shows the difference values for each of the three experimental conditions calculated following the procedure described in Box T4. The

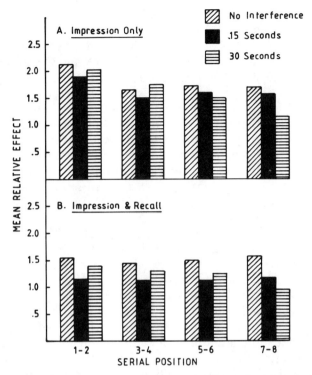

Figure 11. Primacy effects and interference in impression formation. Calculation of differences is demonstrated in Box T 4. Two adjectives occupy each position. Adjectives in one position are both highly favorable items or both highly unfavorable items. (From Riskey, 1979, p. 274. Copyright 1979 by the American Psychological Association. Reprinted by permission)

profiles show a primacy effect in the conditions where interference was presented as well as in the condition lacking interference, because the difference values tend to decrease across positions. Interference by the subtraction task did not increase the primacy effect considerably, although the primacy effect seems to be particularly pronounced in the 30-s interference condition. This result justifies the conclusion that the influence of verbal memory on impression formation is small. While Riskey (1979) obtained recency effects in recall, serial position effects in impression formation were dominated by primacy effects. Consistent with this conclusion, Anderson (1968) hypothesized that impressions are stored in a memory system independent of the verbal memory system. An additional assumption was that an overall impression is continuously adapted to new incoming information (for instance items in a series) without single items of information necessarily being remembered. One might imagine that each single item is processed with respect to the overall judgment without storing the item itself — like a compound problem in arithmetics.

These findings support the hypothesis that position weights decrease across the successive serial positions. Hendrick and Costantini (1970) present direct evidence corroborating this interpretation. Subjects were read lists of six adjectives, three negative and three positive, for instance, *trusting, patient, respectful, withdrawn, silent, helpless*; or *bold, daring, adventurous, shy, passive, timid*. Each subject indicated his/her impression of the hypothetical person on an 8-point scale under two different conditions. In the first condition, the positive traits preceded the negative ones (HL condition). In the second condition the negative traits were read to the subjects first (LH condition). Since 16 different sets of adjectives were read in each condition, each subject had to rate 32 stimulus persons (plus some additional filler items).

In an initial experiment Hendrick and Costantini (1970) determined the primacy effect by calculating the HL−LH difference. In the second experiment two response modes were used. In one condition, subjects were read the complete list before they indicated their judgment (regular condition). In a second condition, subjects had to pronounce each adjective after it was presented, again indicating their evaluation at the end of presentation (pronunciation condition). This new procedure was designed to ensure that subjects paid equal attention to each of the six attributes of the list.

Consistent with the attention decrement hypothesis, the primacy effect was limited to the regular condition. Moreover, the HL−LH difference assumed a negative value in the pronunciation condition, indicating a small recency effect. Hendrick and Costantini remark that this result is consistent with an attention decrement. In addition, it corresponds to the finding that a recency effect results when — prior to the final judgment — ratings are made immediately following each adjective (see Stewart, 1965). Recency effects also emerge when subjects are instructed in advance to recall each trait (Anderson & Hubert, 1963, exp. 2).

Riskey (1979) observed similar results. In one condition he instructed his subjects in advance that recall would be required. The difference values showed neither a primacy effect nor a recency effect (see Figure 11 B). Long interference tasks again produced a primacy effect in impression formation (the statistical interaction position×interference was significant). On the whole, findings indicate that the primacy effect disappears when attention decrement is likely not to take place because of the recall requirement (as an exception to this rule the primacy effect results when long interference tasks were used).

In summary, primacy effects seem to be due to attention decrement so that subjects pay less attention to information later in a series than to earlier information. I will now discuss whether primacy effects depend on the type of serial presentation: that is, on whether information is presented in its natural order as compared to a random sequence. Subsequently I will discuss position effects in the performance domain: Does good performance at the beginning or at the end of a series of tasks produce a primacy effect or a recency effect in the evaluation of the ability of the stimulus person?

The attention decrement hypothesis may explain why Anderson (1968) observed a recency effect in impression formation: he had instructed his judges to pronounce each adjective after it was presented. On the other hand, this experiment differed from others in that judges were told that the serial presentation of the traits was similar to real life because "one ordinarily gets to know a person step by step" (Anderson, 1968, p. 356). This instruction may have augmented the importance of later information, which may have been regarded as particularly representative of the current disposition of the stimulus person (Jones & Goethals, 1972).

In one experiment Jones and Goethals (1972) compared two conditions. In the natural sequence condition it was explained that information about the target person would be presented in the natural order in which it had occurred. In a second condition judges were told that the traits were presented in a random order. Judges watched 21 videotaped vignettes in which the target person made optimistic and pessimistic remarks about human nature. In one condition pessimistic remarks were presented at the beginning (pessimistic-optimistic); in the other condition the optimistic statements dominated at the beginning (optimistic-pessimistic). The total number of optimistic and pessimistic statements was the same for both conditions.

In the random order condition a primacy effect emerged. Thus, the target person was rated as more optimistic when he/she had started with optimistic statements. This effect did not occur in the natural order condition. Free responses indicated that 60% of the subjects in the natural order condition formed hypotheses on how to explain the inconsistent statements of the target person. External reasons were often held responsible for the inconsistencies. By contrast, only 20% of the subjects in the random order condition formed hypotheses about reasons for the inconsistencies. External reasons were not mentioned at all.

A primacy effect may result even given a natural order condition if the entity in question is stable. This fact has been repeatedly demonstrated with regard to ability attributions (Jones, Rock, Shaver, Goethals & Ward, 1968; Thompson, 1972). In the experimental paradigm used, a target person worked on a series of analogies and received feedback indicating whether the answers were right or wrong. The distribution of 15 wrong and 15 correct solutions in three different experimental conditions is depicted in Table 8. In the ascending condition most of the successes (namely two-thirds) are concentrated in the second half of the series, whereas they are concentrated in the first half of the series in the descending condition. No temporal trend is shown in the random order condition.

When subjects were asked to predict the target person's performance in 30 further trials they consistently expected more correct answers in the descending

Table 8. Feedback pattern and ability attribution (from Jones, Rock, Shaver, Goethals & Ward, 1968, pp. 321, 326. Copyright 1968 by the American Psychological Association. Reprinted by permission)

Trials	Prediction of correct answers in 30 trials to follow	
	Experiment 1	Experiment 2
CCCCWCCCWWWCCCWWCWWCCWWW-CWWWWC (descending)	20.2	18.7
CWWWWCWWWCCWWCWWCCCWWW-CCCWCCCC (ascending)	17.2	15.8
CWCWWCWCWCCWWCWWCWCCCWC-WCWWCWC (random)	16.4	15.6

C and W indicate correct and wrong solutions of the target person.

condition than in the remaining conditions (see Table 8). Apparently, the feedback given in the first half of the series influenced the extent to which the ability to solve the problems was attributed to the target person.

Correspondingly, in the descending order perceived intelligence of the target person was regarded as higher than in the ascending order. Subjects tended to recall that the target person solved more problems in the descending than in the ascending condition. This result was obtained when the target person in fact interacted with the subjects as well as when the target person appeared on video.

As far as the primacy effect is concerned, results have to be modified somewhat. Thompson (1972) observed the finding presented in Table 8 for descending and ascending performances only when there was a competitive relationship betwen subject and target person with regard to problem solving. When there was a cooperative relationship in which the amount of money earned depended on equal participation in problem solving, no primacy effect was found.

Thus, these results suggest that tactical considerations concerning impression management play a role when the ability of another person has to be estimated. The term impression management summarizes all attempts to influence the image made by a person in public (Tetlock & Manstead, 1985). According to this view, higher weighting of early performance information is a means for defensive anticipation of later inferiority.

Jones et al. (1968, study 6) obtained different results when subjects had to rate their *own* performance that followed a descending, an ascending, or a random sequence. Higher ratings of one's own performance were given in the *ascending* sequence. Subsequent success seemed to elicit the impression that one would probably succeed or that one is lucky, whereas the descending condition may have made tactical deliberations about impression management salient.

Consistent with this result, Jones and Welsh (1971) found that observing a target person performing may lead to recency effects. Observers watched a video of two persons playing 30 trials of a strategy game. In a control condition both players performed approximately equally. In the experimental condition player X was clearly inferior in the beginning, improved towards the middle of the game, and equalled the other player's performance in the last trial. This ascending performance sequence produced a more positive rating of the player than was obtained in the constant control condition. When the winner of the next game had to be predicted, player X, who had made up for an almost hopeless start, was nominated most often.

In this kind of interpersonal situation later performances are particularly informative because they demonstrate how a person finishes who, after preliminary difficulties, came to terms with a task. When a performance sequence is interpreted in this sense it is reasonable to lay only slight emphasis on the first performances, but to regard subsequent performances as representative of the potential a person possesses to solve future problems. To expect the first events of a sequence to be representative is justified as long as the target of the expectation does not change. When the target person has made him-/herself acquainted with the task or is subject to developmental change, more recent behavior samples are apparently more valid than preceding behavior samples originating from a time when different circumstances prevailed.

To test the effect of instability, subjects were asked to predict aces (Jones, Goethals, Kennington & Severance, 1972, exps. 2, 3). Subjects had to take up 30 cards from a pack of cards in which aces were distributed according to the descending and ascending sequences of Table 8. In the descending sequence subjects tended to recall more aces as being in the second half of the series than had actually been present. On the other hand, in the ascending sequence they tended to recall less aces as being in the second half than had been present. Thus, the frequency of aces was overestimated in the descending sequence and underestimated in the ascending sequence.

In another experiment the implicit assumption of a stable entity – in the example above, *being an ace* – was questioned. Red and blue cards were distributed in a pack so that one color dominated the upper half and the other color dominated the lower half of the pack. Thus, position and colors were correlated. In addition, ascending and descending sequences of aces were again provided, with 20 aces among 40 cards.

When only one color of cards was used or when both colors were randomly distributed across the series, subjects recalled more aces in the descending than in the ascending sequence – a primacy effect. However, the difference between the number of aces recalled in the descending and in the ascending sequence was almost zero when color correlated with position and therefore a (positive or negative) correlation between color and frequency of aces existed. One may conclude that primacy effects are based on the assumption that the entity in question is stable.

Primacy Effect Versus Recency Effect

When order effects were systematically investigated, both primacy and recency effects were obtained. Therefore, one should not postulate a law of primacy. In a comprehensive review of research on order effects, Hovland (1957) noted that primacy and recency coexist. Having acquaintance with a given subject is one factor that moderates the effects of primacy and recency. When acquaintance with the subject is low − as is the case when judging attributes of hypothetical persons − a primacy effect results, whereas a recency effect is obtained when acquaintance with the domain is high − as is the case with attitudes. Hovland (1957) suggests that familiarity with a domain induces the observer to consider all relevant aspects of the matter so that he or she is immunized against premature conclusions. It is reasonable to assume that a person who is well acquainted with a certain problem will be better informed about the advantages and pitfalls of the matter than a person who is confronted with the problem for the first time.

Hovland (1957) then points to another factor which may promote primacy effects. Primacy will dominate impression formation when the information forms a unified whole − for instance, when it describes a person. In contrast, when two communications that are unrelated events are presented, a primacy effect will not be obtained.

On the other hand, recency effects are the more likely the larger the temporal delay between the contradictory information − this result parallels the hypothetical recall function. As a matter of fact, one has to take into account the influence of verbal memory, which was demonstrated when extensive interference promoted the primacy effect (see Figure 10). Worse recall of the last items on a list, as is produced by interference, should strengthen the primacy effect. In addition, research on the attribution of ability has demonstrated that the primacy effect is related to memory influences. The primacy effect is not only fostered by interference, but it is also strengthened by a decrease in attention across a stimulus series. To the extent that it is possible to reduce attention by additional tasks, primacy effects will in most cases (the exception being when there is strong interference) disappear. The belief that one has already heard or seen the most important facts when only the first few items of information have been presented is likely to be an important factor contributing to the primacy effect. Scanning only headlines or the opening paragraphs of the articles in the newspaper before a (possibly premature) judgment is formed is not uncommon. Many primacy effects in everyday life are probably due to this habit. Another factor contributing to primacy is assimilation to an expectation (Jones & Goethals, 1972). The notion that subsequent information is matched to a prior expectation parallels the hypothesis that the early information is dominant because it forms a directed impression (Asch, 1946).

Evidence in favor of assimilation to the expectation is presented in three studies by Zadney and Gerard (1974). In one experiment subjects watched a short stage performance. A student tried to enrol for nine different courses. He was carrying nine different books and articles with him which fell on the floor. Courses and articles could be assigned to three domains: chemistry, music, and psychology. Prior to the stage performance observers had been told that the actor was a student of chemistry, of music, or of psychology. After the performance they had to recall the courses as well as the articles. Recall was selective, since observers of the chemistry student recalled more articles on chemistry than did observers of a music or psychology student. This kind of selective recall is a major factor contributing to assimilation to an expectation (see Chap. 5, "Self-fulfilling prophecies and processes of expectation confirmation").

The same phenomenon is evident in research on prototypes in person perception (see Cantor & Mischel, 1979 a). In an initial study (Cantor & Mischel, 1977) subjects read descriptions of an introverted and of an extroverted person. Each description consisted of ten short sentences ("Laura is energetic"). Subjects had to identify these attributes in a recognition memory task from a list by indicating their degree of confidence when identifying the attributes of each person. When subjects rated sentences containing "extroverted" attributes that did not appear in the original description, they expressed greater confidence that a sentence belonged to the description of the extrovert character than to that of the introvert. The analogous result was found with regard to introverted persons and sentences. These results are in agreement with the concept of prototype-biased memory.

Another study (Cantor & Mischel, 1979 b) showed superior free recall of attributes and behavior of a target person when the target person was consistently presented as extroverted or introverted than in a condition in which an inconsistent description of the target person was used. Correspondence with the prototype fostered correct recall of the items. In addition, "pure" types were characterized in more detail, with a heavy emphasis on trait attributions. For pure types more new aspects were mentioned. In contrast, impressions of inconsistent persons were more often modified by context information. In later experiments the role of prototypes in perception of social situations, stereotypes, and attitudes toward members of a group was demonstrated (Brewer, Dull & Lui, 1981; Cantor, Mischel & Schwartz, 1982; Lord, Lepper & Mackie, 1984; see also Cantor & Mischel, 1979 a). In addition, the role of imaginary self-prototypes has been investigated (Kihlstrom & Cantor, 1984; Singer & Kolligian, 1987; Yarmey & Johnson, 1982). In these experiments selective recognition favored a primacy effect.

When a prototype is activated or an expectation is induced, subsequent information processing is partly biased by the expectation. Jones and Gerard (1967) called this phenomenon the prior entry effect. This effect is also evident in the tendency to look for confirming instead of disconfirming evidence (see Snyder & Gangestad, 1981; see also Chap. 2, "Which data are relevant to assessing a relationship?").

In contrast, recency is an important organizational principle of person perception when there is a logical trend in a development. For instance, a person who is a poor soccer player may be good at handball or may be a successful hurdler. When the type of sport has changed, more recent behavior samples are more valid than earlier samples.

To the extent that the entity in question is unstable due to a systematic tendency in a person's development, recency effects are likely. A subtle example illustrating this is provided by an experiment from Snyder and Uranowitz (1978). Student subjects read an extensive case description of Betty K. The case presented a variety of information concerning sexual relationships and other aspects of life. The information, however, did not allow the subjects to make any conclusions about what information would follow.

When they had read the case, students were either told that Betty K. had married in the meantime or they learned that she was engaged in a lesbian relationship. A control group received no additional communication. One week after they had read the case, the students completed 36 multiple choice questions about the life of Betty K. Response alternatives had been categorized according to their stereotyped lesbian or heterosexual content. Of course, this categorization was not scientifically based. Seventeen items in the questionnaire contained response alternatives categorized as stereotypically lesbian or heterosexual. For instance, the statements that in childhood Betty had been abused by her father and that she was rather unattractive were assigned to the lesbian stereotype.

The result of the recognition memory test demonstrated the effect of the information following the case descriptions. When the lesbian relationship had been mentioned, subjects attributed more stereotypically lesbian alternatives to Betty's life in their reconstruction of the life history narrative than when the heterosexual relationship had been mentioned. The analysis of erroneous answers was particularly instructive. When the lesbian label had been assigned, subjects chose more incorrect lesbian alternatives than when the marriage label had been presented. Correspondingly, the marriage label produced more heterosexual recognition errors. These results were repeatedly replicated using modified experimental conditions (Snyder, 1981), but they were not confirmed in two studies by Bellezza and Bower (1981) and in two studies by Clark and Woll (1981).

One may conclude that subjects sometimes tended to justify the status quo as constituted by the additional information through retrospective reinterpretation – a recency effect. Snyder and Uranowitz (1978) note that the resulting biases may serve to stabilize perception. When the entity in question (that is, the sexual inclinations of Betty K.) had unequivocally developed, preceding information was reinterpreted in accordance with the new status of the entity.

Further evidence pointing to this type of recency effect is provided by experiments on the retrospective reinterpretation of historical events, for instance the violent conflict between the British and the Gurkhas in India (1814). Subjects were asked to judge retrospectively the likelihood of four possible resolutions of the conflict (British victory, Gurkha victory, military stalemate with or without peace settlement). Depending on the experimental condition subjects were first informed about the "actual" resolution of conflict (Fischhoff, 1975). The judged likelihood that things had to turn out as they eventually did exceeded the judged likelihood of the event when no additional information was given by 11%. In retrospect, it may appear that things had to turn out as they eventually did. The influence of factual knowledge even prevailed when subjects were asked to ignore their factual knowledge or to make judgments for persons hypothesized not to possess that knowledge.

"It was bound to happen" is the quintessence of retrospective reinterpretations (Fischhoff, 1980; Snyder & Uranowitz, 1978). They may be regarded as an assimilation to what one already knows about the event in question (Fischhoff, 1975, pp. 297–298) or as an assimilation to expectation (Jones & Goethals, 1972). However, in contrast to the examples of Jones and Goethals (1972), these are expectations elicited by additional information. Thus, things are suddenly seen in a different light.

Summing up, it can be said that assimilation to an expectation may lead to order effects. On the one hand, the expectation may be formed prior to the presentation of single items of information (for instance, through specific knowledge of vocational interests or through prototypes elicited by a person description). Such expectations may selectively influence recall of single items of information. On the other hand, the expectation may be formed after the presentation of a single item of information. For instance, this may be the case when important biographical events occur that suggest a revised interpretation of former events. Reinterpretations may be regarded as the result of a certain development. Given these circumstances, recognition of single items of information may be biased and likelihood estimates of the event may be inflated. Thus, expectations may elicit primacy effects as well as recency effects. Either structuring in advance or reinterpretation may occur. In addition, explaining an event heightens its subjective likelihood (Hirt & Sherman, 1985; Ross et al., 1977; Sherman, Skov, Hervitz & Stock, 1981; Wyer, Srull & Gordon, 1984). Therefore, explanations elicit expectations. Expectations are assimilated to what one knows about the event in question.

The First Impression: Practical Applications

What practical conclusions may be drawn from research on impression formation? Three areas will now be suggested in which an application of research findings seems appropriate.

Accuracy

Impression formation is more accurate than is often supposed. According to a pragmatic perspective (Swann, 1984), one may distinguish between global accuracy and circumscribed accuracy. Global accuracy concerns generalizability of an impression across different observers, different contexts, and a period of time. In contrast, circumscribed accuracy relates only to one observer, one context, or one moment in time. With regard to circumscribed accuracy, the first impression may well be justified (Swann, 1984), and, in fact, coping with the practical problems of everyday life is often more dependent on circumscribed accuracy than on global accuracy.

Experimental studies using contrived stimuli and artificial situations are likely to exaggerate the degree of biased perception in real life (Funder, 1987). In addition, errors in social perception were found to correlate positively with social competence and emotional adjustment among 14-year-olds (Block & Funder, 1986). Therefore, correction of judgment tendencies in lay persons (see Nisbett, Krantz, Jepson & Kunda, 1983) is not necessarily helpful (Funder, 1987).

The review of halo effects ("Illusory correlations between trait characteristics") already demonstrated that a variety of diagnostic information promotes differentiated judgment formation. The biasing effect of stereotypes diminishes when the observer is confronted with individual information about the person in question (see Locksley et al., 1980; see Chap. 3, "Areas of stereotype research"). As a basic rule one may postulate that a target person should be given the opportunity to express him/herself without bias as freely as possible. There should at least be a chance for the target person to correct false expectations of the observers (Swann, 1984). Thus, it becomes obvious that person perception is an integral part of the social interaction between target person and observer (see Chap. 5, "Self-fulfilling prophecies and processes of expectation confirmation").

Perception – and person perception in particular – serves an adaptive function for the human organism: particular attention is paid to information that is relevant to the plans and actions of the actors, because this information gives an adaptive advantage (Holzkamp, 1972; McArthur & Baron, 1983). It is unreasonable to imagine biased person perception and successful coping with the environment at one and the same time. Precise person perception has an adaptive function because it helps to elicit desirable reactions from other persons and helps to avoid negative interpersonal consequences.

We have seen that impression formation is sufficiently precise and adaptive from the pragmatic point of view. Perseverance tendencies appeared to be rational types of information processing, and confirmatory attributions still allowed for corrective feedback. Highly diagnostic information (e.g., *three* behavior examples) received a larger weight when integrated into an overall judgment than information of low diagnostic value (e.g., *one* behavior example). Primacy effects disappeared when the entity in question was unstable and changed across the series (see "Impression formation and order of information"). More detailed discussions of the accuracy problem in judgment formation are given by Cronbach (1955), Funder (1987), Harvey, Town and Yarkin (1981), Kenny and Albright (1987), and Sixtl (1982).

Diagnostic Communications

Impression formation not only represents a basic area of social psychological research within the realm of psychology, but it is also relevant to applied psychology. On the one hand, diagnostic decision-making relies partly on the first impression. On the other hand, psychologists communicate their diagnostic judgments to target persons, who themselves form impressions based on those diagnostic communications.

To a fairly large extent social judgment formation within person perception may be represented by an averaging rule. This notion has some interesting implications. First, extreme information will be moderated by less extreme information. To the extent that the context influences the evaluation of single items of information, one-sided exaggerations that are not representative of context will be corrected and moderated (see "Halo effect versus change of meaning").

Secondly, the plausibility of diagnostic communication decreases when a convincing argument is combined with a less convincing one. Perceived plausibility was higher when only the most convincing argument was presented than when two arguments were given, one of which was only slightly convincing (Bierhoff, Buck & Klein, 1986a). Consider the following example of a depressed pupil. A very plausible explanation of a pupil's depression would be: "The pupil is depressed, because he suffers from puberty-related problems of self-esteem." Less plausible — although still of medium plausibility — is the following explanation: "The pupil is depressed, because he has been reared in an authoritarian as well as in a protective manner." The best explanation was rated more plausible when presented alone than when presented in combination with the medium explanation (Bierhoff et al., 1986a). Therefore it seems evident that one should not provide additional, lower quality arguments when one has already stated the most convincing argument. The persuasive power of the overall explanation does not necessarily increase as a function of argument quantity. As a matter of fact, quite the opposite may be expected. With regard to diagnostic communication one may therefore note that it should stress the most important explanation to achieve highest perceived plausibility (see, for related research, Abelson, Leddo & Gross, 1987; Leddo, Abelson & Gross, 1984; Zuckerman, Eghari & Lambrecht, 1986).

Be Careful with Retrospective Judgments

When an incisive event has happened one often retrospectively interprets the circumstances leading to the event. Consider the following examples:

- One is told that an acquaintance was assigned to a treatment for alcohol addicts.
- One is told that a former classmate is now a member of an extremist political party.

The examples relate to persons the observer already knows. He/she knew several aspects about the person before the event took place. As demonstrated in the section on order of presentation of information, new events influence recall of former events of a target person's biography so that things as they are seem plausible (Snyder, 1981, 1984). When subjects were additionally told that a woman was engaged in a lesbian relationship, they reconstructed her biography from memory to match the lesbian stereotype.

The influence exerted by the knowledge of how things turned out in the end is remarkably robust (Snyder, 1981, 1984):

- "Subsequent clarification" influenced person descriptions given by observers on the basis of the biography.
- Interpretations of individual life events were guided by subsequent information. From the retrospective point of view, biographical events seemed to predict the lesbian development.
- Recall of an interaction that had been observed was biased by the subsequent label. The impression of a target person labeled as lesbian matched the lesbian stereotype.

It has already been emphasized (see "Order of presentation of information") that observers tend retrospectively to overestimate the necessity of the actual development (which may be regarded as retrospective determinism; Fischhoff, 1980). Rationalization of things as they are elicits exaggerated expectations concerning the predictability of events. This problem is also present in the diagnostic process, as for instance in psychoanalysis.

With regard to accuracy in person perception, one may note that retrospective determinism corresponds to circumscribed accuracy, but it does not go along with global accuracy (see "Accuracy"). From a pragmatic point of view (see James, 1908) retrospective reinterpretation may be regarded as contributing to circumscribed accuracy in the given situation and with regard to a specific target person. At the same time, person perception is stabilized, and thus facilitates interaction with the target person (see also Block & Funder, 1986; Funder, 1987).

Such considerations lead to the question of what is to be learned from history (Fischhoff, 1980). Historical knowledge is characterized by the fact that the actual course of events is known. Whatever caused the rise of Hitler, we already know that he seized power in 1933 and are therefore inclined to regard a variety of salient factors in that historical epoch in Germany as causally relevant to the rise of Hitler. Hitler's contemporaries had more difficulties in predicting his rise and some of them could hardly believe it.

One is always right in retrospect. People tend to concentrate on the positive aspects of two events (e.g., economic depression = E_1 and seizure of power by dictators = E_2). However, the joint appearance of two events is not conclusive proof of a correlation between the two (Fiedler, 1985; Fischhoff, 1980; Wason & Johnson-Laird, 1972). Instead, it is also necessary that *not* E_1 occur together with *not* E_2. This part of the correlation between E_1 and E_2 is often overlooked.

Table 9. Examples of high and low correlations

	High correlation		Low correlation	
	Event E_1		Event E_1	
	+	−	+	−
Event E_2 +	44	4	44	14
−	6	30	17	9

Correlation coefficients φ 0.76 and 0.11 for the high and low correlations respectively.

In Table 9 high and low correlations between two events E_1 and E_2 are depicted. For both examples, however, the frequency of $E_1 + E_2$ (+ +) is the same. Thus, it is not possible to infer the correlation between two events from the frequency of the joint event $E_1 + E_2$. It is, instead, important that the occurrences be concentrated on the diagonal. Studies of impression formation often demonstrate that the evaluation of a relationship is not based on an algorithm appropriate for calculating a relationship (see Chap. 2, "How to assess a relationship"). It is only when optimal circumstances are provided that the intuitive understanding of relationships approaches the statistical concept of correlation.

In retrospect people almost always concentrate on the + + cases and do not consider the remaining combinations. Thus, the joint occurrence of two events comes to serve as a clue to their causal relation. Since history is presented as a closed system in which uncertainty is minimized and details are described saliently, dubious retrospective interpretations of events in terms of cause and consequence may result. However, these interpretations are not necessarily justified. In retrospect, events are interpreted as predetermined in a way that foresight did not warrant (Fischhoff, 1975; Fischhoff & Beyth, 1975).

The tendency to appreciate historical details in retrospect may be particularly likely to result in a "correlational overkill", because any event can be explained when a sufficient number of potentially useful predictors is taken into account. Thus, on the basis of random variation plausible explanations may be derived. Unfortunately, such explanations cannot be generalized to different samples (Fischhoff, 1980).

Proceeding from order effects we have now reached an area that extends far beyond person perception. Order effects will be referred to again in Chap. 5, when the impact of self-fulfilling prophecies is discussed. I have shown that one should be very careful in judging retrospectively. In a similar way, it may be dangerous when social interactions evolve under specific premises. For instance, when an actor expects the target person to be hostile and unfriendly, further interaction will be markedly determined by this premise and a tendency to confirm the original expectation will result.

The next chapter discusses the issue of drawing conclusions in person perception. When the processes of impression formation were presented it was inevitable to hint at conclusions and inferences that extend beyond impression formation. However, the next chapter attempts a systematic review of inference processes in person perception. In Chap. 5, the effect of cues on impression formation will be exemplified referring to vocal communication. Social cues may be regarded as the raw material from which impressions are formed. Cues of physical appearance, cues of speech, or cues of the social environment not only determine what diagnostic information enters judgment formation. They also exert an influence on the kind of stereotypes or cognitive schemata used to form an impression about a person. In this sense one may regard social cues as the data matrix basic to social inferences.

Chapter 2

Reasoning in Impression Formation

Hans Werner Bierhoff and Renate Klein

If social cues are taken as the data matrix of impression formation, inferences represent the computer programs. In the first chapter examples of inferences in person perception were given. Inferences based on implicit personality theories from one trait to other traits were demonstrated, for instance, drawing conclusions from the traits *warm* and *cold* about traits that are also located on the *socially good – socially bad* dimension (see Figure 3). With reference to halo effects, interdependencies between various judgmental dimensions of person perception were discussed.

Although inferences are certainly present in person perception, estimates of their impact differ. McArthur and Baron (1983) take the view that inferences are of minor importance since the events themselves may contain all the relevant information. Other authors, however (e.g., Bruner et al., 1958; Swann, 1984), consider inference processes to be very important for person perception. Opposing McArthur and Baron (1983), Swann (1984, p. 472) notes: "On this issue, I endorse the view that virtually all important person perception activity involves inference."

The opposing positions endorsed by McArthur and Baron (1983) and Swann (1984) might be somewhat exaggerated for the sake of a terse presentation. To the extent that there is only little or vague information about the target person, the likelihood of inference processes increases − for instance, inferences guided by stereotypes. Stereotypic inferences are less likely when the target person conveys precise diagnostic information (see Locksley et al. 1980; see also Chap. 3, "Areas of stereotype research"). However, even diagnostic information may instigate inferences concerning different spheres of life about which no information was presented (Deaux & Lewis, 1984).

Inferences in person perception may be observed on a basic level, when relations between two attributes are to be estimated (see "Uncovering relationships"). Inferring the frequency of one attribute from the frequency of another attribute may be represented using a subjective probability model that has been supported empirically (see "Subjective probability models for stereotypes").

Probability judgments may also be used to represent the relationship between an anchor statement and related statements (see "Implicit logic and stereotypes").

Uncovering Relationships

Before relationships are evaluated relevant information has to be gathered. This information then provides the basis for determining the correlation between two attributes. Following Crocker (1981), one may separate several steps that are important in the process of uncovering relationships in social judgments:

- What data are relevant to evaluating a relationship?
- Which samples will be drawn from the relevant data?
- How will data obtained be classified?
- How is the relationship to be assessed?

Following this sequence of steps, we will now discuss how relationships between different items of social information are inferred.

What Data Are Relevant to Assessing a Relationship?

Table 9 contained an example of high and low correlations between dichotomous attributes (e.g., *unattractive-attractive, overweight-standard weight*). For each attribute one level may be regarded as a positive instance and the other level as a negative instance (e.g., *unattractive* as the positive instance and *attractive* as the negative instance). Moreover, one may separate cases that support a relationship between the attributes ($++$ and $--$) from cases contradicting a relationship ($+-$ and $-+$). If, for instance, one assumes a relationship between attractiveness and body weight, an unattractive, overweight person and an attractive, standard weight person both represent confirming cases, whereas a standard weight, unattractive person and an overweight, attractive person represent disconfirming cases.

Four contingencies may be separated (see Bruner et al., 1956):

- Positive confirming (*unattractive, overweight*),
- Positive disconfirming (*unattractive, standard weight*),
- Negative confirming (*attractive, standard weight*),
- Negative disconfirming (*attractive, overweight*).

Starting from this classification it is reasonable to investigate the extent to which positive and negative instances are taken into account when relationships have to be estimated. One may further ask whether people look for confirming or for disconfirming evidence.

It has long been noted that positive instances (representing the hypothesis in question) play an important role in concept formation (Smoke, 1933). However, negative instances were not regarded as hindering, since Smoke (1933) found no significant differences when a fictitious concept had to be learned by positive instances alone or by positive and negative instances.

However, Hovland (1952) criticized Smoke's (1933) approach. Smoke (1933) did not investigate how much relevant information positive or negative instances convey and how information conveyed by different (that is positive or negative) instances is utilized in concept formation. Hovland and Weiss (1953) were able to demonstrate the superiority of positive instances in concept learning. When the amount of information conveyed was held constant across positive and negative instances, a concept was more easily learned when it was exclusively represented by positive instances than when it was represented by negative instances only.

The superiority of positive instances probably results from the fact that most concepts are acquired using positive examples: "Thus, a child learns that the animals in a certain cage at the zoo are 'lions', the marchers in a parade are 'communists', the flowers in a vase are 'roses'" (Smoke, 1933, p. 583).

Correspondingly, relationships in everyday life in most cases are exemplified using positive instances $(+ +)$, but negative instances $(- -)$ are neglected (Fiedler, 1985). Consider the stereotype that women are more interested in fashion than men. The relationship between gender and interest in fashion is mostly demonstrated by pointing to positive cases (women interested in fashion), whereas negative cases (men not interested in fashion) are mostly ignored.

A series of experiments was conducted to investigate what kind of data is gathered when a hypothesis about another person is to be tested (Snyder & Gangestad, 1981). The experiments are summarized in Box 16. For instance, the hypothesis in question either stated that the target person was extroverted or that he/she was introverted.

Box 16. Information search by questioning

In principle, one may differentiate between three strategies to test a hypothesis about another person. One may search for confirmation, for disconfirmation, or for both confirmation and disconfirmation of the hypothesis. Snyder and Swann (1978 b) asked their subjects either to test the hypothesis that a target person was extroverted or to test the hypothesis that he/she was introverted. Subjects had to choose 12 questions from a list of 26. The list of questions may serve as a clue to the underlying research question:

- 11 questions asked for extroverted behavior (e.g., "What would you do if you wanted to liven things up at a party?").
- 10 questions asked for introverted behavior (e.g., "What things do you dislike about loud parties?").
- 5 questions were of neutral content (e.g., "What kinds of charities do you like to contribute to?").

Results showed that participants chose neutral questions under both hypotheses with equal frequency (on average, two out of 12 questions belonged to the neutral category). Beyond this result, distinct preferences emerged:

– Under the extroverted hypothesis mainly extroverted questions were chosen.
– Under the introverted hypothesis subjects preferred introverted questions.

Summing up these findings, one may state that subjects preferred questions that matched the content of the hypothesis. Thus, they tended to gather hypothesis-consistent information, but tended to neglect hypothesis-inconsistent information.

The same pattern of results was replicated in four subsequent studies (Snyder & Swann, 1978b; Snyder & Campbell, 1980). Consistent questions were also preferred when real interviews were conducted and were still preferred when a prize for the best questioning strategy had been announced. In addition, independent observers rated target persons' answers about extroversion/introversion as more extroverted when interviewers had tested the extroversion hypothesis. Target persons who had been interviewed under the introversion hypothesis were rated as more introverted. The independent ratings were always based on the behavior of the target person in the interview. Thus, the confirmatory questioning strategy led to a behavioral confirmation of the hypothesis.

Trope and Bassok (1983) argued against these findings. The questioning behavior of the subjects can be regarded as rational, if it is taken into account that Snyder and Swann (1978b) urged their interviewers to test extreme levels of extroversion and introversion. Assuming that there are different levels of extroversion/introversion, it is most rational to ask confirmatory questions when one wants to test for extreme levels of the attribute. Given these circumstances, confirmatory questions are the most diagnostic. On the other hand, extroverted and introverted questions are equally diagnostic when the boundary between the hypothesized characteristic and the alternative is at the midpoint of the trait dimension.

To illustrate this idea, consider how to test the hypothesis (by questioning) that an object is red. If there are the additional colors yellow and green, it is less informative to ask whether the object in question is green (that is, to ask a disconfirmatory question) than to ask whether it is red. By contrast, if there are only red and yellow objects, the boundary between hypothesis and alternative is located at the center of the "color dimension," and it is equally informative to ask for red or yellow.

In one experiment (Trope & Bassok, 1983, exp. 1) students were asked to design a questionnaire suitable for testing whether a person is polite or impolite. In one condition, students had to test for an extreme level of politeness; in another condition they had to test whether the target person was on the polite side of the trait continuum. Correspondingly, students had to test for extreme impoliteness or to test whether the target person was on the impolite side.

Questions were categorized according to the extent of politeness they implied. In the intermediate boundary condition, there were no differences in the level of politeness the questions implied. The hypothesis effect predicted by Snyder and Swann (1978b) was only obtained when extreme levels of the trait had to be tested.

In a second experiment (Trope & Bassok, 1983, exp. 2) extreme or intermediate boundaries with regard to extroversion/introversion had to be tested. According to a pretest, the questions to be used differed in diagnosticity. The following categories were used:

- Extroverted questions, high diagnosticity (e.g., "Are you usually the initiator in forming new relationships?")
- Extroverted questions, low diagnosticity (e.g., "Do you intervene when someone is pushing in line?")
- Introverted questions, high diagnosticity (e.g., "Do you usually go to movies alone?")
- Introverted questions, low diagnosticity (e.g., "Do you like spending much of your time in libraries?")

The potential interviewers had to select 12 questions from a list of 24 (6 questions in each category) that they would like to ask when testing their hypothesis. All in all, highly diagnostic questions were preferred. In addition, subjects preferred hypothesis-consistent questions to hypothesis-inconsistent ones. Preference for consistent questions was observed in both the extreme and the intermediate boundary conditions.

In another study (Trope, Bassok & Alon, 1984, exp. 1) the questions formulated to test hypotheses on extroversion and introversion were classified according to five categories:

- Biased questions, as used by Snyder and Swann (1978b), that almost force the interviewee to answer in line with the question content
- Introverted questions ("Do you have difficulty making new friends?")
- Extroverted questions ("Do you like parties?")
- Open questions ("What are your hobbies?")
- Bidirectional questions ("Do you prefer classical music or rock music?")

Classification of the questions showed that bidirectional questions were particularly frequent. Biased questions were almost absent. The type of question did not depend on whether the extroverted, the introverted, or no explicit hypothesis was tested.

Results reported by Trope et al. (1984) should not lead to the conclusion that the hypothesis is irrelevant to data selection. Findings, however, indicate that interviewers are capable of asking diagnostic questions. This tendency is especially pronounced when optimal circumstances for questioning are provided.

A more biased selection of questions results when subjects are asked to choose from a group of one-sided, biased questions such as are often used in everyday life. A preference for confirmatory question-asking also prevails when personal involvement influences the search for relevant information. Snyder and Skrypnek (1981) had their subjects consult their personal "library" of self-related knowledge. Student subjects had to assess their own suitability as a summer camp worker. They received a list of relevant attributes a good summer camp worker should possess. In one condition the job description emphasized masculine attributes and activities (athletic, independent, leadership abilities, organizational ability, supervisory ability, fishing, hiking); in another condition the emphasis of the job description lay upon feminine attributes and activities (warm, understanding, cooperative, sensitive to the needs of children, arts of crafts, washing up).

After they had read the relevant attributes students were given 10 min to write down everything that they thought made them suitable for the job. Independent judges rated the written accounts for three factors: masculine qualities, feminine qualities, and qualities neutral to sex role. Descriptions of self-rated suitability as a summer camp worker revealed a confirmatory pattern. Subjects testing the masculine hypothesis listed 5.54 masculine attributes on average, whereas masculine attributes were mentioned only 2.49 times on average when the feminine hypothesis was under scrutiny. Correspondingly, subjects listed more feminine attributes when the feminine hypothesis had to be tested (mean 5.45) than when the masculine hypothesis had to be tested (mean 4.01). This pattern of results emerged for feminine-oriented, masculine-oriented, and androgynous individuals (for this sex role classification see Taylor & Hall, 1982).

One may argue that looking for masculine items in the personal library of knowledge is of comparable diagnosticity to looking for feminine items. However, hypothesis testing was biased in the direction of the hypothesis given. If someone primarily scans his/her library of knowledge for masculine attributes, he/she is likely to neglect important feminine attributes. Moreover, the fourth or fifth masculine attribute is probably less informative than the second or third feminine attribute.

Additional experiments (Snyder & Cantor, 1979) demonstrated that assessments of another person's suitability were also influenced by the hypothesis. Participants read about a week in the life of a woman named Jane. They then had to assess her suitability for an extroverted (sales person) or an introverted job (research librarian). In addition, factual knowledge about the events in the week of Jane's life presented in the biographical sketch was tested. Participants recalled more hypothesis-consistent than hypothesis-inconsistent facts. This tendency was particularly explicit when participants had been told that Jane was applying for the job compared to a condition in which they were told she already had the job. In the latter condition no strong differential recall of consistent versus inconsistent facts emerged.

It is notable that the difference in frequencies of recalled consistent and inconsistent facts correlated highly with assessed suitability ($r = 0.60$). That is, participants who reported relatively more confirming than disconfirming factual material gave higher ratings of Jane's suitability. Actually, Jane's description was characterized by equal frequencies of prototypically extroverted and introverted behavior. Thus, the preference for hypothesis-consistent factual material demonstrates the selectivity of recall. In a second experiment a high correlation between the difference of consistent/inconsistent facts recalled and the rating of suitability ($r = 0.78$) was also obtained.

Snyder and Cantor (1979) noted that job advertisements were almost exclusively framed in terms of relevant, positive attributes the potential job applicant should possess. Only 33 of 7415 job advertisements analyzed noted attributes the applicant should not possess.

Summing up, one may state that suitability dominates non-suitability, since attributes consistent with the job description are particularly prone to be recalled and to be used in deciding about suitability. This bias may result in a neglect of an applicant's attributes that are inconsistent with the job description.

Studies from applied fields of questioning reveal mixed evidence concerning questioning strategies. Sackett (1982) could only partly replicate the findings of Snyder and Swann (1978b; see Box 16) and concluded that professional job interviewers did not follow a biased confirmation strategy, preferring instead neutral questions. Similar results are reported by Strohmer and Newman (1983) with regard to counseling. The majority of their participants selected or formulated unbiased questions. In a similar vein, Hayden (1987) and Strohmer and Chiodo (1984) present findings that are not consistent with a strong confirmatory strategy in questioning.

Lay hypothesis testers as well as professional interviewers seem, in general, to select their questions and their strategies of information search according to some subjective criterion of diagnosticity on the one hand and in line with prior expectations on the other hand. Skov and Sherman (1986) observed a diagnostically oriented strategy that was followed by a preference for hypothesis-confirming data. A similar point was made by Bassok and Trope (1983), who concluded that people generally prefer diagnostic questions to less diagnostic ones. This preference, however, was accompanied by a tendency to prefer trait-consistent questions when only the hypothesized trait was described and not the alternative trait hypothesis.

The findings mentioned up to this point with regard to hypothesis testing indicate that hypothesis-testing behavior depends on the specific hypotheses as well as on a variety of salient expectations. Semin and Strack (1980) argue that participants simply comply with the experimental task and do not test their own hypotheses when selecting confirmatory questions. This argument was supported by Meertens, Koomen, Delpeut and Hager (1984). According to their results, people select questions which are consistent with the most salient expectation at hand. When a rather weak and abstract hypothesis was presented, subjects' selection of questions was influenced by the specific task formulations (experiment 1). Without a task manipulation (i.e., when the subjects were required to establish whether the target person was introvert or extrovert without the instructions being biased to the one or the other conclusion) a vividly described hypothesis led to a hypothesis-confirming questioning strategy (experiment 2). Snyder and White (1981) showed that participants chose disconfirming questions when explicitly asked to falsify a given hypothesis. In contrast, a hypothesis-confirming strategy emerged when they were asked to verify a hypothesis.

Another important factor may be demands emerging from a social interaction. Pennington (1987), for instance, observed that interviewers in a real face-to-face interaction followed a neutral questioning strategy, whereas participants in a paper-and-pencil condition preferred confirmatory questions. The accuracy of social stereotypes was tested using a confirmatory strategy, unless participants were told to consider the impression management implications of their strategies. When confronted with the possibility that the interviewee might rate them as narrow-minded if they asked only confirming questions, participants abandoned the confirmatory strategy and asked for both confirming and disconfirming instances (Snyder, Campbell & Preston, 1982).

Further evidence supporting the notion that information search may be influenced by salient interaction goals comes from a study by Darley, Fleming, Hilton and Swann (1988). Participants in this study expected an interaction with a partner who was described as having "difficulty performing under pressure" and becoming "overly emotional in some stressful situations" (Darley et al., 1988, p. 23). In one condition participants expected a casual conversation with their partner. In another condition they expected to play a video game that required calm and controlled reactions under pressure and that the other person would be their partner.

When given the opportunity to ask their partners some preliminary questions, participants in the video game condition predominantly asked questions in line with their negative expectancy about their partner's behavior. In the casual conversation condition participants asked neutral, expectancy-irrelevant questions.

Another factor which may exert a guiding influence on information search is a person's self-concept. Fong and Markus (1982), for instance, found that extrovert schematics preferred extrovert questions and introvert schematics preferred introvert questions when asked to find out about the personality of other people.

The evidence presented above supports the idea that question selection and formulation as well as information search in general may be guided by salient or task-relevant expectations, some of which may be explicitly stated hypotheses. Obviously, there is a widespread tendency to follow a hypothesis-matching strategy (Higgins & Bargh, 1987). This tendency, however, does not necessarily lead to confirmation of the hypothesis in question (Higgins & Bargh, 1987, p. 402).

A similar argument is advanced by Klayman and Ha (1987). According to their theoretical analysis of hypothesis testing, hypothesis-matching strategies may be regarded as instances of a general "positive test strategy" (Klayman & Ha, 1987, p. 213). For many situations this positive test strategy will serve as a satisfactory heuristic when testing for the truth or falsity of a hypothesis.

Basically, Klayman and Ha (1987) argue that one must discriminate between the hypothesized condition and the actual, "true" condition. Whether a hypothesis-consistent strategy will lead to confirmation or disconfirmation of the hypothesis then depends on the precise relationship between the hypothesized and the true condition. There may be constellations when only a hypothesis-consistent strategy allows for disconfirmation of the hypothesis. Specifically, this will be the case when the hypothesized set of conditions is larger then the actual set of conditions (Klayman & Ha, 1987, pp. 214, 215).

Of course, there are other situations where such a strategy will lead to unjustified confirmation of the hypothesis in question. However, since in most cases the actual relationship between hypothesized and real conditions is not known, a positive test strategy will serve as a reasonably good heuristic in hypothesis testing.

Observers tend to attribute particular relevance to data that are consistent with the hypothesis in question. This tendency leads to an overemphasis on the + + cell in Table 9 (see Crocker, 1982). When asked what kind of evidence they would need to assess the relationship between success in a tennis match and preceding training, subjects preferred a confirmatory strategy. When participants were asked about determining the relationship between winning the match and preceding training they preferred instances that could confirm the assumed relationship ("The number of times you work out the day before a match and win the match"). When they were asked about determining the relationship between losing the match and preceding training, they preferred to ask about "the number of times you work out the day before and lose the match." Positive cases were also preferred when a neutral question about the relationship between training and the *result* of the tennis match was asked. In this condition, however, subjects also asked frequently for other types of evidence (training/lose = + −; no training/win = − +; no training/lose = − −; Crocker, 1982).

These results point to the fact that the type of question asked may influence information search (see Box 16). In addition, the preference for positive instances was also observed using other research approaches. Fiedler (1985, study 4) noted that information search was dominated by positive instances.

For example, judges had to test the hypothesis that a drug ("Aloxan") palliates whooping cough. Four files were provided:

1. Only persons who had taken Aloxan
2. Only persons who had not taken Aloxan
3. Only persons who have whooping cough
4. Only persons who do not have whooping cough

On the front of an index card, for example, was printed that the person had not taken Aloxan (file 2), whereas on the back it was noted whether whooping cough had abated. The first two requests for information revealed a preference for positive cases (files 1 and 3). This tendency was partly compensated for in subsequent requests for information so that the positivity effect was weakened across all information requests and was only observed for file 1. The overall sequence of information search was characterized by an equalizing tendency. That is to say, the initial overemphasis on files 1 and 3 gave way to an equally distributed reliance on all files given.

To sum up, there is a preference for positive cases in hypothesis testing that is especially pronounced during the initial phase of the information search but that may still be found when the information search is terminated. Such a tendency should impede the assessment of a correlation, since a reliable conclusion about the correlation is not possible solely on the basis of the + + cell (see Table 9).

What Kind of Samples Should be Drawn?

Ideally, one draws a random sample from the population if it is not possible to observe all relevant single events. When a random sample is drawn, it is reasonable to expect that the (sufficiently large) sample is representative of the population. However, in social reality the principle of random selection is mostly not taken into account. First, social encounters are selective, since "birds of a feather often flock together." Secondly, single cases exert a strong influence on an overall judgment, the more so when they are presented forcefully. Thirdly, salient persons who attract the observer's attention invoke more inferences than persons outside the focus of attention.

Selectivity of Social Encounters. It is a well-known fact that the structure of social encounters is related to the similarity between the interacting partners, so that similar persons more often interact with each other than dissimilar persons (Clore & Byrne, 1977). Early research by Galton (1870) and Pearson (1903; both cited by Clore & Byrne, 1977) already showed the tendency to associate with similar people. Marital couples showed greater resemblance in several attributes than randomly paired persons. In addition, everyday experience shows that, for instance, social class or ethnic identity are important factors in the frequency of encounters.

Therefore, in most cases one's acquaintances do not represent a random sample of persons that would allow conclusions about the validity of interpersonal hypotheses (e.g., "Overweight persons are unattractive"). On the contrary, one should expect severe regional, ethnic, and socioeconomic selectivity. Misleading conclusions based on such biased samples can only be avoided when the hypothesis is valid for each subsample.

Concrete Versus Abstract Information. Some events are perceived and encoded with all their details, whereas others are merely summarized and may be expressed by a statistical term. Thus, one may distinguish two types of evidence: (1) concrete single case information, and (2) summarizing descriptive statistics. Single cases may exert a considerable influence on judgment formation. The representativeness heuristic states (Tversky & Kahneman, 1974) that classification of an object into a certain category depends on the perceived similarity between object and category. In everyday life, applying the representativeness heuristic often yields good results, for example because many stereotypes which suggest this similarity contain at least a slight amount of truth (see Chap. 3, "Definitions and history of research"). Errors in social judgment only result when expectations about a certain relationship result from overgeneralization.

Since the similarity between object and category plays an important role in assigning an object to a category, single cases that fit the category but are exceptional in important attributes may lead to biased judgments. Such biased judgments often overshadow statistical information. The example in Box 17 demonstrates how a suitable single case can trigger formation of "irrational" judgments and can, thus, be disadvantageous to a whole group of persons. Unfortunately, we are exposed to misleading single cases in the mass media every day.

Box 17. Fascination comes from details
Inductive reasoning based on a limited number of observations is omnipresent in human life. Every weekend, football, basketball, or cricket results are obtained and conclusions are drawn about which teams will end up at the top and about those who will probably fail to remain within the league. Or consider another example: Last summer was cold and rainy. What will the weather be like next summer?

Such generalizations are characterized by the fact that the correct answer will not be known until the event in question has taken place. The top teams are not known till the end of the season and the quality of the next summer can only be assessed next year.

Nevertheless, more or less reasonable considerations may be made. How expectations are derived from the available evidence was investigated by Hamill, Wilson and Nisbett (1980, study 1). In their study a detailed single case history and a summary of statistical information were employed. The case was a 43-year-old woman who had been on welfare and had neglected her children. Children attended school at irregular intervals and finally became addicted to drugs. The woman bought expensive furniture and at the end of the month she had not got enough money to buy the daily food. She had lived in New York for 16 years and had been dependent on welfare for 13 years.

Although this description is consistent with the stereotype of people on welfare, it is not consistent with reality. Only a minority of welfare recipients in the USA are supported for as long as 10 years. Most of them stop receiving welfare after 2–4 years. Thus, the case was atypical of the population of welfare recipients.

Statistical information about welfare recipients was provided in an "Editor's Note" added to the case description. Depending on the condition, the note explained that the average duration of welfare payments was 2 years (atypical condition) or 15 years (typical condition).

In two control groups who were not given the case history, judges either received no information about the average duration of dependence on welfare or they received information consistent with the statistical data. However, no significant differences between the control groups in their attitudes towards welfare recipients emerged.

After presentation of information (or without initial information), attitudes towards welfare recipients were rated on seven scales. For instance, one question was "How hard do people on welfare work to improve their situations?" (1 = not at all hard, 5 = extremely hard). According to the combined attitude index, both control groups – who had not received the negative case description – made more positive evaluations than both experimental groups, who had learned about the case. Remarkably, it was irrelevant whether the Editor's Note had described the case as typical or atypical.

The results described in Box 17 show that a vivid single case may exert a strong influence on the evaluation of a whole group of persons. A single case is not necessarily representative of hundreds or thousands cases, yet judges seem implicitly to assume that the single case provides information relevant to the average member of a group. Even worse with regard to rational information processing is that additional information indicating the representativeness of the single case was neglected. Even in a condition where the single case was apparently atypical of the population in question it strongly influenced the evaluation of this population.

That is to say, with regard to inductive reasoning people tend to neglect important statistical concepts. This tendency is particulary prominent when the population in question is homogeneous, when judgments are made on a subjective dimension instead of on an objective rating scale, and when statistical training of the judges is low (Nisbett et al., 1983).

However, cultural evolution appears to be occurring, in that statistical concepts are nowadays more likely to be taken into account when judgments are made. While in the Middle Ages the representativeness heuristic was widely used, even in the scientific domain, statistical thinking is increasing nowadays, leading to a more widespread use of simple statistical heuristics by the man in the street. The work of Tversky and Kahneman (1974) constitutes a milestone in this cultural evolution (Nisbett et al., 1983).

Salience Effects. Tversky and Kahneman (1974) described another heuristic that may influence selection, registration, and encoding of data: availability. The availability heuristic describes a tendency to assign more weight to information that is easily recalled, easily imagined, or described in concrete details when the likelihood of events is to be estimated. The influence of vividly described single cases (see Box I 7) is probably due to the representativeness and availability heuristics.

In addition, figure-ground phenomena may play a role in information processing. Figural salience of an actor attracts the attention of observers and determines which information is encoded first and easily remembered (see Chap. 4, "Figure/background reversal").

McArthur (1981) assumed that person perception is based on principles similar to those guiding object perception. In both domains observers typically attend to "intense, changing, complex, novel, and unit-forming stimuli" (McArthur, 1981, p. 202). "Figural" persons differing distinctly from their environment should (according to McArthur, 1981) be impressive and easily remembered, trigger strong emotions, and be often regarded as causes of events.

Although empirical evidence for these hypotheses is not conclusive (see McArthur, 1981), figural salience of a person may indeed influence person perception in the expected manner. A series of experiments (McArthur & Post, 1977) suggested that attributions of dispositional/situational causes were influenced by figural salience (see Chap. 4, "Figure/background reversal").

People who have been the focus of attention should be recalled faster, since information concerning these people is easily available. In this sense, Taylor and Fiske (1978) talk about the top-of-the-head phenomenon, which shows that the ideal, random sampling, does not always occur. The top-of-the-head phenomenon, together with selectivity of encounters and emphasis on single case information in judgment formation, fosters biased data gathering.

How Are the Available Data Classified?

Biasing influences of the observer on covariation judgments are identified more easily than influences of the data, which may, for example, be varied by changing the redundancy of the information (Fiedler, 1985). Observer influences can be seen in expectancy effects. These are more thoroughly discussed in Chap. 4 ("Sensitivity for consensus information") and Chap. 5 ("Self-fulfilling prophecies and processes of expectation confirmation"), but for the moment an example will help demonstrate how expectancies may influence classification of data (Box 18). This example also indicates the importance of stereotypes in person perception, which will be more thoroughly discussed in Chap. 3.

Box 18. Authoritarian clerks, liberal students, or: Illusory correlations
To investigate observer influence on the encoding of data, judges were provided with 36 cases in sequence. Each case depicted a student or a clerk holding an authoritarian or liberal opinion on child rearing. Cases were constructed so that there was in fact a zero correlation between attitudinal statements and person category.

After presentation of the 36 cases, subjects had to judge the relative frequency of authoritarian opinions held by clerks and students. The difference between the estimates was 8.1%, indicating that more authoritarian attitudes were attributed to clerks than to students. Thus, the authoritarian clerk stereotype and the liberal student stereotype led to illusory correlations.

Finally, each of the 36 attitudinal statements was shown during a cued-recall test. Subjects were asked to indicate whether the opinion given had been stated by a clerk or by a student. Thus, the number of errors confirming the stereotype and the number of errors not confirming the stereotype could be determined. Confirming errors were present when a liberal statement was erroneously attributed to a student or an authoritarian statement was erroneously attributed to a clerk. Nonconfirming errors were present when a liberal statement was erroneously attributed to a clerk or an authoritarian statement was erroneously attributed to a student.

The percentage of confirming errors exceeded the percentage of nonconfirming errors. The difference between the relative error frequencies was 0.22. Thus, reproduction of an event sequence was biased because of person category stereotypes. According to Taylor and Crocker (1981), a type 1 error had been made.

In addition, even the interpretation of attitudinal statements seemed to be biased by an association of the statement with a clerk or student. Each statement was rated on a 9-point scale according to the extent of liberal or authoritarian attitude expressed. Identical statements were rated as more liberal when attributed to a student than when attributed to a clerk. Thus, one may suspect that a bias due to the stereotypes was already present when the information was perceived and encoded (Fiedler, Hemmeter & Hofmann, 1984).

To sum up, classification of sequences of events that are a conjunction of two dichotomous attributes (e.g., authoritarian/liberal attitudes and clerks/students) is influenced by an implicit consensus (see Box 18). Such implicit assumptions lead to biased recall since expected events are recalled better than unexpected events, and also to biased perception and encoding of the stimulus information.

This expectation effect may be regarded as an illusory correlation. Initially, the concept of illusory correlation was discussed with regard to projective techniques (Chapman & Chapman, 1967, 1969). Projective techniques are likely to elicit illusory correlations since certain answers are expected from clients with certain emotional problems. These expectations are due to widespread and popular prejudices.

The effects of such prejudices were demonstrated with the Draw-a-Man test (Chapman & Chapman, 1967) and the Rorschach test. For instance, Chapman and Chapman (1969) were able to demonstrate that some Rorschach answers were related to a diagnosis of homosexuality with undue frequency because of their semantic associations with homosexuality. Judges read a series of answers to a Rorschach test. Each answer was linked to two diagnoses. For example, the comment on one interpretation was as follows:

> The man who said this
> 1. has sexual feelings toward other men.
> 2. feels sad and depressed much of the time.

No systematic relation between diagnosis and interpretation existed. Each interpretation was linked to each diagnosis with equal frequency. When judges had read the series they were asked whether certain interpretations were particularly frequent with any diagnosis. Judges' answers exhibited a tendency to relate the diagnosis of homosexuality to certain popular answers thought to be indicative of homosexuality.

In spite of missing evidence, illusory correlations contribute to the stabilization of stereotypes (see Box 19 and Chap. 3, "Diagnostic information from single cases"). In a study by Fiedler (1985) it was found that the more pronounced the stereotypes held by the judges the greater the retrospective bias. Illusory correlations in person perception give rise to the question of whether expectancies bias perception, encoding, and recall or only bias recall. Empirical findings support the notion that expectations bias encoding of relevant information (Fiedler et al., 1984; McArthur, 1980).

How Is a Relationship Assessed?

Consider a situation in which a person has gathered data relevant to the relationship between two attributes (e.g., whether a drug was administered and whether an illness was successfully cured). The attributes may be displayed in a 2×2 schema as presented in Table 9. On the one hand, one may ask whether the individual cases were appropriately classified. On the other hand, one may ask whether the evidence gathered is combined appropriately to give an overall judgment of the relationship.

Inhelder and Piaget (1958) were among the first to investigate whether adolescents hold an appropriate notion of correlation. They observed a thorough understanding of correlation among 15-year-olds. However, they presented information in a very clear and well-organized manner and the information used consisted of only few cases.

Other examples also indicate an elementary understanding of correlational relationships. Consider the success of classical conditioning, which may be interpreted as covariation between the unconditioned and conditioned stimuli (UCS and CS; Bindra, 1976). However, successful conditioning depends on optimal learning conditions, disturbing interference being excluded so that the contingency between UCS and CS is particularly clear and salient (Fiedler, 1985; Jennings, Amabile & Ross, 1982). In addition, organisms seem to be particularly sensitive to covariations in their environment that are relevant to them. Other covariations receive less attention.

These examples allow the conclusion that an elementary understanding of correlational relationships is possible – at least given optimal conditions (Crocker, 1981; Smedslund, 1963). Accordingly, Jennings et al. (1982, p. 228) note:

> Every rat who has ever learned to escape in a shuttle box, every child who has ever discerned the advantages of adding sugar to her breakfast cereal, every lover who has discovered that honesty is not always the best policy, every mother who has ever shown a lactation reflex in response to a child's cry, proves that organisms do recognize covariations among environmental stimuli.

The existence of an understanding of simple relationships does not indicate that successful processing of covariation information takes place in complex situations. Smedslund (1963) offered his subjects information on a symptom and a diagnosis based on 100 cases and concluded that adults without statistical training "do not have a cognitive structure isomorphic with the concept of correlation. Their strategies and inferences typically reveal a particularistic, non-statistical approach, or an exclusive dependence on the frequency of + + instances" (Smedslund, 1963, p. 172).

More than half of the female judges indicated that the strength of the relationship is only dependent on the frequency of + + cases: "Not a single subject gave any indication of having understood that the degree of relationship is determined by the ratio of the sum of the + + and − − cases and the sum of the + − and − + cases" (adapted from Smedslund, 1963, p. 169).

This study dealt with relationships between dichotomous variables that may be presented in a 2×2 table. Relationships of this kind are usually expressed by the correlation coefficient Φ (alternative measures of statistical relationships are discussed by Fiedler, 1985). In a more recent study Jennings et al. (1982) investigated subjective estimates of the relationship between quantitative attributes, statistically calculated with the product-moment correlation coefficient. The high variability of estimates showed that there were large individual differences when relationships in bivariate distributions had to be inferred. It was not until the objective strength of the relationship exceeded 0.70 that 75% of the judges supposed the relationship to be larger than zero. On the whole, subjective estimates were rather conservative since even objectively high correlations were considered to be medium-sized.

In spite of the large individual variability of estimates and the conservative judgment tendency, a positive relationship between objective correlation and subjective estimate emerged. This relationship was positively accelerated, since in the lower region a difference of 0.10 was paid hardly any attention whereas a difference of 0.10 in the upper region led to large subjective differences in the relationship estimates.

The relationship between objective correlations and subjective estimates corresponded well to the relationship between objective correlations and an index of forecasting efficiency (see Guilford, 1965). Since a correlation of 0.75 results in an efficiency of 34%, it is clear that the correlations are underestimated on the whole. This is particularly true of lower correlations. Deviations can also be caused by the perceivers' understanding of the instructions (Fiedler, 1985). In addition, their level of cognitive development is important (Allen, Walker, Schroeder & Johnson, 1987) because an adequate understanding of the concept of correlation presupposes formal operational thought (Inhelder & Piaget, 1958).

Studies on the description and estimation of random sequences and controllable events show that perceivers can estimate the extent of a relationship between two events adequately. Perceivers are capable of distinguishing between random sequences and nonrandom dependence. One precondition for this seems to be that the perceivers are made aware at the beginning that in the course of the experiment random sequences may also be presented (Peterson, 1980).

It is possible that perceivers do not expect to be presented with random sequences in psychological experiments. This false expectation can lead to an inadequate differentiation between random sequences and nonrandom dependent events. One result which agrees with this idea is that series of coincidences which were presented without any warning were often perceived as related (Alloy & Abramson, 1979, study 2).

On the other hand, Alloy and Abramson (1979, study 1) found clear indications that perceivers were able to assess the extent of the contingency between two events (i.e., the pressing of a button and the lighting up of a green lamp). The greater the objective relationship between the two events the higher perceivers assessed the controllability of the lighting up of the green lamp by pressing the button to be.

Further experiments (Alloy & Abramson, 1979, studies 3 and 4) showed, however, that the adequacy of the assessment of contingencies by depressed and non-depressed perceivers differed. This was the case when the valence of the events was positive or negative. The valence was manipulated by associating the lighting up of the lamp with winning money and by associating the failure of the lamp to light up with loss of money.

The results showed that:

- Depressed people assessed the contigency on the whole adequately. This was the case for random sequences as well as for series of events in which a dependency between the two events existed.
- Nondepressive people overestimated the extent of their control over series of coincidences when the uncontrollable event was associated with winning money.
- Nondepressive people underestimated the extent of their control when the failure of the green lamp to light up was associated with losses.

To sum up, one can say that perceivers are able to discover nonrandom dependencies in simple series of events. However, they do not apply any formal statistical procedures but follow rough statistical heuristics. It is interesting to note that people who tend to a depressed state of mind do better than non-depressive perceivers, who are less able to recognize the contingency of events. This result points to a relationship between illusions of control and wellbeing (Taylor & Brown, 1988). Referring to Malinowski (1948), Geer, Davison and Gatchel (1970, pp. 737, 738), write: "Man creates his own gods to fill in gaps in his knowledge about a sometimes terrifying environment, creating at least an illusion of control which is presumably comforting." The same idea is behind the writings of Albert Camus.

On the whole, one can say that recognizing noncontingencies is more difficult than recognizing contingencies. Not only the relationship between dichotomous features but also that between quantitative features is represented cognitively. However, there are large interindividual differences. Furthermore, there is a general tendency towards conservative estimates of relationships.

One theoretical interpretation of the results (Alloy & Tabachnik, 1984; see also Alloy, 1988; Goddard & Allan, 1988) assumes that the assessment of a covariation is influenced by existing expectations and by cues present in the current situation specifying the contingencies between events. The relative strength of these two influencing factors seems to determine the accuracy of the assessment of a relationship. The deciding elements seem to be whether the expectations about the contingencies agree with the objective contingencies and whether they are in concord with the situational cues. When faced with a new series of events, one rational information processing technique could be to assimilate the new information about covariations to the existing expectations which have proved to be effective in the past, even if the danger of false judgments exists in the short term (Alloy & Tabachnik, 1984).

Subjective Probability Models of Stereotypes

Chapter 3 deals with stereotypes in detail. Here we want to present two approaches to research on stereotypes which see stereotypes as inference processes. One of these is the approach of McCauley, Stitt and Segal (1980) which uses the Bayes theorem. The second approach is that of Wyer (1977) which is based on logical propositions. Discussion of these approaches is appropriate at this point because they interpret stereotypes as inference processes and because they are not only limited to stereotypes but can be applied to other areas of social judgment.

The Bayes Theorem as a Model of Stereotypes

The results reported in the previous section leave little doubt that in many situations perceivers come to estimates of relationships which correspond roughly to the objective correlation between the events. In the following we want to examine the question of whether this also occurs to a certain extent in the field of stereotypes. Since the attribution of stereotyped characteristics to people involves an element of uncertainty, it seems appropriate to use subjective probabilities of the presence of particular characteristics to measure personal stereotypes.

Stereotypes can be defined as generalizations about a class of people (see Chap. 3, "Definitions and history of research"). The extent of these generalizations can be assessed using subjective probabilities.

Let us look at the following probability judgments:

P (efficient | German) = P (B|A): The percentage of Germans who are efficient.

P (efficient)   = P (B): The percentage of all people in the world who are efficient.

P (German|efficient) = P (A | B): The percentage of efficient people who are German.

P (German)   = P (A): The percentage of people in the world who are German.

The Bayes theorem can be applied to these probability judgments:

$$P(B|A) = P(B) \times P(A|B)/P(A) = P(B) \times LR$$

In Figure 12 the Bayes theorem is illustrated by using Venn diagrams. To what extent the estimate of the efficiency of the Germans $P(B|A)$ deviates from the assessment of the efficiency of all the people in the world $P(B)$ is expressed by the likelihood ratio (LR). If the likelihood ratio is 1, there is no dependence between P (A) and P (B) so that $P(B|A) = P(B)$. If the likelihood ratio is less than 1 or more than 1, this indicates stereotypes because these deviations show that a characteristic is attributed to the group of people in question less or more than the average would lead one to expect. For the likelihood ratio one can say:

$$LR = P(A|B)/P(A) = P(B|A)/P(B) \ .$$

This relationship is also represented by Venn diagrams in Figure 12.

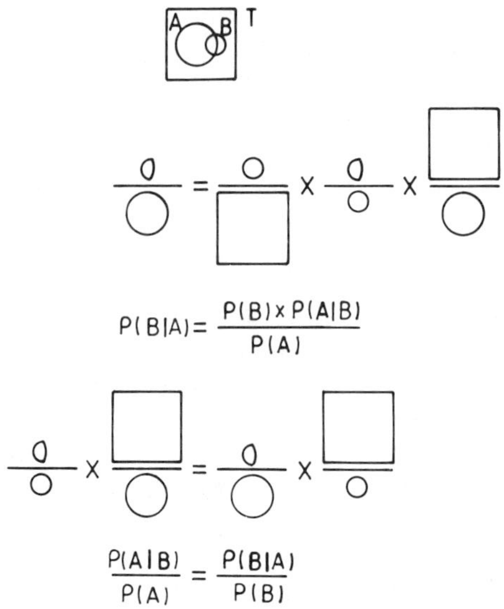

$$P(B|A) = \frac{P(B) \times P(A|B)}{P(A)}$$

$$\frac{P(A|B)}{P(A)} = \frac{P(B|A)}{P(B)}$$

Figure 12. Illustration of the Bayes theorem. Set A represents the members of a group of people while set B represents the people who possess a particular attribute. The total population T refers to all the people in the world. (Modified from McCauley, Stitt & Segal, 1980, p. 198. Copyright 1980 by the American Psychological Association. Adapted by permission).

$P(B|A)/P(B)$ is a useful index of stereotyping. If this index is larger than 1, then the characteristic is overrepresented in the group A (positively distinct). If the index is smaller than 1, then the characteristic is underrepresented in group A (negatively distinct). Instead of comparing a group with everybody in the world, it is also possible to measure the perceived difference between two groups of people (e.g., men and women) using the likelihood ratio (also called diagnostic ratio).

The subjective probabilities for $P(B|A)$ calculated according to the Bayes theorem and the conditional probabilities as assessed directly correlated strongly over a series of nine characteristics attributed to Germans by Americans ($r = 0.91$ for data averaged over 69 female perceivers; McCauley & Stitt, 1978, study 1). Even when the correlations for each individual perceiver were calculated and then subjected to a z-transformation and averaged there was still a strong correlation ($r = 0.73$).

The validity of the likelihood ratio as an index of a stereotyped assessment was tested in a further study (McCauley & Stitt, 1978, study 2) which again was concerned with the stereotype of the Germans. When the female perceivers assessed how typical the nine given characteristics were of Germans, there was a close relationship between these assessments and the likelihood ratio of the characteristic: the higher the likelihood ratio the more typical the characteristic was assessed to be of the Germans.

Further indications of the validity of the likelihood ratio are available in that it was established in the experiment first mentioned that precisely those four characteristics that were found to be especially typical of Germans in a classic study of stereotypes (Karlins, Coffman & Walters, 1969; see Chap. 3, "Definitions and history of research") had the highest likelihood ratios. These characteristics were: efficient (1.27; 46%), extremely nationalistic (1.59; 43%), industrious (1.12; 59%), scientifically minded (1.32; 47%). In parentheses is first the calculated value for the likelihood ratio [= $P(B \mid A)/P(B)$] and second the percentage of Princeton students who rated each of the characteristics as "typically German" (from Karlins et al., 1969). The four characteristics listed achieved the highest percentages and the highest likelihood ratio scores.

These results show that the Bayes theorem can be successfully applied to subjective probability judgments (see also Ajzen, 1971). On the other hand, there have been some less successful applications of the Bayes theorem to social judgment formation (Wyer, 1976). However, these are based on a more complex form of the theorem than that used by Ajzen (1971) and McCauley and Stitt (1978). Hewstone, Benn and Wilson (1988) used deviations from the normative predictions of the Bayes theorem as indicators of biased perceptions of minorities. A comprehensive account of the importance of the Bayes theorem for judgment formation is given in Slovic, Fischhoff and Lichtenstein (1977) and Slovic and Lichtenstein (1971).

Implicit Logic and Stereotypes

In the previous section we considered subjective probabilities of two events. This section will concern itself with the question of how a complex system of statements which can be derived from two basic statements is structured in the field of stereotypes. In this context, judgments about subjective probabilities which refer to the validity of single statements are measured.

The analysis of the system of statements for stereotypes is based on the anchor heuristic (see Chap. 1, "Anchor heuristic"). The system of statements is divided into propositions which can be assimilated to positive and to negative anchors.

The implicit logic of social judgments can be examined using two approaches. Box T5 describes both of these.

Box T5. Two approaches to describing the implicit logic of social judgments
Two aspects of the implicit logic of social judgments have to be differentiated:

1. Generalization on the basis of single pieces of information or specification of general information for a particular case: A number of empirical studies — especially those of Abelson and Kanouse (1966) and Kanouse (1972) — have been concerned with the tendency of perceivers to

generalize or to specify when faced with incomplete evidence. Although in Wyer and Carlston (1979) this question is subsumed under information integration, it seems to be more appropriate to emphasize the close relationship to psycholinguistic analyses because the tendency to generalization/specification with given stimulus material depends on how universally the implicit quantification is interpreted and on whether the definitions are seen conjunctively or disjunctively. Therefore, generalization and specification involve lexical reasoning as defined in Johnson-Laird's models of deduction (Johnson-Laird, 1975).

2. Drawing conclusions when a piece of information about the relationship between several features of a social nature is given: This points to the psychological research on the drawing of conclusions, especially in connection with the application of logical reasoning as summarized by Wason and Johnson-Laird (1972). Besides general models of deduction (see Johnson-Laird, 1975), this also concerns the analysis of the tendency to false reasoning like "affirming the consequent" and "denying the antecedent."

In the following the second approach mentioned in Box T5 will be used to examine the application of logical reasoning in matters of social content. The basic idea of the following analysis is that social categories can be interpreted as concepts which are subject to the same judgment tendencies as have been demonstrated in research on concepts. The same thought was formulated explicitly by McCauley et al. (1980) for stereotypes. First, the theoretical framework will be presented (Box T6) so that we can then report on two empirical studies which seek to test the usefulness of the theoretical framework. In this, we will follow the approach of Wyer (1977), which is also the basis for the empirical studies.

Box T6. Assimilation to an anchor in *if − then* propositions
One can say purely formally that the questions which form the basis of the studies reported on below amount to an analysis of the application of a logical rule to probability judgments. The rule states

$$(X \rightarrow Y) \leftrightarrow (\bar{Y} \rightarrow \bar{X}) \, ,$$

or, in the weaker form,

$$(X \rightarrow Y) \rightarrow (\bar{Y} \rightarrow \bar{X}) \, ,$$

where $\bar{X}$ is the negation of X and $\bar{Y}$ is the negation of Y. Let us look at an example: from the statement "If you smoke, you are damaging your health" one can draw the conclusion "If you are not damaging your health, you do not smoke." Besides the conditionals $X \rightarrow Y$ and $Y \rightarrow X$, six other conditionals can be formulated in which the categories X and Y as well as their negations occur. A summary of these propositions is contained in Table 10.

Table 10. Theoretical framework of the conditional. (Modified from Wyer, 1977, p. 581. Copyright 1977 by Academic Press. Reprinted by permission)

	A+		A−	
	Comparison with $X \rightarrow Y$		Comparison with $X \rightarrow \bar{Y}$	
	Same position	Reverse position	Same position	Reverse position
Same category	$X \rightarrow Y$	$Y \rightarrow X$	$X \rightarrow \bar{Y}$	$\bar{Y} \rightarrow X$
Negated category	$\bar{X} \rightarrow \bar{Y}$	$\bar{Y} \rightarrow \bar{X}$	$\bar{X} \rightarrow Y$	$Y \rightarrow \bar{X}$

A perceiver who has to form judgments in this complex field of statements will probably look for some form of aid. In problem solving such aids are called cognitive heuristics (Sherman & Corty, 1984; Tversky & Kahneman, 1974).

The heuristic of anchor forming is important for the theoretical framework in Table 10. If one follows this heuristic, one takes a certain stimulus as a starting point in a given judgmental field and assimilates other stimuli to this anchor. In Table 10, $X \rightarrow Y$ represents a certain attitude which will be accepted as true. It seems plausible to regard this attitude as the positive anchor. The statements which express a similar assessment should be assimilated to this anchor. That is the case for the conditionals on the left-hand side in Table 10, i.e., the statements which are symmetrical with respect to the occurrence of negations (subject and predicate are both positive or both negative).

The first hypothesis can be summarized as follows: the positive anchor possesses the highest subjective probability of being true. The statements $Y \rightarrow X$, $\bar{X} \rightarrow \bar{Y}$, and $\bar{Y} \rightarrow \bar{X}$ are assimilated to this anchor and are also regarded as having a high probability of being true because their degree of symmetry is the same as that of the anchor proposition (Wyer, 1977).

The second hypothesis relates to the conditionals on the right-hand side in Table 10. The proposition contrary to the positive anchor serves as a negative anchor, i.e., $X \rightarrow \bar{Y}$ (in the example: "If you smoke, you do not damage your health"). This assumption is supported by an additional consideration which will be explained with the help of Table 11.

If one examines a conditional formally, one can find for each one a set for which the conjunctive combination is "prohibited." In the case of $X \rightarrow Y$ (A+) this is the conjunction X & $\bar{Y}$. This combination, forbidden by A+, contains the subject and predicate from $X \rightarrow \bar{Y}$ (A−), i.e., the same categories in the same position. This relationship could dispose perceivers to hold $X \rightarrow \bar{Y}$ for very improbable when $X \rightarrow Y$ is very probable.

The second hypothesis can now be summarized as follows: the negative anchor has the lowest subjective probability of being true. The statements

Table 11. "Prohibition table" for the conditional

	Y		Ȳ	
X	X & Y		X & Ȳ	
		X → Ȳ		X → Y
		Y → X̄		Ȳ → X̄
X̄	X̄ & Y		X̄ & Ȳ	
		Y → X		Ȳ → X
		X̄ → Ȳ		X̄ → Y

In each cell are the two conditionals which are logically equivalent. Each pair of conditionals excludes the corresponding conjunction given in the cell.

Ȳ → X, X̄ → Y, and Y → X̄ are assimilated to X → Ȳ (A−) and are also regarded as having only a relatively slight probability of being true because they are asymmetric. Their degree of symmetry is the same as that of the negative anchor proposition (Wyer, 1977).

The direct result of these two hypotheses is the prediction that the statements on the left-hand side of Table 10 are generally accorded a higher truth content than those on the right-hand side. This anchor main effect means that a division of the statements into two groups comes into effect. Those statements which tend to be regarded as correct and are subsumed under A+ are distinguished from those regarded more as false and subsumed under A−. The greater the mean distance from the positive or negative anchor the more likely it is that a tendency to create a concise attitude will be established.

Three other hypotheses were tested in addition to the two already mentioned. The third hypothesis relates to the effects of the factor *same/ negated category* (see Table 10). One can assume that the occurrence of the same categories as in the anchor would lead the perceiver to take a statement for more probable when the anchor is positive and, conversely, for less probable with a negative anchor. Therefore, there should be a statistical interaction anchor×category when the schema in Table 10 is used as a plan for an analysis of variance.

The fourth hypothesis relates to the effects of the factor *same/reverse position* (see Table 10). The assumption was tested that the similarity of the position (compared with the respective anchor) causes the perceiver to rate the statement as relatively probable (with a positive anchor) or relatively improbable (with a negative anchor). This leads to the expectation of an interaction anchor×position in the analysis of variance.

Finally, a fifth hypothesis can be tested − namely, that the logical equivalence affects the probability judgments. In the case of logical equivalence of the given statement the perceiver should regard the statement as relatively probable (with a positive anchor) or relatively improbable (with a negative anchor). As one can see from Table 10, this hypothesis leads to the expectation of a significant triple interaction anchor × category × position.

To sum up, it can be said that the final three hypotheses characterize in more detail the social judgment processes with respect to the similarity of the categories and positions and to the logical equivalence whereby an assimilation according to A+ or A− is assumed.

The theoretical considerations summarized in Box T 6 give an overview of the role of logical and nonlogical factors in assessing the subjective probabilities of a whole set of statements. Such a set of statements is grouped around certain stereotypes or dogmas which serve as anchors around which related statements can be "rotated." The five hypotheses discussed in Box T 6 were tested in two studies on social stereotypes (see Box 19).

Box 19. Sets of propositions about social matters: what is the consequence of anchor statements?
In two studies (Bierhoff, 1980c) the eight subjective probabilities corresponding to the set of statements in Table 10 were measured in the context of social judgment formation. The two studies were based on different anchor propositions which were seen to contain a lesser (study 1) or a greater (study 2) valuation component.
In study 1 the following statement was given:

When Mary goes to a lot of trouble, John is grateful.

This statement stood at the end of a story about Mary helping John. This scenario told how Mary was helpful in preparing a paper for school. In study 2 the following proposition was given:

If you smoke, you are damaging your health.

The perceivers were asked to assume that the anchor statement was true and then to give their subjective estimates of the probabilities of the eight propositions which can be formed in the set (see Table 10). In study 1 the following propositions were assessed:

When Mary goes to a lot of trouble, John is grateful.
When Mary does not go to a lot of trouble, John is not grateful.
When John is grateful, Mary goes to a lot of trouble.
When John is not grateful, Mary does not go to a lot of trouble.
When Mary goes to a lot of trouble, John is not grateful.
When Mary does not go to a lot of trouble, John is grateful.
When John is not grateful, Mary goes to a lot of trouble.
When John is grateful, Mary does not go to lot of trouble.

In the second study, eight propositions were formulated which were constructed according to the same principles as the propositions used in study 1. The judgments were made on graphical rating scales with the endpoints 0 (very improbable) and 10 (very probable). Twenty-eight subjects took part in study 1 and 21 in study 2.

In both studies there was a strong anchor effect in the sense of assimilation to the positive or negative anchor. In study 1 the means were 0.814 for A+ and 0.182 for A−. In study 2 these means were 0.757 and 0.210. One could argue that these anchor effects were strengthened by including the anchor in the ratings. In order to take account of this objection a comparison was carried out without the two anchor statements, but this was also highly significant.

The results for the first two hypotheses mentioned in Box T6 show that dichotomization of the set of statements does in fact take place, so that propositions grouped around A+ tend to be regarded as true while propositions grouped around A− tend to be seen as false. In this way a major simplification of the assessment of the subjective probabilities for the whole set of statements is achieved.

The third hypothesis referred to the agreement of the "sign" of the category with that of the anchor. In both studies the pattern of the results agreed with the hypothesis (see Figures 13A, 15A), but only in the first study was the statistical interaction anchor × category significant. Propositions with the same categories exhibited higher values with positive anchors and lower values with negative anchors than propositions with negated categories (see the cross-over pattern of the profiles in Figures 13A, 15A). Therefore, one can say that the expected "sign-similarity" effect, which indicates a nonlogical factor influencing the judgment of the set of statements, was demonstrated (see also Wyer, 1977).

The fourth hypothesis (see Box T6) related to the agreement between the positions of the statement and the anchor. The expected interaction

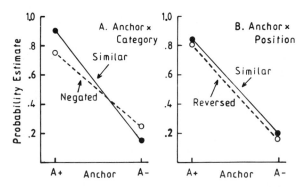

Figure 13A, B. Similarity to anchor propositions in content and form (study 1)

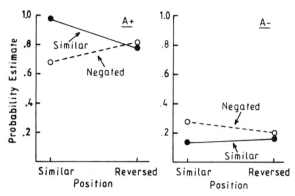

Figure 14. Similarity to anchor propositions in logical implications (study 1)

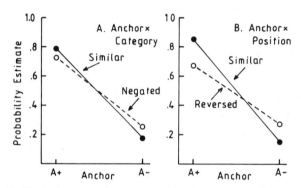

Figure 15 A, B. Similarity to anchor propositions in content and form (study 2)

anchor × position was significant only in the second study. As the graph shows (Figure 15 B), the cross-over pattern of the profiles agrees with the expectation. In the same position, higher subjective probabilities in the area of A + and lower subjective probabilities in the area of A − were found than in the reverse position. However, there was no similar effect in study 1, because the profiles for the same and the reverse position ran parallel to one another (Figure 13 B). Therefore, the influence of position similarity remained limited on the assessments of the health scenarios. It should also be mentioned that in the case of abstract statements Wyer (1977) found indications of the effectiveness of this second nonlogical factor for the assessment of sets of statements.

In the last hypothesis (see Box T6) the influence of the logical equivalence was specified. In Table 11 it was shown that four pairs of logically equivalent propositions are to be found within the set. Equivalent statements should differ only slightly in their subjective probability.

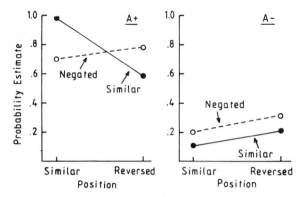

Figure 16. Similarity to anchor propositions in logical implications (study 2)

In agreement with the hypothesis of logical equivalence, there was a significant triple interaction in both studies. As the profiles in Figures 14 and 16 show, the structure of this interaction conformed to expectations. Under A+ there was the characteristic cross-over pattern, which was more pronounced in study 2 than in study 1. The profiles under A− are partially consistent with the expectations as derived from Table 11. Although the direction of the profile under A− in study 1 is, as expected, opposite to that under A+, the profiles in study 2 run parallel to one another and so contradict the hypothesis (see Figures 14, 16). Obviously, the influence of logical equivalence is more pronounced with a positive anchor.

When interpreting the results one should remember that the theoretical analysis led to complex predictions, which are not so trivial that the validation can be dismissed as self-evident. The anchor hypothesis, which resulted in a main effect, is also not obvious. Who would have predicted that the statements $Y \rightarrow X$, $\bar{X} \rightarrow \bar{Y}$, and $\bar{Y} \rightarrow \bar{X}$ would involve very high probability judgments and the statements $\bar{Y} \rightarrow X$, $\bar{X} \rightarrow Y$, and $Y \rightarrow \bar{X}$ very low values? In retrospect, when one knows the pattern of results with the clear mean differences, a lot which one would never have supposed prior to the experiment appears to be trivial (see Fischhoff, 1975; Fischhoff & Beyth, 1975; "I knew it would happen").

In this section we wanted to talk about the relationship between subjective probabilities in a complex set of propositions. The results reported in Box 19 show that the subjective probabilities follow a systematic pattern which can be predicted by a priori dichotomization, nonlogical similarity relationships, and logical equivalence between the pairs of propositions. One can distinguish two clearly distinct blocks of subjective probabilities. As an explanation for this simplifying judgment strategy it was suggested that assimilation to a positive and a negative anchor took place. Since $X \rightarrow Y$ (A+) and $X \rightarrow \bar{Y}$ (A−) are the anchors, the symmetrical statements were rotated to A+ and the asymmetrical to A−. This assimilation cannot be traced back to the effects of logical equivalence since nonequivalent statements were assimilated to A+ and A−.

The results presented in Box 19 show that a generalization of prejudices in the form X → Y can take place. A high subjective probability of X → Y led to a high estimate for Y → X although the statements are not logically equivalent. From the statement "If a person is black, he/she will behave aggressively" one cannot conclude that "If a person behaves aggressively, he/she will be black." In fact such mistakes often occur, negative events (like criminal acts) tending to be attributed to particular groups of people (like immigrants). This overgeneralization contributes to making a stereotype absolute (see Hewstone et al., 1988). Not only are blacks considered to be aggressive but one also thinks that aggressive acts are caused by blacks and one tends to exclude the possibility that white skin and aggression can occur together (see Table 11).

Such a reversal of the relationship is known as "confirming the consequent" (Wason & Johnson-Laird, 1972). Such an overgeneralization also seems to ensure a neatly structured assessment of a set of statements. By assimilating all statements to a positive anchor (A+) with high subjective probability (e.g., blacks behave aggressively) and to a negative anchor (A−) with low subjective probability (blacks do not behave aggressively) seeing things in black and white is encouraged, which is typical for prejudices (see Chap. 3, "Definitions and history of research"). The statement "Whites are aggressive" is assimilated to the A− statement, so the subjective probability of aggression coming from whites can be minimalized. In this way it can happen that what began as simple dogma continues to exist as a closed system of dogmas.

One last thought should be added − the use of the conditional in social judgment formation was interpreted as a problem of propositional inference (aspect 2 in Box T5). The possibility remains that it could also be lexical inference in the sense of aspect 1 (Box T5). It seems possible that future studies may show the following distinction to be justified: Judgmental fields which have a high familiarity may be dealt with more in the sense of lexical inference. On the other hand, attitudes which refer to little known objects or contain rarely used categories which have a low perceptual readiness may tend to be analyzed according to the pattern of propositional logic.

Chapter 3

Stereotypes

Stereotypes are everywhere. Hardly anybody can free him/herself from the temptation of thinking in terms of popular prejudices, whether when talking about the differences between men and women or when comparing the Germans with the French. Some stereotypes are welcomed by the people concerned because they convey a positive social identity or because they are simply good advertising. For example, in an advertisement for food from France it is appropriate that the French have a reputation for knowing something about food. Other stereotypes convey a negative social identity, for example, when the Russians are portrayed as aggressive. Such enemy concepts are an important form of propaganda. If increased defense costs have to be justified, enemy concepts are almost essential because they generate the fear which motivates the members of a society to invest large sums in the military sector. Enemy concepts do not have to agree with reality. It is well known that the Russians have not begun a war of aggression in the last 150 years. Nevertheless, the concept of the Russians still contains the characteristic *aggressive*.

This chapter begins with definitions of stereotypes and how these have changed with time. Then, typical areas of research on stereotypes will be discussed, with particular reference to sex stereotypes and stereotypes concerning physical appearance. The third section presents theories which contribute towards an exploration of stereotypes. The theories will be dealt with according to different general aspects – sociocultural, psychodynamic, and cognitive. Finally, the fourth section is a discussion of the practical applications of research on stereotypes, such as the effects of contact between groups.

Definitions and History of Research

Definitions

Because of the different theoretical approaches which are involved in research on stereotypes it is not surprising that stereotypes have been defined in many different ways. Textbooks on social psychology are a good source of definitions, which can then be compared. Jones and Gerard (1967, p. 719) give the following definition of a stereotype:

> A class of objects is said to be stereotyped when identical characteristics are attributed to any object of that class, regardless of the actual degree of variation within the class. Familiar stereotypes are those sets of characteristics attributed to ethnic and racial groups. Stereotypes usually go along with a positive or negative evaluation of the class of objects.

In this definition emphasis is placed on the overgeneralization and neglect of individual differences. A similar tendency can be seen in the definition of stereotype in Raven and Rubin (1976, p. 517):

> A preconceived idea about the characteristics of some grouping of people; it is often oversimplified, rigid, and uncomplimentary. Once a person is identified with that group, his own individuality tends to be overlooked, and the characteristics of the group are attributed to him with little qualification. (Example: According to common stereotypes, Jews are sometimes viewed as ambitious and clannish; blacks as athletic and musical; professors as absentminded and impractical.)

This definition also contains allusions to a rigid attitude and to the negative, uncomplimentary content of a stereotype. This aspect is even clearer in the following short definition from Wrightsman (1972, p. 610):

> A simplified and standard image (often highly evaluative, inaccurate and rigidified) of a group of people.

This definition is distinguished by the fact that it explicitly refers to the incorrect judgment which leads to a stereotype. Furthermore, it is clear that the author considers stereotypes to be negative. While the definition from Jones and Gerard (1967) is free of any negative judgment, there is a clear value judgment expressed in the definition from Raven and Rubin (1976), and this is even more strongly emphasized by Wrightsman (1972).

The various definitions of stereotypes can be systematically classified. Ashmore and DelBoca (1981) distinguish between several types of definition (see Table 12), as does Brigham (1971). A primary criterion for classification was whether the definition contained a value judgment or not. From the point of view of a cognitive approach such a value judgment would be premature. That does not alter the fact that stereotypes often have negative effects in social reality and lead to distorted and hostile judgments about people or groups of people (Brown, 1965; Campbell, 1967). However, one can describe positive prejudices about a group of people as a stereotype (see Hofstätter, 1966).

In spite of the expected discrepancy among definitions concerning the insertion of a negative evaluation it can be said that there is a general agreement that ethnic stereotypes are a set of opinions about the personal attributes of members of a definable social group. Such "opinions about personal at-

Table 12. What is a stereotype? (Modified from Ashmore & DelBoca, 1981, p. 14; Brigham, 1971. Copyright 1981 by Lawrence Erlbaum Associates. Reprinted by permission)

Without evaluation

Generalization: A simplification of social information processing is achieved through standardization or homogenization in the person perception.

Concept: Stereotypes are seen as special concepts which differ from other concepts only in content and which are rooted in people's normal thinking.

Incorrectly learned: Opinions about groups of people are formed by distorted or unfounded inductive conclusions. These opinions are not justified on the basis of the given "input" and are therefore wrongly coded.

With evaluation

Overgeneralized: The conclusions drawn from the given evidence are exaggerated (e.g., judgments about a social group are based on isolated cases or slight differences are accentuated).

Incorrect: Opinions about groups of people are believed, although they do not agree with reality.

Rigid: Stiff black-and-white thinking dominates and (new) evidence is not considered adequately when revising an opinion.

---

tributes" include, for example, the assigning of characteristics for which there exists a particular consensus in the reference group of the perceiver, so one can talk about a *social* stereotype. On the other hand, *personal* stereotypes are individual opinions about groups of people which can be classified as probability estimates and do not necessarily reflect a consensus in the reference group (McCauley & Stitt, 1978; Secord & Backman, 1964).

According to Ashmore and DelBoca (1981, p. 16), stereotypes can be defined as:

A set of beliefs about the personal attributes of a group of people.

This definition sums up the congruous points in the wide spread of definitions, as shown in Table 12. It does not contain any commitment as to the explanation of stereotypes. This definition has proven to be advantageous since several cognitive, sociocultural, and psychodynamic factors contribute equally to any explanation of stereotypes (Stroebe & Insko, in press).

Since Ashmore and DelBoca (1981) talk in their definition about stereotypes as being beliefs, it seems sensible to distinguish between stereotypes and prejudices (Schäfer, 1988; Stroebe & Insko, in press). Prejudices can be defined as attitudes about the personal characteristics of a group of people.

An opinion can be defined as a probability estimate about the existence of a connection between the attitude object and a characteristic (see Stroebe, 1980). The relationship between an opinion (belief) and an attitude is the same as that between a stereotype and a prejudice. On the one hand, a prejudice contains an evaluation and can therefore be defined as a special case of an attitude. On the other hand, the stereotype introduces a cognitive assessment, which corresponds to a probability estimate about whether a person who belongs to a particular group has a particular set of characteristics. This difference is expressed in Wrightman's short definition of prejudice (1972, p. 608):

> An evaluative reaction to a member of a racial, ethnic or other minority group, which results from the recipient's membership in that group.

In this definition prejudice is limited to ethnic minorities, but this does not seem expedient. Even the emphasis on the minority status of the target person of a prejudice is questionable. Prejudices about men or women − to name but two examples − do not refer to minorities within a society. It would make more sense to talk about a group of people.

Before the history of research on stereotypes is gone into in more depth, here is a brief summary of what the discussion of possible definitions has achieved. Different aspects of stereotypes were emphasized in different definitions − above all generalization or overgeneralization, but also incorrect learning or incorrect opinions which conflict with reality and a tendency to see things in black and white. The definition suggested above as a compromise emphasized the classification of stereotypes as beliefs or opinions, i.e., opinions about the personal characteristics of a group of people. This definition is compatible with each of the definitions recorded in Table 12. Opinions can, for example, be wrong or they can be held too rigidly. They can be deduced from an overgeneralization or can reduce the facts to a single concept.

If stereotypes are understood as a subcategory of opinions, it seems reasonable to think of them as the cognitive components of prejudices. As Jones and Gerard (1967) made clear in their definition, stereotypes suggest a positive or a negative evaluation of the target persons, as expressed in a prejudice. Prejudices about handicapped people (see von Bracken, 1976; Katz, 1981; Richardson, Goodman, Hastorf & Dornbusch, 1961) can be given as examples.

Research History

Synopses of the history of stereotype research have been written by Ashmore and DelBoca (1981), Lilli (1982), Manz (1968), and Schäfer (1988). The term *stereotype* was first used in France in the printing industry in 1798. The English word *type* as in *type face* comes from this linguistic use. The term first appeared in academic usage in connection with psychiatric disorders. Pathological, repeated actions were called stereotypy. This term is still used today. Therefore, a distinction was drawn between stereotyped behavior and stereotyped attitudes. This distinction has been used in recent volumes of *Psychological Abstracts.*

The term stereotypes became relevant for the social sciences when Lippmann (1922), in his book *Public Opinion*, compared stereotypes with "pictures in our heads." According to Lippmann, the high level of complexity of the social environment exceeds the capacity of human information processing. Therefore, simplification strategies are used to interpret complex social information. Seen like this, stereotypes act as a filter and are determined by the cultural group. They help to simplify the complexity in a social reality which is not fully comprehensible.

The first experiments concerning stereotypes were carried out at the end of the 1920s and in the early 1930s. It is informative to look at how the amount of research developed. If one looks at the entries in *Psychological Abstracts* one can see that until the beginning of the 1950s there was only little research. Often there was only one contribution per year and only twice were there five contributions – in 1938 and 1951 (Ashmore & DelBoca, 1981). From the middle of the 1950s onwards there is a continual rise in the number of contributions on stereotypes, which can be seen in the slight rise in the number of contributions relative to the total number of recorded contributions. From 1960 to 1970 the number of contributions on the subject of stereotypes lay between 8 and 32 per annum. The changes in the intensity of research can be seen in Table 13. Until 1977 there was a continual rise, which then changed into a decline in the number of publications. However, the number of publications remained high until 1987, the last year included.

If one looks at this development then it is clear that neither the well-known study from Katz and Braly (1933) nor the publication of a book on the authoritarian personality (Adorno, Frenkel-Brunswik, Levinson & Sanford, 1950, 1964) has had a long-term effect on the development of an interest in stereotype research. The expansion which is to be seen until the 1960s reflects

Table 13. Number of stereotype entries between 1970 and 1987 in *Psychological Abstracts*

Year	Number	Number per 1000 abstracts	Year	Number	Number per 1000 abstracts
1970	16	0.7	1978	144	3.8
1971	53	2.3	1979	159	5.2
1972	50	2.1	1980	179	6.4
1973	89	3.6	1981	153	5.5
1974	93	3.6	1982	94	3.5
1975	119	4.7	1983	92	3.3
1976	164	6.6	1984	109	3.1
1977	203	7.5	1985	114	3.5
			1986	90	2.8
			1987	100	2.8

Until 1973 the information refers to the term *stereotype,* and from 1974 onwards to the term *stereotyped attitudes* which was introduced in addition to the term *stereotyped behavior.* The data on the left-hand side are taken from Ashmore and DelBoca (1981, p. 5).

for the most part the general rise in the number of publications. Only in the 1970s was there a large increase in the number of publications, due mainly to the sharp rise in the number of publications dealing with sex stereotypes (Ashmore & DelBoca, 1981). It was therefore the association of stereotype research with the question of sex differences which led to a real increase in interest on stereotypes (see "Sex stereotypes").

Areas of Stereotype Research

Many stereotypes are aimed at ethnic and racial minorities. Whereas in previous decades Jews and black people were the targets of stereotypes, recently stereotypes about Russians have been particularly acute.

In Chap. 2 ("The Bayes theorem as a model of stereotypes"), the measurement of stereotypes using the likelihood ratio was described in detail. This aspect of stereotype research will be returned to when the theoretical approaches to stereotype research − especially the sociocultural approach − are discussed. In this chapter two further areas will be dealt with as examples of stereotype research: sex stereotypes and stereotypes of physical attractiveness.

Further important areas in which stereotypes play a large role are old people (Branco & Williamson, 1982; Brewer et al. 1981; Lehr, 1980; Rodin & Langer, 1980), people who wear glasses (Harris, Harris & Bochner, 1982; Manz & Lück, 1968), and people who are overweight (Harris et al., 1982). Of course it is possible to name other areas in which stereotypes influence thinking about groups of people. Many of these stereotypes are based on external features which are easily perceived such as hair color, dialect, or profession (Schäfer, 1988).

Sex Stereotypes

In the past two decades the classical division of work between men and women has been questioned more and more. While in the 1950s the role of the woman as mother and housewife seemed to be set (and the man had the role of family breadwinner), trends have become visible in recent years which should lead to a more flexible evaluation of the role of women in society (see Allgeier & McCormick, 1983).

Male and Female Prototypes

In connection with the criticism of the traditional woman's role the question as to which schematic ideas of the picture of women in society exist has become relevant. Rosenkrantz, Vogel, Bee, Broverman and Broverman (1968) tried to measure the stereotypes of men and women (see also Widiger & Settle, 1987). They gave their perceivers 122 bipolar scales, which were in the following form:

not aggressive 1 2 3 4 5 6 7 aggressive

Table 14. Positively valued male and female traits. (From Rosenkrantz, Vogel, Bee, Broverman & Broverman, 1968, p. 291. Copyright 1968 by the American Psychological Association. Reprinted by permission)

Male-valued traits

Aggressive	Feelings not easily hurt
Independent	Adventurous
Unemotional	Makes decisions easily
Hides emotions	Never cries
Objective	Acts as a leader
Easily influenced	Self-confident
Dominant	Not uncomfortable about being aggressive
Likes math and science	Ambitious
Not excitable in a minor crisis	
Active	Able to separate feelings from ideas
Competitive	Not dependent
Logical	Not conceited about appearance
Worldly	Thinks men are superior to women
Skilled in business	Talks freely about sex with men
Direct	
Knows the way of the world	

Female-valued traits

Does not use harsh language	Interested in own appearance
Talkative	Neat in habits
Tactful	Quiet
Gentle	Strong need for security
Aware of feelings of others	Appreciates art and literature
Religious	Expresses tender feelings

These rating scales, which were constructed in the form of a semantic differential, were to be assessed by the judge with regard to the adult male and the
adult female. The technique of the semantic differential has proved to be a
practical way of measuring stereotypes (Ben-Ari & Amir, 1988; Schäfer, 1975,
1983).

On the basis of these judgments the stereotypes of men and women were
determined by compiling the statements for which the male or the female was
assigned a higher value by 75% or more of the subjects. The end poles of the
scales were also assessed as to their social desirability. Table 14 contains a summary of the attributes which, according to the opinions of the male and female
perceivers, differentiated between men and women. The summary is so
organized that on the one hand all attributes which describe men and are
positively valued and on the other hand all attributes which describe women
and are positively valued are included.

Among the 41 scales considered in Table 14 there were 29 whose "male" pole was valued more positively than its "female" pole and only 12 whose "female" pole was valued more positively. Therefore, one can assume that the male stereotype is valued more positively than the female. This result was not replicated by Widiger and Settle (1987). The pattern of results depends on the sampling of the trait terms in the language. Conclusions about the social desirability of masculine and feminine traits depend on the comprehensive sampling of the trait terms in the language or in use in the language (Widiger & Settle, 1987). By contrast, Eagly and Kite (1987) found that stereotypes of nationalities were more similar to stereotypes of the men than of the women belonging to the respective nationalities. This result was explained by the fact that men hold positions of higher status in these societies.

Male characteristics can be summed up with the concept *competence*, while *female* characteristics can be subsumed under the concept *warmth* (Broverman, Vogel, Broverman, Clarkson & Rosenkrantz, 1972; Eagly & Kite, 1987; Spence, Helmreich & Stapp, 1975; Widiger & Settle, 1987).

The assessments which form the basis of the results in Table 14 were made by male and female students, the criterion being reached in 41 scales (see above). Further results show that the perceiver's self-concept tends to agree with the stereotype. That means that even women students, who should be a positively selected sample with regard to women's self-concepts, have a tendency to ascribe to themselves characteristics which have socially less positive value than those which men ascribe to themselves (Rosenkrantz et al., 1968). This result might also depend on the imbalanced 29 : 12 ratio of male-valued to female-valued traits. The results say nothing about the origin of stereotypes of men and women. Besides the influence of socialization (Ruble & Ruble, 1982), there are physical and psychological differences between men and women to be considered. Included in the physical characteristics are physical strength, which is important when technology and automization are less dominant, and the ability to give birth. Rosenkrantz et al. (1968) suspect that physical strength will decline in importance in computerized industrial nations.

Further studies have also found the general pattern of competence versus warmth as stereotypes of men and women (Ellis & Bentler, 1973; McKee & Sherriffs, 1957; Vetter, 1961). Ashmore (1981) comes to the conclusion that the sex stereotype is not so much to be found on a judgment dimension, but on a dimension *hard* (male) and *soft* (female). Bierhoff-Alfermann (1977) interprets these stereotypes as implicit personality theories (see Chap. 1, "Implicit personality theories complete the first impression"). The sex of a person can be used to deduce personality characteristics. In this sense, sex stereotypes can be defined as "structured sets of inferential relations that link personal attributes to the social categories female and male" (Ashmore, 1981, p. 40).

However, everyday experience shows that the implied personality theories about men and women are not so universal that one can say there is only one theory about men and only one theory about women. The man or woman on the street has several prototypes at his or her disposal, which he or she can

Table 15. Male and female prototypes. (Modified from Ashmore, 1981, p. 63. Copyright 1981 by Lawrence Erlbaum Associates. Reprinted by permission)

Sex of perceiver	Prototype	
	Men	Women
Women	Businessmen Knows what he wants Egotist	Nervous Nellie Upper class young woman
Men	Hardworker Under control Tough guy Outspoken Pain in the ass	Girlfriend Neurotic Nurturant Outgoing

apply to men or women. A man can have several prototype ideas about which types are present in a population of women, such as an ideal girlfriend, who personifies the characteristics gentle, sexy, and sensitive, or a moaning neurotic who is perhaps characterized by anxious, confused, and nervous behavior. Or a woman can use for men the prototype of an egocentric who acts without regard for others and is loud and biased.

Ashmore (1981) describes prototypes of men and women which can be formed from the attributes used by Rosenkrantz et al. (1968) and Sherriffs and McKee (1957). Examples of such prototypes are given in Table 15.

According to what cues are present, the judges will apply a specific prototype to a particular man or a particular woman. With the help of this prototype they can deduce characteristics which cannot be deduced by observation. There is an interesting hypothesis that the number of prototypes which exist for a particular target group relates to the amount of contact with and information about the group. The more contact judges have with a target group and the more they know about them the larger should be the number of prototypes available.

Diagnostic Information Versus Sex Stereotypes

A further interesting hypothesis, mentioned above, is that the less pronounced the stimulus component the greater the influence exercised by stereotypes. This general hypothesis carries important implications which agree with the assumption that information from single cases has a greater influence on judgment formation than information based on abstract categories.

As was explained above, concrete individual cases determine to a great extent the opinions formed about a set of facts, while summarized statistical information, which has a higher information value than any individual case, tends to be neglected (see Chap. 2, Box I7). However, this tendency to place more emphasis on concrete individual cases should mean that the importance of stereotypes is relatively small in interactions with concrete people. The concrete person is the individual case while the person's sex, for example, represents a category. The consequence is, therefore, that stereotypes can be neutralized to a large extent by concrete diagnostic information about a person (Locksley et al., 1980). "Accuracy-driven attention to attribute information" leads to "individuating impression formation" (Neuberg & Fiske, 1987). For example, dependency on the outcome of a future interaction (see Chap. 4, "Anticipation of an interaction: the principle of hope") can reduce the influence of stereotypes when inconsistent diagnostic information is available (Erber & Fiske, 1984).

These assumptions contain an important implication. As long as somebody does not know much about a concrete person, then an implicit personality theory should determine which characteristics and behavior will be ascribed to this person, and the selection of a theory can also vary according to the information available. However, as soon as somebody has extensive information about the target, the relevance of a stereotype should be reduced because concrete information about an individual case will now compete with abstract conceptual implications (Brewer & Miller, 1984).

In this context, it is necessary to consider that sex-stereotyped characteristics not only concern personality but also role behavior, profession, and outward appearance (Deaux, 1985; Deaux & Lewis, 1984). There are, for example, typical versions of male and female professions (e.g., truckdriver, town planner vs. elementary schoolteacher, nurse) and roles (head of the house, initiative in sexual matters vs. bringing up children, cooking; see Box I 10). In addition, the typical physical appearance of men and women is different. Physical appearance is closely related to stereotypes (McArthur, 1982).

Box I 10. When sex stereotypes lose influence on social judgment
Deaux and Lewis (1984) gave their perceivers descriptions of men and women which contained only male roles, only female roles, or mixed roles. The perceivers had to say how probable it was that the people described would have "male" and "female" personality traits and exercise a "male" or a "female" profession.

The results of this experiment offered the opportunity to compare diagnostic information about a person (e.g., his or her role behavior) with information about the sex label. The results showed that the diagnostic information completely overshadowed the label information. The information about the role determined the conclusions drawn about male or female personality traits. When male roles were ascribed to the target, there was a strong tendency to assume male characteristics (e.g., independent, active, decisive), while female roles resulted in female characteristics being deduced (e.g., emotional, generous, helpful). However, if a mixed role description was given, then there was no differentiated ascribing of male and female personality traits.

While a sex label had no consistent effect, the effect of the diagnostic information was clear in the conclusions drawn by the perceivers. The concrete description of a person's attributes meant, therefore, that the label information remained unimportant.

This pattern of results was confirmed in two further experiments (Deaux & Lewis, 1984). Information about male or female personality traits dominated over label information when the perceiver was asked to draw conclusions about the role and profession of the target person. If the appearance of the target person was varied by introducing either masculine (big, strong, wide shoulders) or feminine (soft voice, graceful, gentle) attributes, the information about the sex of the target person was almost completely ignored.

If the sex label and the diagnostic information were placed in opposition, the diagnostic information (about physical appearance, role, profession, personality traits) proved on the whole to be more important than the sex for conclusions about the target person. The perceivers were quite prepared to generalize from one area (e.g., role) to another (e.g., profession). It was irrelevant here whether the diagnostic information agreed or conflicted with the sex label. Instead, the judgments were based on consistency of the attributes. Information about the outward appearance of a person was particularly important in determining the definition of a person's sex.

Stereotypes can be seen as expectations which structure social perception (see Berger, Rosenholtz & Zelditch, 1980; Deaux & Major, 1987; Hamilton & Sherman, in press). In answer to the question of whether results have been obtained for expectations in general that are similar to those of Deaux and Lewis (1984) and Erber and Fiske (1984), one immediately thinks of the study by Bruner et al. (1951) in which the effects of expectations in color perception were examined (see Chap. 1, "First come, first served").

Expectations about colors can be caused by particular terms for objects, e.g., tomato (red), tangerine (orange), and lemon (yellow). Under unfavorable perception conditions where the stimulus component was not distinct, the term used had a strong influence on the color perceived. A tomato was graded as redder than a mandarin, whereas a lemon was graded as yellower. However, these expectation effects, which can be interpreted as projections by the perceivers, disappeared to a large extent under favorable perception conditions.

To sum up these results, a "label" effect is present when the stimulus component is indistinct (Neuberg & Fiske, 1987). The same implication could be seen in the experiments on the halo effect (see Chap. 1, "Illusory correlations between trait characteristics"). Weiss (1979) was able to show that perceivers can be influenced in their evaluation of another person by implicit personality theories involving race, age, or profession, especially when the diagnostic information about the person is insufficient. The same conclusion can also be drawn about sex stereotypes, since they seem to play a role especially when insufficient diagnostic information is available.

Physical Attractiveness

In western societies there is a cultural consensus about which people look attractive. For example, specific female facial features correlate with perceived attractiveness (Cunningham, 1986). Large eyes, small nose, small chin, prominent cheekbones, narrow cheeks, high eyebrows, large pupils, and large smile are positively correlated with attractiveness. One can assume that cultural standards of physical attractiveness are widespread (as shown by the high level of agreement among perceivers; Maruyama & Miller, 1981), and it seems justified to speak of a stereotype of attractiveness. It has been shown that even with children the evaluation of attractiveness has a certain stability over a period of 5 years.

Social Desirability

There is good evidence of a stereotype of attractiveness in a study in which photographs of an attractive, a neutral, and an unattractive person were shown to perceivers (Dion, Berscheid & Walster, 1972). The photographs showed either men or women and the perceivers had to assess them on 27 personality traits (e.g., altruistic, honest). Furthermore, five other traits were assessed (e.g., enthusiasm, trustworthiness), the future happiness of the people in the photographs in three areas (in marriage, as parents, at work) was estimated, and conjectures about professional success were made.

In order to increase the generalizability of the results, 12 different series of pictures were used. The physical attractiveness was successfully varied between the series, but extremes were avoided. In general, it was shown that the greater the physical attractiveness, the more positive the assessment. The social desirability of the traits is linearly related to the attractiveness, as are the expected professional status, the estimated marital success, and the conjectured professional success. However, it was thought that neutral people would have more success as parents.

On the basis of these results it can be assumed that there is a positive stereotype of physical attractiveness — "Beautiful is good." However, this was shown to be qualified with regard to parental success, and on the whole the *decrease* in prestige for unattractive people was greater than the *increase* for attractive people. A more recent study (Dermer & Thiel, 1975) indicates that the stereotype of attractiveness is not as positive as one would assume on the basis of the results from Dion et al. (1972). While in the earlier study no extremely attractive or unattractive people were shown, in the second study very (un)attractive people were also assessed. In contrast to the first study, only women were asked and only female stimuli were used. To increase the generalizability of the results two series of pictures were used.

Besides the 27 personality traits, three questions were introduced relating to the middle-class orientation of the target person (materialist?, sympathy with the oppressed?, status-seeking snob?). Furthermore the area of marriage was assessed in more detail: there were questions on the one hand about the danger of divorce and the possibility of extramarital affairs (marriage disaster cluster) and on the other hand about the person's quality as a spouse both generally and sexually.

On the whole the results for social desirability as indicated by chosen traits were similar to those in the previous study. However, they tended to fall more under the rubric "ugly is bad" than "beautiful is good" because the difference between the unattractive and neutral conditions was greater than that between the attractive and neutral conditions. The same phenomenon was to be seen in the study from Dion et al. (1972) in which the assessment of the neutral and of the attractive people was similar, while the unattractive target people fared distinctly worse.

In the additional questions the assessment of the person's quality as a spouse was indeed linearly related to his/her attractiveness, but on the other hand the items in the marriage disaster cluster were particularly highly associated with high attractiveness. It was also clear that supposed middle-class orientation increased monotonically with level of physical attractiveness.

To sum up, it can be said that there was a clear agreement in the assessment of the target women. However, this was not based solely on the tendency to ascribe positive characteristics to attractive women. The assessment of the attractive women was in fact mixed because they were seen not only as socially more desirable but also as women who were vain and materialistic and who were associated with problems concerning divorce and extramarital relationships.

Physical attractiveness is an influential stereotype (Adams, 1982). On the one hand, physical attractiveness acts as reinforcement and, together with other reinforcers (e.g., the similarity of attitudes), determines the degree of affection between men and women (Byrne, Ervin & Lambeth, 1970; Byrne, London & Reeves, 1968). On the other hand, there is evidence that physical attractiveness of a woman reflects on the man in her company (Sigall & Landy, 1973). Accompanied by an attractive girlfriend a man is assessed more positively and is liked more than when accompanied by a woman who is made up to look unattractive.

Like many ethnic stereotypes, physical attractiveness relies on information directly available to the observer. The immediacy of the relevant indicators is an important factor which increases the importance of a stereotype in everyday interactions.

Physical attractiveness not only influences the assessment of a person (and his or her partner) but also affects behavior. In a simple demonstration of the interpersonal effects of physical attractiveness the readiness to help after an accident was measured (West & Brown, 1975). A female student who said that she had been bitten by a rat in an animal laboratory asked passers-by for money for a tetanus injection. The perceptible severity of the injury was varied: either there was no outward sign of the injury or the student wore a first-aid dressing which was soaked in blood. The supplicant was either very attractive or relatively unattractive.

As the results show, with a light injury the physical attractiveness had no influence on the readiness to help the victim with money. In both cases 13 – 14 cents were given on average. The readiness to help was greater faced with a serious injury. In this case the physical attractiveness also played a role, because an attractive woman was given more money (mean 43.3 cents) than an unattractive woman (mean 26.5 cents).

Another study shows that attractive people were given more space than unattractive people (Dabbs & Stokes, 1975). The effect of physical attractiveness on judgments about performance levels is also remarkable (Landy & Sigall, 1974). Male perceivers had to judge a bad or a good essay about the role of television in society. While the female author was not described in the control condition, a photo of her showed that she was attractive in the one and unattractive in the other experimental condition. The judgments on the general quality of a good essay were similar in all three conditions. Therefore no preference was shown towards the attractive authors when performance was high.

However, when performance was low the work of the unattractive author was judged to be particularly poor, while the performance of the attractive author was judged to be relatively good. These results were replicated for white but not for black target people (Maruyama & Miller, 1980). Further studies demonstrated that attractive or unattractive pupils do not differ on the whole in their actual performance (Maruyama & Miller, 1981).

Physical Attractiveness and Social Interaction

Stereotypes can influence social interaction. How does the stereotype of physical attractiveness affect social interaction between men and women? The answer to this question gives an indication about how it happens that stereotypes do contain a kernel of truth, as has been mentioned on different occasions (Allport, 1954; Campbell, 1967).

If stereotypes structure the expectations of a perceiver (A) about a recipient (B), then it can be assumed that stereotypes create their own reality. They influence A's way of behaving towards B, so that B's behavior may be influenced by A's stereotype (Darley & Fazio, 1980; Deaux & Major, 1987; Snyder, 1984).

This consideration was tested by Snyder et al. (1977) for the stereotype of physical attractiveness. In the previous section it was demonstrated that the stereotype of physical attractiveness is characterized mainly by social desirability. If a target person is attractive, he or she is ascribed more socially desirable characteristics than if a target person is unattractive. Empirical studies show accordingly that an attractive person is subject to more positive stimulation (Davis, Rainey & Brock, 1976). The positive stereotype can be confirmed by positive attention inasmuch as the target person (B) behaves according to the signals given by A (see Box I 11).

Box I 11. Stereotypes gain reality in social interaction
To test whether behavioral confirmation of stereotypes occurs, Snyder et al. (1977) recorded conversations, which were 10 min long, between male-female pairs, whereby each voice was recorded on its own track. The interaction partners talked to each other over the telephone without having met previously. There was therefore the possibility of deceiving the men as to the appearance of the target person. A Polaroid photo had allegedly been taken in the experimental situation. To increase the plausibility of this statement a photo was taken of each man, which would supposedly be shown to the interlocuter. No picture was taken of the woman. Instead, a photo of an attractive or of an unattractive woman was shown to the men so that they would believe that their interlocuter was more or less attractive.

As was to be expected in the light of previous results the first impression made on the basis of the attractive and unattractive photos differed. In particular, the conviviality of the attractive women was estimated to be greater. The women's comments during the conversation were analyzed afterwards by perceivers. The perceivers had to assess the women on the same characteristics as those assessed by the men on the basis of their first impression. In 17 of the 21 characteristics the difference between the assessments of the attractive and unattractive women tended in the same direction as the first impression. Where the men believed in a difference, the women showed an effect.

In order to gain an idea as to how these differences in the behavior of the women, who in reality did not differ systematically in their attractiveness, came about, the men's conversation behavior was also analysed. The analysis showed that the men who expected an attractive interlocuter were assessed as being more sociable, sexually attractive, interesting, and witty than men who expected an unattractive partner. The increased conviviality of the men towards the attractive women was the mediating variable for the women's reciprocal behavior, who also rated the behavior of the men who thought they were conversing with an attractive partner as more genuine.

These results are particularly interesting because they show how stereotypes gain reality in social interaction. What begins as a stereotype leads in fact to corroboration of the stereotyped views (see also Chap. 5, "Self-fulfilling prophecies and processes of expectation confirmation").

The results in Box I 11 demonstrate the possibility that stereotypes verify themselves because they create a social reality which makes behavior corresponding to the stereotypes probable. Historical examples suggest the same:

if a group of people are forbidden to set up as craftsmen, this group will tend to take up financial dealings, which explains the origin of the stereotype that these people are avaricious. Or if a particular ethnic group is banned from entering higher education and universities, this results in a slight impairment of their intellectual faculties, which concurs with the stereotype that this ethnic group is intellectually not too gifted.

Another variant of the self-fulfilling prophecy is that the stereotype of aggressiveness can give rise to hostile interactive behavior, which in turn makes the aggressive behavior awaited on the basis of the stereotype more probable (see Snyder & Swann, 1978a, whose study on reciprocal animosity is presented more fully in Chap. 5, Box I 21).

Sex stereotypes can also be self-confirming, since they cause the behavior they contain. In an important study Skrypnek and Snyder (1982) demonstrated that ideas about typical sex roles can function as self-fulfilling prophecies (see Box I 12).

Box I 12. Toughness in negotiations depends on the sex of the opponent Skrypnek and Snyder (1982) asked pairs consisting of a man and a woman to negotiate with one another. The partners negotiated using a signal system which prevented direct facial contact so that the real sex of the person could not be ascertained. The negotiations were about who should perform which of two tasks. In one condition the men assumed correctly that they were negotiating with a woman. In the second the men were given the impression that they were interacting with a man. In reality, however, they were negotiating with a woman in both conditions. One result of the study was that the men made fewer concessions when they thought their interaction partner was a woman than when they assumed their interaction partner to be a man.

This study, which will be discussed again in Chap. 5 (" 'Forcing' expectations through"), leads to the conclusion that the true core of sex stereotypes can at least in part be caused by self-fulfilling prophecies. Men behave towards women in a way which tends to confirm the stereotype of a woman. By expressing a more masculine task preference to the "female" negotiator than to the "male" negotiator, the men forced the woman in the female condition in a more expressive direction as regards the choice of tasks than in the male condition. In this way the conditions were created for translating the different competence expectations of men and women into reality (see Deaux & Major, 1987; Spence & Helmreich, 1978).

In connection with this it is worth noting that the expectation effects caused by the label *man* or *woman* only persisted for women who ascribed to themselves an expressive or a balanced (i.e., neither particularly expressive nor particulary instrumental) attitude. In the case of instrumentally orientated women the effect of the label did not last. They returned instead, as soon as they could, to behavior which corresponded to their self-concept.

One aspect of this result is that instrumentally orientated people proved to be less easy to influence than expressively orientated people. Another aspect is that expressively orientated people tend to be easier to manipulate than instrumentally orientated people. Women who negotiated in the male condition were motivated at a later point in time to instrumental behavior although they had an expressive self-concept. Perhaps showing oneself open to social influence is one aspect of an expressive self-concept (see Spence & Helmreich, 1978).

Swann and Ely (1984) assumed that self-fulfilling prophecies and tendencies which aim at confirmation and verification of the target person's self-concept often stand in contradiction to and conflict with one another. Self-fulfilling prophecies appear to exercise an influence over the behavior of the target person, especially when the acting person is certain that his or her expectations about the target person are right (Snyder, 1984; Swann, 1987). This condition was met in the studies on self-fulfilling prophecies in stereotypes concerning the physical attractiveness or sex of target person, since the participant could hardly doubt that the target person was attractive/unattractive or male/female. The experimental procedure was carefully planned so that everybody was certain to be deceived by the label or physical appearance.

Theories About Stereotypes

Inadequacy of Stereotypes

An important question of general theoretical and practical interest concerns the adequacy or inadequacy of the descriptive content of stereotypes. In Table 12 a distinction was made between definitions of stereotypes with and without a value judgment. A negative evaluation of stereotypes – for example, as inaccurate, irrational overgeneralizations which serve to justify social discrimination – assumes that the falsity of stereotypes in general can be proved.

The arguments against stereotypes which can be used in this context have been discussed by Brown (1965), Campbell (1967), McCauley et al. (1980), and Peabody (1985). One criticism is that stereotypes are not fair to the individual case. This is justified insofar as individual cases cannot be sufficiently represented by a judgment summing up a group of people. On the other hand, this criticism of stereotypes is not fundamental. Every summary of information, be it as averages or relative frequencies, abstracts from underlying details. Summarizing judgments which estimate a descriptive characteristic value do not appear to be incorrect or false unless the estimate is distorted or misleading.

The continuation of this criticism is that stereotypes make false statements as regards contents. In the literature there are only few indications that stereotypes specify features which are quite independent of, or indeed the opposite of, the features of the target group. Campbell (1967) tried to take into account the stimulus dependency of stereotypes by assuming that every stereotype consists of a stimulus component, which stems from genuine differences between ethnic groups, and of a projective component (see below). Distortions of the true features are then to be expected when the stimulus component is weak − because, for instance, there is hardly any contact with the ethnic group or because only misleading information about the ethnic group is given − and the projective component dominates − because, for instance, personal experience is characterized by frustration and a scapegoat is sought (Secord & Backman, 1964; Wills, 1981).

The third criticism is that stereotypes are often ethnocentric. Ethnocentrism means that the norms of one's own ethnic group are seen as definitive for all people in the world. Many stereotypes arise from an ethnocentric viewpoint and disturb the coexistence of ethnic groups because hostile projections develop which hinder peaceful cooperation. LeVine and Campbell (1972) described different aspects of enemy concepts which have their roots in ethnocentrism. The ingroup appears from an ethnocentric point of view as virtuous and superior, as strong and cooperative, while the outgroup is seen as despicable and inferior, weak and unreliable. Ethnic stereotypes which are part of a general ethnocentrism can be a stumbling block for the peaceful coexistence of ethnic groups and contribute to the escalation of conflict.

One problem of many stereotypes is that they often suggest genetic differences. Genuine differences, as are often observed between ethnic groups, can often be caused by a number of environmental factors (such as nutrition, climate, upbringing, affluence, and tradition) whose effects are easily underestimated. Ethnic stereotypes often suggest a false chain of cause and effect.

Since race is a concrete, visible, and colored feature, the cause of real differences between ethnic groups is easily sought in race. It is well known from research that concrete information is more convincing than abstract information (Borgida & Nisbett, 1977; Hamill et al. 1980). Environmental disadvantages and constraints arising from the social structure can only be ascertained through reflection because they are involved and complex and often exercise an indirect influence. While such an influence can hardly be seen on the surface, race is a feature which is present at the same time and in the same space as the interaction and, as in a conditioned response, is associated with the behavior of the interaction partner (Campbell, 1967).

In order to understand the negative consequences of ethnic stereotypes it is important to realize the tempting easiness with which racial features can offer an explanation for the underprivileged situation of an ethnic group. Often, differences in achievement levels between ethnic groups can be cursorily explained by race, although they are probably the result of a long historical development. If, for example, black Americans achieved considerably lower intelligence test scores in comparison with white Americans, then it would seem obvious to make the race responsible for these differences. But the first explanation to suggest itself need not be the right one, since black Americans look back on a long history of deprivation, and since there is a connection between cultural deprivation and intelligence.

On the other hand, the example shows that the stereotype that blacks are stupid is not totally without justification. School achievement and the results of intelligence tests among black Americans are indeed lower than those among white Americans (Miller & Zabrack, 1975). However, the stereotype exaggerates the actual differences and ignores the fact that the intelligence distributions of blacks and whites overlap.

Stereotypes do not have to be pure fabrication. Instead, there is much to suggest that they take up the real differences between cultures and peoples. As mentioned above, Campbell (1967) distinguishes between the stimulus component of a stereotype and the projection component: Real group differences are included in the *stimulus component*. Contrasts seem to be particularly important, such as that between the extroverted Americans and the reserved English. The bigger the real difference between groups, as regards appearance and habits, the easier it is to process such a contrast into a stereotype (Campbell, 1967). Cultural certainties are included in the *projection component*, as are wishful thinking and other motivational influences such as transference of aggressive impulses. If the stimulus component is only weak then the projections, which have their origin in the perceiving person, gain progressively in importance.

In this context Campbell (1967) refers to a latent reciprocity of stereotypes. An example can illustrate this phenomenon. The English and Americans tend to differ in their openness towards social contacts. Whereas the English, for example, see themselves as people who value the privacy of the individual highly, the Americans consider the English to be snobby, cold, and unfriendly. On the other hand, Americans see themselves as sociable and friendly. The distorted picture of this behavior appears in the image which the English have of the Americans, when they emphasize that the Americans do not keep their distance and behave obtrusively (Campbell, 1967). That which is suppressed in one's own culture becomes with great ease the object of mockery and scorn.

The latent reciprocity of stereotypes leads to some universal stereotypes which are based on the fact that every group has an ethnocentric point of view. Some examples of such universal stereotypes were compiled by Campbell (1967):

— *We* have self-esteem and respect the traditions of our culture; *the others* are self-centred and egoistic.
— *We* are honest and trustworthy; *the others* cheat us if they can.
— *We* are moral and clean; *the others* are immoral and unclean.

If two ethnic groups debased each other in this way and to this extent, an onlooker might gain the impression that the participants were in a lunatic asylum. From the viewpoint of the participants, however, it looks different: on the one hand they do not know much about each other, about concrete behavior and attitudes (Eagly & Kite, 1987; Stapf, Stroebe & Jonas, 1986), and, on the other hand, projective attitudes out of one's own culture influence the picture of the other culture lopsidedly so that an awareness which is distorted in one direction arises.

These introductory comments represent a warning against simple condemnation of stereotypes. The inadequacy of stereotypes becomes clear above all in some of the universal stereotypes mentioned above, which can be easily condensed into an enemy concept. For many ethnic stereotypes, however, there is evidence that they have at least a certain validity (see Peabody, 1985). In the following sections three theoretical viewpoints will be described (see Ashmore & DelBoca, 1981), which were already anticipated by Lippmann (1922):

- Sociocultural: stereotypes are a part of our cultural system (e.g., Katz & Braly, 1933).
- Motivational: stereotypes can be explained by personality structures (e.g., Adorno et al., 1950/1964) or by the desire to increase the standing of the ingroup (e.g., Tajfel & Turner, 1979).
- Cognitive: stereotypes arise as a consequence of particular features of human information processing (e.g., Tajfel & Wilkens, 1963).

Sociocultural Perspective

The sociocultural perspective can be demonstrated best by the methods used to reach an agreement about the characteristics of an ethnic group as seen by a culturally homogeneous group of perceivers. Since stereotypes are seen as a part of a cultural system, the object of the exercise is to describe the cultural consensus, e.g., on ethnic and national stereotypes. Theoretical analyses are then concerned with how the consensus about certain contents and evaluations arises.

Katz and Braly (1933) developed a simple method with which a consensus about the attribution of characteristics to ethnic groups could be measured. Eighty-four characteristics (e.g., intelligent, no sense of humor) were presented in a list. The perceivers, students of the University of Princeton, had to say to what extent these characteristics were applicable to ten national or ethnic groups. These classifications were made for Americans, Chinese, Germans, English, Irish, Italians, Japanese, Jews, black Americans, and Turks. Finally, the perceivers had to say which of the chosen characteristics they would consider to be the five most typical of the respective ethnic group. Similar studies have been carried out in German-speaking countries by Sodhi and Bergius (1953), Bergius, Werbik, and Winter (1970), and Dannenberg and Winter (1975).

The Princeton study was repeated at the same university in 1951 (Gilbert, 1951) and 1967 (Karlins et al., 1969). Since it is instructive to see how the stereotype of black Americans has changed, Table 16 contains the results illustrating the stereotype of the typical black American.

Table 16. The traits of "Negroes" as seen by white American students. (Karlins, Coffman & Walters, 1969, p. 5. Copyright 1969 by the American Psychological Association. Reprinted by permission)

Trait	% Checking trait		
	1933	1951	1967
Superstitious	84	41	*13*
Lazy	75	31	*26*
Happy-go-lucky	38	17	*27*
Ignorant	38	24	11
Musical	26	33	*47*
Ostentatious	26	11	*25*
Very religious	24	17	8
Stupid	22	10	4
Physically dirty	17	–	3
Naive	14	–	4
Slovenly	13	–	5
Unreliable	12	–	6
Pleasure loving	–	19	*26*
Sensitive	–	–	*17*
Gregarious	–	–	*17*
Talkative	–	–	*14*
Imitative	–	–	*13*

The percentages in italics represent the ten traits most often named in 1967. Only traits which were selected as typical by the students are included.

There is some debate about the quality of these data (Sigall & Page, 1971) because social desirability needs of the students might distort the response. The results of Sigall and Page (1971) indicate that black Americans are assigned less favorable stereotypes when the influence of social desirability is reduced. Sigall and Page (1971) add a disclaimer (p. 253): "In sum, we should state explicitly that we make no claims to have demonstrated the Karlins et al. findings to be artifactual." McCauley and Stitt (1978) carried out a study using the likelihood ratio (see Chap. 2, "The Bayes theorem as a model of stereotypes") and typicalness rankings (nine traits were ranked as to how typical they were of Germans) as measures of the stereotype of Germans. The likelihood ratio and the rankings were highly correlated. This result supports the validity of the Katz and Braly paradigm. The four traits with the highest likelihood ratios (extremely nationalistic, scientifically minded, efficient and industrious) were also most applicable to Germans according to the checklist method (Karlins et al., 1969). One of the most recent studies using the checklist method for the measurement of ethnic stereotypes was conducted by Eagly and Kite (1987).

It is noticeable that the consensus tends to be in the middle (see Table 16). Only few traits were seen by more than 40% of the perceivers as typical for black Americans. Secord and Backman (1964) reported on a study in which perceivers had to estimate to what extent attributes which the authors considered would define a black American and personality characteristics were very typical, fairly typical, or not typical of black Americans. While there was a high degree of consensus as regards the three defining attributes *curly hair*, *dark skin*, and *thick lips* (which were judged by 96%, 94%, and 87% of the perceivers to be very characteristic), the agreement about personality traits was lower and reached a maximum of 46% (for *deeply religious*) in the category *very typical*.

Furthermore, it was observed that many perceivers ascribed attributes which were used by only a few other perceivers. Therefore, it seems appropriate to say that *personal* stereotypes of ethnic groups should be taken into consideration in addition to the consensus on *social* stereotypes when discussing personality traits (see Chap. 2, "The Bayes theorem as a model of stereotypes").

Peabody (1985) suggested differentiating between two aspects of ascribing characteristics to nations. First, the descriptive contents of the characteristics which are seen as typical for a target group are important. Secondly, it has to be taken into account whether a characteristic which is attributed to a target group is positively or negatively valued.

This distinction can be made clear, for example, with the help of the four traits *thrifty, generous, miserly, extravagant*. From a descriptive point of view, the traits *thrifty* and *miserly* on the one hand and the traits *generous* and *extravagant* on the other are similar, the two pairs building a polar contrast. From the point of view of an evaluation, the traits *thrifty* and *generous* on the one hand and the traits *miserly* and *extravagant* on the other hand are similar because one pair expresses a positive and the other a negative evaluation.

English, German, French, Italian, Austrian, and Finnish subjects judged themselves (autostereotype) and other nations (heterostereotypes) on semantic differentials which were named by pairs of opposites like *thrifty-extravagant* and *miserly-generous*. The main study took place in 1969/1970. If a nationality was judged as *thrifty* and also as *miserly* then obviously the descriptive aspect was dominant. If a nationality was judged as *thrifty* and also as *generous* then the evaluation aspect dominated. All groups of judges rated the English, Germans, French, Italians, Americans, and Russians.

The results showed that the assessments of national stereotypes could be traced back to three dimensions of which the two more important ones were descriptive. The first descriptive dimension was called "tight vs. loose control over impulse-expression." The trait *thrifty* can be assigned to the *tight* pole and generous to the *loose* pole. The second descriptive dimension was called "self-assertiveness." An example of two trait pairs which can be assigned to this dimension is *peaceful-aggressive* or *passive-energetic*. *Peaceful* and *passive* were assigned to the *non-assertive* pole, while *aggressive* and *energetic* were on the *assertive* pole, although the evaluation was in each case opposite.

Furthermore, an evaluative dimension was found which expressed the tendency to ascribe mainly positive or mainly negative characteristics to a particular nationality. This dimension can be explained as a halo effect (Eagly & Kite, 1987; Hofstätter, 1966). It represents the judgment aspect which contributes to a "friend or foe" picture.

Peabody (1985) reports that the differences between the ratings given by one group of judges to different target groups were appreciably bigger than the differences between the ratings given by different groups of judges to one target group. While the same group of judges (e.g., the English) rated different nations differently, there was a convergent tendency in the ratings of the same nation by different groups of judges. This result was interpreted as showing that different groups of judges agree to a large extent in the attribution of national stereotypes.

An example is the heterostereotype of the Germans. According to Peabody's results (1985), the Germans were described by all other nations as impulse controlled (but not ascetic) and relatively assertive. The assessment of the German autostereotype agreed with the outgroup judgment on the first descriptive dimension but a difference was clear on the second dimension, since the Germans described themselves as considerably less assertive than the non-German judges did.

A comparison of the stereotypes of different nations led Peabody (1985) to the conclusion that the English and Americans on the one hand and the French and Italians on the other hand were perceived relatively similarly. The consensus about the Anglo-American nations could be traced back to their common Calvinist tradition, while the agreement on the stereotypes of the French and Italians could be due to the Catholic-Latin tradition, according to Peabody (1985).

These observations are based on the assumption that the heterostereotypes represent to a certain extent genuine differences between nationalities. This assumption was supported by the result that there was a consensus on the assessment of single nations.

As for the evaluative judgments, there were no consistent indications that a nation gave itself preference over other nations. Instead, there was even a reversal of the expected relationship in the case of the Germans and the French, since they both judged themselves less favorably than they did other nations (and also less favorably than they were judged by other nations).

It is interesting to compare these results with those from a study on autostereotypes and heterostereotypes among inhabitants of Berlin and Vienna (Hofstätter, 1966). A sample consisting of inhabitants of both towns rated themselves and the comparative group using 24 semantic differentials with seven steps, the endpoints of which were marked by pairs of opposites (e.g., soft-hard). The self-concept of the Berliners differed from that of the Viennese in that the former tended to ascribe themselves "male" traits, while the latter tended to ascribe themselves "female" traits. Furthermore, it was shown that the heterostereotypes resembled the autostereotypes. However, the heterostereotypes tended to be more negative than the autostereotypes. The Viennese rated the Berliners as more aggressive, while the Viennese were assessed by the Berliners as being more sleepy (Hofstätter, 1966). It is also worth mentioning that the Viennese autostereotype approached the Austrian self-assessment, while the autostereotype of the Berliners was similar to the German self-concepts.

How do these ethnic stereotypes come about? Hofstätter (1966) draws attention to the importance of the social roles which the target people play: "Our thesis is that the specific simplifications which we use to characterize our fellow human beings reflect the prevailing social structure" (p. 376). The assumptions which Eagly (1987) and Eagly and Steffen (1984) make about the formation of stereotypes go in the same direction, as they base their social-structure analysis on the hypothesis that stereotypes reflect the typical social roles in which the target people are observed. Starting from this hypothesis, Eagly (1987) traced the differences in the judgment of men and women with regards to competence and warmth (see Table 14) back to the fact that women tend to have the role of a nonworking person (housewife) while men tend to play a working role.

In agreement with this analysis, Eagly and Steffen (1984) were able to show that equally few female traits were attributed to women and men when they had a working role, whereas both were attributed with just as many female traits when they were not working and were doing the housework. Conversely, more or less male traits were attributed in accordance with the role, and this was to a large extent independent of the sex of the target person. Typical sex stereotypes were only found when it was not specified if the person was working or not.

These results show that diagnostic information − here, about employment − asserted itself over sex stereotypes (see "Diagnostic information versus sex stereotypes"). The results can also be interpreted as demonstrating that sex stereotypes reflect correctly the social structure of work distribution in society (Eagly, 1987; Eagly & Kite, 1987). Since sex is correlated with employment, the perceivers drew the conclusion that features which correlate with employment were typical for men and women (Eagly & Steffen, 1984). This is an example of an inadmissible causal interpretation of a correlation.

Motivational Perspective

The motivational perspective includes explanations based on a psychodynamic approach and also those which emphasize the importance of a positive social identity and of realistic conflicts. These two approaches have in common that a depreciation of other ethnic groups and a positive evaluation of the ingroup are to be expected for motivational reasons.

Psychodynamic Approach

The classic psychodynamic approach was developed through the research on the authoritarian personality (Adorno et al., 1950/1964). It is not possible here to give a comprehensive overview of the theory of the authoritarian personality that includes all the empirical results, criticism, and further developments (see Altemeyer, 1981; Brown, 1965; Schäfer & Six, 1978). Instead, selected aspects of this theory which are directly relevant for stereotypes and prejudices will be examined here.

Questionnaire techniques as well as in-depth clinical interviews have been used to examine the authoritarian personality. The questionnaire scales were intended to measure four traits (in parentheses for each of the scales is an example of a typical statement from Adorno et al., 1950/1964).

- *Antisemitism* ("No matter how Americanized a Jew may seem to be, there is always something basically Jewish underneath, a loyalty to Jewry and a manner that is never totally changed," p. 63).
- *Ethnocentrism* ("America may not be perfect, but the American Way has brought us about as close as human beings can get to a perfect society," p. 117).
- *Political and economic conservatism* ("A child should learn early in life the value of a dollar and the importance of ambition, efficiency, and determination", p. 158).
- *Authoritarianism or Fascism* ("Obedience and respect for authority are the most important virtues children should learn," p. 227).

The contents of the scales for the measurement of antisemitism and ethnocentrism are related to ethnic stereotypes. While the antisemitism scale measures depreciative attitudes toward Jews, the target groups in the ethnocentrism scale are minorities like black people and religious sects as well as the ingroup. The conservatism scale is intended to measure the right-wing/left-wing orientation, whereby right-wing positions are characterized by an insistence on traditional values and left-wing positions contain a positive attitude to trade unions, general medical care by state institutions, and economic planning. Therefore, conservatism differs in content from ethnocentrism and antisemitism.

The authoritarianism scale is, unlike the other three scales, a personality scale. Different areas which are similar in their subject matter were used for this scale: conventionalism, submission to authority (the statement above is an example of this), aggression in defense of ones own values, aversion to personal weaknesses, superstition, emphasis on strength and dominance, cynicism regarding human nature, exaggerated attention to imaginary dangers, and exaggerated concern about sexual morality.

Although the contents of the authoritarianism scale are very heterogeneous, a satisfactory correlation was found between the individual items and the total score on the scale. It was also established that the authoritarianism scale correlated positively with the attitude scales. The high correlation between authoritarianism and ethnocentrism is particularly interesting here because it suggests that stereotyped attitudes towards the ingroup and minorities are related to the personality structure of the subjects.

In the clinical interviews it was possible to gain an overall picture of the personality of the subjects. The comparison of the answers of people with a high ethnocentrism score (in the top quartile of the distribution) with the answers of people with a low ethnocentrism score (in the bottom quartile) is particularly instructive. The answers were later coded into different categories. The two extreme groups differed in their self-assessment.

While prejudiced people were relatively uncritical of themselves, people with a low ethnocentrism score tended to be more critical of themselves. Because prejudiced people attributed negative characteristics to the minorities, it is possible that they project their sexual and aggressive wishes and endeavours outwards.

Another characteristic of prejudiced people was their fixation on affluence and success, which Fromm (1976) described fittingly as a "to-have orientation." One interpretation assumes that prejudiced people had parents who emphasized success, discipline, and career strongly in order to fulfill vicariously their own unfulfilled wish to get on in life. A brutal and inconsiderate upbringing caused anger and frustration, which was manifested in aggressive impulses. Since these impulses could not be expressed to the child's strict parents, they were displaced onto people or groups of people who were to a certain extent legitimatized objects of aggression. Such people are members of minorities, e.g., Jews or black people, who serve as scapegoats, as seen from a psychoanalytic viewpoint.

The question as to whether the concept of an authoritarian personality is tenable will not be discussed here. Criticism has been directed at the quality of the measurement instruments, the selection of subjects, and the evaluation of the data. But the basic idea of a motivational cause for ethnic stereotypes has been used in later approaches (e.g., Campbell, 1967).

It is appropriate to examine the phenomenon of ethnocentrism here in more detail. The term ethnocentrism comes from Sumner (1906), who meant by this the more positive judgment of the ingroup in comparison to the outgroups on the relevant dimensions (e.g., virtues, values, strengths, and bravery). Campbell (1967) proposed in connection with this the hypothesis that universal stereotypes arise from the tendency of every group to think ethnocentrically (see "Inadequacy of stereotypes").

Extensive anthropological studies show that the ingroup is in general judged as better than alien ethnic groups (Brewer, 1979; Campbell, 1967). In one of these studies, for example, two to five informants in 20 communities were interviewed about their perception of other ethnic groups. A total of 95 ethnic groups were described, of which 54 were direct neighbors and 41 lived further away. It was shown that the own ethnic group was judged as more virtuous and more hardworking, independent of the distance. In addition, there were indications that neighbors were judged in a more differentiated manner than groups living further away. Evaluating neighbors on different dimensions (e.g., fear, liking, trust) produced lower intercorrelations than evaluating people living further away, who tended to be assessed as generally positive ("our friends") or generally negative ("our enemies").

On the whole, it has been shown that the judgment of moral value and trustworthiness is distorted for the in- and outgroup, so that the ingroup is preferred, being seen as honest, peaceful, and virtuous (Campbell, 1967). Such a distortion can contribute to the escalation of conflicts because the attacks of one side, which see them as justified demonstrations of strength, are interpreted by the other side as acts of terrible immorality — as happened in the Vietnam war (Brewer, 1979).

In the section on the sociocultural perspective it was mentioned that such ethnocentric trends were not to be seen in the present judgment tendencies of the Germans and the French. Perhaps the special historical circumstances, especially the two world wars, are responsible for the decline in these two countries of the ethnocentric tendencies which contributed to the outbreak of these wars.

Social Identity

The social identity theory of Tajfel and Turner (Tajfel, 1978, 1982; Tajfel & Turner, 1979, 1986; Turner, 1984; Turner & Oakes, 1986) concludes that ethnocentric tendencies manifest themselves in stereotypes (see Brewer & Miller, 1984). Social identity is that part of the self-concept which is derived from the membership in social groups. In this context *groups* mean sets of individuals who belong to the same social category, maintain a consensus on group values, and are emotionally linked to one another.

A fundamental assumption of this theory is that individuals strive for a positive social identity. Features of the ingroup such as affluence, race, sex, and success determine whether the social identity is assessed as positive or negative in comparison with other groups. If the ingroup stands out positively from the comparison-groups, the social identity is assessed as positive. If the ingroup appears to be weaker, less adequate, and less developed than other groups, the ingroup stands out negatively from the other groups and the social identity is assessed as negative (Mummendey, 1985).

Finally, the assumption was made that a positive social identity leads to the wish to preserve the status quo, while a negative social identity leads to the aspiration for a change in the status quo. On the one hand, the individual can try to be accepted into a positively distinct group. On the other hand, there is the possibility of improving the image of the own group.

By using the concept of legitimacy the theory tries to take into account the fact that obviously not all inferior individuals strive to join a positively distinct group. If an inferior person feels that he/she is treated fairly, the person can come to terms with his/her inferiority. Resistance is then to be expected if a person believes that illegitimate methods have contributed to the emergence of his or her unfavorable situation.

A survey of participants in court cases shows that losers are prepared to recognize that procedural justice was applied (Tyler, 1986). The evaluation of the judge, for example, was influenced by the perceived procedural justice of the proceedings as well as by the actual results. On the one hand, this indicates that something which has positive consequences appears to be legitimate. On the other hand, it has to be taken into consideration that the perceived legitimacy also depends on whether the proceedings were fair, and this is independent of the outcome.

In general, there are several possible ways for an individual to react to negative distinctiveness of his or her group. It is possible to aim for individual mobility or to put up collective resistance. Another possibility is social creativity. If a particular comparison between the in- and outgroup is unfavorable, then there should be a tendency to prefer those comparison dimensions which the groups differ on and at the same time are advantageous for the ingroup (see Eiser & van der Pligt, 1984). Even if the ingroup is militarily inferior, its artistic achievements may surpass those of the outgroups. Another area in which a positive social identity can be gained is competitive sport with its international competitions.

Illusory correlations and selective recall as well as retrospective reinterpreting on the basis of stereotypes are further aids which can contribute to the consolidation of the threatened social status of a group. In this respect one can say that ethnic stereotypes often have the function of securing the positive distinctiveness of the ingroup by degrading other groups in an ethnocentric perspective. The possibility of a downward social comparison is used chiefly by those who feel themselves threatened in their subjective well-being (see Schönbach, Gollwitzer, Stiepel & Wagner, 1981; Wills, 1981).

Positive distinctiveness in the ingroup in comparison with outgroups should contribute to an increase in the social identity of the members of the ingroup. The perception of one's own superiority could increase individual satisfaction. Negative distinctiveness should decrease the social identity. If the circumstances are seen as stable and there is no hope of change, the level of anger should be relatively low even if the perceived justification for the discrimination is low (and of course also if the perceived legitimacy of the status quo is high). These conclusions are in line with the results of research on justice which show that deprivation causes frustration if a better alternative is apparent and if deprivation appears not to be justified (Folger, 1986).

If stereotypes are seen in the context of social comparisons, indications can be found as to their function (in the sense of securing a positive social identity). Social comparisons relate to the achievements of other groups of people as well as to the possible ways of reaching these achievements. This is the question of the "referent instrumentalities" (Folger, 1986) which refer to the features of a world imagined as an alternative and which are to be interpreted as mental constructions about the way in which things could be improved. The idea of referent instrumentalities leads to the question of whether the actual methods are less legitimate than the imagined possibilities. If such a difference in legitimacy can be confirmed, then deprivation should cause bitterness and moral outrage.

In a later paper, Turner and Oakes (1986) added to the social identity theory the "self-categorization" theory which assumes that ingroup/outgroup categorization leads to an enhancement of stereotyping, ingroup bias, and ethnocentrism. The emergence of social identity enhances a process called depersonalization of individual self-perception which corresponds to stereotyped self-perception on the social dimensions which invite ingroup/outgroup comparisons.

One implication of the revised theory is that the depersonalized self-perception elicits the expectation that ingroup members behave similarly in a given situation and perceive identical social situations with a high consensus. In addition, it is assumed that a high consensus between ingroup members facilitates external attribution in the sense that the shared response proves the existence of the social situation as interpreted (see Chap. 4, "Commonsense attribution").

The social identity theory is closely related to the realistic conflict theory (Sherif, Harvey, White, Hood & Sherif, 1961), which is based on the assumption that conflicts of interest over scarce resources elicit stereotypes and discrimination. From this viewpoint, distortions in social perception are caused by competition for scarce resources. The theory was supported in three field experiments with boys who visited a summer camp. These studies are probably the most important experiments on intergroup discrimination. The results indicate that competition between groups elicits hostility towards the outgroup and solidarity within the ingroup. If one takes the characteristics of the most intense intergroup conflicts occurring at present in the world (e.g., Northern Ireland, the Israeli-Palestinian conflict) into account, the conclusion seems justified that the realistic conflict theory is an appropriate account of the roots of these conflicts. The social identity theory specifies the psychological consequences of competition between groups (e.g., formation of positive social identity, social creativity, perceived injustice).

Cognitive Perspective

Stereotypes can be seen as being guided by a cognitive mechanism whose main function is to reduce the complexity of the social environment. Therefore, one can say that stereotypes release perceivers from their uncertainty and allow quick decisions (Hofstätter, 1966), as was assumed by Lippmann (1922) in his pioneering book.

There are various aspects to the cognitive mechanism of stereotypes, two of which will be discussed below in more detail: the classification of people according to particular features like skin color or sex, and the tendency to make retrospective errors as a consequence of illusory correlations.

Categorization of Groups of People

Human information processing is characterized by concept formation (see Bruner et al., 1956, Chap. 1). Concepts involve a division of a set of instances into two or more classes which can be contrasted – for example, edible mushrooms and poisonous mushrooms.

In the experiment of Tajfel and Wilkes (1963), the idea was taken up that the categorizing of objects into two classes leads to the difference between the classes of objects on a judgment dimension being accentuated. The hypothesis was formulated as follows (p. 102):

> When a classification in terms of an attribute other than the physical dimension which is being judged is superimposed on a series of stimuli in such a way that one part of the physical series tends to fall consistently into one class, and the other into the other class, judgements of physical magnitudes of the stimuli falling into the distinct classes will show a shift in the directions determined by the class membership of the stimuli, when compared with judgements of a series identical with respect to this physical dimension, on which such a classification is not superimposed.

This hypothesis was tested by letting subjects estimate the length of lines which were shown six times each. In the condition in which a classification was superimposed the lines were marked A or B. When the superimposed classification was consistent with the length the shorter lines (16.2, 17.0, 17.9, and 18.8 cm) were marked A and the longer lines (19.7, 20.7, 21.7, and 22.8 cm) B. The length of the lines was graded so that the difference was about 5% of the length of the neighboring lines. The consistently classified condition was compared with a condition in which a classification was also superimposed but this time it was allocated randomly so that each line of a given length was classified alternately A or B in the successive presentations. There was also a control condition in which no classification was used.

The results show that the difference between the estimates of the length of the lines measuring 18.8 cm and 19.7 cm was greater when a consistent classification was given than when either a random classification or no classification was used. On the other hand, there was no indication that the consistent classification resulted in an increase in similarity of the length estimates within the classes.

Although they had worked with estimates of length, Tajfel and Wilkes (1963, p. 113) were aware that their results could have direct implications for social perception. They were of the opinion that the results represented a simplified example of stereotyped judgments since stereotypes are characterized by the exaggeration of certain differences between groups of people. In this context, the authors put forward the theory that social judgment processes can be traced back to relatively simple principles of psychophysical judgment processes.

Further studies have supported this theory (Lilli, 1982). An illustrative example of such a study is discussed in Box I 13.

Box I 13. The minimal group paradigm

The study was on the behavior of recruits to the German Federal Army (Dann & Doise, 1974). A random classification was made by asking soldiers to judge a series of electron-microscopic pictures of blood cells. Ostensibly on the basis of their preference for certain pictures but in reality randomly the soldiers were divided into an X and a Y category. They were only told, however, which category they had been allocated to without their knowing how other recruits had been divided into the two categories.

In a later stage of the experiment the recruits had the opportunity to divide money between people of their own group and people of the other group, without knowing who the recipients were. In a competitive condition they were told the profit would be divided equally between the members of the group. In a cooperative condition it was announced that the total profit would be divided equally among all participants in the experiment. With a low incentive the subjects were led to expect a profit of between DM 0.50 ($ 0.25) and DM 1.00 ($ 0.50) per person. With a high incentive it was said that the profit would be between DM 5.00 ($ 2.50) and DM 10.00 ($ 5.00) per person.

In the decision phase the recruits were presented with a series of matrices with which the tendency to intergroup discrimination was to be measured. Here I will only describe one type of matrix, which measured the tendency to maximize the difference between the profits of the in- and the outgroup. This tendency can be termed competition orientation, since here it is established whether a tendency exists to maximize the relative advantage of one's own group without considering the absolute level of profit (see Kelley & Thibaut, 1978).

Two matrices with the help of which the competitive tendency was compared with the tendency to maximize the individual and collective profit are shown in Table 17. Both matrices are identical except that the assignment of the rows to the in- and to the outgroup has been exchanged. In the upper matrix the alternative on the far left (16/19) is most favorable insofar as it maximizes one's profit (19), the collective profit (35), and the difference (+3). However, the wish to minimize the difference — as in the lower matrix — is maximized by the middle alternative. In the lower matrix the alternative on the far right is the most favorable from the point of view of maximizing the difference (+3). However, from the point of view of maximizing the individual or collective profit the alternative on the far left, which also implies maximizing the difference in favor of the other group, is the most favorable (+3).

In order to measure the intergroup discrimination in the condition using a random classification the difference between the decisions based on two related matrices [see Table 17; row 2 (own group) — row 2 (other group)] was calculated. The difference in all experimental conditions was positive, which indicates that on the whole there is a tendency to discriminate in favor of one's own group even if the total profits or one's

Table 17. Payoff matrices. (From Dann and Doise, 1974, p. 10. Copyright 1974 by Verlag Hans Huber. Reprinted by permission)

Matrix I	Outgroup (1)	16	15	14	13	12	11	10
	Ingroup (2)	19[a,b,c]	17	15	13[d]	11	9	7
Matrix II	Ingroup (1)	16	15	14	13	12	11	10
	Outgroup (2)	19[a,b]	17	15	13[d]	11	9	7[c]

[a] Alternative which maximizes the collective payoff.
[b] Alternative which is most favorable to ingroup.
[c] Alternative which maximizes the difference in favor of the ingroup.
[d] Alternative which minimizes the differences between ingroup and outgroup.
The difference between the upper and the lower matrix is that the rows have been exchanged so that the row 1 represents the outgroup once and the ingroup once.

own profit cannot be maximized by doing so. This tendency was greater in the competition condition than in the cooperation condition (3.545 vs. 0.715) and tended to be stronger if large instead of small incentives were given (2.58 vs. 1.68).

As a consequence of the categorization a discrimination between the in- and the outgroup in favor of the ingroup arose, which can be explained by an emphasis on the differences which were found on one dimension (see also Eiser & Stroebe, 1972; Lilli, 1982).

Taylor, Fiske, Etcoff and Ruderman (1978) advanced seven hypotheses:

1. Physical and social features such as race and sex are used to categorize people and structure the information about these people.
2. Therefore, differences in the ingroup are minimized and differences between the groups exaggerated.
3. Within a group behavior is interpreted in stereotyped terms.
4. The fewer the number of members in a subgroup, the greater the amount of attention the subgroup can be expected to attract.
5. The greater the familiarity with a group, the greater the amount of attention this group should receive.
6. The fewer the number of members in a subgroup, the greater the number of stereotyped attributes ascribed to the individuals in the subgroup.
7. Social groups are stereotyped as a function of the proportion of different subgroup members.

These hypotheses were tested experimentally in a conversation between six stimulus people. In one experiment, for example, three white and three black people discussed an advertising campaign. While the judges listened to the conversation a picture of the person currently speaking was shown. Therefore, it was possible to attribute a remark to a white or to a black person.

During the discussion each person made six suggestions as to how the advertising campaign could be organized. After the discussion the judges had to say who had made which suggestion. An error analysis was carried out. The question was whether errors were random or whether intragroup errors (blacks are confused with blacks and whites with whites) occur more often than intergroup errors (whites are confused with blacks and vice versa) − as would be expected if use of stereotypes were schematic. The results were in agreement with the first two hypotheses. Intragroup errors occurred more often than intergroup errors (see also Box 18).

In a second experiment the same pattern of results was found for a discussion group made up of three women and three men. In a third experiment indications were found that the third and fourth hypotheses are correct. Once again discussion groups made up of six people were observed. Men were rated as more influential, confident, and analytical than women. Furthermore, there were indications that a sex group attracted more attention if it consisted of fewer people (see Chap. 4, "Figure/background reversal").

While the fifth and sixth hypotheses could not be confirmed there were results which supported the seventh hypothesis. The more men in the group, the more competent and successful the group as a whole was assessed as being. Furthermore, it was assumed that it was more unlikely that a trade union would be successful if more women were in the group.

The emphasis on group differences arose above all when evaluative judgment dimensions were used or when the incentive was high (Brewer, 1979; Dann & Doise, 1974). This fits in with the experimental results showing that attitude judgments become polarized when the judges identify themselves with the positively labeled end of the scale (see Eiser & van der Pligt, 1984). On the other hand, the difference is minimized if one's own position agrees with the negatively labeled end of the scale.

A distinction between the in- and the outgroup is made above all when the ingroup can be assigned to the positive end of the scale. This conclusion is highly plausible because it is not to be expected that somebody emphasizes a difference (e.g., on the education dimension) if he or she has an unfavorable position on the judgment dimension.

Retrospective Errors and Illusory Correlations

In Chap. 1 ("Cognitive representation of persons") it was said that schematic conceptions of social reality (such as expectations, perceptual sensitization, prototypes, and stereotypes) have a high resistance to change. This high resistance to change is not surprising because a rational strategy cannot give up successful schemata (see Alloy & Tabachnik, 1984). If a perceptual schema has proved itself to be useful it is hardly sensible to give it up merely because one countercommunication has contradicted it.

A trend to persistence can be caused by the retrospective reinterpretation of past events, which strengthens the durability of stereotypes. The distorting influence of illusory correlations (see Chap. 2, "How are the available data classified?") seems to be especially relevant for the maintenance of stereotypes.

Illusory correlations can hinder the unbiased judgment of events. Hamilton and Rose (1980) assumed that a tendency to overestimate the frequency of the co-occurrence of two features exists with associatively linked features. Illusory correlations refer to distorted judgments of the degree of association between two variables in a stimulus sequence (Hamilton & Sherman, in press).

In this sense a stereotyped expectation causes distorted processing of information about members of the group so that associatively linked stimulus pairs are recalled as occurring more often than stimulus pairs inconsistent with expectations. The result of such a distortion is that the stereotype is confirmed although no corresponding relationship is present in the data. Illusory correlations of this type are based on semantic associations (McArthur & Friedman, 1980; Fiedler et al., 1984).

This phenomenon was demonstrated using the example of occupation stereotypes (Hamilton & Rose, 1980). A stimulus set consisted of 24 people who were allocated to three occupational groups. One stimulus set consisted only of male occupations, while the other contained only female occupations. In each stimulus set the people were assigned eight characteristics. Two of the characteristics were typical for each occupational group while two further characteristics were neutral. For example, the following stimuli were presented for the male occupations: accountants (perfectionist, timid), doctors (thoughtful, wealthy), salesmen (enthusiastic, talkative). The neutral characteristics were *courteous* and *boring*.

Important was the fact that each of the eight characteristics was paired exactly twice with the members of each occupational group; i.e., two of the eight stimulus people were described with the characteristic *perfectionist*, for example. Each characteristic was equally probable in each occupational group of a stimulus set. A female and a male stimulus set were constructed according to the basic principle of equal frequency of each characteristic per occupational group as described above. The perceivers assessed, for each stimulus set, how often a characteristic had described the members of each occupational group in the set. This was done separately for all eight characteristics listed alphabetically.

The frequency estimates proved to be distorted by the stereotyped connections between occupational groups and characteristics, since stereotyped characteristics were seen as describing the appropriate occupational group more often. Since each characteristic was assigned equally often to each occupational group, this overestimate of stereotyped connections can be interpreted as an example of illusory correlations (Hamilton & Rose, 1980, study 2).

In this example a positive illusory correlation was found, but in a further study the opposite − a negative illusory correlation − was demonstrated. Here, characteristics were used which, according to the stereotype, were incongruent with the occupational groups. Those which contradicted expectations were assessed as occurring relatively seldom (Hamilton & Rose, 1980, study 3).

Another type of illusory correlation is based on shared infrequency (McArthur & Friedman, 1980). For example, subjects read 39 sentences in which a stimulus person who behaved desirably or undesirably was identified by category membership (group A or group B; Hamilton & Gifford, 1976). One category was overrepresented (two-thirds A, one-third B). In addition, desirable behavior was more frequent than undesirable behavior. There was no relationship between category membership and desirability of behavior (the frequencies were: A-desirable 18, A-undesirable 8, B-desirable 9, B-undesirable 4). However, the frequency of co-occurrence of the relatively infrequent events (group B and undesirable behavior) was overestimated. This type of erroneous judgment, which is based on the co-occurrence of distinctive events (shared infrequency), is discussed in more detail by Hamilton & Sherman (in press).

Stereotype Research — Practical Applications

The practical relevance of research on stereotypes is obvious, but before I discuss individual applications I will summarize the most important results of the research.

Stereotypes can be traced back to several processes which often complement each other. Conceptual thinking leads to a classification and organization of the social environment, which can cause one to overestimate the real differences between social groups. In addition, perceived differences between social groups are linked to values. Because of the basically ethnocentric positions, the constellation of characteristics seen as typical of the ingroup is described in positive terms, while the constellation of characteristics which appears to be typical of other groups is couched in negative terms.

If such flexibility in the use of words does not lead to success because the ingroup is clearly inferior on one dimension, then comparisons on this dimension will be neglected. If the ingroup is clearly superior on one dimension, the comparison on this dimension will be preferred. This selectivity of comparisons is one aspect of the striving towards a positive social distinctiveness for the ingroup.

When stereotypes are established different mechanisms help to maintain them. First, there are self-fulfilling prophecies which justify features which originally were at best only a tendency. Selective memories and restructuring of memories to agree with the stereotype are further processes which ensure the stability of stereotypes. Finally, one must remember that stereotypes reflect and strengthen the distribution of roles in society (e.g., with respect to labor distribution between men and women). If stereotypes are based on the distribution of roles in society, if does not seem very promising to try to dismantle stereotypes through contact between groups or by education. Since stereotypes represent simplifications, they will be supported and reinforced as long as the distribution of roles (e.g., between men and women) continues to exist. Observers learn again and again that typical features are associated, for example, with sex. Probably a change in the role distribution will lead to the dismantling of stereotypes based on the distribution of roles.

Enemy concepts of other people also prove to be relatively stable. This high resistance to change is not surprising because a rational information processing strategy must be based on the retention of successful schemata (see Alloy & Tabachnik, 1984). They can only be revised in a long-term process. Wolf (1979) drew attention to the fact that prejudices can be questioned when new information becomes available. Simple education, however, is not enough (Sampson, 1971). It is necessary to discuss prejudices critically and individually. Therefore, therapeutic and quasi-therapeutic approaches would seem appropriate.

One cannot expect a miracle from programs aimed at changing attitudes which operate in the natural environment of the target group. Studies of Israeli tourists in Egypt (Ben-Ari & Amir, 1988) and American exchange students in France and Germany (Stroebe, Lenkert & Jonas, 1988) led to the conclusion that exchange programs have positive as well as negative effects on intergroup attitudes and national stereotypes.

Ben-Ari and Amir (1988) asked Israelis to assess social characteristics (e.g., friendly, honest) and perceived competence (e.g., efficient, intellectual) of Egyptians before and after a visit in Egypt. Results indicated positive pre-post changes in the social domain and negative changes in the intellectual domain. Since the social evaluations were more positive than the intellectual evaluations from the beginning, these results indicate that the direction of change correlated with the original position: when the original attitude was positive the tour fostered a more positive attitude, while the opposite change was observed when the original attitude was unfavorable (see Brickman, Redfield, Harrison & Crandall, 1972; Perlman & Oskamp, 1971).

In a study of American exchange students who stayed in France or Germany for a year, only little support for the assumption that a stay abroad leads to less stereotyped thinking was found (Stroebe et al., 1988). On the contrary, especially the American students in France exhibited a more negative image of France after spending a year in the country. In addition, general attitudes towards the people, country and culture tended to worsen. These results are a warning against simplistic assumptions about the favorable effects of intercultural contacts. But it should be noted that the American students were a special group in the sense that they had positive attitudes about their host countries at the beginning. Their expectations might have been too high. As a consequence, disappointments may have been inevitable. In addition, personal experience might foster a more differentiated view of both positive and negative aspects of other cultures.

An overview (Six & Schäfer, 1985) shows that role-playing, educational programs, and behavior-modification methods (e.g., group therapy) are effective in modifying stereotypes. An informative approach which includes describing similarities and differences to be expected between the ingroup and the outgroup might be an important prerequisite for overcoming the cultural gap which usually exists between different countries (Stephan & Stephan, 1984). Intercultural understanding is promoted when differences are described in the context of similarities and when the presentation of possible differences emphasizes respect and appreciation of ethnic traditions.

The Role of Contact Between Groups

One possible way of correcting false stereotypes lies in racially mixed interaction. However, the results of such contact depend on the atmosphere in which contact takes place and on how intensive it is. Amir (1969, 1976; Ben-Ari & Amir, 1988) lists factors which can ensure a positive outcome of contact between members of different groups:

- Equal status of the participants
- Superiors, teachers, and parents support racially mixed contact
- Not only superficial but also personal, deep friendship is made possible
- The contact takes place in a rewarding, relaxed social context
- The participants cooperate to solve a common problem
- The members of both groups rate each other positively before interaction begins

It is clear that on the whole in racially mixed meetings these conditions are only insufficiently met. Therefore, it is not surprising that the success of mixed schools in racial integration has remained small (see Gerard & Miller, 1975; Stephan & Feagin, 1979).

However, integration programs which fulfill important preconditions for effectively combatting ethnic stereotypes have more success (Aronson, Stephan, Sikes, Blaney & Snapp, 1978). Creating a cooperative task is seen as an important prerequisite for successfully reducing prejudiced attitudes (see Johnson, Johnson & Maruyama, 1984; Sherif, 1979). Social contact between racially mixed groups must be carefully planned in order to be able to avoid setbacks (Stroebe et al., 1988).

A further strategy is to develop inconsistent status characteristics. The theory of status-organizing processes (Berger et al., 1980) includes the hypothesis that inconsistent status characteristics in the interaction partners lead to their accepting an equality norm. If, for example, black skin color in comparison to white skin color represents a diffuse negative status, a particular skill which the black — but not the white — children have learned is a positive status characteristic. Various techniques for training expectations are aimed at giving the apparently inferior group positive status characteristics so that increased equality is achieved in interaction with the apparently superior group. In racially mixed groups of people the integrative effect of such status manipulation is increased when the teaching staff is also racially mixed (see Berger et al., 1980).

Other results indicate that actual contact is not absolutely necessary to reduce ethnic stereotypes. In a study of a white housing estate into which black people had moved it was shown that, after 1 year, prejudices against black people were reduced even if no explicit contact with black neighbors had taken place. The conversations of the white inhabitants amongst themselves involved an exchange of information about the black neighbors which became more positive with time. It was important for the reduction of negative stereotypes that unfavorable expectations about violence and loss in value of their property were not fulfilled (Hamilton & Bishop, 1976).

Label Effects

Studies on impression formation have shown that certain labels can change the perception of a person. A speaker who is described as warm caused more participation than a speaker stigmatized as cold (Kelley, 1950; Widmeyer & Loy, 1988).

In the same way, the labels *black* and *white* distort impression formation. White perceivers who observed an interview without being able to see the skin color of the interviewer clearly believed that they agreed with the interviewer less when they were informed that the interviewer was black not white (Dienstbier, 1972).

Therapists who observed an interview on experiences at work described the same behavior of an interviewee as either pathological or as well adapted depending on whether the interviewee had been described as a patient or as an applicant (Langer & Abelson, 1974). Furthermore, it can be shown that labels are accepted by stigmatized people and their subsequent behavior can deteriorate (Langer & Benevento, 1978).

Since one generally cannot hide age and race, to name but two features which give rise to stereotypes, the influence of the label can be felt permanently. Therefore, it is not surprising that middle-class black people report that in interacting with white people they place an emphasis on making a good impression through language and appearance in order to avoid the negative label effect (Pettigrew, 1981).

Particularly in superficial contact between different racial groups there is the danger that stereotyped expectations of the other race are "awakened" and strengthened by contact (Ben-Ari & Amir, 1988). Superficial contacts activate the scripts associated with the other race so that stereotypes become more entrenched (Rose, 1981). On the other hand, more personal contacts offer the possibility of neutralizing or correcting the stereotype. In addition, cognitive training with an emphasis on similarities, realistic expectations, and positive information might facilitate change in the same direction (Ben-Ari & Amir, 1988; Stroebe et al. 1988).

Diagnostic Information From Single Cases

A number of indications show that intensive contact with members of another ethnic group reduces prejudices (Rose, 1981). A study by Gurwitz and Dodge (1977) showed that a stereotype was more likely to be corrected if a single person from the outgroup disproved a prejudice several times than if three people disproved a stereotype once each. Conversely, the stereotype was strengthened more when three people provided confirmation than when one person confirmed the stereotype several times.

Stereotypes can be neutralized by diagnostic information from single cases (Deaux & Lewis, 1984; see also Locksley et al., 1980; Locksley, Hepburn & Ortitz, 1982; Neuberg & Fiske, 1987). Social contact between groups can therefore reduce the negative effect of stereotypes. This requires, however, that the contact between the members of two groups be intensive and personal so that relevant diagnostic information is likely to be exchanged.

This limitation has a further implication. Personal contact does not necessarily contribute to the dismantling of stereotypes because the target person, either because of cultural differences or because of self-fulfilling prophecies, might exemplify the negative characteristics which the perceiver despises (Ben-Ari & Amir, 1988). Ethnic stereotypes which are based on a kernel of truth can only be neutralized by diagnostic information if the diagnostic information contradicts the category information which is contained in the stereotype.

Several Prototypes Instead of One Universal Stereotype

It is unrealistic to assume that stereotypes of black people, men/women, or old people are applied universally and unspecifically. It is to be expected that the universal stereotype can be divided into several prototypes (Ashmore, 1981; Taylor, 1981). Such prototypes allow greater flexibility in interacting with another group than can one universal stereotype (Pettigrew, 1981) and foster more differentiated representations of the outgroups (Stroebe et al., 1988).

The presence of several prototypes is of course no excuse for denigrating attitudes towards particular groups of people. But a complex system of stereotypes contributes to less "pigeonhole" thinking. Differentiating a stereotype into several prototypes is at least a step in the right direction – persons are not judged according to their membership of an ethnic or social group but according to individual characteristics.

Contrast Effects

One can conclude with some certainty from the many studies in which contrast effects were created (see Manis & Armstrong, 1971; Manis & Paskewitz, 1984 a, b; Simpson & Ostrom, 1975) that the judgment of a group of people is influenced by the context, i.e., which other groups are judged at the same time (see Pettigrew, 1981). If, for example, black civil rights campaigners are assessed, their rating should be more positive if militant black organizations (like the Black Muslims) were judged beforehand. This phenomenon is called a contrast effect.

Such contrast effects are present in all aspects of political judgment formation. One is often surprised, for example, which trifles are rated as sensations. But when serious problems arise, such as the question of whether the oil supply can be secured, the problems which previously stirred people's emotions for the most part lose their importance. The importance of a topic obviously depends on which other topics are under discussion (Sherman, Ahlm, Berman & Lynn, 1978).

An extreme example can illustrate this line of thought: If the famous men from Mars invaded the earth one day, the many prejudices between human beings would melt down to just a handful, since all humans are very similar if an alien from Mars is used as the yardstick.

Contrasts can occur between the auto- and the heterostereotype. An example of this is the picture of the typical employer as seen by a "normal" employee compared with the autostereotype of this employee (Bergler, 1976). While the employee's heterostereotype of the employer contains features such as businesslike, self-confident, versatile, serious, and loud, characteristics like emotional, self-critical, steady, cheerful, and quiet are emphasized in the employee's autostereotype. However, the heterostereotype of the typical employer and the autostereotype of a company executive would tend to overlap.

Chapter 4

Attribution: Theories

Attributions are subjective estimates which are related to an analysis of causality. The meaning of *cause* has been discussed extensively in philosophy and methodology (Cook & Campbell, 1979; Einhorn & Hogarth, 1986; Nagel, 1961; Shaver, 1985; Stegmüller, 1969). Stegmüller (1969) states that the cause of an event Y consists of all antecedent conditions which allow a deductive explanation of the event. The deductive explanation refers to laws. Stegmüller (1969) adds a number of distinctions (e.g., deterministic and statistical laws, qualitative, comparative, or quantitative laws, laws which describe a process in time, and laws which describe a state at a given point on the time continuum) which allow us to speak of different forms of cause-effect relationships.

In addition, an interesting question is what is the scope of causal thinking? With regard to this question a valuable distinction has been drawn between causes as antecedent conditions of an effect and reasons as a purpose or goal (Buss, 1978; Locke & Pennington, 1982). While causes refer to the processes which bring about the effect, reasons are described in terms of intentions and purposeful behavior and include accounts of the appraisal and justification of behavior. Reasons represent a special class of causes (Locke & Pennington, 1982). The distinction between cause and reason is reminiscent of Heider's distinction between impersonal and personal causality (see "The naive analysis of behavior").

Empirical studies on attribution behavior fall into both categories. While studies on the rational information processing of observers (e.g., Hewstone & Jaspars, 1987; Hansen, 1980; McArthur, 1972) are concerned with perceived causes, studies on the justifications and rationalizations of actors who fail at a task (e.g., Bradley, 1978; Stevens & Jones, 1976; Tetlock & Levi, 1982) are concerned with perceived reasons. The study of reasons is also closely related to the attribution of intention, responsibility, and blame (Fincham & Jaspars, 1980; Shaver, 1985).

A related idea is expressed by Stegmüller (1969) who argues that the term *cause* changes its meaning in everyday life depending on the practical goals.

If the focus is on the realization of a desired goal, cause means a sufficient condition which brings about the effect. If the focus is on the avoidance of an event or its elimination, causes are described as necessary conditions (Stegmüller, 1969). In formal logic, necessary conditions must be given for an event to occur, while sufficient conditions, if present, guarantee that the effect occurs. For necessary causes: given the effect, the cause must be present. For sufficient causes: given the cause, the effect must be present (see "Causal relations"). Necessary causes have the logical structure of a reversed conditional (replication), while sufficient causes have the logical structure of a conditional (implication). A necessary and sufficient cause refers to the logical biconditional (see Table 20). Reversed conditional, conditional, and biconditional can all be regarded as forms of causal relationships (see Hewstone & Jaspars, 1987).

Mill (1846) devised several methods of causal analysis which are described here in the notation from Mayntz, Holm and Hübner (1969): the method of agreement is based on the idea that several factors could cause an effect. These independent variables are X, A, B, and C. The effect is called Y. Each of the independent variables might be present (e.g., A) or absent (e.g., $\sim$A). Now, consider two empirical results:

$$X, A, B, C \rightarrow Y$$

$$X, \sim A, \sim B, \sim C \rightarrow Y$$

Because Y is still present when A, B, and C are not present, X is assumed to be the cause of Y. (Note that $\rightarrow$ denotes the logical implication). The second method − the method of difference − is based on the following idea: the effect is present when variable X is present and absent when variable X is absent. Therefore, X is considered to be the cause of Y:

$$X, A, B, C \rightarrow Y$$

$$\sim X, A, B, C \rightarrow \sim Y$$

The method of difference is the paradigm for Kelley's analysis of variance (ANOVA) model. In his theory of causal attribution Kelley (1967, p. 194) stated: "The effect is attributed to that condition which is present when the effect is present and which is absent when the effect is absent."

Weiner (1986) suggests that *why* questions refer to the search for causes. He discusses the situational conditions under which *why* questions are asked in everyday life. He refers to studies which measure in one way or another the occurrence of spontaneous attributional activity. One possibility is to code newspaper reports of public events according to the types of attributions used.

The study by Lau and Russell (1980; see also Lau, 1984) is representative of this approach. Lau and Russell coded newspaper reports of football games according to stability and internality of explanations. They found that unexpected events tended to elicit more attributional activity than expected events.

In addition, there was a tendency to attribute expected events more to stable causes than unexpected events although unstable causes were in general much more popular than stable causes.

Försterling and Groeneveld (1983) found that the defeat of one party in a political election in the Federal Republic of Germany elicited more attributions than the political success of the competing party. Försterling and Groeneveld (1983) analyzed newspaper reports of explanations of election results given by the parties who lost or won. The election had resulted in wins for the CDU (Christian Democratic Union) and losses for the SPD (Social Democratic Party of Germany). It is interesting to note that the SPD statements included more external attributions while the CDU-statements included more internal attributions. In addition, CDU-politicians applied more stable attributions and referred more to controllable causes while SPD politicians applied more variable attributions and referred more to uncontrollable causes. This attributional pattern is an example of a self-serving bias (see "Motivational influences on the attribution process"). While in Lau and Russell's study (1980) internal and unstable attributions dominated, Försterling and Groeneveld (1983) reported that external and unstable attributions were most popular. The kind of attribution seems to depend, at least in part, on the event which is to be explained (Lau, 1984).

Weiner (1986) summarized the available studies on the factors which facilitate attributional activities (see also Weiner, 1985a). The conclusion is that *why* questions emerge especially for negative events, for unexpected events, and for important events. The evidence for negative events is in agreement with studies which show that negatively evaluated persons elicit a more differentiated perception than positively evaluated persons (Bierhoff, 1980a; Irwin, Tripodi & Bieri, 1967).

For example, in the study by Bierhoff (1980a) results indicated that the degree of explanation varied inversely with the evaluation of the stimulus person's behavior. Negatively evaluated behavior was explained more comprehensively than positively evaluated behavior. One possibility is that negative behavior is threatening for the perceiver. The threat inherent in the negative behavior might motivate a search for plausible explanations in order to make sure that the perceiver is able to avoid the negative consequences (see also Fiske, 1980).

Events which lead to negative consequences may elicit blame attribution. The question "Who is responsible for damage?" is central to a discussion of moral responsibility in legal philosophy (Fincham & Jaspars, 1980; Shaver, 1985). These issues will be dealt with in the section "Attribution of responsibility and blame".

The evidence for unexpected events is in agreement with Jones and Davis (1965) and Jones and McGillis (1976), who assumed that events of low prior probability are used for dispositional attributions. Behavior which is seen as having high social desirability seems to demand an explanation in terms of situational determinants. The question of importance is more or less self-evident because it is more likely that attention is directed towards important than towards unimportant events.

Another question is related to the content of attributions. Weiner's summary (1986) of the evidence shows that the number of specific causes of an event is nearly infinite. This is true for achievement as well as for poverty or sickness. If, for example, "Bill took Jane to an expensive Italian restaurant" (see Wimer & Kelley, 1982) it is possible to argue that Bill didn't know how expensive the restaurant was, that Bill wanted to impress Jane, that Bill enjoys a good meal, that the expensive restaurant was the only Italian restaurant around and that Bill likes to eat Italian food, that Jane wanted proof of Bill's love, etc. The causes of a specific event can be highly idiosyncratic.

Although it is difficult to specify how much attributional activity occurs in daily life, the results indicate that important, negative, and unexpected events are likely to elicit causal attributions. In addition, factor analysis and multidimensional scaling techniques show that the large number of causes which can be applied in an attempt to explain an event can be reduced to a small number of attributional dimensions (see below).

What is the place of attribution processes in theories of attribution? A possible answer can be found in Kelley and Michela's (1980) distinction between *attribution theories* and *attributional theories* (see Figure 17). Attributions are conceived as mediating variables which transform the attributional "input" into behavioral consequences.

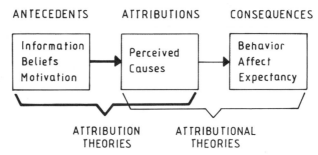

Figure 17. Model of the attribution field. (After Kelley & Michela, 1980, p. 459. Reproduced, with permission, from the *Annual Review of Psychology*, Vol. 31. Copyright 1980 by Annual Reviews Inc.)

If, for example, asked how consistency of information affects the certainty with which person and stimulus attributions can be made, one can use attribution theories (e.g., Kelley's ANOVA model) to answer this question. Person attributions refer to dispositions or characteristics of the target person, while stimulus attributions refer to situational determinants which might influence the actions of the target person. If, however, the question is how person attribution for an act of assistance affects later helpfulness, attributional

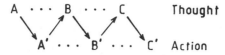

Figure 18. Behavior sequence and attributions from an interactionist perspective. (Modified from Weiner, 1976, p. 284. Copyright 1976 by Bernard Weiner. Reprinted by permission)

theories are relevant (e.g., Bem's self-perception theory). This distinction between attribution theories and attributional theories is mainly of heuristic value (Harvey & Weary, 1984) and should not be taken as evidence for a dichotomy between cognition and behavior (Eiser, 1983). For example, self-perception theory can function either as an attribution theory (the question being "What can I infer from my behavior?") or as an attributional theory (the question being "What does my self-perception imply about my future behavior?").

In attribution theory attributions are not seen as epiphenomena which accompany actions. Instead they are treated as cognitive processes which influence the course of action and are influenced by feedback during and after action (Weiner, 1976). Therefore, the assumption that actions and attributions are mutually dependent (see Figure 18) replaces a dualistic conception (see Box T7).

Box T7. Actions and attributions
The mutual dependence of actions and attributions is depicted in Figure 18. Attributions are not the only determinants of social behavior and are not always the most important. If, for example, the actors in a social episode respond to each other's actions, the interaction context influences considerably the development of the relationship. A similar idea was formulated by Jones and Thibaut (1958) when they put social perception in relationship to the interaction context. The consideration of the social context in which an action takes place leads to the general framework shown in Figure 19.

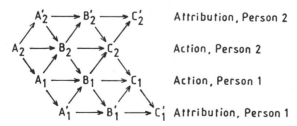

Figure 19. Extended interactionist perspective: actions and attributions in a social context. (From Bierhoff & Bierhoff-Alfermann, 1983, p. 95. Copyright 1983 by Verlag für Psychologie – C.J. Hogrefe. Reprinted by permission)

Jones and Gerard (1967) described different patterns of social interaction. If one differentiates accordingly between primary and secondary influences, there are numerous ways in which social interdependence can be expressed. Figure 19 would be a presentation of a case in which both interaction parties are under a social influence while at the same time the influence of their attributions and intentions on their own behavior is clear and in the ideal case equally strong. Furthermore, the social influence is equally strong compared with the influence of the attributions, which themselves are influenced by actions as well as by earlier attributions. Other cases are of course also possible. For example, person 1 may be more strongly influenced by person 2 than vice versa and person 2 may be more influenced by attributions than person 1 (see Bierhoff & Bierhoff-Alfermann, 1983).

Here one must add that in Figure 19 the actual relationships are still oversimplified. One has to take into consideration that, besides the direct influences (e.g., $A_1 - A'_1$ or $B_1 - C_2$), second and higher order influences can also occur (e.g., $A'_1 - C'_1$; $B'_2 - C_1$; $A'_2 - B'_1$). A more differentiated analysis can be necessary. This could be so if the question was asked of how the attributions of person 1 influence those of person 2 (see Heider, 1958, Chap. 3) or how person 1 believes that he/she can make him/herself popular with person 2 by using an appropriate self-presentation (see Jones, 1964; Jones & Wortman, 1973; Tetlock & Manstead, 1985).

Figure 19 was intended to introduce the social context in Weiner's interactive perspective (see Figure 18). The sequence of actions and attributions during the behavioral episode can be divided into four phases (see Weiner, 1976, p. 286):

1. Motivational arousal together with the registration of new information and/or the onset of a new intent
2. Instrumental activity and persistence of goal-directed behavior, combined with cognitive activities related to the attainment of the goal (social comparisons, information processing, etc.)
3. Goal attainment or nonattainment together with cognitive activities during goal expression
4. Behavioral consequences of goal activity together with postgoal thoughts (evaluation with respect to goal, modification of strategy to fit future events, etc.).

Just as it appears to be necessary to introduce the social context in order to complete Weiner's interactive perspective, so it is desirable to place the attribution process in the context of the behavioral episode as a whole (Eiser, 1983). Attribution processes are relevant to all four phases: for example, the attribution of intentions and freedom of choice (phase 1), the explanation of continuing behavior with a naive psychological theory (phase 2), attributions in connection with ingratiation and control (phase 3), and retrospective conclusions about the cause of an event (e.g., whether internally or externally determined) and responsibility attributions (phase 4).

Kruglanski, Hamel, Maides and Schwartz (1978; see also Kruglanski, 1980) understand attributions to be a naive epistemology, analogous to scientific epistemology. Such a theory of knowledge can be characterized by content, logic, and course of epistemological behavior. Content is based on the terms used and the relationships which are formed between them (e.g., causal). Logic means that consistency of terms can be described using procedures from propositional logic. Course of epistemological behavior refers to the sequence of inferences which serve the goal of increasing knowledge.

Causal attributions permit the maintenance of perceived control under certain conditions (Fiske & Taylor, 1984). If you put the result of an action down to chance, for example, this gives you no indications about actions of the actor to be expected in the future. This is different, however, in the case of a causal explanation by observers which concerns dispositions to be found in the actor's person. Here, the result, together with the explanation, leads to expectations about the results of the actor's future actions in a given situation (Yarkin, Harvey & Bloxom, 1981). In contrast, actors' self-attributions are influenced by their concern with flexibility of behavior (Snyder & Wicklund, 1981) because they are motivated to broaden the range of causes and to increase their freedom of choice (Wicklund, 1974).

The cognitive side of the motivational process is central to attribution research. This does not mean that motives are completely ignored in attribution research. Firstly, the attribution process itself has to have underlying motives (see Kruglanski et al., 1978; Pittman & D'Agostino, 1985; Snyder & Wicklund, 1981), for example, the wish to gain more knowledge, to increase the predictability of social events, or to render interpersonal relationships more controllable. Secondly, the importance of motivational distortions compared with rational attributions is under discussion (Bradley, 1978; Gollwitzer, Earle & Stephan, 1982; Shaver, 1985; Tetlock & Levi, 1982). It would be surprising to find that causal attributions is the only area of human behavior where motivational influences are not relevant (Shaver, 1985). Therefore, attributions must be understood in their motivational context (see "Motivational influences on the attribution process").

The rest of this chapter is organized as follows. Firstly, causal relations and the naive analysis of behavior as described by Heider (1958) and Weiner (1972, 1986) are discussed. Next, causal schemata are described which are applied when only a single observation can be made. This includes the analysis of configuration concepts of multiple necessary causes and multiple sufficient causes. Also relevant here are processes which are closely related to these concepts, especially discounting and augmentation. I shall also consider the systematic analysis of covariation between causes and effects. The covariation principle is applied when repeated observations are available. In describing the covariation concept I will distinguish between a multidimensional approach which takes several dimensions into consideration simultaneously and a one-dimensional approach which considers each dimension individually. Following this, the theory of correspondent inference (Jones & Davis, 1965) and the self-

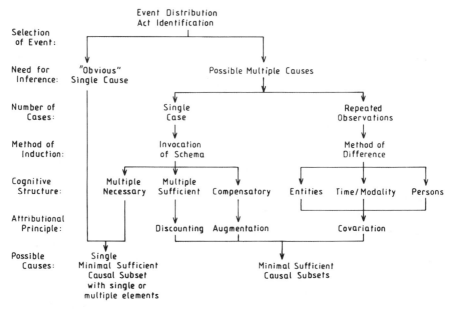

Figure 20. Model of the attribution process. (After Shaver, 1985, p. 60. Copyright 1985 by Springer-Verlag. Adapted by permission)

perception theory (Bem, 1967) are presented. This is followed by an analysis of the different attributional tendencies in actors and observers and a discussion of the importance of attention for causal attribution. Finally, motivational influences on the process of attribution and responsibility attributions will be considered.

Figure 20 summarizes different attributional processes which are discussed in the next sections. The starting point is an event or event distribution which is categorized at a specific level of act identification (see Vallacher & Wegner, 1985, 1987). The term "event distribution" is used because different persons (e.g., actors and observers) may perceive an event in slightly different ways. The concepts mentioned in Figure 20 will be discussed in detail in the following sections.

Causal Relations

Different types of relations between a cause and an effect are basic to causal understanding (Alloy, Abramson, Metalsky & Hartlage, 1988; Bindra, 1976). Both man and animals have information about correlated events in the environment. For example, Pavlov's dogs learnt a contingency between a sound and food. These relationships can be quantified by conditional probabilities. The difference between the conditional and the simple probability of the joint occurrence of cause and effect shows what value that cause has as a predictor for the effect (Bindra, 1976).

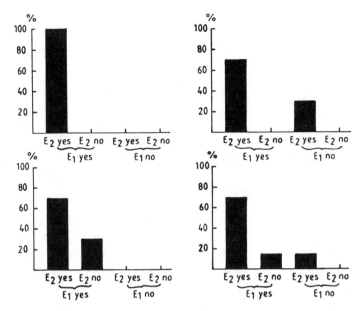

Figure 21. Hypothetical distributions of relative frequencies of observation of two events. E_1 and E_2 represent a cause and an effect. The relative frequency of the occurrence/nonoccurrence of E (in %) is given in the first/second column. *Top left,* the case in which E_1 is a necessary and sufficient condition for E_2; *top right,* E_1 is a sufficient condition for E_2; *bottom left,* E_1 is a necessary condition for E_2; *bottom right,* E_1 is a contributory condition for E_2. (Modified from *"A Theory of Intelligent Behavior"* (p. 127) by D. Bindra. New York: John Wiley & Sons, Ltd. Copyright 1976 by John Wiley & Sons, Ltd. Reprinted by permission)

If one tabulates the frequencies of occurrence of an event in a 2×2 schema, four different types of causal relationships can be identified (Figure 21). In case 1 cause E_1 is a necessary and sufficient condition for the occurrence of effect E_2. In case 2 E_1 is not a necessary, only a sufficient condition for the occurrence of E_2. In the third case E_1 is necessary but not sufficient for E_2. In the last case E_1 is neither necessary nor sufficient but does contribute to the likelihood of the effect E_2 (Bindra, 1976). These types of causal relationships represent the simplest knowledge about causation.

More elaborate accounts of causal attributions which are directly related to conditional probabilities are presented by Ajzen and Fishbein (1975, 1983; see also Fincham & Jaspars, 1983; Fischhoff & Lichtenstein, 1978). A treatment of this theory which is based on the Bayes theorem (see Chap. 2, "A model of subjective probabilities of stereotypes"), is beyond the scope of this book.

The Naive Analysis of Behavior

Heider's book (1958) on the psychology of interpersonal relationships contains a pioneering analysis of implicit theories explaining behavior. The "commonsense" theory emphasizes the attribution of dispositional, invariant characteristics. An action is put down to factors in the environment and factors in the person, which represent effective forces the addition of which is assumed to determine the actions of a person. The action outcome x is dependent on the effective forces of the person and the environment — in Heider's (1958, p. 82) terms: $x = f$ (ff person, ff environment).

The effective personal force is assumed to consist of the multiplication of a power and a motivational factor (see Darley & Goethals, 1980). While ability is the most important factor of power, motivation is determined by the perceived intentions (*trying*) and the exertion (how hard the person is trying). The multiplicative combination makes clear that the effective personal force should be zero when either the power or the *trying* is zero. In Heider's (1958, p. 83) terms: $x = f$ (trying, power, environment).

The outcome of an action is determined not only by dispositional factors, but also by situational influences. Heider (1958, p. 86) assumes that the dispositional power together with the environmental force determine whether an action can be carried out or not: $can = f$ (power, ability — difficulty of environmental factors). An easy task can be solved by a person with little ability. The solution of a difficult task requires great ability. The *can* as well as the *trying* then determine together the outcome of the action. In Heider's (1958, p. 86) terms: $x = f$ (trying, can). Furthermore, Heider (1958) assumes that the *can* can best be proved by actual behavior (p. 87): "Actions speak louder than words" (see Box T 8).

Box T8. "Actions speak louder than words"
The assumption that "actions speak louder than words" was confirmed in two studies in which perceivers had to judge the abilities of a target person (Reeder & Fulks, 1980). Good and poor performances led to extreme conclusions about the ability of the target person if they manifested themselves

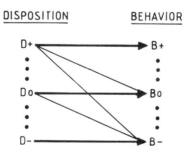

Figure 22. Hierarchically restrictive schema of attribution. $+$, 0, and $-$ stand for very high, moderate, and very low levels of the disposition or behavior. The *bold arrows* describe the dominant schema of the conclusions while the *thin arrows* represent alternative conclusions. (After Reeder & Brewer, 1979, p. 68. Copyright 1979 by the American Psychological Association. Adapted by permission)

in behavior rather than in verbal remarks by the target about his/her performance.

Furthermore, a tendency was visible according to which good performance suggested high ability on the part of the actor whereas poor performance only led to the conclusion of low ability when the situational pressure favored good performance. When the situation suggested showing poor performance for tactical reasons, this was not interpreted as low ability (Reeder & Fulks, 1980; see also Reeder, 1985; Reeder & Brewer, 1979; Snyder & Wicklund, 1981).

These results can be traced back to a hierarchically restrictive schema of attribution (see Figure 22) since the observer seems to reckon with the possibility that someone who shows poor performance is presenting himself as worse than he/she is. Conversely, it is assumed that someone of low ability is not in a position to produce a good performance. A similar asymmetry can be seen for extroversion: extroverts are credited more often with the ability to behave introvertly than introverts with the ability to behave extrovertly.

Heider (1958, p. 82) gives an instructive example of the naive analysis of action. A person is rowing a boat across a lake. What are appropriate causal attributions for this action? Heider describes some options: "He is *trying* to row the boat across the lake"; "He has the *ability* to row the boat across the lake"; "He *can* row the boat across the lake"; "He *wants* to row the boat across the lake"; "It is *difficult* to row the boat across the lake"; "Today there is a good *opportunity* for him to row the boat across the lake"; "It is sheer *luck* that he succeeded in rowing the boat across the lake." These causal descriptions were analyzed more fully by Weiner (1972, 1986; see "Attributional theories of achievement behavior and depression").

Heider (1958, pp. 100–109) analyzed in some detail the distinction between personal and impersonal causality. Personal causality is identified with intentionality. It is characterized by two aspects: equifinality and local causality. Equifinality describes a case where several independent means are each a sufficient condition to reach the goal region. Therefore, equifinality is defined as invariance of the end and variability of the means. The goal may in principle be achieved by different methods which are equivalent in the sense that they can serve to reach the goal. Personal causality does not hinge on one method of realization. The goal is reached by the method which is most appropriate under the given circumstances. Local causality refers to the fact that the person controls the means which are used to reach the goal.

Intentional actions involve the use of means for achieving some other objective. They are performed by actors who believe that they have the ability and knowledge to reach the objective and who want the objective to be realized (Shaver, 1985, pp. 121–122). *Want* refers to motivational forces which are directed toward reaching a certain state of affairs (Heider, 1958, pp. 16–17).

Heider (1958, p. 109) notes that the concept of trying is closely related to personal causality and motivation. Impersonal causation, in contrast, is characterized by multifinality. That means that an impersonal event will lead to different effects depending on the circumstances. For example, a falling stone might hit a man or might fall into the water and cause a wave. More will be said about intentional actions in the section "Attribution of responsibility and blame".

It is impossible to cover all the ideas Heider (1958) presents in his pioneering book. An excellent presentation of many of his ideas can be found in Shaver (1985). A collection of Heider's later contributions on causal attributions can be found in *Fritz Heider's Notebooks*, which have been edited by Benesh-Weiner (see also Benesh & Weiner, 1982).

Attributional Theories of Achievement Behavior and Depression

The naive analysis of behavior was developed further by Weiner, Frieze, Kukla, Reed, Rest and Rosenbaum (1972) and Weiner (1972, 1979, 1985b, 1986) with respect to success and failure in achievement situations. Weiner et al. (1972) and Weiner (1972) drew a now classic distinction between stable and variable causes as well as between internal (dispositional) and external (situational) causes of performance (see Box T9).

Box T9. Basic attributional dimensions in achievement situations
The internal/external distinction is reminiscent of Heider's assumption that the outcome of an action depends on a combination of an effective personal force and an effective environmental force. Heider (1958) divided the personal force further into a power (ability) factor and a motivational factor which refers to the actor's intention (trying) and the intensity of the effort (exertion).

The stability dimension was also included in Heider's analysis. He considered task difficulty as an invariant characteristic and luck as a more variable external factor. Weiner and his coworkers combined both dimensions in a 2×2 framework. Although the cell entries were first labeled ability (internal, stable), effort (internal, unstable), task difficulty (external, stable),

Table 18. Classification schema of perceived causes of achievement. (From Weiner, 1986, p. 47. Copyright 1986 by Springer-Verlag. Reprinted by permission)

	Internal	External
Stable	Aptitude	Objective task characteristics
Unstable	Temporary exertion	Chance

and luck (external, unstable), Weiner (1986) proposed the labels shown in Table 18 because he wanted to avoid possible misunderstandings especially with regard to ability and effort. Ability is amenable to modification (and therefore unstable) if learning is possible and effort is often conceived as a dispositional term because it can be related to traits like laziness.

Later the 2×2 schema was extended by addition of a controllability dimension (Weiner, 1979). A cause is perceived as controllable when it can be volitionally manipulated. Uncontrollable causes are understood to be factors which escape conscious influence. An example of this dichotomy would be arriving late because of oversleeping (controllable) or because of a physical handicap (uncontrollable). Another example of a controllable cause is effort and of an uncontrollable cause is mood.

The striving for control was also mentioned by Heider (1958) in his naive analysis of action. This is not surprising given Heider's special interest in dispositional attributions, which he related to the striving for a "stable, predictable, and controllable world" (p. 80). Perceived invariances like abilities and traits were regarded as the reference points for understanding the social world. From a different viewpoint, the just world theory (Lerner, 1980) stresses the importance of people's motivation to control what happens to them. In a similar vein, defensive attribution (see "Motivational influences on the attribution process") might be understood on the basis of the need to exercise control over one's fate (Chaikin & Darley, 1973).

Weiner (1986) discusses the merits and problems associated with a third attribution dimension. While the striving for personal control is a deep-rooted motive in human beings (see Kelley, 1972a; Lefcourt, 1976; Seligman, 1975), it proves to be problematic to speak of controllable external factors, as this seems to be self-contradictory. Although it is possible to think of controllable external factors in the sense of factors controllable by others, this flexibility in the use of the concept of personal control seems to be unwarranted. Therefore, the conclusion seems to be justified that the controllability dimension can be crossed with the stability dimension in the

Table 19. Examples of perceived causes for failure in an examination

	Internal		External/ uncontrollable
	Controllable	Uncontrollable	
Stable	Low interest in the subject	Examination anxiety	High task difficulty
Unstable	Distraction by new girl-/ boyfriend	Sickness	Bad luck

domain of internal causes but not in the domain of external causes. External causes are uncontrollable by definition.

Table 19 contains examples of perceived causes of failure as an illustration of the resulting classification schema. It should be added that the three dimensions are not completely independent as perceived facets of the causes of behavior.

While the distinction between internality, stability, and controllability (Weiner, 1986) seems to be theoretically valid, the three dimensions do not exhaust the possibilities of causal dimensions. For example, Abramson, Seligman and Teasdale (1978), who also used the dimensions of internality and stability for the classification of attributions after failure, added the dimension of globality of attributions (see also Alloy et al., 1988). While global causes are relevant for a wide variety of outcomes, specific causes affect only a specific set of outcomes.

For example, the attribution of failure in a math examination to low intelligence is global while attribution of the failure to lack of numerical fluency is specific. Abramson et al. (1978) assume that internality, stability, and globality are orthogonal dimensions of causal attributions. Later work has demonstrated that these causal dimensions are very useful for the understanding of depression (Peterson & Seligman, 1984; see Box I 14).

Box I 14. Depressogenic attributional style
Seligman and his coworkers assumed that a depressogenic attributional style — attributing negative events to internal, stable, and global factors — is a risk factor for depression in adults (Seligman, Abramson, Semmel & von Baeyer, 1979) and children (Seligman, Peterson, Kaslow, Tannenbaum, Alloy & Abramson, 1984). A specially devised Attributional Style Questionnaire (Peterson, Semmel, von Baeyer, Abramson, Metalsky & Seligman, 1982) was used to measure individual tendencies towards internal versus external, stable versus unstable, and global versus specific attributions for positive and negative events. The Attributional Style Questionnaire is a self-report instrument which presents six hypothetical positive and negative events. Respondents are asked to write down the major cause of each hypothetical event and assess the internality, stability, and globality of the cause on rating scales.

The attributional reformulation of the learned helplessness model (the hopelessness theory of depression) elicited mixed empirical results (an alternative model was suggested by Pyszczynski & Greenberg, 1987). In a summary of 61 investigations, Peterson, Villanova and Raps (1985) found that 26 out of 49 (53%) supported the internality-depression link, 16 studies out of 35 (46%) supported the stability-depression link, and 21 out of 27 studies (78%) supported the globality-depression link. Support for the depressogenic attributional style hypothesis was found in 26 out of 35 studies (74%). Support for the hypothesis was stronger when the investigators employed large sample sizes, when the number of events sampled was large, and when hypothetical events were used (as in the Attributional Style Questionnaire). A critical analysis of the relationship between depressogenic attributional style, negative life events, hopelessness, and depression is presented by Alloy et al. (1988).

Anderson (1983 a) investigated the causal structures for different situations involving success and failure. Subjects read brief descriptions of 20 achievement situations and generated plausible causes for the target person's outcome. An example of such a situation is: "X has just won a game of Scrabble [the word game]." Only the first cause which a student generated was used in an additional study. This time students assessed the changeability, locus within or outside the person, globality, stability, intentionality, and controllability of the 63 causes generated. In general, these dimensional ratings were highly correlated. For example, the correlation between locus and stability was 0.66, which is highly significant. Only globality and stability were nearly unrelated.

These results are in agreement with Carroll and Payne's analysis of the "think out loud" protocols of judicial experts who evaluated offenders (summarized in Carroll, 1978). They found that attributions frequently fell into the internal-stable cell. In another study (Carroll, 1978), the causes of an offense given by members of the Pennsylvania Board of Probation and Parole in open-ended assessments on a posthearing questionnaire were coded with regard to internality, stability, and intentionality. Results indicated that internality and stability were highly correlated because high internality was usually associated with high stability of a cause. In general, the degree of correlation between causal dimensions seems to be content specific. Judgments of the causes of crimes seem to elicit very high correlations between internality and stability because trait attributions for crimes are very popular. In other content areas the correlation should be lower.

Although the attributional dimensions tend to be correlated, it is not necessary to abandon the whole multidimensional approach. For example, Carroll and Payne (1976) assumed that the internal/external distinction is more related to seriousness of the crime and severity of punishment while the stability dimension is more closely related to expected recidivism (see Carroll & Wiener, 1982). This is in agreement with Weiner et al. (1972), who assumed that internality is related to affective reactions and stability to expectations.

Empirical studies using factor analysis or multidimensional scaling of causal attributions identified nearly unanimously a dimension of internality (e.g., Meyer & Koelbl, 1982; Wimer & Kelley, 1982; Michela, Peplau & Weeks, 1982). In addition, most of the studies found a stability dimension (e.g., Meyer & Koelbl, 1982; Michela et al., 1982) and a dimension which might be labeled controllability (e.g., Anderson, 1983a; Meyer & Koelbl, 1982).

Studies using the Attributional Style Questionnaire (Peterson et al., 1982) show that it is possible to measure reliably the dimensions stability, internality, and globality. The intercorrelations of the scale are, especially for negative events, quite low (between 0.18 and 0.45). Therefore, these results indicate that the three dimensions should be treated independently of each other.

Wimer and Kelley (1982) and Weiner (1986) discuss the similarities and differences between controllability and intentionality. The two dimensions are highly intercorrelated. People usually exert control over what they intend. But this is not necessarily the case. A student might intend to invest all his effort in studying for the next exams, but some friends may interfere with these intentions. Therefore, it is useful to differentiate between intent and control on a conceptual level. The results of Wimer and Kelley (1982) indicate that intentionality is perceived to be located within the person, with the emphasis on motivational properties. Controllability was related to duration and awareness, controllable causes being perceived as being of shorter duration and involving greater awareness. Weiner (1986) subsumes both dimensions under the label *controllability* although he acknowledges that both dimensions have different associations.

With regard to globality, Weiner (1986) assumes that, like stability, it is related to generalizability. While stability concerns the question of consistency over time, globality refers to consistency over situations. The empirical correlation between these dimensions was 0.45 for negative events and 0.59 for positive events in the study by Peterson et al. (1982). Both dimensions have a common denominator because consistency over time is in everyday life confounded with consistency over situations.

It is beyond the scope of this presentation to go into further details of Weiner's attribution model of achievement-related behavior. A simplified version of his theory is shown in Figure 23. Inspection shows that causal attributions determine expectancy and affect. Specifically, the stability dimension is assumed to influence expectancies and internality (and controllability) determines affective reactions (see also Weiner, 1985b). The achievement motive may influence the predominant attributional dimension which a person is inclined to use. In addition, children might respond with optimism and hope or pessimism and negative self-cognitions after failure (mastery-oriented children vs. helpless children; Dweck & Leggett, 1988).

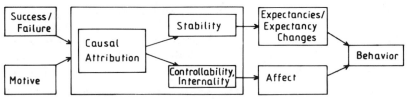

Figure 23. Schematic representation of Weiner's model of achievement-related behavior. (After Schmalt, 1986, p. 88. Copyright 1986 by Verlag W. Kohlhammer. Adapted by permission)

These are only a few comments on the multidimensional analysis of attributions and the relationship between attributional dimensions and behavior (attributional theories). Most evidence is available for Weiner's attributional theory of achievement behavior (Dweck & Goetz, 1978; Weiner, 1985b, 1986), the hopelessness theory of depression (Abramson et al., 1978; Alloy et al., 1988), Fincham's theory of attribution in close relationships (Fincham, 1985; Fincham & Bradbury, 1987; see also "Attributions in close relationships"), and Carroll and Payne's (1976) attributional theory of judicial decisions (see also Carroll & Wiener, 1982). In addition, there is evidence that judgments about giving help are related to the controllability of the cause of the dependency (Barnes, Ickes & Kidd, 1979; Ickes & Kidd, 1976; Meyer & Mulherin, 1980; Weiner, 1980a, b).

Finally, the importance of causal attributions for affective reactions toward the event is stressed by Weiner (e.g., Weiner, Russell & Lerman, 1978, 1979). For example, Weiner (1980a) found that judges infer affective reactions from perceived controllability of the fate of the person in need (e.g., high controllability → anger). These reactions then influence judgments about giving help (e.g., anger → not helpful; pity → helpful). Therefore, the general model is based on the assumption "that attributions guide feelings and feelings direct behavior" (Weiner, 1980a, p. 681).

Causal Schemata

Causal relationships are the relationships between a cause and an effect. Causal schemata are the relationships between two (or more) possible causes and one effect. They are used above all when complex material has to be explained without a systematic collection of data, such as an experimenter would have, being available (Kelley, 1973). While the covariation principle is used when repeated observations were made, configuration concepts are applied when only a single observation is available.

Kelley (1972b, p. 151) defines a causal schema as "a general conception the person has about how certain kinds of causes interact to produce a specific kind of effect. Each schema can be described in terms of a hypothetical matrix of data which summarizes the attributor's beliefs and assumptions about the distribution of the effect over various combinations of the causal factors." Kelley (1972b, p. 152) states further that causal schemata contain statements as to how information is used to draw causal conclusions. They are a repertoire of abstract ideas about causal connections.

Which schemata are included in this repertoire? Two of the truth functions included in Table 20 (see also Staudenmayer, 1975) have received particular attention: the schema of multiple necessary causes (8) and the schema of multiple sufficient causes (2). Other different truth functions deserve similar interest. That is especially true for schemata 7 and 10 as well as for schemata 5 and 3, which are called biconditional and exclusive disjunction on the one

Table 20. Possible truth functions in the two-valued propositional logic

		1	2	3	4	5	6	7	8	9	10	11	12	13	14	15	16
p	q	t	t	t	t	t	t	t	t	f	f	f	f	f	f	f	f
p	q̄	t	t	t	t	f	f	f	f	t	t	t	t	f	f	f	f
p̄	q	t	t	f	f	t	t	f	f	t	t	f	f	t	t	f	f
p̄	q̄	t	f	t	f	t	f	t	f	t	f	t	f	t	f	t	f

p and q stand for two propositions. A bar over p or q symbolizes a negation of a statement; t and f stand for true and false.

hand and conditional and reversed conditional on the other in propositional logic (Bierhoff & Bierhoff-Alfermann, 1983).

Schema of Multiple Necessary Causes

Causal schemata can be described as rules of propositional logic (Bierhoff & Bierhoff-Alfermann, 1983). The schema of multiple necessary causes states – in accordance with the conjunctive connection of causes (truth function 8 in Table 20) – that the effect only occurs when both causes are present. One cause in the absence of the second cannot elicit the effect. The quintessence is that the effect depends on the presence of both causal factors. Kelley (1972b) hypothesized about the circumstances under which the application of this schema was especially likely. What qualities should the effect have if it is to be attributed to two available causes at the same time? The answer is that the more extreme an effect, the more likely is a conjunctive connection of causes. Conversely, effects which lie in the middle should be traced back to only one of the causal factors more often than not.

Evidence has been found for the adequacy of this hypothesis (Cunningham & Kelley, 1975; Kun & Weiner, 1973) – unexpected, unusual events are more likely to be explained by several causes than ordinary, everyday events. The subjective logic is clear: one assumes that one single cause is not sufficient to explain an unusual event. One has to postulate an interaction between several factors in order to do justice to such an event (see Box T 10).

Box T 10. Emergent effects and resultant effects
A simple method of demonstrating schemata of multiple necessary causes was used by Cunningham and Kelley (1975). They presented the perceivers with subject-verb-object sentences describing interpersonal relationships (such as "Ted feels himself to be inferior to Norm" or "Tom helps Phil"). The sentences contained either a moderate or an extreme modifier ("Tom feels himself to be slightly inferior to Norm" versus "Tom helps Phil a great deal").

For each statement two possible causes were given, one of which (*a*) related to the actor and the second (*b*) to the target person who was named as object of the action. The perceivers had to decide on a 7-point scale to what extent *both* causes *a* and *b* must have been present in the individual cases. A high score on this rating meant that the schema of multiple necessary causes had been used.

A main effect of extremity was evident, viewed over all the interpersonal events presented: more extreme events were traced back more often to both causes. (However, this effect was not equally evident for all cases. While it was significant for the verb *helps*, for example, *feels inferior to* produced a zero effect. Nevertheless, the general trend of the mean differences lay clearly in the expected direction.)

If causal attributions for extreme events follow the schema of multiple necessary causes, two cases can be distinguished. In addition, extreme events are sometimes explained by only one cause (patterns 3 and 4).

1. The generalization with respect to target persons and actors increases with the size of the event: i.e., one believes that the actor behaves towards other target persons in the same way and that other actors show the same behavior to the given target person. This characterizes a schema of multiple necessary causes in which each factor alone has a small effect but both together have a large effect ("resultant effect schema"; see Table 21). An example of this is the statement "The Labour Party candidate beat his opponent by an overwhelming margin in the recent by-election in Durham." The extreme effect has multiple necessary causes (e.g., strength of the winner, weakness of the loser). The winner is expected to win against other opponents and the loser is expected to lose against other opponents.

2. The generalization with respect to target persons and actors decreases with an increase in the magnitude of the event. In this case only the specific combination of both factors leads to the effect ("emergent effect schema"; see Table 22). An example of this is the statement "Charles likes Ed." The mutual liking is specific for the combination of two given people Charles

Table 21. Resultant effect schema. (Reprinted with permission from Cunningham & Kelley, 1975, *Journal of Personality*, Vol. 43, No. 1, p. 76. Copyright 1975 by Duke University Press)

		Cause A	
		Absent	Present
Cause B	Present	E	EE
	Absent		E

E, effect; EE, resultant effect.

Table 22. Emergent effect schema. (Reprinted with permission from Cunningham & Kelley, 1975, *Journal of Personality*, Vol. 43, No. 1, p. 76. Copyright 1975 by Duke University Press)

		Cause A	
		Absent	Present
Cause B	Present		E
	Absent		

E, emergent effect.

and Ed and allows no generalization to other combinations of people. The emergent effect schema is applied when the effect appears "out of nowhere" and has multiple necessary causes (Cunningham & Kelley, 1975).

3. The perceived causation is determined by an attribution to the actor. With increasing magnitude of the event the perceiver generalizes to other possible target persons. For example, in the case "Ted feels himself to be greatly inferior to Norm" the generalization is that Ted feels himself to be greatly inferior to other target persons. Only one cause, i.e., that connected with the actor, increases in importance because of the greater extremity. Therefore, a schema of multiple necessary causes is not invoked.

4. Finally, in the last case an attribution to the target person is to be expected. With increasing magnitude of the event the perceiver generalizes more to other actors. At the same time, only the cause which relates to the target person should be increased in importance by greater extremity. The results from the statement "Fred dominates Bill" tend in this direction.

Schema of Multiple Sufficient Causes

The schema of multiple sufficient causes states that each cause taken by itself, as well as the combination of both, can explain the effect. The truth function used is the inclusive disjunction. If an effect is present, one cannot conclude with certainty whether a given cause, e.g., a positively valued in comparison with a negatively valued factor, led to the effect or not (see Table 23).

The study by Thibaut and Riecken (1955) is one of the first empirical studies in which attribution principles are evident. Since the results have been replicated (Ring, 1964; Strickland, 1958; Kruglanski, 1970), the study will be described briefly.

Three people were involved. One had a high status and another a low status relative to the perceiver. After the perceiver had asked both people for help and both had complied, the perceiver had to judge to what extent each of the people asked had agreed voluntarily or because of external pressure.

Table 23. Causal schema for multiple sufficient causes. (From Kelley, 1972b, p. 152. Copyright 1972 General Learning Press. Reprinted by permission of Silver Burdett and Ginn)

		Cause A	
		Absent	Present
Cause B	Present	E	E
	Absent		E

E, effect.

In the case of high status an internal attribution was preferred and the behavior was more often put down to a voluntary decision. In the case of low status the behavior was mostly explained by an external cause.

In the latter instance the perceiver can conceive two possible reasons for the compliance of the low status person. Either the difference in status means that someone with low status feels forced to comply, or a person helps of his/her own accord. Here are two plausible causes to choose from, either of which, alone or in combination, could have caused the compliance. Therefore, the perceiver should apply the schema of multiple sufficient causes.

While these results concern the relationship between antecedents and causal attribution, other results refer to the relationship between the antecedents and consequences of causal attribution. It is interesting to see that the change in the evaluation of the two people between the beginning and the end of the experiment was different. The change was more positive for a high status than for a low status person. Someone who, because his status is high, appears to help for internal reasons gains more respect than someone who appears to give in to environmental pressure (Bierhoff & Bierhoff-Alfermann, 1983).

Discounting and Augmentation

If two causes could each individually have caused one effect, a degree of uncertainty arises when answering the question of which cause is responsible for the effect. This uncertainty has important consequences which Kelley (1972a) described using the principle of discounting. This says that a given cause (e.g., a positively valued cause of another person's behavior) is discounted if a second plausible cause (e.g., a less positively valued explanation) is available. Empirical studies have shown that people do judge according to this principle quite early in childhood (see "Discounting"). Up till now I have assumed that the cause which appears plausible favors the effect, brings it about, or facilitates its occurrence. But one has to divide the causes according to whether they facilitate or suppress and hinder the occurrence of the effect (Kelley, 1972a, b). If an effect occurs while an impeding and a supporting cause are in force, the strength of the supporting cause is rated particularly highly (in comparison to the case in which only the supporting cause is plausible). This direct compensation of an impeding cause by a supporting one leads to the augmentation of the supporting cause (Bierhoff & Bierhoff-Alfermann, 1983).

Augmentation

The importance of the principle of augmentation was tested in performance situations (Kun, 1977) and in interpersonal conflict situations (Enzle, Hansen & Lowe, 1975). It was also demonstrated at the level of purely perceptual judgments (Kassin & Lowe, 1979) by testing the causal perception of movements of geometric figures (see Box I 15).

Box I15. A perceptual approach to the augmentation principle
Series of movements by geometric figures were used by Heider and Simmel (1944) in a classic study to examine causal judgments. A typical scene with two triangles and a circle as well as a large, opened rectangle is shown in Figure 24. In a cartoon film the geometric figures moved in such a way that it looked as if they were entering the rectangle, chasing each other, or fighting one another. It is hardly surprising that the perceivers, when they were instructed to interpret the film as well as when they were instructed to interpret the movements as actions by people, gave anthropomorphic descriptions.

In a similar approach, Michotte (1963) asked the question under which conditions of visual stimulation causal concepts were used in the verbal description. In a typical experimental procedure two colored rectangles

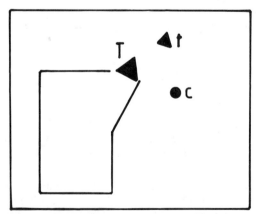

Figure 24. Cartoon picture to investigate phenomenal causality. (From *"The Psychology of Interpersonal Relations"* (p. 31) by F. Heider, New York: John Wiley & Sons, Ltd. Copyright 1958 by John Wiley & Sons, Ltd. Reprinted by permission)

were shown. Rectangle A, which is on the left of rectangle B, begins to move in the direction of B. When A reaches rectangle B, B begins to move at the same speed as A, so that they appear to touch one another for a moment before disappearing. Under these circumstances the impression aroused in the perceivers is almost unanimously that A bumped into rectangle B or carried B while B appeared to be completely passive.

An approach based on perception has from a methodological point of view certain advantages for the analysis of causal schemata: one can avoid for the most part verbal communication problems as could occur in studies like those by Cunningham and Kelley (1975) or McArthur (1972). Normative expectations about the relationship between the actors or events are also avoided.

Continuing the approach of Heider and Simmel (1944) and especially that of Michotte (1963), Kassin and Lowe (1979) showed children of different ages (preschool, second grade, fourth grade) an 8-s-long cartoon film in which two triangles were shown moving towards a house (Figure 25). While one triangle had a clear path, the other had to move a heavy obstacle out of the way. Both triangles were moving for the same length of time and entered the house at the same time.

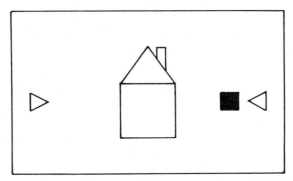

Figure 25. Cartoon picture to demonstrate the augmentation principle. (After Kassin & Lowe, 1979, p. 730. Reproduced from *Child Development*, Vol. 50, No. 3. Copyright 1979 by the Society for Research in Child Development. Reprinted by permission)

The results show that preschool children already have an elementary understanding of augmentation. Of these children, 93% said that the triangle which moves an obstacle out of the way tries harder to reach the house (second grade 87%; fourth grade 100%). For the ages tested, age differences were only found in the verbal explanations which followed these judgments. Although preschool children applied the principle of augmentation on an elementary level, they could often not give an adequate explanation for their choice (40% adequate explanations in comparison to 67% and 100% in the second and fourth grades).

Augmentation can be extended from all-or-nothing comparisons to graded comparisons (Kun, 1977). One could, for instance, show obstacles of different sizes in Figure 25 to express different degrees of hindrance. In this case there was a clear developmental trend in the cross-sectional comparison (Kassin & Lowe, 1979): only 33% of the preschool children answered according to the extended principle (in comparison to 73% and 93% in the second and fourth grades). There was a similar trend in the use of suitable explanations for the choice of the triangle which makes more effort to reach the house.

The augmentation principle might lead to a bonus effect when a reward is made dependent on certain preconditions. For example, in the conditional "If you do X, then you'll get Y" the reward Y is dependent on carrying out X. An inhibitory cause is introduced which must be overcome to reach Y. Therefore, the augmentation principle comes into play. The prediction is that Y should be more attractive when it is made contingent on X than when no contingency exists (Boggiano & Main, 1986; Lepper, Sagotsky, Dafoe & Greene, 1982).

In several empirical studies this augmentation hypothesis was confirmed. For example, children were asked to play some puzzle games. In one condition, the experimenter introduced a contingency between two puzzles: "*If* you play the maze, *then* you will get a chance to play the hidden-picture puzzle" (from Boggiano & Main, 1986, p. 1117). In the second condition, no contingency was mentioned. In both conditions the children played with each puzzle. Afterwards children could select the puzzle they preferred. The predicted enhancement effect was obtained, children in the contingent condition being more likely to choose the bonus activity as a last game.

The augmentation principle is invoked in many situations. Suls, Witenberg and Gutkin (1981) asked students to evaluate actors who helped a target person who had either helped before or had refused to help. While positive reciprocity should facilitate the willingness to help, prior refusal of help should inhibit the willingness to help. In accordance with the augmentation principle, students evaluated the actor who was helpful in an inhibitory context more favorably than an actor who had previously received help.

Discounting

Kun (1977) deduced from the comparison of direct and inverse compensation that the augmentation principle should be learned first by children. This hypothesis agrees with the fact that perceivers have difficulties drawing correct conclusions out of negative evidence (Wason & Johnson-Laird, 1972). The discounting principle should be learned second.

In a study by Kassin, Lowe and Gibbons (1980) which used the perceptual approach by Michotte (1963), nursery school children as well as children from the second, fourth and sixth grades and college students watched cartoon films in which it was shown how two triangles moved towards a house at the same speed and how they arrived simultaneously. One triangle was "carried" by a

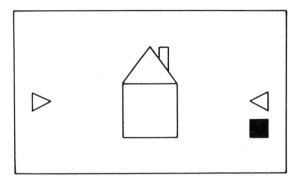

Figure 26. Cartoon picture to illustrate the discounting principle. (After Kassin, Lowe & Gibbons, 1980, p. 723. Copyright 1980 by the American Psychological Association. Adapted by permission)

black square insomuch as it began to move when the square had approached it and was located directly under the triangle (see Figure 26).

Only from the second grade upwards was successful application of the discounting principle observed; in answer to the question of which triangle wanted to get to the house more, the children pointed more often than one would expect by chance to the triangle which had not been "carried." Furthermore, there was an increase in the number of appropriate explanations between the fourth grade and college from 12.5% via 43.75% (sixth grade) to 75%. In comparison to the results from Kassin and Lowe (1979), who used a comparable experimental paradigm for the augmentation principle (see "Augmentation"), it can now be seen that understanding the discounting principle begins later, since the augmentation principle can be used correctly even by pre-school children. In the same vein, Shultz, Butkowsky, Pearce and Shanfield (1975) found that discounting was used by 9- and 13-year-old children but not by 5-year-olds.

When short stories are used to study the augmentation and discounting principles, information processing is more complex than in the elementary perception studies by Kassin and his colleagues. Nevertheless, Smith (1975) found a considerable increase in the adequate use of the discounting principle up to the fourth grade. Preschool children seemed to guess randomly.

It seems to be important for such an experimental approach that comprehension and remembering are guaranteed, especially for younger children whose working memory is relatively small (Ruble & Rholes, 1981). Random guessing can be caused by inability to remember or to understand. In fact, if one ensures an appropriate form of communication, one can show that preschool children also give answers consistent with the schema. If one summarizes the choices between pairs of stories (each of which were contrasted with one another and featured boys who played with or without expecting a reward for this), there is a small group of preschool children (ca. 10% − 20%) who use the discounting principle consistently while a larger group (55% − 70%) uses an additive model (Karniol & Ross, 1976a). In answer to the question "Which boy really wanted to play with toy X?" the "adders" named the boy whose mother had promised him a reward (while the "discounters" named the other boy who played of his own accord).

So one can find two groups of lay theorists in this preschool group. The one group follows the central idea of classic conditioning while the others answer according to the attribution theory (Karniol & Ross, 1976b). However, the proportion of adders decreases with increasing age (63.2% − 54.5% − 9.1% in the first, second, and third grades respectively according to Karniol & Ross, 1979), and the attribution theorists gain the upper hand (10.5% − 27.2% − 63.6% in the respective grades).

Which processes are behind the move away from the additive model to the discounting model? One possibility is that it depends on which meaning is accorded to the reward (Ruble & Rholes, 1981). Karniol and Ross (1979) report on two experiments which support the hypothesis that adders see the reward as a positive incentive which increases the attractiveness of the toy while discounters see a (manipulative) influence in a reward. One consequence of this is that preschool children tend to reject the additive model and apply the discounting model when they clearly recognize the manipulative intention of the reward.

To sum up, one can say that the use of the discounting principle was observed in the second grade, especially when elementary perception processes were observed, and can even be found in preschool children if the manipulative intention of an action is made clear. This suggests that causal schemata are not used automatically in everyday life but that the application of the schema depends on the interpretation of the social/physical context (Karniol & Ross, 1979; Kassin et al., 1980 in the comparison of experiments 1 and 2). When stories were used the discounting principle was used by children aged 9 and above (Shultz et al., 1975).

The discounting of the importance of a cause as soon as a second plausible cause occurs appears to be logical and rational judgment behavior because the effect remains the same while the number of plausible causes increases. If one imagines a rational information processor who endeavors to take all relevant information into consideration, the proportion of the explanation put down to a given cause should decrease as the number of plausible alternative explanations increases (Bierhoff & Bierhoff-Alfermann, 1983).

This logic is comparable with the functioning of a beam balance. The effect is put on the one side while the causes are on the other side to "weigh up" the effect. If the weight of the effect remains the same then the addition of the second cause must be linked to a reduction in the weight of the first cause so that the balance is maintained. The augmentation principle can also be illustrated with this analogy. In this case the weight of the effect increases, so the weight of the available explanations for the occurrence of the effect has to increase to achieve equilibrium.

The effects of the discounting principle are illustrated by the use of superfluous rewards and deterrents. Extrinsic rewards undermine intrinsic interest in performing an activity in children and adults (Deci & Ryan, 1980; Lepper & Greene, 1978; see "Self-perception"). This overjustification effect is based in part on the tendency to see a rewarded activity as a means to an end. Extrinsic rewards discount intrinsic interest as a possible cause for performing the rewarded activity. This overjustification effect occurs when superfluous extrinsic incentives are used (Lepper, Sagotsky, Dafoe & Greene, 1982). Studies on the bonus effect also illustrate the negative consequences of imposing extrinsic incentives because they show that the *then* activity is evaluated favorably while the *if* activity is devalued (Boggiano & Main, 1986; Lepper et al., 1982, see "Augmentation").

The imposition of superfluous extrinsic constraints can have a detrimental effect on self-perception when they are used to deter the performance of an unattractive activity of low social desirability. In this case, two cognitions compete with each other: "I didn't want to do it" versus "I didn't do it because of the threat." As a consequence the first cognition is discounted.

This principle was applied in a study of cheating (Wilson & Lassiter, 1982). Students participated in a knowledge test and were presumably not motivated to cheat. In two experimental conditions the experimenter imposed a constraint before leaving the room. In the mild threat condition he said only "Please don't look at the answers until I come back." In the severe threat condition he added that the data could be ruined by cheating and that he would look in periodically. In the control group no comments were made.

In a second session which was held 8–20 days later an achievement test was administered which was very difficult and purportedly a measure of intelligence. Subjects were instructed to answer the questions in the given order and to work for only 1 min on each of the eight questions. It was assumed that the motivation to cheat in this test was strong. The experimenter left the test room and observed through a one-way mirror whether the subject followed the instructions. The number of times that subjects returned to earlier questions was the measure of cheating.

The results indicated that cheating was most common in the high threat condition and less common in the low threat condition. Control subjects cheated least. Superfluous threats used in the first session increased the tendency to cheat in the second session. The threats undermined the tendency of subjects to behave honestly in test situations. Subjects' attributions about their failure to cheat during the first session were assessed. While in the control condition internal attributions prevailed, in the severe threat condition external attributions were dominant. Subjects inferred from the imposition of threats the absence of intrinsic causes. These results illustrate the discounting principle because the presence of superfluous extrinsic constraints reduced the influence of intrinsic motives not to cheat. Powerful external constraints may backfire.

Discounting was also relevant for person perception when judges were asked to assess the likelihood of an actor cheating in the future who had not cheated in a situation where cheating was not probable (Lassiter, 1986). In a severe threat condition the likelihood of cheating in the future was assumed to be higher than in a low threat condition. In the control condition the perceived likelihood of cheating was lowest. Superfluous external constraints led to a discounting of internal reasons for not cheating.

Augmentation and Discounting in Concert

If one takes both the discounting and the augmentation principles into consideration, one can construct a hierarchy of the strength accorded to a particular facilitative cause in the face of a given effect (Bierhoff & Bierhoff-Alfermann, 1983, p. 107):

- Facilitative cause + strongly inhibitory cause (strongest)
- Facilitative cause + slightly inhibitory cause
- Facilitative cause alone
- Facilitative cause + slightly facilitative cause
- Facilitative cause + strongly facilitative cause (weakest).

The upwards deviations from the assessed strength of a facilitative cause that occurs alone are explained by the augmentation principle and the downwards deviations by the discounting principle.

Quattrone and Jones (1978) examined the effectiveness of both principles in a motivational context using the wish for positive self-presentation and for ingratiation. How does one prove that one has a particular ability and how does one exhibit this positive fact when it is definite that one has this ability (see Box I 16)?

Box I16. Attributional strategies in self-presentation

Let's assume there are three facilitative and three inhibitory factors available which relate to the existence of an ability (such as the ability to take on a role in a play). In each of these groups of three factors, one factor is very positively valued, one is neutral, and one is very negatively valued. (For example, a positive facilitative cause might be that you can refer to a number of positive reviews which you have received in the past. A negative inhibitory cause might be that in an article you yourself had described the role which you want to play as implausible and sentimental).

If someone has clearly proven his/her ability (e.g., with a performance in which he/she played the role with great success), he/she should only mention the most positive of the conducive causes. Mentioning the other two causes would reduce the importance of the most positive cause (i.e., discounting).

On the other hand, the augmentation principle leads people to like to be able to mention inhibitory factors when bringing evidence of one's ability. In these circumstances one has gained the ability despite adverse circumstances and therefore created the impressive picture of "heroic" achievement in the self-presentation.

If, however, the ability in question cannot be clearly proven, a self-presentation dilemma arises: one tries to make the ability seem probable by mentioning facilitative causes of differing quality and must then accept that a discounting of the most positive cause occurs and the overall impression is not so good. Furthermore, one must not mention inhibitory causes because this could lead to doubts as to whether one has the ability at all. This analysis leads to the assumption that there are systematic differences in self-presentation depending on whether conclusive evidence is available or not. If one ignores the positive conducive cause for a moment (which should be mentioned very often in both conditions), one should find that the other conducive causes are emphasized when conclusive evidence is not available. Conversely, when all necessary evidence is available the inhibitory causes should be stressed. This prediction results from a combination of the augmentation and discounting principles.

In order to test this hypothesis, subjects were required to select from a given pool of information facts to be disclosed to a hypothetical target person (e.g., the play's director). The subjects had to judge their willingness to disclose a particular fact on a 27-point scale (-13 to $+13$). The mean values for willingness to emphasize facilitative or inhibitory factors can be seen in Table 24.

Table 24. Tendency to emphasize facilitative and inhibitory influencing factors. (After Quattrone & Jones, 1978, p. 523. Reprinted, with permission, from *Journal of Experimental Social Psychology*, Vol. 14, No. 6. Copyright 1978 by Academic Press)

	Conclusive evidence	
	Not available	Available
Facilitative factors	3.96[a]	-1.21[b,c]
Inhibitory factors	-3.77[c]	-1.01[b]

Means which have no common superscript differ significantly ($p < 0.05$). The most facilitative factor was not included in the facilitative factors.

In the study by Quattrone and Jones (1978; Box I 16) one condition in which self-presentation and behavior (e.g., actual suitability for a given task) quite clearly correspond is compared with a condition in which correspondence is dubious. If there is correspondence, neutral and negative facilitative causes are held back while at the same time the self-presentation is augmented by mentioning inhibitory causes – a strategy which employs the discounting and the augmentation principle simultaneously.

It is interesting to note that the augmentation principle is also used if one expects not to be able to prove one's ability in the near future (see Wortman,

Costanzo & Witt, 1973) or if one thinks one has failed. In this case, mentioning inhibitory causes functions as an apology for a (possible) failure. This is a self-presentation strategy which can have the character of a self-created handicap if one falls back on, for example, drugs or alcohol as a justification for (possible) failure (Arkin & Baumgardner, 1985; Berglas & Jones, 1978; Jones, 1980). Self-handicapping may also take the form of selecting very difficult tasks after unexpected success with a first task (Greenberg, 1985).

Berglas and Jones (1978) used an analogy test which contained either mostly insoluble or mostly soluble items. Nevertheless, in both cases the impression was created by positive feedback that the items had been dealt with successfully. Before a further intellectual performance test the subjects were given the opportunity to take a performance-boosting or performance-blocking drug. Men (but not women) preferred the performance-blocking drug after success with the insoluble items (= noncontingent success; see also Kolditz & Arkin, 1982).

Uncertainty about success and perceived lack of control seem to cause an anxious attempt to externalize failure in future performance tests (i.e., to blame the performance-blocking drug). Paradoxically, the wish to maintain a positive performance level about which one is very uncertain, motivates a strategy of self-handicap, which makes failure in the future almost certain.

Greenberg (1985) arranged a successful performance with a first set of tasks and congratulated his subjects on their success. The success was achieved with soluble tasks (contingent success) or with insoluble tasks (noncontingent success). In addition, the performance was described as personally relevant or personally irrelevant. In the personally relevant condition this led to an increase in effort; however, this increase was greater in the contingent than in the noncontingent condition. This effect was reversed for the subjects in the personally irrelevant condition. Noncontingent success in an area of achievement central to a person's self-concept led to the selection of very difficult tasks which made failure highly likely.

Quattrone and Jones (1978) show that ordinary people can employ appropriate self-presentation strategies more or less consciously. The results from Berglas and Jones (1978) lead one to suppose that a subtle application of the augmentation principle is a possible cause for a history of drug or alcohol abuse. If someone has created a self-handicap, success reaches heroic proportions while failure is attributed externally and becomes pardonable without the person having to alter his/her positive self-image. This is especially true if the creation of the self-handicap is not private but public and observed (Kolditz & Arkin, 1982).

Discounting and augmentation are compensatory processes (Kassin et al., 1980; Kun, 1977). For a given effect, change in one cause is compensated by change in another cause. This happens as direct compensation in the case of augmentation (the greater the hindrance the more stimulation is necessary to create the effect) and as inverse compensation in the case of discounting (stronger external causes are compensated, for example, by weaker internal causes).

The logic of the discounting and augmentation principles is analogous to that of the beam balance (see above). Anderson (1974) presents similar arguments on an algebraic level and talks of an adding model. Several studies (Festinger & Carlsmith, 1959; Jones, Davis & Gergen, 1961; Kruglanski, 1970; Mills & Jellison, 1967; Strickland, 1958) can be analyzed in an elegant fashion on the basis of this qualitative algebraic model (see Anderson, 1974).

A quantitative analysis of the effects of situational constraints on attitude attribution can be found in the study by Himmelfarb and Anderson (1975; Box I 17).

Box I 17. Pro-pacifist versus pro-militaristic opinions
Himmelfarb and Anderson (1975) asked their subjects to infer the standing of a stimulus person on a militaristic-pacifist attitude scale. Subjects read three statements which were attributed to a stimulus person. Two of the statements were militaristic in content and the third statement was pacifist. In a "high choice" condition each statement was described as the stimulus person's own opinion. In a second condition, the two militaristic statements were said to have been formulated freely by the stimulus person while the pacifist statement was said to be the result of an instruction to write a pro-pacifist statement. In a third condition, subjects learned that the stimulus person had been instructed to write pro-militaristic statements. These manipulations of free choice should influence the weight which is attached to each statement when forming an overall impression of the stimulus person's attitude (Himmelfarb & Anderson, 1975). The pacifist statement should be discounted (i.e., given low weight in the overall inference) when it is described in the second condition as corresponding to situational constraint. Therefore, the overall impression should be distorted in the militaristic direction. In contrast, the importance of the pacifist statement should be augmented when it is described in the third condition as conflicting with the situational constraint. Therefore, the overall impression should be distorted in the pacifist direction.

These predictions were confirmed by the empirical results. Compared with the high-choice condition, subjects inferred a more militaristic attitude in the second condition and a more pacifist attitude in the third condition. These results − and additional data which are reported by Himmelfarb and Anderson (1975) − agree with the assumption that manipulation of choice influences the weight parameter in the integration process. It seems intuitively plausible to assume that observers take into account high or low choice of the actor to produce the attitude statements by weighting the evidence differently.

Insufficient Discounting

Even if the discounting principle seems to follow an algebraic rule, this rule is possibly applied only insufficiently by people in everyday life. As a secondary result of three studies on the theory of correspondent inferences, Jones and Harris (1967) established that perceivers attributed more responsibility to an actor for an action than seemed rational. In two of the experiments perceivers had to assess the attitude of a student who had presented a pro- or an anti-Castro opinion in a 200-word essay. There were ten 7-point scales available relating to Castro and Cuba. A score of 10 means a maximal attribution of antipathy while a score of 70 signaled a maximal attribution of sympathy. Relevant here are the two experimental conditions in which the perceiver discovered that the author had been instructed to write the essay. In the anti condition the instruction was: "Based on the last week's discussion and lectures, wright a short cogent *criticism* of Castro's Cuba as if you were giving the opening statement in a debate." (Jones & Harris, 1967, p. 4). In the pro condition the word *defense* replaced *criticism*.

In spite of the obvious fact that the essays had been written in response to an instruction, the writer who had written a pro essay was attributed a more positive attitude towards Castro. The means (44.1 and 22.9 in experiment 1 and 41.3 and 23.7 in experiment 2) differed significantly.

Jones (1979) drew attention to numerous experiments in which the effect occurred (see Jones, Worchel, Goethals & Grumet, 1971; Jones, Riggs & Quattrone, 1979; Miller, 1976; Snyder & Jones, 1974). Cantor, Pittman and Jones (1982) showed that the correspondent inference was generalized to related attitude dimensions. Snyder and Frankel (1976) showed that an emotional cue is dissociated from the situation and attributed to the participating persons as a disposition. A situation in which it is plausible to be afraid elicits more dispositional attribution of fear. What has become evident in these studies is that an opinion expressed serves as an indication of an underlying attitude, even if this opinion was expressed under duress. This cue function of an expressed opinion only ceases to be effective when the author uses ready-made arguments or when someone merely copies a given text (Snyder & Jones, 1974). In the same vein, situational cues of emotionality elicit a tendency to identify a person with the surrounding situational context.

The tendency to draw conclusions about underlying attitudes on the basis of context-dependent behavior is so prevalent that it could be called a fundamental attribution error (Ross, 1977). The anchor heuristic – as described by Tversky and Kahneman (1974) – can be used to explain this effect (Jones, 1979). According to this, there is a tendency in judgment formation to form an anchor and to accommodate further information whereby, however, the accommodation is not sufficient (Bierhoff & Bierhoff-Alfermann, 1983; Quattrone, 1982; Tversky & Kahneman, 1974).

What is then the anchor in the attribution of attitudes? According to Jones (1979) and Quattrone (1982), a direct link is made from the action (that is the opinion expressed) to the actor (that is to the underlying attitude). This correspondent link forms an anchor which is then adjusted by considering the situational constraints or contextual influences, but, according to the heuristic, only inadequately. If, however, free choice is given, adjustment to the situational constraints is not necessary and the correspondent link determines the final judgment.

In a situation in which external pressures make complete discounting of the internal cause plausible, the position expressed in the opinion is used to a certain extent to diagnose the true attitude. Even when there is extremely high external pressure, perceivers assume a high degree of autonomy, although only a small number of actors can elude the situational pressure (Bierbrauer, 1979). Another example of insufficient discounting is to be seen in dissonance reduction after behavior not in accordance with one's own attitudes (e.g., Festinger & Carlsmith, 1959). In typical dissonance situations the actor believes his/her behavior was not fully justified by the external circumstances, although in reality nearly all the persons gave in to the external pressure and did not behave according to their attitudes.

The fundamental attribution error is amplified when the diagnostic information is given first and the context information last (Jones et al., 1979). In this case the attribution of attitudes is no more extreme in a free choice situation than under duress! Here the discounting principle is largely neglected (see Figure 27) and the tendency to underestimate the effect of exercised pressure becomes dominant (see Miller, Mayerson, Pogue & Whitehouse, 1977).

The phenomenon of insufficient discounting can also be explained with the help of a complex model of information processing (Lopes, 1972). Such a model, which is fitted to the data, takes into consideration inter alia the discrepancy between the expected and the actual behavior (Jones et al., 1971).

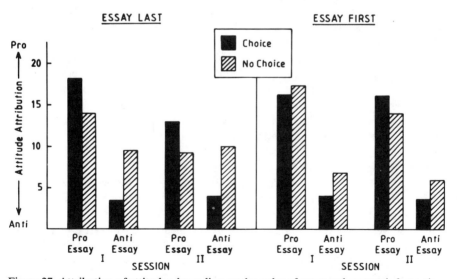

Figure 27. Attribution of attitudes depending on the order of essay and context information. (After Jones, Riggs & Quattrone, 1979, p. 1232. Copyright 1979 by the American Psychological Association. Adapted by permission)

The importance of the discrepancy increases with the size of the deviation from the expectation, and the importance of the diagnostic information decreases when the freedom of choice is small (see Himmelfarb & Anderson, 1975). Such a model provides a good quantitative prediction of results. Whether if reflects the subjective judgmental logic remains to be shown in future studies.

Gilbert and Jones (1986) offered another interpretation of the fundamental attribution error which they prefer to call "bias toward correspondent inference." They interpreted the phenomenon as part of the process of subjective reality construction. People are assumed to build their own social world by eliciting exactly that behavior in their interaction partners which they consider to be diagnostic of these people. From this perspective, the bias toward correspondent inference contributes to self-fulfilling prophecies (see Chap. 5, "Self-fulfilling prophecies and processes of expectation confirmation").

Gilbert and Jones (1986) presented experimental evidence which demonstrates that people are not always aware of the fact that they induce a specific attitude in other people which they then assume to be the true attitude of these other people. Similar considerations apply to the controversy about the consistency of human behavior. By selecting and influencing their social environment people frequently manage to live in a stable and predictable world which is, at least in part, the result of their own activities and inclinations.

Gilbert and Jones (1986) add a comment on the relationship between situational constraints and dispositional attributions. In accordance with Johnson, Jemmott and Pettigrew (1984), they assume that dispositional attribution, a basic perceptual process, takes place automatically and fast while causal analysis, a higher order process, takes place slowly and corrects only insufficiently for situational constraints which were neglected in dispositional attributions.

Others are of the opinion that the evidence for the fundamental attribution error is not fully convincing (e.g., Kelley & Michela, 1980; Harvey et al., 1981). Jellison and Green (1981) assume that the fundamental attribution error is due to a tendency in humans to overestimate the importance of internal causes. In addition, observers are said to prefer internality because they want to make sure that others are responsible for what they are doing. This might be an important issue when people blame others for their conduct (Shaver, 1985; see "Attribution of responsibility and blame").

Miller, Schmidt, Meyer & Colella (1984) investigated the possibility that the overattribution phenomenon is due to artifacts which are built into the experimental paradigm of studies on attitude attribution. They found evidence that observers who reproduce the fundamental attribution error in their inferences of attitudes are at the same time aware of the usefulness of high-choice behavior. Their dispositional attributions are in part explained by pressure in the experimental situation which dictates taking the essay content into account when drawing an inference. Because the essay is the only evidence on the attitude of the target person, subjects might assume that the experimenter wants them to use this information even in the conditions of high situational constraint.

Similar arguments are raised in response to studies which show that subjects do not take base-rate information into account when predicting behavior of target persons (Fiedler, 1980). The similarity rests on the fact that in a "no choice" condition the base-rate of the constrained behavior can be considered to be 100% because everybody complies with the pressure. This is equivalent to high consensus, which should lead to a situational attribution being highly probable (the behavior was caused by external pressures and cannot be seen as diagnostic of the dispositions of the actor). These issues are discussed more fully in the section "Sensitivity to consensus information".

The anchor heuristic appears to offer a plausible explanation for the effect of "behavior engulfing the field" (Heider, 1958, p. 54). Further studies should be devoted to the problem of under what conditions the bias toward correspondent inference dominates (Ajzen, Dalto & Blyth, 1979). It might be that its occurrence is especially likely when observers have limited and ambiguous information about the target person's attitude structure available.

The Covariation Principle

Let us begin with an example (modified from Hilton & Slugoski, 1986):

(Fact) *Sally comes out in a rash from the Beauty Cream.*
(Low consensus) *Other people do not come out in a rash from the Beauty Cream.*
(High distinctiveness) *Sally does not come out in a rash from other creams.*
(High consistency) *Sally has regularly come out in a rash from the Beauty Cream in the past.*

The question is, what is the cause of Sally's rash? Is it because of Sally herself or because of the cream or because of a combination of unfortunate circumstances? In order to answer this question the event as described in the first sentence is compared on several dimensions. *Consensus* information refers to how other people react to the cream. *Distinctiveness* information is about creams other than the special Beauty Cream. Finally, *consistency* information relates to Sally's reaction to the Beauty Cream in the past.

On the basis of the three dimensions consensus, distinctiveness, and consistency, Kelley (1967) developed his ANOVA model of causal attribution, which built on the theoretical analysis of Heider (1958). The parallel between experimental design and the analysis of attributions was first suggested by Heider and referred to the method of difference devised by Mill (see above). Kelley (1967, 1973) invented the principle of covariation as a direct analogue to the method of difference. He emphasized that his attribution model was similar to an analysis of variance (hence ANOVA model).

Two approaches have been used for the empirical study of the covariational definition of causality. Some authors have focused on the information configurations described in the ANOVA model (Hewstone & Jaspars, 1987; Hilton & Slugoski, 1986; Jaspars, 1983; Orvis, Cunningham & Kelley, 1975). Others were primarily interested in the separate effects of each dimension on causal attributions (Hansen, 1980; McArthur, 1972; Zuckerman, 1978). In the following, both approaches will be discussed in succession.

Unexpected Contrasts

The "multidimensional" approach, based on the same approach as in the original account by Kelley (1967), takes all three dimensions into consideration simultaneously in order to make predictions as to whether attributions will be to the person, the situation, the circumstances, or a combination of these. This version of the covariation theory assumes that attributions always occur when an unusual or "abnormal" situation arises (Hilton & Slugoski, 1986; see Box T 11).

> *Box T11.* Logical model of the attribution process
> Hilton and Slugoski (1986) assume that the person directs his/her attention towards the dimension on which an unexpected contrast occurs (abnormal conditions focus model). This model was developed on the basis of a "logical model" of attribution (Hewstone & Jaspars, 1987; Jaspars, 1983; Jaspars, Hewstone & Fincham, 1983). In the logical model predictions are based on an analysis of necessary and sufficient causes for the occurrence of an effect (see "Causal relations"). A causal inference is made by inferring whether the stimulus, the person, the circumstances, or a combination of these are necessary and sufficient conditions for the occurrence of the effect. The rules of this abnormal conditions focus model are as follows:
>
> — The person, the stimulus, and the circumstances are necessary conditions and can therefore be seen as potential causes for this event.
> — If there is a low consensus (only the target person has a special experience), the person is the abnormal condition which causes the event.
> — If there is high distinctiveness (only this stimulus creates a special experience), the stimulus is the abnormal condition which causes the event.
> — If there is low consistency (only these special circumstances create a special experience), the given circumstances are the abnormal condition which creates the event.
>
> If a necessary condition does not deviate as defined by the rules, it is not considered in the causal attribution. The model enables a complete analysis of all the conditions specified in the covariation model (see Table 25).
> The abnormal conditions focus model agrees with the predictions made by Jaspars et al. (1983) on the basis of a logical analysis of necessary and

Table 25. Complete predictions for the logical model. (From Hilton & Slugoski, 1986, p. 79. Copyright 1986 by the American Psychological Association. Reprinted by permission)

Configuration (consensus/ distinctiveness/ consistency)	Abnormal condition(s)	Accompanying conditions	Perceived cause(s)
HHH	S	PC	S
HHL	SC	P	SC
HLH	–	PSC	–
HLL	C	PS	C
LHH	PS	C	PS
LHL	PSC	–	PSC
LLH	P	SC	P
LLL	PC	S	PC

S, stimulus; P, person; C, circumstances; H, high; L, low.

sufficient causes. The advantage is that it is considerably less complicated to derive the eight hypotheses.

The predictions of the model are intuitively easily comprehensible. Let us look, for example, at the classical cases in which the perceived cause should be either only the stimulus or only the person (lines 1 and 7 in Table 25). The configuration HHH means, for example, that everybody comes out in a rash from the Beauty Cream, that only this cream causes a rash, and that the rash reoccurs with every application. In this case it is plausible to say that the cream is "guilty." This particular cream causes all users to come out in a rash every time!

The configuration LLH is also easy to understand: only Sally comes out in a rash regularly and this is not only the case with the Beauty Cream. It does not depend, therefore, on the particular cream or the particular day but it depends on *Sally* using the cream that the reaction occurs!

Empirical tests of the model tend to confirm the model's predictions (see Hewstone & Jaspars, 1987). However, there were deviations in the comparison of the HLH and the LHL configuration when normal routine events were given (Hilton & Slugoski, 1986). The comparison of these configurations is of particular interest because no special causal attribution was predicted for HLH (all conditions were average) while three causal attributions are plausible simultaneously for LHL (it is because of the person as well as because of the situation and also because of the circumstances) since there is a contrast on each dimension.

In the first case all persons react to all stimuli of the same class in the same way. In the second case only Sally reacts to one particular stimulus in the class in a particular way, but this only on one particular occasion.

The deviation was that in the case of events which are unusual (e.g., "Sally does not buy anything when she goes to the supermarket") HLH information is assessed as being more and LHL information as less informative. This pattern of judgment for the HLH configuration is understandable insomuch as an unusual event which occurs regularly for many people and can be generalized for all stimuli in a class says something about the stimulus situation as well as about the people. It seems sensible to put unexpected behavior embedded in the HLH configuration down to the person as well as to the stimulus situation (Hilton & Slugoski, 1986).

Hewstone and Jaspars (1987) discuss several problems of the logical model in accounting for the empirical data. One problem is the formulation for the "circumstance" attribution. For example, Hilton and Slugoski (1986, exp. 2) used the term "particular occasion." The response language contributes to the variance in the attribution judgments (Hewstone, 1983).

In addition, the fact that people make attributions to the person, the stimulus, and a combination of both with high frequencies in the HLH configuration (Jaspars, 1983) is problematic because, from a theoretical viewpoint, no specific attribution is possible. In the HLH configuration the effect does not covary with any of the dimensions. Nevertheless, people attribute HLH events to specific causes and combinations of causes.

One possibility is that the logical model (see Box T 11) does not describe the attribution process completely. This point was elaborated by Pruitt and Insko (1980), who emphasized the factor of whether the actor agrees with others in their evaluation of comparison objects. Kelley (1967) explicitly took into account the agreement between the actor and others in their evaluation of the target object. This agreement or disagreement is described as high or low consensus. But since the actor and others might also agree or disagree with regard to the comparison objects it is intuitively plausible to include this dimension of comparison-object consensus (see Box T 12).

Box T 12. Target-object consensus versus comparison-object consensus
Pruitt and Insko (1980) mention everyday situations in which such consensus information is used spontaneously. For example, the fact that the actor likes the movie "The Color Purple" might be more impressive if the audience is informed that in the past the actor agreed with other people in their evaluation of movies. This example illustrates the idea that high comparison-object consensus might increase the plausibility of an object attribution. Just as high target-object consensus is an indicator of external attributions, high comparison-object consensus might emphasize the objectivity of the actor's evaluations.

In contrast, low comparison-object consensus might, like low target-object consensus, encourage a person attribution. In the example above, an actor who in the past only infrequently agreed with other people with

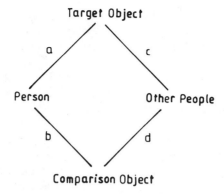

Figure 28. Representation of the diamond model. (Modified from Pruitt & Insko, 1980, p. 42. Copyright 1980 by the American Psychological Association. Adapted by permission)

regard to the evaluation of movies might be perceived as a person whose judgments on movies are highly idiosyncratic and therefore an expression of his or her personal inclinations or interests.

Pruitt and Insko (1980) named their revised ANOVA model the "diamond model" because a graphical representation of the model resembles a diamond (see Figure 28). The illustration shows that the diamond model, like Kelley's model, includes four elements: the person, other people, the target object, and other similar objects. Usually a certain similarity between the actor and the other people is assumed. While Kelley only considered the connections a, b, and c, the diamond model also includes a connection d.

It is instructive to describe the dimensions of distinctiveness, consensus, and consistency with reference to Figure 28. Distinctiveness is determined by a comparison between connections a and b. Target-object consensus is inferred from connections a and c. Comparison-object consensus refers to a comparison between connections b and d. Finally, consistency is the only dimension of the model which refers to a single dimension. While Kelley (1967) focused on the consistency of connection a, it is certainly plausible to speak of consistency with regard to connections b, c, and d. For example, other people might be consistent or inconsistent in their evaluation of comparison objects.

In a 2×2×2×2 design, Pruitt and Insko (1980) varied distinctiveness, target-object consensus, comparison-object consensus, and consistency (in Kelley's sense). They used a between-subjects design. Their results are based on 384 students. The causal attributions were measured by two methods. Firstly, three 7-point rating scales were used to assess the person, the target object (in one scenario the evaluation of a restaurant, in a second scenario the liking of a television series), and the special circumstances as possible causes. Secondly, subjects gave their judgments in percentages by dividing 100% between the three possible causes. In general, both scenarios and both methods of measurement led to similar results.

Following Kelley (1967) and in agreement with the predictions derived from the logical model (Table 25), Pruitt and Insko (1980) assumed that a HHH configuration elicits strong object attributions while a LLH configuration fosters a strong person attribution. In accordance with the results of Orvis, Cunningham and Kelley (1975), Pruitt and Insko (1980) assumed that the circumstance attributions are primarily dependent on consistency information with low consistency leading to high circumstance attribution. In general, these predictions were confirmed. They are supplemented by the fact that the highest object attribution was obtained in the HHH plus high comparison-object consensus (57.7% on the percentage measure) and the highest person attribution in the LLH plus low comparison-object consensus condition (59.3% on the percentage measure). However, the HHH plus low comparison-object consensus condition produced nearly as high object attributions (49.8%) and the LLH plus high comparison-object consensus condition also resulted in high person attributions (53.2%).

These results support the multidimensional predictions contained in Table 25 and expand the pattern of results by including comparison-object consensus. As expected, this additional variable produced somewhat stronger effects than are obtained on the basis of target-object consensus alone. Pruitt and Insko (1980) also analyzed their data from the viewpoint of the influence of each information dimension separately (which is called a commonsense attribution analysis in the next section). The results show that distinctiveness, target-object consensus, and consistency influence person attributions and object attributions. For example, person attributions were greater with low distinctiveness, low target-object consensus, and high consistency. In addition, high comparison-object consensus resulted in higher agent attributions than low comparison-object consensus. Therefore, target-object consensus and comparison-object consensus influenced the inference process in the same direction.

Situational attributions were also influenced by the independent variables. They were greater with high distinctiveness, high target-object consensus, and high consistency. In addition, they were greater with high comparison-object consensus. This pattern of results shows that explicit information about high comparison-object consensus is able to strenghten the effect of high target-object consensus by increasing object attributions.

The circumstance attributions were closely related to consistency information. While high consistency was translated into low circumstance attributions, low consistency resulted in high attributions to the circumstances. These attributions were not influenced by comparison-object consistency. This analysis in terms of each information dimension leads to the unidimensional approach which is described more fully in the next section.

Commonsense Attribution

While the first approach explicitly involves multidimensionality of causal attribution, the second approach concentrates on the individual effects of the three dimensions on the causal attribution. What is the influence on causal attribution if there is high instead of low consensus? What is the effect if the distinctiveness is low?

This second approach is noteworthy in that it can be assumed that many attributions are not the result of a multidimensional analysis but instead the result of a one-dimensional observation. Considering several dimensions is time-consuming and often not practical. Hansen (1980) presented a comprehensive theoretical and empirical analysis, the most important points of which will be summarized here.

The quintessence of commonsense attribution is that internal attributions are mainly determined by distinctiveness information while external attributions are largely dependent on consensus information. Circumstantial attributions are mainly determined by consistency information.

First, *internal* attributions: conclusions about the abilities and dispositions of the actors can be made directly on the basis of the information that there is *low* distinctiveness. The conducive cause of the events can be localized directly in the person.

Next, *external* attributions: if there is *high* consensus this suggests that the stimulus caused the effect. Since everybody was affected by the stimulus in the same way, it is plausible to regard the stimulus as the cause of these effects.

Finally, it has been shown that *circumstantial* attributions are elicited above all when the consistency is low. *Low* consistency means that the effect only occurs on a particular occasion, which suggests that the special circumstances were decisive.

These assumptions are supported by empirical results. Going back to the predictions in Table 25, it can be seen that the typical attribution pattern for external attributions is the HHH configuration, while the LLH configuration is typical for internal attributions and the HLL configuration for circumstantial attributions. One should add, on the basis of the experimental results from Hansen (1980), that in the HHH configuration the high consensus is the deciding factor for the external attribution, that in the LLH configuration the low distinctiveness is important for the internal attribution, and that in the HLL configuration the low consistency allows circumstantial attribution.

Hansen (1985) and Hansen and Hall (1985) have extended the analysis of commonsense attributions by including the augmentation and the discounting principles. Two examples from sport serve to illustrate these principles (Hansen & Hall, 1985). If two players stand firm when faced with one opponent, the ability of one of these players will be assessed as being lower than if one player alone was in the defense (discounting principle). If one player stands firm in the face of a team of several players, his ability will be regarded as higher than if he succeeds against one single player (augmentation principle).

Hansen and Hall (1985) were able to show that the discounting principle was used more intensively, the more competing conducive causes there were (e.g., the more fellow players). On the other hand, it was established that the augmentation principle was considerably less important and did not influence attribution judgments as much as the discounting principle did. Furthermore, it was demonstrated that one of four winners was rated as weaker than a single winner while one of four losers was not perceived as weaker than a single loser. Conducive causes were therefore taken more into account than inhibitory causes when their strength varied. While winners receive the attention of the public, losers are assigned collectively to the category of the losers without analyzing in any depth why they lost.

The psychology of commonsense attribution can be summed up as follows (see Hansen, 1985): low distinctiveness elicits strong dispositional attribution, which decreases when low consensus becomes doubtful and several people experience the same as the target person. The dispositional attribution is supplemented by situational attribution when everybody experiences the same. On the other hand, high consensus elicits a situational attribution which becomes stronger the fewer the number of people predisposed to the effect. For example, if fearless people are put to flight by a stimulus, the fearsomeness of the stimulus must be greater than when fearful people are put to flight.

Person attribution is greatest when low distinctiveness coincides with low consensus, because the personal facilitative force is augmented by a stimulus inhibitory force; situational attribution is strongest when high consensus which is not expected on the basis of dispositional predisposition occurs, because the stimulus facilitative force is augmented by a personal inhibitory force. In the first case the behavior of the target person is unexpected; in the second the strong effect of the stimulus is surprising.

Sensitivity to Consensus Information

The importance of consensus for commonsense attributions has been debated intensively. While in the original ANOVA model (Kelley, 1967) there is no reason to assume that consensus is less influential than distinctiveness as a factor for determining internal/external attributions, empirical studies cast some doubt on the effectiveness of consensus information in molding attribution judgments and predictions.

McArthur (1972, 1976) employed agent-verb-target sentences (e.g., "John laughs at the comedian") to test predictions from Kelley's ANOVA model. She added information about distinctiveness, consensus, and consistency (e.g., "John does not laugh at almost any other comedian" − high distinctiveness). Students were asked to indicate whether the event was caused by the agent, the target, the circumstances, or a combination of these causes. McArthur (1972, 1976) reported that consensus information carried less weight than distinctiveness information. Overall, only 2.9% of the variance was explained by consensus while distinctiveness explained 10.16% and consistency 20.03%. This pattern of results does not mean that consensus was unimportant because the results differed for the four attribution variables. Consensus explained 6.25% of the variance of agent attributions and 5.17% of the variance of target attributions.

Additional data (McArthur, 1976) indicated that for agent attributions in the context of person-person descriptions (e.g., "woman conceals boy" as opposed to thing-person "blanket conceals boy", person-thing "woman conceals book", or thing-thing "blanket conceals book") consensus information was as influential as distinctiveness information. In addition, target attributions of person-person events were substantially influenced by consensus. On the whole, both studies by McArthur show that distinctiveness is weighted more than consensus and that consensus had a substantial impact on agent attributions and target attributions. This was especially pronounced for descriptions of person-person interactions.

Hewstone and Jaspars (1983) used a questionnaire format similar to that used by McArthur. They added the information that the comparison persons who constitute high or low consensus were similar to the subject. Subjects were told that agents and others were of the same sex. By emphasizing the similarity between actor and comparison persons, a "unit" relationship should be created (Heider, 1958). Therefore, the weight of the consensus information should increase. In line with this reasoning, Hewstone and Jaspars found that consensus explained considerably more variance in their study than in the original study by McArthur (1972).

The most impressive evidence against the hypothesis that consensus influences attribution judgments in the Kelley model was presented in a series of studies on the reduction of depressive feelings by Nisbett, Borgida, Crandall and Reed (1976). The first study was concerned with the negative mood experienced by some students on Sunday evenings. The authors assumed that disphoric moods at the end of the week could be attacked by information indicating that nearly all students experience the same depressive moods. This high consensus information should be used to infer that the special situation of a Sunday evening is responsible for the disphoric mood, and so should inhibit internal attributions and, as a consequence, reduce disphoric feelings. The data indicated that the high consensus messsage was not successful. Learning that other students feel as depressed as oneself did not reduce disphoric feelings.

In a second study the authors tried to reduce depressive feelings in chronically depressed students by externalizing the cause of the depressive state. The endeavor was futile. An additional study showed that the stress experienced by first-year faculty members could not be reduced by information which indicated that negative emotional reactions in the first year of employment are the norm. While some people seemed to react positively to this attempt to externalize the problem, others tended to react negatively. In a fourth experiment subjects were asked to evaluate different crackers. The tasting test served as a pretext to allow subjects to drink a "neutralizing solution" between trials. Subjects later learnt that they had drunken much more or much less than other subjects who had participated in the study earlier. This evidence did not influence ratings of the taste of the solution, nor the estimate of the subject's thirst before the test, nor the degree of thirst estimated to have been induced by the crackers. These results are surprising because subjects who saw that they had drunk more of the solution than others should be inclined to infer that the crackers had made them especially thirsty and/or that they had been thirsty from the beginning, while subjects who saw that they had drunk less than others should infer that they had not been so thirsty at the beginning and/or that the crackers had not made them very thirsty.

Nisbett and Borgida (1975) went even further. They gave subjects correct base-rate information about the willingness of subjects to endure as large an electric shock as they could tolerate. This base-rate information indicated truthfully that many people will endure a very strong electric shock in such a situation (see Nisbett & Schachter, 1966). Additional data indicated that naive subjects assume that most people would only endure a moderate electric shock. The judgments of the students showed that they ignored the base-rate information in their predictions for two or three target subjects. In their prediction about the behavior likely in target cases they followed their implicit assumption of what people do even though objective information which summarized a large amount of data about subjects' behavior was made available to them. But it must be added that the descriptions of the target persons seem to be biased towards indicating that they try to avoid embarrassing experiences because one target person was portrayed as "prone to anxiety and fears of rejection" (Nisbett & Borgida, 1975, p. 937).

While abstract information in the form of a statistical summary of the evidence was not effective in influencing subjects' estimates, two concrete cases which referred to the behavior in the shock experiment of specific target persons who were described as accepting a strong electric shock proved to be effective. Concrete information seemed to triumph over implicit assumptions. Subsequent studies (Borgida & Nisbett, 1977; Hamill et al., 1980) confirmed that concrete case information was more influential in determining subjects' viewpoints than abstract base-rate information.

The objective value of a source of data seems to be neglected in many situations (Nisbett, Krantz, Jepson & Fong, 1982; Nisbett & Ross, 1980). This pattern of results corresponds to the representativeness heuristic (Tversky & Kahneman, 1974), which conjectures that people are inclined to neglect base-rate information when they make predictions about the category membership of a target person and that they instead infer category membership from perceived similarity (e.g., semantic similarity) between target person and category. When subjects can base their judgment on base-rate information and on a brief personality sketch (which nevertheless is informative with regard to what the target person might do; see Fiedler, 1980), they are usually inclined to neglect the base-rate information and to form their prediction primarily on the basis of the personality sketch (Carroll & Siegler, 1977; Tversky &

Kahneman, 1974). Base-rate information is analogous to consensus information because both reveal how many people act in a specified manner. In addition, extensive single case information is related to distinctiveness information and consistency information refers to the reliability of the data (Nisbett & Borgida, 1975; McArthur, 1976).

The results on the impact of consensus and statistical base-rate information can be interpreted as a failure on the part of subjects to use sample-based consensus information. A number of studies are available which shed further light on this issue (e.g., DiVitto & McArthur, 1978; Hansen, 1976; Hansen & Donoghue, 1977; Hansen & Lowe, 1976; Hansen & Stonner, 1978; Major, 1980; Wells & Harvey, 1977; Zuckerman, 1978). For example, the studies of Hansen and his coworkers indicate that observers are more efficient in using base-rate information on consensus than actors themselves. In addition, explicit consensus information tends to be discounted when the representativeness of the sample is questionable while consensus information based on random samples is used in making judgments (Hansen & Donoghue, 1977; Wells & Harvey, 1977). Results of a cross-sectional study by DiVitto and McArthur (1978) with first, third, and sixth graders and college students show that the ability to use consensus information improves with age. College students gave the highest percentage of model-consistent attributions. Those who have not attained the formal operational level (in Piaget's sense; Inhelder & Piaget, 1958) have difficulties in applying the covariation principle (Allen et al., 1987).

Another question concerns the kind of inference that is determined by consensus information. On the basis of the ANOVA model at least attributions to the person, to the situation, and to the circumstances must be considered. In a replication of the cracker-tasting study by Nisbett et al. (1976), Hansen and Stonner (1978) asked actors and observers to assess how thirsty the actor was prior to the experiment. Actors and observers inferred equally often that when the actor drank more of the neutralizing solution he/she had been more thirsty than the sample had been on average. This result disagrees with the negative conclusion of Nisbett et al. (1976) because even actors used sample-based consensus information. A possible explanation for these discrepant results is that the sample information may have had more impact in the study by Hansen and Stonner (1978). This is a reasonable assumption because the subjects of Nisbett et al. (1976) saw the bottles of other participants "accidentally" while Hansen and Stonner (1978) presented data on the amount drunk with the help of a graphic illustration.

In a later experiment (Hansen, 1980, exp. 5), distinctiveness, consensus, and consistency were manipulated using an experimental design similar to that used by McArthur (1972). Subjects were exposed to one-sentence descriptions of behavior (e.g., "Person X beats the opponent in the chess game," "Person X cried during the movie"). They received several pieces of additional information in random order, e.g., "Person X beats most opponents" (low distinctiveness), "Most people beat this opponent" (high consensus), "Person X usually beats this opponent" (high consistency). This carefully planned study revealed the importance of consensus information for target attributions. High consensus resulted in a strong situational attribution while low consensus led to a weak situational attribution. Distinctiveness did not matter for these target attributions. In contrast, agent attributions were strongly influenced by distinctiveness information. Low distinctiveness resulted in high person attributions while high distinctiveness led to low person attributions. This effect was especially pronounced for low consensus (a similar interaction effect was reported by McArthur, 1976). Circumstance attributions were mainly determined by consistency information. This effect was reduced for the low consensus condition. Combined with high consensus, low consistency led to high circumstance attributions, while high consistency did not. Instead, high consistency elicited more agent attributions and more target attributions.

To sum up, consensus was the main determinant of situational attributions and explained 24% of the variance of this dependent variable (1% was explained by distinctiveness and 5% by consistency). Distinctiveness was the main determinant of person attributions and explained 31% of the variance (14% was explained by consensus and 5% by consistency). A rereading of the results of DiVitto and McArthur (1978) shows that they found the same pattern. In these studies subjects judged as observers. Other studies show that consensus information is effective in influencing target attributions (Hewstone & Jaspars, 1987; Orvis et al., 1975; Pruitt & Insko, 1980; Zuckerman, 1978) and that a given situational attribution elicits the inference of higher consensus than a given dispositional attribution (Zuckerman & Mann, 1979).

Another line of research indicates that the impact of consensus information depends on the order in which the information is presented. In the experiments by Ruble and Feldman (1976) and Zuckerman (1978), consensus had less influence when the relevant information was given first than when it was given last. It is interesting to note that McArthur (1972) gave consensus information, distinctiveness information, and consistency information in that order (Ruble & Feldman, 1976).

Another issue is which kind of information is chosen from three general categories of information (distinctiveness, consensus, and consistency) when subjects are given a description of behavior (for example a fight between two prisoners in experiment 1, high effort invested into a particular project in experiment 2; Major, 1980) and are asked to attribute the behavior to the agent, the target, the circumstances, or a combination of these causes. Preattribution information acquisition emphasized distinctiveness and especially consistency information more than consensus information, although consensus was certainly not ignored (Major, 1980). But there might be a real tendency in people to organize their information search more in terms of the focus of their search − the agent − than in terms of what other people do in the same situation. Given the tendency of observers to focus their attention on the actor, the observer subjects in the studies of Major (1980) were more inclined to choose information which was related to the actor than to choose information which was related to other prisoners' behavior towards the target person.

Kassin (1979) drew attention to the difference between explicit and implicit consensus; this is easily understood with reference to the study by Nisbett and Borgida (1975), who informed their subjects truthfully that people are inclined to try high electric shocks in an experimental situation while subjects in general believe that people will avoid high electric shocks in such a situation. Therefore, the explicit base-rate information was in disagreement with implicit assumptions subjects brought with them into the laboratory. In other words, explicit consensus diverged from implicit consensus, which was based on prior expectations. Explicit consensus information is not the only source of evidence which people use for their consensus estimates. From this follows the hypothesis that people tend to ignore explicit consensus information when it is highly discrepant with implicit consensus (Kassin, 1979). For example, people might regard discrepant explicit consensus information as biased and reject it as unimportant. Jones and McGillis (1976) discuss the possibility that extremely unexpected behavior is rejected as evidence for attributions because prior expectations render the discrepant behavior as highly unlikely. For example, the message that eight out of ten blacks demand race discrimination is at variance with what people know about their social world. Why should they take into account base-rate information which they regard as complete nonsense?

Another possibility is suggested by the results of an experiment by Kassin (1981), who tested the influence of implicit consensus on base-rate estimates which were obtained after the presentation of 50 cases. Implicit consensus was manipulated via prior expectations. In one situation it was highly likely that help would be given, while in a second situation it was highly unlikely. Subjects read about the behavior of 50 persons who did or did not help. The base-rate of helping was 50%. High prior expectancies of helping resulted in a relatively high base-rate estimate (61.9%), while low prior expectancies of helping produced a low average base-rate estimate (43%).

The amount of influence exercised by consensus information depends on a number of variables. Consensus effects are stronger when actor and comparison persons are in a unit relationship (Hewstone & Jaspars, 1983), when the application of the base-rate information does not require extensive computation (Carroll & Siegler, 1977), and when the base-rate sample is described as representative (Hansen and Donoghue, 1977; Wells & Harvey, 1977). Another issue is whether subjects encounter several values of the consensus variable or only one value, as in the studies where consensus proved to be ineffective. Sample-based information is used – although not in perfect agreement with normative statistical theory – when judges read several examples with different consensus values (Fischhoff, Slovic & Lichtenstein, 1979).

Kassin (1979) concluded that base-rate information will be ignored when it contradicts normative expectations. Evidence (Hewstone & Jaspars, 1988) indicates that the competition between explicit and implicit consensus frequently results in a "victory" of the explicit information over prior expectancies. For example, Hewstone and Jaspars (1988) varied implicit consensus by using stereotypical male and female behavior items. They attributed stereotypical or counterstereotypical behavior to a male or female stimulus person. Using a technique similar to McArthur's, they added information about explicit consensus and whether consistency was high or low.

Results indicated that agent attributions were higher with low rather than with high consensus and with high rather than low consistency. Situational attributions were higher with high rather than with low consensus and with high rather than low consistency. Implicit consensus (i.e., stereotypical beliefs) did not influence these attributions. In a second experiment evidence was found which indicated that implicit consensus only influenced agent attributions when no information about explicit consensus was available.

To sum up, explicit consensus information seems to exert a powerful influence on attributions, especially situational attributions, given that certain preconditions (sensitivity of the judges, representativeness of the sample, similarity between actor and comparison persons) are met. Implicit consensus might interfere with explicit consensus, especially when the explicit information is hard to believe. Information search seems to be biased towards the agent in the event. Although the similarity between Tversky and Kahneman's account (1974) of the representativeness heuristic and the missing effect of consensus information in the Nisbett et al. (1976) studies is tempting, neither the empirical results as a whole nor a theoretical analysis justify the conclusion that consensus information is in general neglected in human information processing (Bar-Hillel & Fischhoff, 1981; Fiedler, 1980; Ginosar & Trope, 1980; Manis, Dovalina, Avis & Cardoze, 1980; Manis, Avis & Cardoze, 1981). Some objections against this conclusion are inherent in attribution theory. For example, the hypothesis that person attributions should be reduced by high consensus information rests on the assumption that the effect to be explained can have only one cause. Such an assumption complies with a multiple sufficient cause schema (Kelley, 1972b) which states that a simple cause can elicit the event. But especially with regard to events of great magnitude like those in the studies of Nisbett and Borgida (1975) it is likely that another schema – the multiple necessary cause schema – is applied which assumes that the combination of several causes is necessary to cause the effect. Empirical evidence indicates (Cunningham & Kelley, 1975; Kun & Weiner, 1973) that extreme effects tend to be explained by a combination of causes following a multiple necessary cause scheme (see "Schema of multiple necessary causes"). If a multiple necessary cause schema is considered appropriate, it is totally understandable that subjects do not discount person attributions when high consensus invites a situational attribution (Fiedler, 1980).

In addition, Tversky and Kahneman's results (1974) were found in the context of tricky mathematical tasks. It is not clear whether they be can generalized to social situations. This question must be raised because in the typical experimental tasks which demonstrate subjects' ignorance of base-rate information the subjects' attention is systematically diverted from the statistical information (Fiedler, 1980). When the focus is on the statistical information the likelihood that it will be taken into account in the final attributional judgment is high. For example, successive presentation of the consensus information is more effective than the simultaneous mode of presentation which is used in most studies in the McArthur tradition (Feldman, Higgins, Karlovac & Ruble, 1976). A successive mode of presentation should emphasize the importance of the consensus information. The likelihood of the formation of consensus-related hypotheses should be directly related to the amount of attention which is directed toward the consensus information (McArthur, 1981) and the salience of the consensus information (Fischhoff et al., 1979). Both enhance the sensitivity of subjects to differences in base-rates (Fiedler, 1980). Subjects use subjective hypotheses about the meaning of an experimental task which guide their information processing in the experimental situation. When they are led to think that consensus information is important, for instance by being told that base-rates are related causally to the prediction (Ajzen, 1977; Tversky & Kahneman, 1980) the likelihood is high that the consensus information molds the final judgment. People are inclined to rely on information which is perceived to have a causal relation to the event. This reliance on causal information shows the importance of causal attributions for social cognition in general.

Studies on the effectiveness of consensus have addressed different issues, whereby three lines of research must be distinguished. One line of research concentrates on the importance of consensus information when no competing items of single case information are present. The results indicate that consensus information is taken into consideration by judges who make internal and, especially, external attributions. The second line of research contrasts explicit and implicit consensus. The results indicate that explicit consensus is used as a basis for attribution even when contradictory expectancies and stereotypes are at work. Finally, the third line of research investigates the influence of base-rate information when contradictory individuating information is available. Worthless or unreliable individuating information seems to be ignored insofar as the base-rates determine the predictions (Bar-Hillel & Fischhoff, 1981). Only when seemingly diagnostic individuating information is available are base-rates ignored and do people judge on the basis of representativeness. In these cases subjects are offered seemingly useful items of individuating information which resemble the prediction task. Apparent high diagnosticity of single case information modifies the influence of consensus information on prediction.

The Theory of Correspondent Inference

The presentation of the hierarchically restrictive schema of attribution (Figure 22) gave a first glimpse of the theory of correspondent inference (Jones & Davis, 1965; Jones & McGillis, 1976). If one ignores the thin arrows in Figure 22, what is left is a schema of correspondent inference in which every behavioral classification has a corresponding dispositional level. In such a "fully restrictive schema" (Reeder & Brewer, 1979) a very good performance when solving math problems, for example, is equated with high mathematical ability, whereas a poor performance corresponds to low ability.

The use of such a schema of attribution should be especially likely when unexpected behavior is being observed (Jones & Davis, 1965; Reeder & Brewer, 1979). While standard behavior which lies within the norms should not be very informative about the person, one assumes that behavior which, for example, has a low social desirability gives more information about the person's dispositions. If there is high consensus about particular behavior (e.g., neatness in the office) among the target persons, then the fact that a person exhibits such behavior (e.g., that an office clerk tidies his/her desk) is of little value for any conclusion about the individual tendencies of this person.

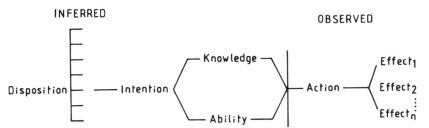

Figure 29. Process of correspondent inference. (After Jones & Davis, 1965, p. 222. Reproduced, with permission, from the *Advances in Experimental Social Psychology*, Vol. 2. Copyright 1965 by Academic Press)

Jones and Davis (1965) state various conditions necessary for correspondent inference (see Figure 29): a central precondition is freedom of choice, which ensures that the action was actually intended (and not forced by outer influences). Further preconditions are knowledge of the effects of an action and the perceived ability of the target person actually to achieve the observed effect. These suppositions suggest that correspondent inferences involve ascribing responsibility based on the question of whether the target person could have acted other than he/she did (Hamilton, 1980). Responsibility, intention, ability, and knowledge are implied factors which have to be inferred from social cues.

The theory is completed by some further hypotheses which relate to the evaluation of social cues for attribution. An important cue is low social desirability, which is also described with the term low prior probability of behavior, and low valence effects. In addition, a correspondent inference can be deduced when an action has a specific effect which is typical only for this action and not for its alternative (= noncommon effect). When the number of noncommon effects is low and the expected valence is low the action should be attributed to a disposition of the actor. The hypothesis was confirmed for a number of noncommon effects (Ajzen & Holmes, 1976).

Furthermore, it is assumed that hedonic relevance and personalism contribute to an intensifying of personal attribution. Hedonic relevance is given when the observers do not have a neutral attitude towards the result of the action but either approve or disapprove (see Chaikin & Cooper, 1973). The personalism factor becomes important when the observers are personally affected by the action of the target person (see "Motivational influences on the attribution process").

In this context it should be mentioned that the freedom of choice in the attribution of attitudes only had an effect when the behavior was unexpected (Jones et al., 1971). If an essay was not written voluntarily, the likelihood that it became the basis of a correspondent inference was lower than when the essay had been written without duress. This result has been confirmed in several experiments (see "Insufficient discounting").

However, even forced behavior can become the basis of a correspondent inference − although mostly in a diminished form − especially when the context information about the duress is given later (Jones et al., 1979). The empirical evidence for the correspondent inference theory is not very strong. Studies on attitude attribution revealed the phenomenon of bias toward correspondent inference. But only weak evidence was found for a link between decision freedom and intensity of attitude attribution when unexpected behavior is observed. While Jones and Harris (1967) and Jones et al. (1971) found a tendency in the predicted direction, Ajzen (1971) found disconfirming evidence because trait inference magnitude was more strongly affected by prior probability with low decision freedom (compared with high decision freedom).

In addition, observers seem to be influenced by motivational biases. Studies on causal attributions for (un)reliable behavior of a stimulus person (Bierhoff & Kramp, 1988) reveal that unexpected behavior is attributed either to situational factors or to dispositional causes depending on the content of the behavior. Unexpected *reliable* behavior was primarily explained by dispositional factors while unexpected *unreliable* behavior was primarily ascribed to situational factors. While Stevens and Jones (1976) showed that defensive attributional tendencies distort ANOVA-type judgments, these results indicate that observers are willing to attribute unexpected behavior to situational influences, presumably because they do not accept the implication that the stimulus person's unreliable behavior is likely to continue in the future. Only unexpected reliable behavior was attributed to the person in accordance with correspondent inferences, i.e., a person who was in the past unreliable and unexpectedly behaved reliable was perceived as being a reliable person.

Another problem of correspondent inference theory is related to the issue of credibility. Unexpected behavior may cause the observer to doubt whether the agent really meant what he/she did or said (Jones & McGillis, 1976). For example, a student who demands more stringent standards for examinations in an improvised speech is not necessarily perceived as a workaholic. It might be that the student's speech is interpreted as role-playing or that he/she is joking. But hardly anybody would infer that the student is a tough person who seeks challenges during his/her academic career. This inference is especially unlikely if the student argued in the past for lowering the examination standards.

After a certain threshold point unexpected behavior is no longer taken at face value. The question is where the threshold lies. How much discrepancy between prior probability and actual behavior is necessary for skepticism to arise? This question leads to a mute point of the theory which makes it hard to falsify its hypotheses.

Another problem is that the correspondent inference theory predicts low prior probability of behavior to be a cue for dispositional attributions, and this is at variance with ANOVA model predictions. The logical model (see "Unexpected contrasts") implies that high consistency facilitates person attributions (and object attributions). Jones and McGillis (1976) assume that low prior probability is based on prior knowledge of the actor. Therefore, low prior probability is equivalent to low consistency. The evidence which indicates that low consistency is related to circumstance attributions and not to person attributions is quite strong (Hansen, 1980; Pruitt & Insko, 1980).

These considerations lead to a new understanding of the role of unexpected behavior in attributions. Low prior probability might be less a cue for dispositional attributions but more a cue for engaging in an attributional search (Erber & Fiske, 1984). In the study of newspaper reports, Lau and Russell (1980) found that unexpected events elicited a greater number of attributions than expected events. The study by Pyszczynski and Greenberg (1981) led to the conclusion that attributional search increases with the uncertainty of the observer (see also Weiner, 1985a, 1986). Low prior probability of observed behavior seems to motivate a search for a plausible explanation which might either be located in the person or in the situation.

In addition, the idea of low prior probability was translated into the logic of the ANOVA model in the abnormal conditions focus model by Hilton and Slugoski (1986; see "Unexpected contrasts"). They assumed that observers focus on abnormal states in their search for the cause of an event. For example, in the HHH configuration neither does the person's behavior differ from what other persons do nor does the present moment differ from past moments (see Table 25). But the object differs from other objects (high distinctiveness). In a sense, the object has unexpected qualities with respect to comparison objects. The tendency of the LLH configuration to elicit person attributions can be explained with the same logic (Hilton & Slugoski, 1986).

Self-Perception

Interpersonal perception was discussed above in some detail, especially in the context of insufficient discounting, the theory of correspondent inference, and the ANOVA model. Now I shall go into some of the possible differences between interpersonal perception and self-perception. Before that a brief summary of Bem's self-perception theory (1967) is given.

The discussion of such differences appears in fact to have been the most important topic of attribution research in the 1970s. When Bem (1972, p. 42) guessed that the testing of actor/observer differences would determine the direction of research in the following years, he was clearly right.

Bem (1967) developed self-perception theory as an alternative explanation for dissonance phenomena (e.g., Festinger & Carlsmith, 1959). In the long run self-perception theory became more important as a general theory of self-attribution. In addition, the theory alluded to important aspects of the individual's social life (e.g., intrinsic motivation, misattribution of arousal, and individual differences in self-presentation) that were investigated from the viewpoint of self-perception.

The basic postulate of the theory is that people infer their internal states (e.g., attitudes, fatigue, or hunger) partially from observation of their own behavior *and* of the controlling conditions present. The controlling conditions might or might not offer sufficient justification for the behavior. For example, a person who helps children from poor families to learn math is sufficiently motivated by a salary as a teacher in special education. But the helping behavior is less justified by controlling conditions when only minimal rewards can be expected. In this case the individual might infer with some confidence that the teacher is a helpful person. Note that this explanation is based on the logic of the discounting principle (Kelley, 1972a) because an internal state is discounted by external incentives in the case of the teacher.

A general rule of self-perception theory is that people will infer an intrinsic motivation for their activities when no obvious external incentives are apparent. In contrast, when strong external incentives for an activity are present the intrinsic motivation should be reduced. This "overjustification effect" has important consequences. Incentive systems which use contingent rewards to motivate desired behavior patterns run into the danger that the prior internal interest is undermined. This seems to happen again and again in elementary school. Many school activities are intrinsically interesting for the pupils. The grade system introduces a strong external reward system for conforming to teacher expectations. The pupils tend to show a reduction in their intrinsic interest because they discount their intrinsic motivation, which "competes" with the reinforcement system of the school. After a while many pupils need the pressure of grades to learn successfully because their intrinsic interest in learning has been reduced substantially.

Self-perception theory presents a hypothesis which equates self-perception and interpersonal perception under certain conditions: "To the extent that internal cues are weak, ambiguous, or uninterpretable, the individual is functionally in the same position as an outside observer, an observer who must necessarily rely upon those same external cues to infer the individual's inner states" (Bem, 1972, p. 2). Note that this hypothesis rests on the assumption that internal cues are weak. Only then should self-perception and interpersonal perception follow the same rules.

The example of overjustification may illustrate this hypothesis. An outside observer (e.g., the teacher) is inclined to assume that pupils are motivated by grades because the grade system is an effective reinforcement system which is able to motivate pupils to participate in dull tasks. In the same vein, the pupil is inclined to infer that he/she is motivated by the grades because the grades offer a plausible explanation for learning behavior in school. Therefore, "the individual is functionally in the same position as an outside observer."

The undermining of intrinsic interest by extrinsic rewards was demonstrated in a study by Lepper et al. (1973) with preschool children who had an intrinsic interest in drawing. In the expected-reward condition they could earn an award (a certificate with a gold seal and ribbon) for doing what they liked to do: drawing. In the no-award condition, no reward was offered for the drawing activity. A retest was arranged which allowed children to play with the drawing material if they wanted. While children in the control group devoted nearly 16.7% of their time on average to drawing, this percentage was much lower in the expected-reward group (8.6%).

Deci (1971, 1972; Deci & Ryan, 1980) showed in his empirical studies that contingent rewards reduce intrinsic motivation in adults. A large number of studies show that extrinsic incentives reduce intrinsic motivation (e.g., Folger, Rosenfield & Hays, 1978; Greene, Sternberg & Lepper, 1976; Ross, 1975; Ross, Karniol & Rothstein, 1976). Salient surveillance (Lepper & Greene, 1975) and time limits (Amabile, DeJong & Lepper, 1976) may also result in a reduction of intrinsic interest. In addition, extrinsic incentives for an activity which is perceived as a means to an end tend to reduce intrinsic motivation (Lepper & Greene, 1978). Therefore, a change of label might suffice to reduce or heighten intrinsic interest in a task (e.g., "work" vs. "play").

After the basic relationship between oversufficient reward and motivation was confirmed, experimenters concentrated on the boundary conditions of this effect. For example, Boggiano and Ruble (1979) demonstrated in their study of children that rewards do not necessarily undermine intrinsic motivation. They compared the effects of contingent rewards which were only given when a specified performance standard was met and noncontingent rewards which were given for participating in the task. The detrimental effects of rewards on intrinsic motivation was visible in the noncontingent reward conditions. In contrast, contingent rewards did not have such detrimental effects (but they also had no positive effects on intrinsic motivation; see also Boggiano & Ruble, 1986).

Another line of research which is closely related to the self-perception theory focuses on misattributions of arousal. In a classic experiment Schachter and Singer (1962) showed that physiological arousal which was elicited by an epinephrine injection was interpreted as anger or a euphoric feeling depending on the social context. When a second person demonstrated anger the aroused subject was inclined to feel angry. When a second person behaved euphorically the aroused subject also felt this way (for further discussion of the Schachter theory, see Reisenzein, 1983).

Later studies demonstrated that misattribution can be induced by confounding two sources of arousal (Zillmann, 1971, 1978, 1979). In his excitation-transfer paradigm Zillmann showed that subjects who were physiologically aroused by physical training misattributed their arousal to another salient source, e.g., provocation by an aggressor, and retaliated more strongly. This transfer effect was only observed when the temporal distance between physical training and provocation was short (e.g., 5 min).

In other misattribution experiments placebo pills are used which are said to heighten or reduce physiological arousal (e.g., Coke, Batson & McDavis, 1978; Thornton, Hogate, Moirs, Pinette & Presly, 1986). For example, people who encounter a victim who needs help are more helpful when they took a placebo pill in advance which was supposed to be relaxing than subjects who thought that the placebo was arousing (Coke et al., 1978). Supposedly relaxed subjects were aroused by the victim's fate and interpreted their arousal as empathy while supposedly aroused subjects attributed the arousal caused by the victim's fate to the pill.

Misattribution can be understood within the framework of self-attribution theory. Subjects try to explain their physiological arousal by whatever cues are salient in the situation. When, for example, an arousing pill offers a plausible explanation for the arousal felt, the arousal is thought to be a result of the pill. When a relaxing pill offers no sufficient explanation for the arousal felt, the needy person is labeled as the cause of the arousal, which is then called empathy. While in the second case only one salient cause is present, in the first case the arousal which stems from the confrontation with the victim's fate is misattributed to the pill.

Another interest which was fostered by self-perception theory involves individual differences in the tendency for self-monitoring (Snyder, 1974, 1987; Gangestad & Snyder, 1985). High self-monitors are described as people who tend to observe closely what social cues the situation contains and to act accordingly. Low self-monitors, who presumably focus more on their internal states, act more in correspondence to their attitudes. Self-monitoring describes a continuum which is related to the general orientation of an individual. Some are inclined to use the social cues excessively in order to infer their feelings and attitudes while others rely more heavily on their internal states.

Another interest which was stimulated by self-perception theory concerns actor-observer differences. Bem (1972) predicted certain differences which are related to the fact that the actor has more information about the consistency of his/her behavior than the observer. The actor has more historical knowledge than the observer. In addition, the actor might be motivated to protect his/her self-esteem by defensive attributions.

Another possibility suggested by Jones and Nisbett (1972) is that actors and observers have different perceptual perspectives. While actors see their environment as a "gestalt", observers see the actor as a "gestalt."

If different perspectives for actors and observers could be proven, this would be a result of great practical and theoretical value. From a theoretical point of view, a revision of Bem's self-perception theory would be necessary because then self-perception could at best only be partially equated with interpersonal perception (see Bem, 1972). On a practical level, an analysis of conflicts such as take place between teacher and pupil or between court and defendant would be possible because, if actors and observers are shown to have different perspectives, then contradictory interpretations of a certain behavior (e.g., a pupil cheating in a class test) should occur solely on the basis of this divergence.

Differing Perception of Causes by Actors and Observers

Actors and observers have different role requirements: while the actor is concerned with maximizing his/her performance under the given environmental influences and constraints, the observer is more concerned with the actor and whether he/she acts in agreement or disagreement with other persons in the same situation (Hansen & Lowe, 1976). This is tantamount to saying that actors have to take distinctiveness information into account while observers are especially interested in consensus information (see "Sensitivity to consensus information").

This pattern of results leads to the conclusion that actors focus on the differential impact of different situations on their behavior while observers are interested in differences between actors in a given situation (Watson, 1982). Observers tend to ignore the question of cross-situational consistency while actors focus on their own behavior under different situational constraints. These different orientations might be interpreted as a desire to control one's social life (Watson, 1982). Actors have an advantage in focusing on the task requirements, which is functional for successful performance. Observers are concerned with whether the agent is a reliable and trustful person. They draw distinctions between different persons on relevant trait dimensions like trustworthiness and reliableness which are essential for interpersonal exchange.

This explanation, which is based on the human need to control one's environment, is closely related to Kelley's (1972a) hypothesis that attribution is motivated by the desire to exert control over one's fate. In a similar vein, Wortman (1976, p. 42), summarizing studies on freedom of choice, wrote: "Taken as a whole, these studies indicate that people like to believe that their behavior is under their own control and can be modified according to their own needs." This perceived-control view is not the only explanation for actor-observer differences (see below). It is quite possible that several factors contribute to these differences.

What are the main differences between attributions by actors and by observers? Heider (1958), who spoke of "polar tendencies in attribution", wrote (p. 157): "The person tends to attribute his own reactions to the object world, and those of another, when they differ from his own, to personal characteristics." In a similar vein, Jones and Nisbett (1972, p. 80) state that "there is a pervasive tendency for actors to attribute their actions to situational requirements, whereas observers tend to attribute the same actions to stable personal dispositions." The perceptions of causes by actors and observers differ, therefore, with regard to the tendency towards person attributions and object attributions. Actor attributions to the situation should be more pronounced than observer attributions to the situation. In addition, observer attributions to dispositions should be more pronounced than actor attributions to dispositions. Furthermore, a general tendency for person attributions might be present for both actors and observers (Watson, 1982).

As an example of actor-observer differences, the results of a study on perceived causes of altruistic behavior (Bierhoff, Klein & Kramp, 1987) are instructive. Subjects were asked to write down the reasons why they themselves would be inclined to help or not to help in emergencies. In addition, they were asked to list the reasons why people in general would help or not help in emergency situations. The open answers were coded for person attributions and situational attributions. Results indicated that person attributions were much more common as a response to the second than to the first question. The results are summarized in Figure 30. In addition to showing that strong actor-observer differences are found in this paradigm, it is also obvious that situational attributions are generally more frequent than person attributions. This result is a warning against the assumption that person attributions are in general more popular than situational attributions. The general level of person and situational attributions seems to depend on the content area and the specific question formulations used.

The differences between actors and observers in their causal attributions were investigated further by Nisbett, Caputo, Legant and Marecek (1973). In one study (exp. 1) they asked college students to volunteer to work on a weekend. They offered either $ 1.50 per hour or $ 0.50 per hour (in the following these incentive differences are ignored). An observer was present during the interview. After the decision, actors and observers were asked what their prediction about the actor's future behavior in similar situations was. It was assumed that dispositional attributions would be reflected in the tendency to

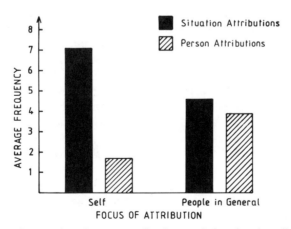

Figure 30. Average frequencies of person attributions and situational attributions for helping in emergencies. (Adapted from Bierhoff, Klein & Kramp, 1987, p. 91)

generalize the behavior of the actor to similar situations (e.g., volunteering to canvass for the United Fund). Observers, who should prefer dispositional attributions, should tend to assume that conforming actors will volunteer in a similar situation and that refusing actors will not volunteer in a similar situation. In contrast, actors should be less inclined to extrapolate their decision to future situations.

This hypothesis was confirmed because actors did not make different predictions about the likelihood of volunteering in the future after they had agreed to the request or refused, while observers assumed that an actor who agreed was more likely to agree to a future request than an actor who refused.

A general characteristic of the means in all conditions was that actors and observers tended on the whole to predict that the actor would not agree to a future request. Even observers who observed a conforming student thought it was "neither likely nor unlikely" that the actor would volunteer time to canvass for the United Fund (Watson, 1982). This alludes to the possibility that the ratings of subjects reflect their uncertainty because they had insufficient information to make predictions with confidence. It is plausible to assume that observers tend to use the middle response when they are uncertain because their information is not sufficient to justify a dispositional attribution. Other possibilities are that the middle response is used to indicate stimulus ambiguity or an average attribution (neutrality; Goldberg, 1978, 1981).

Nisbett et al. (1973) asked subjects in another study (exp. 3) whether trait terms provided an appropriate description of themselves and of various others (best friend, father, admired friend of the same age, television announcer). Specifically, subjects indicated for 20 situations whether the trait, its antonym, or low consistency ("it depends on the situation") was typical of the target person. The situational option was chosen more often in the self-description task than in the interpersonal task. (The second experiment by Nisbett et al., 1973, will be discussed later).

A more comprehensive study with the same basic design was performed by Goldberg (1978). Subjects were asked to describe themselves and three others (one person they liked, one person they disliked, and one person about whom they had no specific feelings). These descriptions were made using 2800 trait terms, divided into 14 lists of 200 terms. These trait terms, which were used by 14 samples, were reduced to 731 familiar trait terms. Subjects had three response alternatives: 0 was chosen when the word was not an accurate description of the target person and 2 was chosen when the word was an accurate description. 1 was labeled as "the word is only partly or occasionally descriptive" and was considered to be a situational attribution. The proportion of situational attributions for the familiar trait words was highest (0.44) for descriptions of self, while the neutral other (0.41), the well-liked other (0.34), and the disliked other (0.33) elicited fewer situational attributions. The same pattern of results emerged for the set of 2800 trait terms. Over 90% of the 2800 trait terms showed the expected pattern of situational responses. The same pattern of results emerged in a second study in which the situational option had the wording "the word is only occasionally descriptive — in other words, if it depends on the situation."

Although these results confirming the Jones and Nisbett (1972) hypothesis of actor-observer differences were quite impressive, Goldberg expressed some reservations as to the meaning of situational attributions. In a subsequent series of studies Goldberg (1981) allowed the subjects to indicate explicitly what they meant when using the middle response, which had indicated a situational attribution in the studies by Goldberg (1978). The response format offered the two alternatives that the trait term was or was not an accurate description of the target person. In the middle of the scale four alternatives were specified: "average or middle," "it depends on the situation," "I'm uncertain: I just don't know the person that well," or "the term is unclear or ambiguous: I don't understand it." This response format avoids the confounding of "pure" situational attributions with neutrality, uncertainty, and ambiguity.

The results, based on 833 subjects and the descriptions of the self, the ideal person, and 12 different peer targets, indicate that the Jones and Nisbett hypothesis (1972) was confirmed using the unconfounded situational measure. Therefore, the actor-observer difference cannot be explained as an artifact of the dependent measures. Watson (1982) found in his meta-analysis of studies on actor-observer differences that 24 of 26 empirical comparisons were in the predicted direction. Therefore, this attributional bias is a robust phenomenon. It is evident in the tendency of actors to use more situational attributions than observers. In contrast, observers seem not to use more person attributions than actors. Note that situational and person attributions are not necessarily highly correlated (Solomon, 1978). In summary, the actor-observer hypothesis received support in these empirical studies. The difference between actors and observers is primarily revealed in situational attributions while trait attributions seem to be less influenced by the role of the respondent.

Actor-observer differences are also revealed in the use of different linguistic categories. Semin and Fiedler (1988) described a taxonomy of interpersonal verbs and adjectives. They identified four linguistic categories:

- Descriptive action verbs (e.g., *kick, phone, talk*) which refer to at least one physically invariant feature of the action
- Interpretive action verbs (e.g., *attack, help, imitate*) which refer to a general class of behavior
- State verbs (e.g., *admire, envy, like*) which refer to mental or emotional states
- Adjectives (e.g., *altruistic, fair, jealous*) which refer to abstract descriptions of persons.

Semin and Fiedler (1988) asked their subjects to rate sentences which contained these interpersonal verbs and adjectives on five dimensions (subject informativeness, situative informativeness, endurability, verifiability, and disputability) which were assumed to be related to the dimension of concreteness-abstractness. It was assumed that the four linguistic categories varied on the concrete-abstract dimension with descriptive action verbs at the concrete pole, adjectives at the abstract pole, and interpretive action verbs more concrete than state verbs. The results of a discriminant analysis confirmed this assumption. The four semantic categories were found to be on one dimension in the predicted order. The basic dimension was best represented by situative informativeness (i.e., how much the interpersonal term reveals about the concrete situation of the subject) and endurability.

In an analysis of open answers by actors and observers, causal attributions for behavior were coded according to these four linguistic categories. Fiedler and Semin (1988) reanalyzed written material from a study by Nisbett et al. (1973, exp. 2). In that study male students were asked to explain why they liked the girl they had dated most regularly and why they had chosen their major. In addition, they had to explain why their best friend liked the girl he had dated most regularly and why he had chosen his major.

Nisbett et al. (1973) coded the open answers for the degree to which they expressed person attributions and attributions to the entity (e.g., the girl). Self-attributions emphasized entity attributions more strongly than attributions for the friend's behavior. Semin and Fiedler (1988) reanalyzed these protocols using their classification scheme of interpersonal terms. While actors used more descriptive action verbs, observers used more adjectives, state verbs, and interpretive action verbs. Therefore, the linguistic categories observers used were more abstract, while actors tended to explain their behavior in terms of neutral action descriptions. The semantics of explaining behavior obviously depends on the role requirements. One might speculate that actors code interpersonal events in different semantic categories to those used by observers. This should be related to the tendency of the actors to stress distinctiveness information and the tendency of the observers to emphasize consensus information (see Hansen & Lowe, 1976). The semantic side of the enterprise of speaking about distinctiveness information seems to be concreteness, while speaking about the differences between people (consensus information) seems to force the speaker to use more abstract, trait-like semantic categories.

Watson (1982) discusses four theoretical explanations of actor-observer differences:

1. Actors have more information available than observers. It might be argued that a high amount of information — especially with regard to consistency over time — leads to more situational attributions.
2. Actors have a different visual orientation than observers because the visual fields have different centers. It might be argued that a causal explanation is identified with the center of the visual field.
3. Actors and observers distribute their attention differently. While actors look at the environment observers focus on the actor as a salient stimulus. Therefore, actors should attribute more causal importance to the situation, while observers should emphasize the actor as a causal agent.
4. Actors and observers have different interaction goals. While actors are motivated to control environmental stimuli to ensure effective action,

observers focus on the question of what the specific characteristics of the actor are compared with comparison others. Observers, then, strive for control over people.

Another explanation is that actor-observer differences are related to differential usage of semantic categories (Fiedler & Semin, 1988). In the following we will focus on the "information level" explanation and the "salience" explanation because most of the data are relevant to these theoretical accounts. The semantic interpretation and the control approach were discussed above. The "visual orientation" hypothesis, which is based on results by Storms (1973), will be discussed in the context of the salience explanation. Note that these different explanations do not exclude each other. It might be possible to combine their predictions of actor-observer differences.

Information Level and Accuracy of Attribution

It seems reasonable to assume that actors and observers base their attributory conclusions on different levels of information. An actor knows on the whole more since he/she can compare present behavior with similar situations in the past. The actor can assess the temporal consistency better than the observer can (see the ANOVA model). Therefore, the actor should reach more appropriate attributions than the observer can (Monson, 1983; Monson & Snyder, 1977). When a pattern of behavior is highly consistent, a dispositional inference is likely (especially when distinctiveness is low) whereas a circumstantial attribution should be inferred if the behavior varies according to point in time.

The fact that an actor has more and better evidence available than the observer leads to the hypothesis that actors should give more situational attributions than observers do when the behavior in question is actually under the control of the situation. Conversely, actors should attribute more to dispositions than observers do when their behavior is under dispositional control (Monson & Snyder, 1977). While the first part of this prediction agrees with the Jones and Nisbett hypothesis (1972), the second part reverses this hypothesis!

Why has it then often been found that observers deduce more dispositional dependence than actors do? A simple answer would be that the behavior under examination has stood mainly under situational control so that actors have in fact produced the more accurate attributions. On the other hand, it has been observed in a context in which the actor has been clearly responsible for the course of the interaction that actors give more dispositional factors as causes than passive observers do (Miller & Norman, 1975). Actors attribute themselves more responsibility and assume stronger dispositions in their behavior than observers do (see also Miller & Porter, 1980, study 3).

A further aspect should be taken into consideration in order to be able to judge the Monson and Snyder hypothesis (1977) adequately: actors should attribute more to dispositions when they have been able to choose the situation freely. However, it is obvious that in typical experiments no free choice of situation is possible, so it would seem plausible that actors would prefer a situational attribution under these circumstances. They do not have any choice and the attributions by actors should take the realization or nonrealization of their intentions into account more than the attributions by observers do.

Monson and Snyder (1977) mention six factors which cause actors to attribute especially often to the situation. Their behavior is elicited by an experimental manipulation, is conducted in a context in which they exercise little control, is supported by situational cues which elicit a discounting of dispositional causes (discounting principle), differs from previous behavior insomuch as the experimental situation is new, is inconsistent with previous self-attribution (again because of the novelty of the experimental situation), and has no previous history.

On the other hand, a dispositional attribution should be preferred by actors when natural conditions are given, when control of behavior exists, when no conductive situational cues dominate, and when there is similarity of behavior, consistency of self-attribution, and a relationship to a larger causal chain with dominant dispositional causes (Monson & Snyder, 1977).

A number of experimenters do not find the expected actor-observer differences. It is, for instance, a fact that when an observer is instructed to put himself in the shoes of the actor, he/she attributes more to the situation than a neutral observer does (Finney, Merrifield & Helm, 1976; Galper, 1976; Regan & Totten, 1975). While this empathy effect can still be explained by a change of perspective on the part of the observer (the observer tries to see things from the actor's point of view and therefore looks at his surroundings) other deviating results are less easy to explain. A number of studies have given indications that actors prefer a dispositional explanation more than observers do (Calder, Ross & Insko, 1973; Langer & Roth, 1975; Wolosin, Sherman & Mynatt, 1972), and this especially after success (Ross, Bierbrauer & Polly, 1974; Snyder, Stephan & Rosenfield, 1976; Wolosin, Sherman & Till, 1973; see "Social interaction, responsibility, and egotism).

The hypothesis of Monson and Snyder (1977) implies that observers' degree of familiarity with the target person should influence observers' attributions. Length of acquaintance should correlate positively with situational attributions. This derivation was confirmed in the study by Goldberg (1981). Familiarity was related to the use of the unconfounded situational response option. Although the correlation of 0.18 was not very high, it was highly significant. The attributional bias of observers was especially strong for unfamiliar target persons.

Figure/Background Reversal

A plausible assumption is that the points of view of actors and observers differ systematically. The actor is central to the orientation of the observer, while the surrounding situation appears to be central to the orientation of the actor. The consequence of this analysis is that a change in the orientation should also lead to a change in the behavioral interpretation (Storms, 1973). To test this hypothesis a discussion between two actors was stage-managed and observed by two perceivers. Both of the actors were filmed. During the 5-min discussion each of the observers was instructed to observe one of the actors.

At the end of the discussion both the actors and the observers were shown the video of the discussion. Two conditions were created for the actors: an actor watched either the video of the other actor (actor-same orientation) or the video of himself (actor-new orientation). Similarly, two conditions were created for the observers. The observer saw either the video of the actor he had observed (observer-same orientation) or the video of the second actor (observer-new orientation). In a control condition no video was shown at the end.

Using an index of the relative strength of dispositional versus situational attributions, the expected difference between observer and actor was found in the control condition. The same pattern of results was found in the conditions with the same orientation: the actor attributed more often to the situation while the observer rated more according to dispositions. Important is the fact that these differences were reversed in the conditions with a new orientation: the actors used more dispositional attributions than the observers.

These results are in agreement with the hypothesis that actor-observer differences are the result of their different visual perspectives. A figure/background reversal seems to have taken place between actor and observer which elicits divergent perception of the causes of behavior. Similar conclusions result from the fact that people who are put in a state of intensive self-observation (high objective self-consciousness) prefer a dispositional attribution more strongly in comparison to observers (Arkin & Duval, 1975).

This explanation amounts to differing information processing by actors and observers (Jones, 1976; Jones & Nisbett, 1972; Watson, 1982). An observer sees the behavior of the actor as dynamic and the visual field as dominant whereas actors stress the influence of the situation more strongly. The causal origin is sought where the focus of attention lies (Bierhoff & Bierhoff-Alfermann, 1983).

If the causal origin varies with the focus of attention, then even the seating arrangement of the observers should have an effect on the causal attribution. The person one is looking at is assigned a greater causal importance when a conversation between two actors is being observed (Fiske, Kenny & Taylor, 1982, study 2; Taylor, Crocker, Fiske, Sprinzen & Winkler, 1979, study 1; Taylor & Fiske, 1975, study 1).

In order to test this hypothesis, six observers were sat in different positions around two actors holding a conversation. Two perceivers looked directly at actor A and two at B, while the two remaining perceivers sat at the side and could see both of the actors. All the observers saw the same discussion and had to judge the causal importance of each actor (i.e., how much the individual actors had influenced the course of the discussion, had determined the information exchanged, and had influenced the behavior of the other actor).

Using a summarizing attribution index derived from the four ratings it was shown that an observer attributed the actor he had been watching with the greater causal role while no corresponding differences occurred in the case of the observers sitting on the side. Another important aspect was that the results obtained by Storms (1973), who used a dispositional/situational index, could not be replicated. Visual orientation only influenced the perceived causal role of actors. Problems with the measurement of attributional variables in salience research are discussed by Taylor and Fiske (1981) and Srull (1984).

A further study (Taylor, Fiske, Close, Anderson & Ruderman, 1977, quoted by Taylor & Fiske, 1978) succeeded in demonstrating a further implication of the hypothesis for the focusing of attention. If in a group of people there is one person who stands out because of some deviating feature (e.g., the only woman, the only black, or the only man), this person should receive over-proportional attention. Consequently, a disproportionately large influence should be attributed to the person with solo-status. The combination of six people in a group was varied systematically in order to test the effects of solo status. The solo person was attributed with disproportionately great influence, whether this person was male, female, or black.

In a series of studies (McArthur & Post, 1977) in which the focus of attention was also varied, the results agreed only in part with those from Taylor and Fiske (1975). In the first study the results were similar since a greater causal role, in the sense of Taylor and Fiske (1975), was attributed to a conversation partner illuminated by a bright light. In two further studies it was shown (as in study 1) that the dispositional dependence of behavior (in the sense of Storms, 1973) was greater when the actor moved around on his chair (instead of sitting still) or wore a loudly patterned shirt (instead of a plain gray one). Brightness, movement, or complexity probably aroused more attention, which then caused an increased dispositional attribution.

In two further experiments these conditions were reversed. This time groups of four instead of two were observed. Novelty within the context was varied in that one actor wore a shirt which was a different color to that of the other three participants (two of whom remained reticent). Another variation of novelty within the context consisted of the gender of the participants, one participant being of a different sex from the others. In both these experiments the person with solo status was attributed with less dispositional dependence!

These results are understandable if one assumes that in the three versus one studies the solo person forms a Gestalt, as does the group of three, the latter forming a unit on the basis of the law of similarity (see Haber & Hershenson, 1973). A reinterpretation of the Jones and Nisbett hypothesis (1972) is necessary here: it is not the focus of attention relative to the actor which is decisive but the prominence of the actor's environment. If the actor's environment does not receive any attention, dispositional attributions are likely while, conversely, stronger situational causes are perceived when the actor's environment is prominent (e.g., because it itself is perceived as a figure). The extent of the dominance of the dispositional attributions stands in inverse proportion to the prominence of the actor's surroundings. A number of experimental results (Arkin & Duval, 1975; Storms, 1973; Taylor & Fiske, 1975) can be explained by this new hypothesis (McArthur & Post, 1977).

A further implication is that in self-perception one should overestimate one's own causal role when one directs one's attention to oneself, as is the case when a state of objective self-awareness is created, for instance, by a mirror (see Duval & Wicklund, 1972). When the surroundings are pushed out of the center of attention in this way there is an increase in the self-attribution of responsibility (see Duval & Hensley, 1976). That is the case when a subject has to judge on the basis of a hypothetical description of a car accident to what extent he/she or another imaginary person was responsible for the event (Duval, 1972, in Duval & Wicklund, 1972). Conversely, less causal responsibility is attributed to oneself when self-focusing is reduced by motor activity (Duval & Wicklund, 1973). Taking into consideration Gestalt psychological laws on unit building, especially the law of similarity, the "focus of attention-causal attribution" hypothesis was formulated (Duval & Hensley, 1976); according to this, the focus of attention influences causal attribution. Objects and events which occupy the same position on the focusing dimension should be placed in a causal relationship to one another. If the focus of attention is directed to a car accident and at the same time self-attention is increased, the self-attribution of causality should increase.

Since one obviously attributes to the first thing which comes into one's head, Taylor and Fiske (1978) coined the term "top of the head" phenomenon. An important cause for the phenomenon − especially when there is time pressure (Strack, Erber & Wicklund, 1982) − might be the accessibility of categories in one's memory (Higgins et al., 1977). Perceivers who have activated, for example, animosity or friendliness as concepts (during a sentence construction task) later use these concepts more often when they have to attribute characteristics to a person (see Chap. 1, "Social cognition"). These effects are dependent on the strength of the category activation and the length of time between activation and presentation of the relevant information or attribution of the characteristics. Perceivers might refer to their prior knowledge about what constitutes a causal relationship. Fiske et al. (1982, study 2) showed that salience effects were mediated by causally relevant recall. Perceivers seem to employ a memory search for confirmatory and disconfirmatory evidence of a causal relationship. Measurement problems in the empirical testing of the process of causal attribution are discussed by Fincham and Jaspars (1980), Srull (1984), and Taylor and Fiske (1981).

It is possible that stimulus salience leads to increased attention (Fiske, 1980; Langer, Taylor, Fiske & Chanowitz, 1976) and that paying attention leads to increased category accessibility (see Bruner, 1957a), which then makes a causal attribution probable (Strack et al., 1982). Another possibility is that salience effects could be traced back to concept-coding strategies and the recall of these concepts (McArthur, 1980; Smith & Miller, 1979). In sum, actor-observer differences seem to be caused by different processes. Among these are striving for control, differential schemata of the situation, and differing degrees of familiarity which lead to information being processed at different levels. In passing, it should be mentioned that actor-observer differences are not robust under all methods of measurement. For example, Goldberg (1981) reported that the differences vanished when the number of response options on the dispositional scale was increased. Other problems involve the measurement of the dependent variable, which should be based on a valid attribution scale (Fiske et al., 1982).

Nevertheless, actor-observer differences in attributions seem to be a "real" phenomenon. West, Gunn and Chernicky (1975) found that people who were induced to commit Watergate-style actions gave more situational attributions for their decision (to take part or to refuse to cooperate) than role players who imagined themselves in the situation. The latter saw personal dispositions as more effective when it was a matter of whether they agreed with the suggestion of carrying out a burglary or not.

Motivational Influences on the Attribution Process

In a relaxed atmosphere the conditions for rational information processing are favorable. But a glance at attributions after a personal disaster shows that attribution is often "hot cognition." In fact, it is often a question of fate whether an event in one's own life or in the lives of other people is attributed internally or externally, stably or variably, globally or specifically (Janoff-Bulman & Brickman, 1982). Three degrees of involvement can be distinguished (Knight & Vallacher, 1981):

- Low: passive and distant observation of the actor
- Middle: observation of an actor with whom an interaction is anticipated
- High: observation of an interaction partner during an interaction with the person

Anticipation of an Interaction: The Principle of Hope

If one expects to meet another person soon in order to work together on a task or to hold a conversation, a dependency on the behavior of that person is created (see Berscheid, Graziano, Monson & Dermer, 1976). Women students, for example, expected to go out several times in the next few weeks with one of three male students who had been chosen by chance. Obviously, the success of the date depended mainly on whether one got on well with the partner. This outcome dependency should contribute to a desire for control being activated which finds expression in increased attention and possibly also in a wish-fulfilling assessment of the partner. The principle of hope has proved to be a central motive in outcome dependency (Berscheid & Graziano, 1979).

Attribution processes can be set in motion by control deprivation (Pittman & Pittman, 1980; Swann, Stephenson & Pittman, 1981). In addition, a person who might be threatening arouses increased attention (Bierhoff, 1980a; Fiske, 1980; Irwin et al., 1967). The anticipation of an interaction with a stranger is threatening insomuch as one does not know what sort of a person he/she will turn out to be: carping, or entertaining and friendly. One can supplement this thought with the hypothesis that outcome dependency is one of the factors that sets the "attribution machinery" in motion (Berscheid et al., 1976). In one of the first studies in which the anticipation of interaction was taken into consideration (Davis & Jones, 1960), it was shown that the anticipation of a conversation with another person who one had previously offended on the instructions of the experimenter completely suppressed the negative consequences of such behavior (namely a derogation of the other in the sense of the dissonance theory). The mere possibility of being able to talk to someone about the fact that the offence was not genuine was sufficient to neutralize the dissonance. This result makes it clear that the expectation of an interaction influences the formation of social judgments considerably (see also Erber & Fiske, 1984; Neuberg & Fiske, 1987).

The tendency to wish-fulfilling anticipation became clear in studies in which the anticipation of an interaction with another person led to an increase in the attractiveness of this person (Berscheid, Boye & Darley, 1968; Darley & Berscheid, 1967). When, for example, female students were presented with personality descriptions of two possible female partners, one of whom was allocated to them for a discussion of attitudes towards marriage, the judgment of the partner's important characteristics was more favorable than the judgment of important characteristics of the person who was not described as a future discussion partner. This was especially so when she had previously been described with negative characteristics. Furthermore, it was found that 35% of students who had expected a negative partner chose the negatively described woman as their discussion partner even when they were later given a free choice between a positively characterized and the negative partner because of an initial "error" – the negative partner was chosen by only 10% of the female students in a control group (Berscheid et al., 1968).

These results are supplemented by the fact that people of the opposite sex who came into consideration as a possible partner for a date were paid more attention, remembered better, and attributed with more characteristics (like warm-cold, weak-strong; Berscheid et al., 1976). Furthermore, it was again found that anticipated interaction partners were liked more. These results show that outcome dependency elicits more attention and a more positive assessment of the partner, probably because of a desire for control and wish-fulfillment.

In a further study (Miller & Marks, 1982), the tendency towards wish-fulfillment when anticipating an interaction could be seen in the fact that with anticipation the perceived similarity of attitudes to a subject of discussion is rated particularly highly. It is plausible to assume that the exaggerated assessment of the similarity of the future interaction partner's attitudes contributed to a reduction in the amount of conflict and differences of opinion expected for the discussion. In this way the students fulfilled their wish for harmonious relationships through their assessment. This increase in the perceived similarity related only to the subject intended for discussion.

It is notable that precisely those people who themselves had a clear point of view (and therefore had to fear being drawn into a controversial discussion) assessed the similarity of attitudes as particularly high. In this reversal of the theory of social comparisons, it should be noted that similarity was projected onto persons who came into consideration as comparison persons. The aim of attribution appears in this case to be to increase the expectation of social support in social interaction (see Jones & Thibaut, 1958, who called this orientation value maintenance).

The function of social support for one's own position and the desire to maintain optimism about possibilities for control and wish-fulfillment in a pending interaction became clear in a study which made it possible to measure the different implications of positive or negative behavior on the part of an expected interaction partner (Knight & Vallacher, 1981). The future interaction partner was observed in an interview in which he presented himself as a friendly or unpleasant discussion partner. In the positive condition he praised the questions asked of him ("That's a good question") while in the negative condition he criticized the interviewer ("That's not a very good question"). The perceivers, who also expected to have to interview this person, attributed the person's behavior to the dispositions of the interviewee when the behavior was positive and to the context of the interview when it was negative.

These results follow the principle of hope: if the future partner presents himself as a pleasant discussion partner, one can hope for a friendly interaction if one puts his behavior down to his person. In this way the benevolent behavior is given stability over time and one can expect that the interaction partner will also prove to be socially competent in the future. If the future partner presents himself as hostile and ironic, one can maintain a glimmer of hope for the following conversation by attributing his behavior to situational influences which can probably be eliminated when a new conversation partner asks the questions.

Social Interaction, Responsibility, and Egotism

Causal attributions have different meanings depending on the involvement of the perceiver (see Bradley, 1978). While a passive onlooker like an applied scientist is interested in understanding the causes of the actor's behavior (and uses the covariation principle to this end), there is a desire to maintain the hope for a harmonious relationship if an interaction is anticipated. Finally, when the observer is the actor him/herself, the desire to defend one's self-value replaces the principle of hope (Knight & Vallacher, 1981). In the case of positive behavior on the part of the partner this means that the observer is motivated to attribute the cause for this to him/herself. By contrast, faced with hostile behavior on the part of the partner the observer will tend to concentrate on the partner's characteristics as causes. This asymmetrical attribution pattern can be called egotism (Snyder, Stephan & Rosenfield, 1976, 1978).

In the case of attributional egotism, a tendency can be seen to claim responsibility for good events for oneself and to deny responsibility for bad events. This is a motive which structures attribution so that the self-value is increased after success and protected after failure in order to ensure the best possible impression of oneself. Egotism occurs given two conditions that must necessarily be fulfilled (Snyder et al., 1978): the consequences of the action must be ascribed to the person (i.e., internally attributed) and the internal attribution has to affect the self-value. That is the case when the success/failure is relevant to one's own self (e.g., because it occurred in a valid intelligence test and not in some minor area). Correspondingly, no egotism is found in hypothetical situations (Kammer, 1984).

Motivational distortions in causal attribution have been demonstrated using various paradigms (for a summary see Bierhoff & Bierhoff-Alfermann, 1983). Either a particular task had to be taught whereby the pupil either learned successfully or failed to do so (Beckman, 1970; Ross et al., 1974); or in performance situations success and failure were elicited which could be explained internally or externally (Bierhoff-Alfermann, Bartels, Michels, Pätzold & Souren, 1980; Lau, 1984; Riess, Rosenfield, Melburg & Tedeschi, 1981; Stevens & Jones, 1976); or the attributions of actors and observers were compared (Schlenker, 1975; Stephan, Burnam & Aronson, 1979). While the first design is less successful than the others (see Miller & Ross, 1975), the data seen as a whole support a motivational bias interpretation of attributions (Bradley, 1978; Shaver, 1985; Zuckerman, 1979). In addition, a tendency for biased search for social comparison information is in agreement with a motivational bias interpretation (Pyszczynski, Greenberg & LaPrelle, 1985).

Knight and Vallacher (1981) found a clear egotism effect (see also Miller, 1976; Stevens & Jones, 1976). When the observers questioned an interview partner the interviewee reacted benevolently or disapprovingly towards the interviewer. The interviewers ascribed the disapproving behavior more than the benevolent behavior to the person of the interviewee. If the partner behaved pleasantly, the interviewers preferred to ascribe this positive effect to the situation and therefore flattered themselves. However, if the partner behaved ironically and coldly, the interviewers attributed this negative behavior more to the person of the interviewee and thus protected their own self-value. The results for high involvement of the observer show a reversal of the pattern of results obtained when an interaction was anticipated (see above). While somebody anticipating an interaction ascribed positive behavior more to the interviewee (in the sense of the principle of hope), the same behavior in an actual interview situation was ascribed less to the interviewee (egotism and increase in self-worth). Egotism can be seen as a special case of rationalizing tendencies as described in psychoanalysis in connection with defense mechanisms. The resulting motivational distortion of attribution can be interpreted as dissonance reduction. If, for example, a failure is relevant to the self-concept, a contradiction arises, provided that a positive self-value exists. These contradictory thoughts in a central area of the personality motivate the wish to minimize the responsibility for negative results (see Snyder et al., 1978).

The egotism hypothesis offers an alternative explanation for behavioral deficits after uncontrollable failures (Frankel & Snyder, 1978). The failure in the first series of tasks threatens the self-value. This threat to the self-value continues when a new series of tasks is presented because a new failure is possible. In order to have a favorable attribution tactic for the expected new failure, the "helpless" persons reduce their efforts so that they will not have to attribute a further failure to their low intellectual abilities. This explanation constitutes an alternative to the theory of learned helplessness (Abramson et al., 1978; see "Attributional theories of achievement behavior and depression").

Just as a failure can be explained externally by drugs or alcohol (and so remains harmless for one's own self-concept; see "Augmentation and discounting in concert"), so can failure in a task be explained subjectively by saying one did not really make an effort. The lack of effort becomes an alibi for the failure (Hormuth, 1986). This performance-inhibiting effect can be avoided if the series of tasks done after the helplessness training are described as more difficult (Frankel & Snyder, 1978). Then the item difficulty represents a plausible and for the self-value a harmless explanation of a possible failure, so a reduction in effort is no longer necessary. In this case the item difficulty serves as a possible alibi.

What has already been mentioned in connection with the occurrence of self handicaps ("Augmentation and discounting in concert") will be emphasized here once again: attributional egotism can have long-term negative effects even if the self-esteem is protected in the short term. The denial of failure worsens the realistic self-assessment of one's own abilities and therefore also the chances that an actor sets him/herself goals which he/she can actually reach. Only if one accepts failures one can find out where one's own limits lie. A person who accepts his/her failures as failures is better able to exercise control, overcome personal defeats, and avoid fatal mistakes (like that made by drug addicts who think they can control their use of drugs; Janoff-Bulman & Brickman, 1982).

Which Motives Elicit Self-Serving Biases?

Tetlock and Levi (1982) make a distinction between four theoretical positions which identify specific motivational influences on the attribution process:

1. *The self-esteem position:* Success and failure elicit specific tendencies which serve to protect the self-esteem after unfavorable outcomes and enhance self-esteem after favorable outcomes. The prediction is that success is primarily explained by internal attribution (e.g., aptitude) and

failure is explained by external attribution (e.g., chance). There is strong empirical evidence which supports this egotism prediction of asymmetrical causal attributions (e.g., Gollwitzer et al., 1982; Knight & Vallacher, 1981; Snyder et al., 1978; Stevens & Jones, 1976; Weary, 1980; see also "Social interaction, responsibility, and egotism"). In addition, self-serving biases influence the social comparison process (Pyszczynski et al., 1985). Finally, self-esteem maintenance influences close interpersonal relationships (Tesser, 1980).

2. *The self-presentation position*: People strive for positive self-presentation in public. Self-presentation is directed toward socially desirable social identities (Schlenker & Leary, 1982). Therefore, people are motivated to reduce the personal implications of failure by externalizing the causes of unfavorable outcomes. In contrast, after success they are motivated to maximize the credit they receive for the favorable outcome (Weary & Arkin, 1981). Although various methods are available for assessing self-presentational concerns, the general idea is that people's responses are influenced by considerations of situational appropriateness and claims for socially desirable identities (Tetlock & Manstead, 1985). Whether self-serving biases are the result of ego-defensive motives or self-presentational concerns is not clear, although the results from Greenberg, Pyszczynski and Solomon (1982), who explicitly introduced a public-private distinction into their design, speak more for the validity of an egotism interpretation (see also Riess et al, 1981).

3. *The just-world position*: Lerner (1980) presented evidence which indicates that people are motivated to believe that everyone gets what he/she deserves. The belief in a just world might motivate the victims of misfortune. In addition, it might explain the tendency to make defensive attributions, as described by Shaver (1970). In his experiments Shaver noted a tendency for perpetrators who had caused an automobile accident and were similar to the subject to be judged as more careful and less negligent than dissimilar target persons. Relevant others were blamed less than persons who were personally dissimilar. Although the experiment by Shaver (1970) was criticized as inconclusive by Fincham and Jaspars (1980), later experiments by Thornton (1984) and Thornton et al. (1986) showed the generalizability of the findings. Personally similar victims were perceived as less responsible than dissimilar victims using a measure of characterological responsibility (e.g., "Can the victim be considered responsible to some extent for being sexually assaulted because of the kind of person she is?"; Thornton, 1984, p. 726). This result fits with the defensive attribution hypothesis: observers of another person's misfortune defend their belief that they themselves might not suffer a similar fate by distorting their responsibility attributions. This need should be strong when observer and victim are personally similar because observers might feel that they are effectively accusing themselves by accusing the victim (Chaikin & Darley, 1973). For example, when the observer was supposed to be a supervisor in

a future experiment, he was reluctant to say that a supervisor was responsible for a mistake (Chaikin & Darley, 1973). In addition, Thornton (1984) and Thornton et al. (1986) found support for the notion that defensive attributions involve emotional arousal. When an opportunity for misattribution which could account for negative emotional responses was present, attribution of responsibility to the victim was reduced.

4. *The effective control position*: Kelley (1972a) and Fiske and Taylor (1984) assumed that causal attributions have the function of enhancing the understanding of one's social world. Chaikin and Darley (1973) argued that notions of defensive attribution and belief in a just world go back to the need to protect one's own safety and to secure order and justice in one's own life (see also Heider, 1958). Miller, Norman and Wright (1978) argue that observers are motivated to increase their effective control (see also Miller & Norman, 1975; Snyder & Wicklund, 1981). To be able to negotiate effectively with another person it is an advantage to believe that the behavior of the other person is predictable. Using the future-interaction paradigm (see "Anticipation of an interaction: the principle of hope") it was found that "active" observers who expected to meet the player in a prisoner's dilemma game in a later session believed that they could infer more about the personality of the target person than "passive" observers who did not expect to play against the target person. Outcome dependency leads to increased attention being directed toward the future interaction partner (Berscheid et al., 1976; Erber & Fiske, 1984).

Although the evidence for motivational influences on causal attributions is impressive, alternative explanations in terms of information-processing concepts are possible (Ajzen & Fishbein, 1983; Miller & Norman, 1975; Tetlock & Levi, 1982). People in the role of actors might process the available information differently from people in the role of observers. They might pay more attention, use smaller perceptual units (see Newtson, 1976; Newtson & Rindner, 1979), or compare actual outcomes with what they had expected (Feather & Simon, 1971). For example, Simon and Feather (1973) summarize four studies which show that expected outcomes are explained by internal stable factors (e.g., knowledge) and unexpected outcomes are attributed to variable external factors (e.g., luck). It might be that subjects in most situations expect to succeed at a task. Therefore, failure would constitute an unexpected outcome which is attributed to external sources. Although this explanation demonstrates that it is possible to explain the asymmetrical attribution pattern in information processing terms, Simon and Feather (1973) found additional tendencies in student's achievement attributions which are not fully consistent with such a conclusion. Success was attributed more to ability than failure (irrespective of expectancy) and failure was attributed more to chance than success.

In addition, people might use cognitive heuristics (Tversky & Kahneman, 1974) for making causal attributions. Representativeness should enhance dispositional attributions if there is a high degree of similarity between behavior (e.g., hitting a person) and trait (e.g., aggressiveness). Ajzen and Fishbein (1983) equate representativeness with high diagnosticity. Availability should support the use of "primed" causal attributions which are activated by prior experiences (Higgins et al., 1977). Anchoring could explain the perseverance of attributional responses when the evidence has changed. These cognitive heuristics might be used as possible explanations of self-serving biases. For example, availability might cause an internal attribution for success and an external attribution for failure. People functioning as actors might be accustomed to explaining success with aptitudes instead of situational pressures or to explaining failure with special circumstances instead of traits. This is especially likely because self-presentation leads to the same asymmetrical attribution pattern in public. Anchoring could also explain asymmetrical attributions if we are willing to assume that people start their explanation of success and failure with the most prominent explanation and then only insufficiently adapt to the given evidence. When a task is perceived as difficult, success is congruent with high ability while failure is congruent with high task difficulty (Ajzen & Fishbein, 1983). It is possible that people expect difficult tasks in experimental settings and therefore are inclined to attribute a favorable outcome to internal factors and an unfavorable outcome to external factors.

These arguments illustrate the general point that it will probably always be possible to construct an information-processing explanation for "motivational" influences on attribution processes (possible exceptions are the results by Gollwitzer et al., 1982, and Thornton, 1984). Therefore, other criteria should be used. For example, it is highly unlikely that motivational influences are not present when people are concerned with causal attributions because motivational influences seem to pervade all human life (Shaver, 1985). It would require a complicated theory to justify the conclusion that motives are not relevant for causal attributions. On the other hand, the sheer number of possible cognitive explanations casts doubt on the parsimony of the information-processing approach (Tetlock & Levi, 1982).

Attributions in Close Relationships

Intimate relationships between spouses or friends are associated with positive as well as with negative experiences for each partner. The question arises of how people account for their disagreements and problems as well as for their agreements and successes in a close relationship. Because attributions in close relationships are presumably influenced by motivational factors they represent a good example of self-serving biases.

Orvis, Kelley and Butler (1976) investigated attributional conflicts in couples. They analyzed free responses by members of 41 couples and coded their responses in causal categories derived from the written answers. The results were complex. Orvis et al. (1976) compared the actor's attribution for disagreements with the attribution the actor believed his/her partner would give. Actors tended to explain their behavior by circumstances (e.g., temporary financial problems, lack of time), background characteristics and objects, and actors' states and preferences. Partners tended to explain the behavior of the actors more with the actors' characteristics (e.g., inability) and actors' negative attitudes toward the partner. These results were summarized as follows: "The partner tends to see the particular action as part of a more general pattern of behavior, whereas the actor may view it as a single incident" (Orvis et al., 1976, p. 363).

Kelley (1979) emphasized the role of dispositional attributions in the escalation of conflict. While actors tend to excuse negative behavior or justify it, partners prefer a dispositional attribution which is strongly biased in the negative direction. The explanations of the actors refer to intentionality while the explanations of the partners refer to a state-trait dimension (Passer, Kelley & Michela, 1978). Further analyses indicate that the actors' explanations mostly imply a positive attitude toward the partner while the explanations of the partner mostly imply a negative attitude toward the partner on the part of the actor.

In a later series of studies Thompson and Kelley (1981) noted that couples exhibit an egocentric bias (see Ross & Sicoly, 1979). For various activities (e.g., planning leisure activities, conducting a conversation, resolving conflicts, waiting for the other, taking the other's needs into account) the partners tended to overestimate their individual contribution, resulting in a sum which was higher than 100%. Thompson and Kelley (1981) assume that people who are asked about their and their partners' contribution to common activities engage in a two-step process: first, they ask "How often do I do this activity?" and secondly, "How often does my partner do this activity?" (Thompson & Kelley, 1981, p. 476). Because in many cases only the first question is considered seriously, one's own contributions are overestimated.

Thompson and Kelley (1981, study 3) found that the more positive the relationship was judged, the more positive was the assessment of the partner's contribution to resolving conflicts and to conducting a conversation. In addition, the success of the relationship was rated as greater when subjects tended to blame themselves for negative consequences for the partner. Fincham, Beach and Baucom (1987) used a different paradigm. They compared attributions for positive and negative behavior in distressed and nondistressed couples. Couples who were seeking marriage guidance were defined as distressed. They were compared with a sample of couples who responded to an advertisement. Subjects read a checklist of events, checked those which had occurred during the last 24 h, indicated whether the impact of the event was negative, neutral, or positive, and wrote down the most important cause of the behavior, which was then rated according to internality, stability, and globality. These dimensions are taken from Abramson et al.'s (1978) attributional model of helplessness (see "Attributional theories of achievement behavior and depression"). Fincham et al. (1987) therefore applied the dimensions of causal attributions in the helplessness model to close relationships. The assumption is that distress in couples resembles closely the experience of helplessness (Fincham, 1985).

The results indicate that women in distressed relationships tend to exhibit a negative attribution bias in that they used more benevolent attributions for their own behavior than for the partner's behavior. No significant differences were found for men. In a second study evidence was found that nondistressed spouses exhibited a positive bias, making more benevolent attributions with regard to the partner than with regard to themselves, while distressed spouses exhibited a negative bias, making more benevolent attributions with regard to themselves. These differences were mainly related to the globality dimension. Distressed spouses assume that the causes of negative behavior are more global than nondistressed spouses do. The reverse is true of positive behavior (Fincham, 1985).

In addition, perceived intentionality is related to conflict escalation in couples (Fincham, 1985). The assumption that the actor intended to harm the partner contributes to a negative spiral which leads to derogating meta-attributions – explanations for explanations (Orvis et al., 1976). For example, the spouses might conclude from negative behavioral episodes and the excuses of the partner that the partner is not trustworthy or that the partner is egocentric. In contrast, the attribution of a benevolent intention might foster the development of trust (Lindskold, 1978).

Additional data indicate that marital satisfaction in women can be predicted on the basis of attributions using the dimensions of globality, stability, and internality (Fincham & Bradbury, 1987). The results for men are less clear.

In general, the question of whether attributions are a determinant of marital satisfaction and happiness or whether attributions are a covariate of marital satisfaction is hard to settle (Fincham & Bradbury, 1988). It is plausible to assume that when the relationship deteriorates a negative attributional bias is elicited. Causal connections might be bidirectional, leading from happiness to attributions and from attributions to happiness (Fletcher, Fincham, Cramer & Heron, 1987). Although the issue of causal dependence between attributions and satisfaction is not settled, the importance of attributions for the success of close relationships is obvious. Negative attributions might intensify a conflict while benevolent attributions might reduce the tendency towards conflict escalation.

Attribution of Responsibility and Blame

Causal attribution and responsibility attribution must be differentiated on a conceptual level (Fincham & Jaspars, 1980). Causal attributions concern the relationship between the behavior and dispositions of the person. Attributions of responsibility concern the relationship between act and outcome. In addition, Fincham and Jaspars (1980) postulate a sequence of dependent variables consisting of causation, responsibility, blame, and punishment (see also Fincham & Shultz, 1981). Each dependent variable in the sequence seems to be a necessary condition for the next one. For example, responsibility attribution precedes blaming, and blaming precedes punishment. Similar arguments are presented by Shaver and Drown (1986). They define a cause as a subset of antecedents which are a sufficient condition for the occurrence of the effect. Responsibility refers to the outcome of an action and is explained on the basis of Heider's model of attribution of responsibility (see below). Attributions of blameworthiness take the actor's justifications and excuses, which are either accepted as valid or rejected as invalid, into account.

Another problem is related to the fact that most of the research on attribution of responsibility has focused on negative outcomes. In the same vein, theories of attribution of responsibility are primarily developed for the analysis of responsibility attributions after negative behavior. Piaget (1932), in his book on moral development, also stressed the responses to negative events more than the responses to positive events. His analysis of moral judgments focuses on wrongdoing, blaming, and punishment. Fincham and Jaspars (1980) suggest that the language for judging positive events is less differentiated than the language for judging negative events.

Negative events evoke a number of questions (Montada, 1986): Who is responsible for the outcome? Who has suffered damage? Who is to blame? Who must compensate damage? Montada (1986) emphasizes that causal attributions and attributions of responsibility differ in that the latter depend on justifications and excuses. Justifications reject the accusation that the actor's behavior was morally wrong, while excuses refer to mitigating influences.

Heider (1958, pp. 113, 114) presented an intriguing stage model of attribution of responsibility (see Box T 13).

Box T 13. Stage model of responsibility attribution
Heider (1958) assumed that responsibility can be attributed at various levels:

Association: A person is held responsible for any effect which is connected with him or her. This primitive form of responsibility attribution is typical for young children, but not limited to children. Especially in stress situations adults are inclined to hold other people who were present during the negative event responsible. For example, helpers who assist an accident victim are sometimes held responsible for the fate of the victim merely because they are associated with the negative outcome.

Causality: A person is held responsible for all effects which were caused by that person. At this stage, causality is equated with responsibility. Such an equation is obviously the result of a rather crude understanding of the concept of responsibility (objective responsibility; Piaget, 1932). For example, unintended aftereffects which arise after an act and which were not foreseeable are ascribed to the actor.

Foreseeability: The actor is held responsible for all effects and aftereffects which could be foreseen although they were not necessarily intended. This stage describes a pragmatic understanding of responsibility. Foreseeability is a cue which indicates that the actor was aware of possible negative outcomes.

Intentionality: The actor is held responsible for all effects and aftereffects which he/she intended to produce. This stage equates responsibility with personal causality. Equifinality and local causality are given (see above). Ascription of responsibility is in accordance with subjective responsibility (Piaget, 1932).

Justifiability: A final stage represents the most sophisticated understanding of responsibility. A person is held responsible to the extent that no justifications and excuses mitigate perceived responsibility. For example, the hostile act of a person may be understood as a justified response after prior provocation.

While the five stages in the order given represent increasing levels of sophistication, the perceived intensity of responsibility should be characterized by increasing responsibility in the following order (Fishbein & Ajzen, 1973): association, causality, foreseeability, justifiability, and intentionality. The reversal of justifiability and intentionality is due to the expected reduction of responsibility after justification. Fishbein and Ajzen (1973) suggested that the five levels form a Guttman scale, which indicates that the attribution of responsibility is unidimensional. This unidimensional approach was confirmed by the empirical results of Fincham and Jaspars (1979), who found the Guttman-type pattern in all age groups investigated (second graders, fourth graders, sixth graders, eighth graders, adults). They used a blame scale (e.g., "How much should the actor be blamed for the boy getting hurt?") and a causal attribution scale (e.g., "How much was the actor the cause of (reason for) the boy getting hurt?"). Only the attribution of blameworthiness constituted a Guttman scale with increased intensity of blaming at the higher levels. The attribution of causality also showed an increase over the five levels.

For the attribution of blameworthiness the vertical spread of the data was larger for adults than for young children. This indicates that adults made sharper distinctions between the conditions than young children, who nevertheless proved to be ready to take intentionality cues into account in their overall judgment of blameworthiness.

It might have been more consistent with Heider's model to investigate attributions of responsibility instead of attributions of blameworthiness (Shaver & Drown, 1986). Nevertheless, the results offer fresh insights into the dynamics of attributions of blameworthiness. Foreseeability, intention, and lack of mitigating circumstances constitute the factors which intensify perceived blame (see also Brewer, 1977; Fincham & Jaspars, 1983).

The attribution of responsibility and blameworthiness is a complex issue, especially if real-life examples are analyzed. The complex network of effects and aftereffects must be taken into consideration. In addition, external influences which covary with the action are important. These influences might intensify the effects which follow from the actor's behavior. Finally, causal chains must be taken into account (Brewer, 1977; Brickman, Ryan & Wortman, 1975; Fincham & Jaspars, 1980; Fincham & Shultz, 1981; Vinokur & Ajzen, 1982). Attributions of responsibility are not only influenced by the internality of the ultimate cause. The internality of intermediate causes also counts, although less weight is given to intermediate causes than to ultimate causes (Fincham & Jaspars, 1980; Vinokur & Ajzen, 1982). In everyday life, negative outcomes are frequently the result of a complex interplay of ultimate and intermediate causes. In such situations more sophisticated concepts of responsibility must be applied than those described in the attribution literature.

The finding that the attribution of internal causes for negative outcomes leads to more severe punishment (Carroll & Payne, 1977) is in agreement with the results of Brickman et al. (1975) and the stage model of attribution of responsibility by Heider (1958), because internality should increase attributions of responsibility (at the causality level). In addition, people tend to confound internality with intentionality (Anderson, 1983a). Assessments of internality are highly correlated with assessments of intentionality. Therefore, it is quite likely that people infer from internality a certain degree of intentionality. If internality is a cue for high intentionality, it is quite reasonable for people to blame the actor after an internal attribution is made.

Another issue is the diffusion of responsibility in bureaucratic organizations (Hamilton, 1986). People seem to entertain different ideas about the responsibility of subordinates who are involved in crimes (e.g., the My Lai massacre or Nazi concentration camps). Future research should be undertaken to develop procedures which strengthen the individual's readiness to accept responsibility. Studies on the diffusion of responsibility in emergency situations indicate that it is possible to focus responsibility on a person (Schwartz & Ben David, 1976; Staub, 1970) but, in general, tendencies toward diffusion of responsibility are quite strong and pervasive even among people of the same status (Latané & Darley, 1976; Schwartz & Gottlieb, 1976).

Issues of attributions of responsibility were well handled in the work of Fincham and Jaspars (1980) and Shaver (1985). The interested reader is referred to these authors for a more comprehensive analysis of the topic.

Chapter 5

Attribution: Applications

With a few exceptions (e.g., Kelley, 1950; Messé, Stollak, Larson & Michaels, 1979; Sherman et al., 1978), the behavioral consequences of person perception have been neglected. However, in the last few years several studies have been carried out to analyze directly the connection between person perception and social interaction. These studies were motivated by sociological theories about the applying of labels in the field of mental illness and psychiatric hospitals, about the effect of "total institutions" (Goffman, 1961), and about self-fulfilling prophecies (Merton, 1968). Psychologists have also noted that human behavior can be guided by definitions of the situation which do not necessarily have to agree with the objective facts (see Thomae, 1970).

Before turning to the question of how preconceived expectations and suppositions which structure person perception find expression in social interaction, I will first try to list the possible conditions in which a close relationship between person perception and behavior is to be expected. Since there are no comparable results in connection with impression formation, I will use results which illustrate how attitudes find expression in behavior.

The controversy about consistency of attitudes and behavior (see Zanna, Higgins & Herman, 1982) shows that attitudes are not necessarily converted into the corresponding behavior. Instead, one has to take certain factors into consideration (see Bierhoff, 1988):

- The level of abstraction of the measured attitude should correspond to that of the behavior measured. One can predict the actual frequency of church-going with greater accuracy from the attitude to church-going than from the attitude to religion (Fishbein & Ajzen, 1975).
- Individual differences must be taken into consideration. People who pay a lot of attention to the outer effect caused by their behavior (high self-monitoring individuals: Snyder, 1987) show less attitude-behavior consistency than people who are less interested in achieving good "impression management."

- A further factor which can have implications for behavior is the consistency between feelings and the assessment of consequences. If the cognitive-emotional consistency is high, the corresponding behavior is more likely to result than when this consistency is low (Chaiken & Baldwin, 1981). Therefore, the degree of structuring or schematizing of an attitude has a direct influence on the probability of a certain type of behavior. Less clearly articulated attitudes have less clear behavioral consequences and are therefore more easily manipulated.
- It has also been established that direct contact with the attitude-object has a positive effect on the attitude-behavior consistency. In general, stable and clearly defined attitudes are based on direct experience and attitudes developed in this way are relatively valid for behavior prediction (Regan & Fazio, 1977; Fazio & Zanna, 1981).
- Self-focus increases the validity of attitude reports (Wicklund, 1982). If people articulate their attitudes after examining their internal standards, they will provide more valid data about themselves than those who have not gone to the trouble of an intensive self-exploration. Correspondingly, someone whose self-focus is low is more easily influenced and his/her feelings are easier to manipulate.
- If a person is of the opinion that he/she is somebody who acts according to his/her convictions, the attitude-behavior consistency is greater (Snyder & Kendzierski, 1982). This attitude can be described as the "doer" self-concept. Such a self-concept contains the belief that one is a person who acts as one thinks.

These conditions influence how well one can predict a person's behavior from his/her attitudes. Since corresponding studies on person perception are rare, it seems permissible to transfer the results on attitude-behavior consistency to the field of person perception (with great care nevertheless). As will be shown, a number of plausible assumptions can be made here — however, these will need further examination.

What can one learn from the research on attitudes? First of all, it is obviously important that the level of abstraction in impression formation should correspond to that in social interaction if one wants to attempt to predict social interaction from impression formation (see Fishbein & Ajzen, 1975; Stroebe & Insko, in press). From the above-mentioned empirical results a number of further generalizations for person perception are possible: high self-monitoring individuals should be more pragmatic in social interaction than people who place less emphasis on self-portrayal (Snyder, 1987). Empirical results (Berscheid et al., 1976) tend in the same direction and show that high self-monitoring individuals registered information about a future interaction partner more exactly and that as students their heterosexual friendships lasted for a shorter time (Snyder & Simpson, 1984). In addition, high self-monitoring individuals paid more attention to physical appearance of a dating partner than low self-monitoring individuals. High self-monitoring individuals seem to be more influenced by images of potential dating partners with whom they may be seen (see Chap. 3, "Physical attractiveness").

Further factors which should influence the transformation of an impression into social behavior relate to the degree of articulation of the impression and to the self-concept of the perceiver. If someone proves generally to be temperamental and variable in his/her behavior, he/she should show less consistency between person perception and social interaction than someone who prefers stable behavior. A clearly articulated impression of another person which is the result of "individuating impression formation processes" (Neuberg & Fiske, 1987) should influence the social interaction with this person more strongly than a superficial stereotype (Swann & Ely, 1984). If an impression is based on direct interaction with another person (or on the anticipation of outcome dependency) it should influence behavior more strongly than if it only relies on hearsay (Neuberg & Fiske, 1987; Swann & Ely, 1984). In addition, a high self-focus during impression formation should lead to more consistency between impression and social interaction than a low self-focus. Finally, as for the self-concept of the perceiver, it can be assumed that a doer motivation causes higher impression-behavior consistency (see "Self-control and altruistic behavior"). On the other hand, one must take into account that perceivers influence the self-concept of the interaction partners by their expectations, which they communicate to the interaction partner (see "Self-fulfilling prophecies and processes of expectation confirmation").

Surprisingly, these hypotheses have only been insufficiently tested for person perception. They represent, however, plausible generalizations from the field of attitude research in which the question of behavioral implications has been considered in more depth. In particular, the studies by Mark Snyder, W. B. Swann, and their colleagues have helped research to move from social perception towards social reality (see Snyder & Swann, 1978a; Snyder, 1984; Swann, 1984, 1987; see also Deaux & Major, 1987; Jones, 1986; Miller & Turnbull, 1986).

Before this approach is dealt with in more detail, it will be shown in the next section how social perception affects performance aspiration and altruistic behavior. These two areas will demonstrate by way of example what role self-perception and attribution processes play in social motives. Other areas in which similar connections can be found are, for example, aggression and hostility as well as justice and fairness. In the section on reciprocity is an example demonstrating how aggressive behavior can be conveyed by behavior confirmation and the principle of reciprocity.

Social Motives and Attribution: Achievement Behavior and Helping

Performance and altruism are determined by attribution processes in many ways. Here one need only call to mind how success and failure are explained causally (see Bar-Tal, 1978; Davis & Stephan, 1980; Simon & Feather, 1973; Weiner, 1986; see Chap. 4, "Attributional theories of achievement behavior and depression") and also the importance of internal/external explanations for the plight of a victim when considering the readiness to help (Berkowitz, 1969; Ickes & Kidd, 1976; Meyer & Mulherin, 1980; Weiner, 1980b).

In this section I will concentrate on two particular questions:

1. How are intelligence and motivation assessed when information about performance and ability is available? How is a person assessed as regards performance-relevant attributes when his/her performance is known?
2. Can one create the self-concept of a helpful person with the help of "character attributions"? Here we are interested in the influence of terms which are used as labels to characterize a person (see Chap. 3, "Label effects"). Do such labels lead to self-fulfilling prophecies?

Performance Attribution

Heider (1958) described the "naive" judgment of performance as the product of ability and motivation (see Chap. 4, "The naive analysis of behavior"). The two most important theories which took Heider's work as a starting point were the ANOVA theory (Kelley, 1967) and the theory of correspondent inferences (Jones & Davis, 1965; See Chap. 4). Kepka and Brickman (1971) used both theories to make predictions about performance attribution (see Box I 18).

> *Box I 18.* Attribution of intelligence and motivation in schools
> On the basis of Weiner's classification schema (see Table 18) one can see that aptitude (ability) and motivation (temporary exertion) differ in that aptitude represents a structural component (high stability) and temporary exertion (effort) a dynamic component (low stability). Structural components like intelligence are relatively stable over a period of time while dynamic components can be variably graded. A person can invest all his/her energy in achieving an aim or can do something with the minimum of effort. The actual performance obviously depends on both the structural and the dynamic components.
>
> Kepka and Brickman (1971) hypothesized that the structural components can be predicted using the ANOVA theory (see Chap. 4, "The covariation principle"), while the dynamic components can be predicted on the basis of the high information content of unexpected behavior as explained by Jones and Davis (1965; see Chap. 4, "The theory of correspondent inference").
>
> When observers have to assess the intelligence of a target person they can assume that this structural characteristic might be measured incorrectly by a once-only measurement. Since, however, intelligence is relatively stable over time, observers might tend to collect as many indications and as much evidence as possible and add this together in a summarizing judgment.

Furthermore, the observer's subjective security that he/she is on the right path is greater if several sources of information are consistent. Consistency over time and over modalities is an important criterion for the ascription of a trait in the ANOVA theory.

On the other hand, the observer might tend to take the prior expectation of the performance level into consideration when assessing the target person's effort. If, for example, a target person is of average ability but achieves a high performance, the observer should conclude with a high subjective certainty that the target person's efforts were high. When there is a discrepancy between ability and performance the observer should attribute this to a large extent to effort. (In contrast, the observer attributes performance to ability if ability and achievement are consistent.)

In two studies with 270 and 160 subjects, respectively, the intelligence of a hypothetical target person was assessed. Furthermore, the judges had to say how sure they were in their judgments. In the first study the mean grade in school was described as above average, average, or below average. The ability (as measured by a school performance test) was then described as well above average, average, or well below average.

How was the target person perceived in the performance-relevant areas? The intelligence assessment followed a simple rule: the better the average grade and the better the test score, the higher the perceived intelligence. The certainty of the judgment depended only on the test performance, uncertainty being greatest when the test performance was average.

The ascribed motivation was higher the higher the grades. However, it is interesting to note that the ascribed motivation was lower the higher the test performance. If the mean grade was fixed (e.g., high) the estimated motivation was greater the lower the ability. Here, the certainty of the judgments depended on the mean grade (not on the ability, as with intelligence) so that the uncertainty was highest with average grades. In addition, there was more certainty in the conditions in which the grades and the test results were inconsistent than in the conditions where there was consistency.

These results were replicated in the second study. Furthermore, by incorporating conditions in which information was given only about the grades or only about the test performance it was demonstrated that judgment formation about intelligence probably follows an averaging rule. The intelligence assessments were more extreme (in a positive or a negative direction) when no additional information about mean grades was given, only information about high or low ability. The same information when combined with information about mean grades led to less extreme judgments (as is typical for the averaging model of information integration; Anderson, 1981). On a 7-point scale the average values given two pieces of information were 5.50 (high ability, average grades), 4.70 (average ability, average grades), and 3.95 (low ability, average grades), while the comparable mean values given only one piece of information were 5.90 (high ability), 4.70 (average ability), and 3.20 (low ability).

To sum up, one can say that intelligence and motivation are estimated according to different principles. While the perceived intelligence was determined by an adding rule, there was a compensatory judgment pattern for motivation inasmuch as for a particular grade level the perceived motivation was greater the lower the ability.

This compensatory schema may have far-reaching implications: if a good performance is attributed to effort this could be hiding the idea that the target person's ability is only average. This "hard-working but stupid" stereotype fits the compensatory judgment schema of the judges (see Box 118). It has been shown in studies in which students were asked if they would rather be very able and not very committed or not very able and highly committed that ability is preferred to effort (Nicholls, 1976; Covington & Omelich, 1979a). However, the students found it best to be able and hard-working and worst to be neither able nor hard-working (Covington & Omelich, 1979a).

This pattern of results could be caused by effort's being a "double-edged" sword. Feelings after failure were more negative when the failure occurred after great effort than when it occurred after only slight effort (Covington & Omelich, 1979b). From this point of view high motivation can be threatening for the ego because after failure the conclusion that low ability was responsible would seem to be unavoidable. This could be the reason for the trend towards apathy in school among many pupils.

There is a similar tendency to be seen in results showing that unexpected successes lead to an inclination to create self-handicaps in order to have a plausible explanation for later failures without threatening one's self-esteem (Berglas & Jones, 1978). In one study it was shown that unexpected successes led to subjects taking drugs which reduced efficiency and could serve as an excuse for later failures (see Chap. 4, "Augmentation and discounting in concert").

What about the applicability of Kepka and Brickman's results (1971) for schools in general? In the studies mentioned, hypothetical scenarios were presented. In a further study (Felson & Bohrnstedt, 1980) teachers assessed the intelligence and motivation of pupils actually in their class. Data on the average grades and the pupils' scores in an intelligence test were also available, but this information was not explicitly given to the teachers.

The analysis showed that the assessment of intelligence *and* the assessment of motivation are determined additively by the grade and the IQ score. The better the grade and the better the IQ score the higher the teachers assessed the intelligence and motivation of their pupils.

There was no evidence for a negative correlation between the estimated motivation and the estimated intelligence. On the contrary, there was a tendency towards a slight positive correlation. Somebody who was assessed as more intelligent tended to appear more motivated. Furthermore, there was evidence that the consistency principle of the ANOVA theory determined the estimated certainty of the judgments more than low prior probabilities.

When grades and assessed ability were consistent there was a greater certainty about the judgment of motivation and intelligence. Furthermore, the certainty of the judgment was higher for good grades than for bad grades and higher for extreme grades (extremely good or extremely bad) than for average grades.

The greater certainty of judgment about extreme grades represents an indirect confirmation of Jones and Davis (1965) if one assumes that extreme performances are less likely than average ones. This pattern of results and the additive judgment formation for ability corresponds to the results of Kepka and Brickman (1971). The clearest differences in the results were in the compensatory relationship between ability and effort for a particular grade and the greater certainty of judgment when faced with discrepancies between grades and test scores. Felson and Bohrnstedt (1980) suggest that such results only occur when the judges have explicit information about ability. There is a big difference between the situation where an instruction says the ability of the target person in this scenario is definitely low and the situation in which an intelligence test, which the teacher does not have in front of him/her when forming the judgment, indicates that the ability of a particular pupil is low. In the latter case the information is not so prominent during the judgment formation as in the former case. It is possible that low ability is only compensated by a presumably high level of motivation when the discrepancy between ability and achievement is very obvious, if not all too obvious, to the observer.

Self-control and Altruistic Behavior

Many authors have considered the question of how altruistic behavior is acquired (see Bierhoff, 1980b; Bilsky, 1988; Eisenberg, 1982, 1986; Staub, 1978/1979; Staub, Bar-Tal, Karylowski & Reykowski, 1984). The theories which have been discussed most in this context are the imitation of models and a learning paradigm of altruism based on conditioning processes and conveyed through empathy.

If one carries through the idea that someone's self-concept can be directly manipulated there is a further possibility for the socialization of altruism. I mentioned briefly the experiment which aimed to establish a "doer" self-concept in people in order to increase their readiness to act according to their beliefs (Snyder & Kendzierski, 1982). In the same way, it is possible to arouse the self-concept of a tidy person by character attribution (see Box I 19).

In this we are anticipating the next section which deals with processes of expectation confirmation in person perception (see also Box T 2). An expectation which an actor expresses about a target person may possibly contribute to the occurrence of the expected behavior. Character attributions can be interpreted as processes of expectation confirmation. In contrast to everyday situations when self-fulfilling prophecies occur, expectations are expressed specifically and deliberately if the intention is to trigger a character attribution. The person who expresses a particular expectation of a target person projects a concrete impression onto the target person. This impression, however, is only simulated so that the actual behavior of the target person might approach the simulated impression.

Box I 19. Character attribution of self-control

How can children be brought to pay more attention to math? Miller, Brickman and Bolen (1975) tried five methods:

1. *Attribution of Ability:* Whatever their actual performance in math, the pupils were told repeatedly that they were good at math and had excellent arithmetic skills.
2. *Attribution of Motivation:* The pupils in this group were told repeatedly that they were working very hard in math and that their efforts were highly satisfactory.
3. *Persuasion of Ability:* The pupils in this condition were made aware of how good it is to learn new math skills.
4. *Persuasion of Motivation:* The pupils in this condition were encouraged to try harder.
5. *Reinforcement Control:* The pupils in this condition were rewarded often for their progress.

The different strategies were used for 1 week by the teachers in school classes of second-grade pupils. A math test to measure the pupils' knowledge was given before, immediately after, and 1 week after the treatment. The correctly answered items were taken as a measure of the knowledge of math. The results of the individual groups are shown in

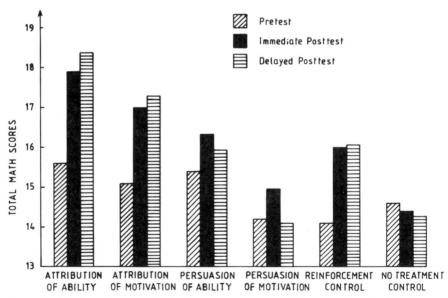

Figure 31. Math performance dependent on persuasion, reinforcement, and attribution. Each test consisted of 20 items. There was one school week between each test. (After Miller, Brickman & Bolen, 1975, p. 436. Copyright 1975 by the American Psychological Association. Adapted by permission)

Figure 31. A control group which received none of the treatments was introduced for comparison. The persuasion techniques used had proved to be the most effective in earlier studies aimed at influencing people by direct persuasion. Therefore, this was a particularly "strict" test of the superiority of attribution techniques.

As one can see from Figure 31, the two attribution techniques were especially effective inasmuch as they caused a clear increase in the math performance. This is particularly true for attribution of ability but also for attribution of performance. The superiority of these strategies can also be seen in the fact that there was no drop in performance between the second and third tests (as happened in the conditions which used persuasion techniques).

In a second study (Miller et al., 1975) it was again demonstrated that character attributions are particularly effective education techniques for schools. One group of pupils were told that their classroom was particularly neat, they were ecology-minded, and their rubbish was thrown into the wastebasket as it should be. In the second group the teacher explained that they should not drop litter on the floor. In addition, a role play was used to emphasize this exhortation. Both programs were carried out intensively over 7 days. Before and after the treatment phase the experimenters observed how many children threw candy wrappers onto the floor or into the wastebasket. While the "clean-up" behavior of the pupils in the control group and persuasion group was relatively poor (1 week after the program only about 39% used the wastebasket) there was a stronger effect in the attribution group — over 80% followed the motto "Don't Litter."

Explicit labels (like "You are tidy") express the observers' expectations about the type of person in front of them. The target persons appear to accept their expectation and behave accordingly (Box I 19). While persuasion techniques, even when applied extensively, produced only mixed results, a labeling strategy led to an effective change in behavior.

These results can be put down to the fact that the self-concept of the children was changed. Because they were told again and again by people in authority that they were neat and tidy they integrated this characterization into their self-concept after initial protest and behaved accordingly thereafter. The weakness of other strategies seems to be that they are not so successful in modifying the self-concept in the desired manner.

Character attributions appeared to be so promising that they were tested in other fields. In an attempt to increase altruistic behavior, an initial act of assistance was put down to compliance when faced with external pressure or to sympathy (Batson, Harris, McCaul, Davis & Schmidt, 1979). One real subject and a confederate were asked for help. The confederate agreed immediately and either said her readiness to help was because she did not want to leave a fellow student in the lurch and did not want him to be at a disadvantage because of her not helping or said it was because she did not have any choice but to give in to the request.

Even though only 40 women took part in the experiment it can be said that the results speak for a label effect on later readiness to help. After the real subjects had agreed to help the fellow student, they were given a form in which a local organization was asking for volunteers to work with them. While 60% of the students were prepared to help when the "sympathy" label had previously been used, only 25% were prepared to in the "compliance" condition. However, these results show mainly that in the latter condition a reduction in the readiness to help occurred, because in a pretest in which only the form was handed out 50% agreed to help. Because of the small number of subjects the results remain ambiguous in this point.

A further result was also interesting: the readiness of the confederate to help as perceived by the real subject was greater when she explained her readiness to help with sympathy than with compliance. In the perception of a helpful person the reason why someone helps is important (see Chap. 4, "Discounting"). Similar results were found in a study by Goranson and Berkowitz (1966). When help was voluntary rather than forced the readiness to help was perceived as being greater. The effects of altruistic labels are further illustrated in Box I20.

Box I20. Character attribution and helpfulness
While the study from Batson et al. (1979) was on too small a scale to allow wider-ranging conclusions, a more thorough study of the effects of character attribution on altruism was presented by Grusec and Redler (1980). In an earlier study (Grusec, Kuczynski, Rushton & Simutis, 1978) with 126 7- to 10-year-olds it was found that a model aroused more readiness to help when the first act of assistance was explained internally instead of externally. The model commented either "I guess you shared because you're the kind of person who likes to help other people. You must really like to help others . . ." (character attribution) or "I guess you shared because you thought I expected you to. Yes, you're right . . ." (external attribution).

In a later study (Grusec & Redler, 1980) the results of three experiments were reported which showed in particular the long-term effects of the use of labels. The authors assumed that susceptibility to character attribution varies with age. They believed that it would be particularly easy to manipulate the self-concept of 7- to 8-year-old children because in this age group there should be a greater consistency between self-concept and behavior than among younger children. On the other hand, older children should have a more established idea of their altruistic self-concept, which could be more resistant towards character attributions.

In the first experiment with 60 7- to 8-year-old children a training program to influence the readiness to help was carried out. The children played with a bowling game and won eight times in 20 rounds. After each win the children took two marbles, of which they could donate one to poor children. If they did not donate one of their own accord, they were encouraged to do so by the experimenter. After the game followed either the attribution condition or the reinforcement condition. In the first case the experimenter remarked: "I guess you're the kind of person who likes to help others whenever you can. Yes, you are a very nice and helpful person." In the reinforcement condition the comment was: "It was good that you gave some of your marbles to those poor children. Yes, that was a nice and helpful thing to do."

Following the training phase four opportunities were planned to test the children's altruism:

— The child played 20 rounds of bowling in which he/she won eight times.
— The child was given 12 colored pencils, some of which he/she could give to the children who had not taken part in the experiment.
— One week later the experimenter repeated the same remarks to the children according to the attribution or the reinforcement condition. Then the child could either play with an attractive toy or fold cards for the experimenter.
— One to two weeks later the children were given the opportunity to draw pictures and collect craft materials for children in hospital.

The results, which are summarized in Table 26, also contain the data for the control group who took part in the same tests of altruism without hearing the comments of the experimenter used for the attribution and reinforcement conditions. To sum up, it can be said that immediately after the training in a situation comparable to the training phase (test 1) there was an increased degree of altruism in both experimental groups when compared with the control group. But the superiority of the attribution strategy with respect to the generalizability is already clear in test 2. This superiority

Table 26. Average readiness to help in five posttests. (After Grusec & Redler, 1980, p. 528. Copyright 1980 by the American Psychological Association. Adapted by permission)

	Attribution		Reinforcement		Control	
	Boys	Girls	Boys	Girls	Boys	Girls
Test 1 (marbles)	7.2	8.2	7.0	5.8	2.8	3.9
Test 2 (colored pencils)	5.1	6.5	3.3	2.3	2.4	2.3
Test 3 (cards)	3.9	5.4	1.1	2.5	0.9	3.2
Test 4 (drawing)	1.9	3.4	0.9	2.3	1.1	1.8
Test 5 (craft materials)	4	5	0	2	1	3

In each column are the results for ten children. For the first four tests the average number of objects is given. For test 5 the number of children who collected any craft materials whatsoever is given.

remains in the delayed tests, in which the reinforcement condition cannot be distinguished from the control condition.

It should also be mentioned that in the last two posttests, and in particular in test 5, there was a sex effect, the girls being more ready to help than the boys. In a second experiment the main results were confirmed for a group of 48 8-year-olds, a generalizing of the training situation to "true" altruism being observed over a longer period of time. However, in a group of 48 5-year-olds the attribution training had no long-term effects although a short-term effect of the reinforcement and attribution training was noticeable. Finally, in a third experiment with 60 children with an average age of 11 years it was shown that the altruism training increased the donating of marbles and the sharing of colored pencils in comparison with the control group. This was so for reinforcement and attribution. Delayed posttests were not carried out here.

To sum up, it can be said that the self-concept and self-control – especially in children – can be influenced by specific attribution communications. This is particularly so when one is able to link these communications to important persons in authority. Expectations which are conveyed through the consensus of the larger social network and remain consistent over a longer period of time appear to be especially effective. Such expectations have the effect of self-fulfilling prophecies.

Self-fulfilling Prophecies and Processes of Expectation Confirmation

Interest in processes of expectation confirmation is based on two developments in sociological research:

1. Merton (1968) described the phenomenon of self-fulfilling prophecies by referring to how the social definition of a situation had repercussions for social interaction in this situation:

> The self-fulfilling prophecy is, in the beginning, a *false* definition of the situation evoking a new behavior which makes the originally false conception come *true*. The specious validity of the self-fulfilling prophecy perpetuates a reign of error. For the prophet will cite the actual course of events as proof that he was right from the very beginning. (Merton, 1968, p. 477).

2. Scheff (1974) and Becker (1963) presented a labeling theory of deviant behavior which was not based on the motivation of the deviant (unlike Merton, 1968, in his anomie theory). Instead it started with the social perception of those who call other people deviant:

> The deviant is one to whom that label has successfully been applied; deviant behavior is behavior that people so label. (Becker, 1963, p. 9; see Yarkin et al., 1981).

Self-fulfilling prophecies can be traced back to an observer who forms an expectation about the behavior of a target person in a way which corresponds to his expectation (Jones, 1986; Miller & Turnbull, 1986). If the observer acts in correspondence with expectations, then it is possible for these expectations to be converted into social reality (Messé et al., 1979). The observer then sees his interpretation confirmed and the target person may infer a self-concept via self-perception which resembles the false expectation of the observer. This process of expectation confirmation was presented schematically in Chap. 1 ("First come, first served") because it is an example of a primacy effect.

Reciprocity

The process of expectation confirmation can be illustrated with the help of an empirical demonstration of aggressive behavior (Box I 21). It should not be left unsaid that the results presented in Box I 21 lead to pessimistic conclusions. If an actor − no matter how − reaches the hypothesis that a target person tends to hostility this will produce the tendency in the actor to demonstrate (preventive) hostility, which should then elicit the expected behavior from the target person. Worse is the implication that the target person transfers the hostile behavior to new situations so that the initial hypothesis about hostility can soon receive multiple confirmation. Finally, the target person may come to the conclusion that he/she is an aggressive person. What begins as a false definition of a situation can manifest itself in the behavior of the target person following a change in the self-concept.

Box I 21. How reciprocal hostility can begin
In a study by Snyder and Swann (1978 a) a target person interacted with an actor/perceiver (the so-called labeling perceiver) who had previously received personality information about the target person. Needless to say, this information about the hostile (e.g., aggressive, competitive) or nonhostile (e.g., passive, cooperative) character of the target person was fictitious. The interaction consisted, among other things, of the use of a "noise weapon" which one could set at different noise levels (1 = inoffensive; 6 = offensively irritating). The perceiver and the target person were engaged in a competition to react as quickly as possible to a signal light. For three rounds each (over a total of 24 rounds) either the perceiver or the target person had the noise weapon, which they could set at the beginning of each round so that the opponent would be more or less strongly disturbed by the noise relayed over headphones.

After this first contest the target person took part in a second contest under the same conditions with a "naive" perceiver who had not been informed in any way about the personality of the target person. The target person was told that the use of the noise weapon was totally dependent on the personality of the user (dispositional attribution) or on the opponent (situational attribution). If dispositional attribution is used, a generalization about the expected hostile/nonhostile behavior in later interactions should result because the target person can then attribute his/her behavior to his/her own self-concept ("I am more aggressive than I previously assumed"; see "Self-control and altruistic behavior").

First of all, labeling perceivers showed more hostile behavior if they expected to be interacting with a hostile rather than a nonhostile target person. Consequently, target persons who had been labeled *hostile* used the noise weapon more than those who had been characterized *nonhostile*. This behavioral reciprocity was a self-fulfilling prophecy. A false situational definition had been established. Therefore, the labeling perceiver rated the behavior of the target person as more aggressive when the label *hostile* was used at the beginning. Without being aware of their own role during the contest, the labeling perceivers assumed that the aggressive behavior characterized the personality of the target person.

As for the following interaction with the naive perceiver, here the attribution focus became clear. If the attribution was situational, there was no difference between the hostile and nonhostile target persons. However, the behavioral differences resulting from the label were perpetuated if a dispositional attribution was suggested. Then the *hostile* target person showed more hostile behavior in the second interaction with the naive perceiver, as shown by the level of use of the noise weapon. Consequently, the perceivers said in a final assessment of the impression they had of the target person that they rated the *hostile* target person as more aggressive than the *nonhostile* target person.

While Merton (1968) described how a false situational definition can lead to behavioral confirmation, Snyder and Swann (1978a) showed that in addition to the behavioral confirmation a self-perception effect which contributes to a generalization of the social behavior elicited by the expectation must also be considered (see "Self-perception and self-concept of the target person").

As we have seen, the target person's hostile behavior can be caused by the perceiver's expectation that the target person is a hostile person. Analogous to hostile behavior, it has been shown that the expectation that the target person is competitive results in the target person's being genuinely competitive (Kelley & Stahelski, 1970). In these examples it seems plausible to trace the expectation confirmation back to the reciprocal behavior of the target person towards the perceiver (Darley & Fazio, 1980). Because of his/her expectations, the perceiver behaves in a hostile or competitive way which then "forces" the target person to answer in kind.

Nonverbal Communication

Besides reciprocity various other communication processes play a role in behavioral confirmation of an expectation. After these communicative processes have been illustrated, I will turn again to the question of to what extent interpersonal expectations can influence the self-concept of the target person.

First, I want to demonstrate how expectations are "realized" through nonverbal behavior. While the wording chosen by an interaction partner is usually under conscious control, this is often not the case for nonverbal behavior accompanying speech. Nevertheless, nonverbal comunication offers an important means of influencing the course of an interaction (see Scherer, 1979).

Word, Zanna and Cooper (1974) tested the hypothesis that black job applicants were treated with more reserve by white interviewers than were white applicants and that this approach led to the blacks' presenting themselves in a less favorable light in the interview (see Box I22). This hypothesis implies that blacks create an impression in white perceivers which triggers an attempt to increase the distance between the perceiver and the target person.

Box I22. Immediacy in social interaction
In the first experiment the interaction behavior of white interviewers towards job applicants was examined. It was shown that the interviewers placed their chair farther away from black applicants than from white applicants; they also conducted a shorter interview with these applicants and used fewer complete sentences.

In a second experiment these features of the interview behavior were systematically varied. In one condition the (white) interviewer behaved less immediately, conducted a shorter interview and spoke in a less connected manner. In the second condition more immediacy was introduced into the social interaction with the applicants. This time all the applicants were white students.

The video recording of the interview was assessed by observers as to how favorable the impression made by the applicant was. When the interview behavior was immediate the impression was rated as more positive than when immediacy was lacking (as was typical for the interaction with black applicants).

The comparison of the results from the two experiments shows that the interaction of black and white persons was characterized by a self-fulfilling prophecy. Black applicants were treated with less immediacy and this interaction behavior led to their presenting themselves less favorably in comparison to white applicants. Black skin color seems to function as a stigma in that avoidance behavior is elicited from white interaction partners. It is possible that one reason for higher unemployment among blacks (among others like lower standards of education and prejudices) is that the achievements of black people who present themselves in interactions with white people are assessed less positively merely because blacks are restricted in their self-presentation by the interaction behavior of whites.

Other studies (Chaikin, Sigler & Derlega, 1974; Rubovits & Maehr, 1971) show that expectation effects also occur in the content of school learning. These experiments studied which verbal and nonverbal behaviors contribute to the teachers' suppositions becoming a prophecy confirmed by the pupils' behavior (see "Teacher expectation effects").

Yarkin et al. (1981) induced expectations about the mental health of a person which was either described as positive or negative (or no information was given). Subjects who expected the person to be extroverted and content established more eye contact with her during a conversation than subjects who expected her to be socially isolated and depressive. This tendency was especially pronounced for subjects who had completed an attribution measure after viewing a videotape which showed the stimulus person. Presumably the attributional activity strengthened the effect of the expectations on the course of social interaction (see Town & Harvey, 1981).

"Forcing" Expectations Through

Expectation confirmation can be communicated via several channels. Besides reciprocity and nonverbal signals it is possible that the observer imposes his/her expectations of the target person directly on to the latter. This possibility will be illustrated here using as examples two tactics which both put pressure on the target person to behave in a manner consistent with the expectations of the observer. The first tactic involves verbal manipulation in a conversation between observer and target person (see Box 16). If an interviewer uses manipulative questions there is the danger that the interviewee's self-presentation will be restricted in an unacceptable way. Such manipulative questioning techniques – for example, during the cross-examination of defendants and witnesses in court – can lead to false conclusions being suggested. A judge who has formed the hypothesis that a defendant is a squabbler could be tempted to ask questions referring to episodes in which squabbling is not improbable. Such a questioning strategy could lead to the defendant not having sufficient opportunity to present episodes in which he did not embody the hypothetical type. A possibly wrong situational definition by the judge can thus be confirmed by the defendant's statements.

If two-sided questions are used in an interview to test the hypothesis that a person is extrovert or introvert, there is evidence to suggest that expectation confirmation takes place when, on the one hand, the interviewer is convinced of his/her expectations while, on the other hand, the target person is uncertain of his/her own self-assessment (see Box 123). High certainty in the perceiver and high uncertainty in the target person with regard to the characteristics of the target person intensifies the expectation confirmation and reduces the resistance of the target person.

Box 123. Self-verification versus expectation confirmation
Swann and Ely (1984) tested whether a process of expectation confirmation can be disturbed by processes of self-verification. They observed the effects

of a real-life interview between two people (see Snyder & Swann, 1978 b, study 2). In contrast to the earlier study, the interviewers chose their questions from a set of open questions (instead of manipulative questions). The interview was conducted in three stages in each of which five out of 12 questions had to be chosen. Six of the questions on each list probed for evidence of extroversion (e.g., "Do you like to go to big parties?") and six for evidence of introversion (e.g., "Do you have trouble meeting people and making friends?").

After the self-assessment by the interviewee of his/her extroversion the interviewer was given a personality description leading him/her to expect an introvert or an extrovert interviewee. In fact, the description contradicted the self-assessment so that introverted people were described as extroverted (and vice versa).

In one experimental condition the impression was given that the information on the interviewee was very reliable. In the second experimental condition it was presented as if it was not too reliable. Furthermore, a distinction was made in the data analysis between those target persons whose self-assessments were very definite and those who were relatively uncertain.

The results show that in the first round with the interviewers who had a high expectation certainty, a confirmatory questioning technique was preferred. In all three rounds expectation confirmation only occurred for the behavior of the interviewee who was assessed for extroversion by naive perceivers when high certainty in the expectation coincided with low certainty in the interviewee about his/her self-assessment. When the interviewer was uncertain, or when the interviewee was certain about the self-assessment, then self-verification prevailed so that extroverted persons seemed extrovert and introverted persons introvert.

A further way of forcing expectations onto people is to act first and to express the expectation in the first action. This tactic resembles the advantage which a player has in particular types of games when he/she draws first (so-called pre-emption; see Kelley & Thibaut, 1978).

This tactic can be seen in use when men acting as perceivers and women as target persons have to negotiate which of them will perform each of two tasks. In a study by Skrypnek and Snyder (1982), one of the tasks corresponded more to the male stereotype (e.g., installing a light switch) while the other corresponded more to the female stereotype (e.g., ironing a shirt). Although the men always negotiated with women, they were given the impression in the one condition that the partner was a man, while the men in the second condition believed correctly that they were negotiating with a woman. When able to react first, men chose the male task more often when faced with "women" than with "men" (see Box I 12).

Character Attributions

Finally, it is also possible that expectations can be confirmed by character attributions (Miller et al., 1975; see also "Self-control and altruistic behavior"). The explicit communication of a label to somebody — whether negative as with deviant behavior or positive as with self-control and altruistic behavior — represents a "cognitive manipulation of his self-concept" (Kraut, 1973, p. 552). This mediating process will be discussed again in the section on the effects of teachers' expectations.

Expectation Confirmation and Self-Verification: Two Contrary Processes

When the mutual expectations of the interaction partners are misleading, this results in formation of false impressions, which can lead to the imagined social reality actually coming into existence (Darley & Fazio, 1980). Snyder (1984) used the term "belief creates reality" in this context. For a long time the importance of "belief-creates-reality" processes in everyday social behavior could not be adequately assessed.

One difficulty in estimating the importance of self-fulfilling prophecies in everyday situations lies in the fact that one can often only inadequately assess to what extent the "natural" behavior of the target person can defend itself against an expectation (Swann, 1987). The person who is the target of an expectation can correct the falsified impression formation through his/her concrete behavior, at least when certain conditions are fulfilled.

The study by Swann and Ely (1984; see Box I 23) shows that the expectations of the interviewer only have a minimal effect on the interview behavior of the target person if the self-concept of the target person is secure and stable. This indicates that expectation confirmation is often hampered by self-verification processes. One precondition for successful self-verification by a person who is the target of an expectation is that free communication must be possible. In none of the conditions of the experiment by Swann and Ely (1984) was, for example, an "introverted" expectation observed to lead to an extroverted target person behaving in an introverted manner. When the conditions were favorable for expectation confirmation (i.e., low certainty of the target person combined with high expectation certainty of the interviewer), the self-concept could at best be neutralized.

The probability that an expectation holds its own increases the fewer the number of contradictory cues occurring in the social interaction. If, for example, the target person is not seen in a face-to-face interaction and if only minimal information about him/her is available, an expectation can most easily hold its own.

The conditions in experimental studies in which expectation effects have been demonstrated resemble this favorable starting situation. In the studies by Jones and Panitch (1971) and Kelley and Stahelski (1970) the target persons could only show something of their "true" personality through their moves in a game. If social interaction is reduced to moves in an experimental game the target person has hardly any means of correcting the presuppositions of the interaction partner.

The possibilities are greater when the person who has formed a false impression and the target person meet in a face-to-face interaction and, for example, have a conversation together. Since communication is not limited in such a face-to-face interaction, the probability is far greater that the target person can correct a false impression.

The probability of a false expectation being corrected is particularly high when the target person knows that he/she has been inadequately assessed by the observers (Hilton & Darley, 1985; Swann & Read, 1981; Swann & Hill, 1982). Here the target person can consciously oppose the false impression. In one experiment (Swann & Read, 1981) people who thought themselves to be likable were told that another person thought they were unlikable. This information elicited behavior in the social interaction which was suited to creating the picture of a likable person.

Such processes which maintain one's own self-concept are called self-verification processes (Swann, 1987). The combination of the processes of expectation confirmation (initiated by the observer) and of self-verification (initiated by the target person) can be characterized in two hypotheses:

1. The more limited the target person's communication possibilities, the weaker the processes of self-verification should be in proportion to the processes of expectation confirmation. Self-verification is dependent on free and undisturbed communication which allows the target person to manifest his/her "true" self.
2. The better the target person is informed that the observers have formed a distorted impression of him/her, the stronger his/her motivation to correct the false impression should be. This should be the case especially when the false impression refers to a central part of the self-concept, e.g., reliability and honesty.

In Box 124 an experiment is described (Bierhoff & Schreiber, 1988) in which the aim was to measure the effects of false expectations on conflict resolution. The areas of cooperation and competition are obvious choices, as classic studies show that self-fulfilling prophecies are to be found here − at least under conditions of limited communication (Jones & Panitch, 1971; Kelley & Stahelski, 1970).

We tried to set up a conflict situation in which free communication between observer and target person was possible. On the other hand, we wanted to avoid increasing the resistance to the expectation on the part of the target person, as probably happened in the studies by Hilton and Darley (1985), who informed their target persons about the false impression formed by the observers. We wanted to create an experimental situation in which processes of self-verification were neither suppressed nor reinforced.

Box 124. Expectation confirmation influences development of trust

Two interaction partners had to agree on a resolution of a conflict in a discussion. The perceived interpersonal orientation of the partner was varied by giving information from a fictitious questionnaire before the beginning of the negotiation. The students negotiated everyday problems in which they had to represent opposing interests. A resolution to the conflict could be reached by one side giving in, by reaching a compromise, or by creative solutions.

In the 90 negotiations two negotiating partners sat face-to-face. It was possible to exchange suggestions, opinions, and demands freely. The students of each negotiating pair were asked to come to different rooms in the laboratory. They filled in a questionnaire in which they had to assess eight different interpersonal situations according to their own preferences. The main aim of this questionnaire was to make the information about the interpersonal orientation of the partner credible.

Three forms of personality information were used:

1. The partners were described as strongly competitive, egoistic, and aggressive (= competition orientation).
2. The partners were described as ready to cooperate, interested in mutual help, democratic, and ready to compromise (cooperative orientation).
3. The partners were described as selfless and altruistic (altruistic orientation).

Both people in a pair were given the same information about the attitude of the partner. After the fictitious information the negotiating partners were told about the subject they were going to negotiate. The base information for each partner was different since they were supposed to take on two different roles. The subject of negotiation involved a conflict of interests between the two parties. An example of a subject of negotiation is the question of whether a student coming from another university can have all his/her courses recognized at the new university. While one negotiating partner played the role of the student, the other negotiated in the role of the professor who has certain discretionary powers to recognize courses taken at other universities although he/she is bound by certain regulations. A total of four different subjects of negotiation were used to test the generalization of the expectation confirmation effects. The students were motivated to take a hard line in the negotiations by telling them that the aim of the study was to establish whether they were able to support a particular standpoint in an argument successfully.

Before the negotiation began the students assessed their negotiating partners, who they at this time only knew from the personality profile, with respect to trust, friendliness, and liking. After the negotiation the trust in the partner was reassessed. Before the negotiation began the students chose a chair which they could place anywhere in a marked area. In this way it was possible to measure the spatial distance chosen. Because the negotiation was recorded on video it was possible to analyze the verbal and nonverbal behavior during the negotiation. Further dependent variables were the duration of the negotiation and the negotiating partners' overall impressions of the negotiation.

The personality information had a significant effect on the assessments of trust before and after the negotiation and of friendliness and liking. This effect meant principally that trust, friendliness, and liking were assessed as being lower in the competition condition than in the other two groups.

A repeated-measures analysis of the trust assessments showed that an increase in trust had taken place, as is to be expected in such situations (see Schneider, 1976; Zand, 1972). This increase in trust was observed equally in all three experimental conditions. At the same time, the above-mentioned effect of the personality information was significant (see Figure 32).

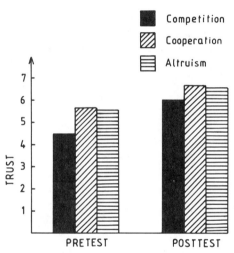

Figure 32. Effects of personality information and time of measurement on the perceived trust (0, low; 9, high)

There was a significant effect of the personality information on the spatial distance for the 90 pairs. While the partners sat fairly closely together in the altruistic condition, the distances were greater with the cooperative and competition orientation.

The following significant effects were found for nonverbal features, which can be seen as possible stress indicators:

— With the competition orientation more head movements were observed than in the other two conditions.
— There was a significant interaction of personality information and sex with respect to the overlapping of speech acts. This effect was mainly

due to women with a cooperative expectation and men with an altruistic expectation showing the lowest frequency of overlapping.

The overall impression was most favorable in the altruistic condition, while it was most negative in the cooperative condition. There was a significant effect of the personality information on the duration of the negotiation — in the competitive condition the negotiation lasted longer than in the cooperative or in the altruistic conditions. This effect was, however, only observed in some of the conflict situations.

The effects of the personality information can be followed chronologically in this study. The information had its first effect on the trust scale which followed immediately after fictitious feedback. One could see in these assessments that less trust was shown towards the competition-orientated partners. In the next step the negotiating partners were led together into a room. When asked to position their chairs those subjects with an altruistic expectation chose a shorter distance than in the other two conditions. At this point the students had the opportunity to collect the first accurate information about their partner (e.g., about appearance, which is very important for the self-presentation; see Swann, 1987). Some of the nonverbal negotiation characteristics reflect the effects of the induced expectations. This is interesting because in other comparable studies no nonverbal effects were observed (see Hilton & Darley, 1985).

The length of the negotiation represents an overall measure of the intensity of the negotiation (see Müller, 1980). The longer duration in the competition condition shows that subjects with this expectation negotiated with more vigor. As the final trust rating and the rating of the overall impression show, the induced expectation had not been completely neutralized by the end of the interaction. Interpretation of the partner's argumentation was probably biased in the light of the expectation. Many arguments open a whole spectrum of meanings which can be applied to what was said. The same arguments were probably interpreted differently, as a sign of competition or as a sign of cooperation or altruism.

The sex differences in the nonverbal measures could possibly explain the fact that altruistic and cooperative expectancy conditions together sometimes formed the opposite pole to the competition condition (e.g., for distance) and sometimes lay apart because the cooperative condition approximated the competition condition.

The results of the study described in Box 124 show that expectations exert complex influences in situations which allow free communication between observer and target person. The strength of the influences is far from being overwhelming. Obviously, processes of self-verification contradict the influence of fictitious expectations. Nevertheless, certain traces of the original expectations were found which determined important aspects of the negotiations.

Self-perception and Self-concept of the Target Person

However expectation effects are conveyed, it is possible that at the end of such a process lies a modification of the self-perception and self-concept of the target person. Evidence can be found in two studies in which it was shown that hostile behavior on the part of the target person persevered when he/she was faced with a new interaction partner (Snyder & Swann, 1978 a) and that women still orientated their task choice according to the label *man* or *woman*, even when they chose first (Skrypnek & Snyder, 1982).

In another study (Fazio et al., 1981) the circle from the self-fulfilling prophecy to the self-perception of the target person was completed. When a target person was forced in an extroverted or an introverted direction by manipulative questions, the self-assessment shifted correspondingly in the expected direction. What began as one-sided questioning led to an internalized disposition in the target person.

In a later study (Riggs, Monach, Ogburn & Pahides, 1983) this conclusion was corroborated. Thirty-one students were confronted with either extrovert or introvert questions. Afterwards they assessed their extroversion. Then they waited with an accomplice of the experimenter who behaved either in an extroverted or in an introverted way and then assessed their personal extroversion once again. The results showed that the "extroverted" rated themselves as more extrovert than the "introverted" even after the waiting period. The influence of the confirmatory questions remained apparent even when the students were confronted in the waiting period by behavior on the part of the accomplice which contradicted the direction of the questions.

Expectations cannot move mountains. If a target person has an articulate, secure self-assessment, an expectation about the extroversion/introversion of the target person which contradicts his/her actual extroversion cannot assert itself (Swann & Ely, 1984; Box I 23). Target persons are at pains to keep their self-concept stable (Swann & Read, 1981 b). People tended to look for confirmatory social feedback, elicit it, and remember it selectively (for a summary see Swann, 1987).

Optimal conditions for self-verification by the target person occur when the perceiver asks open questions which are not manipulative and when the target person can answer these questions about his/her self-concept explicitly. In such a situation he/she will convince a perceiver who began with a contradictory expectation of the target's self-concept (Swann & Ely, 1984). On the other hand, expectation confirmation on the part of the perceiver is more likely when he/she asks manipulative questions (Fazio et al., 1981) or is subjectively quite certain about his/her expectation, while the target person is completely uncertain about his/her disposition. This is the case, for example, when a teacher receives information about the performance capacity of a school beginner who is relatively uncertain how much he/she can achieve.

Self-fulfilling prophecies can be observed in many areas of life (Darley & Fazio, 1980; Jones, 1986; Miller & Turnbull, 1986; Snyder, 1984). In Chap. 3

("Physical attractiveness") it was described how physical attractiveness structured interactions between men and women. When women talked with men
who had a picture of an attractive interlocuter in front of them, they were more
stimulating, more personal in the conversation, and more content than when
they spoke with men who had a picture of an unattractive woman in front of
them. Furthermore, there was a suggestion of an influence on the self-concept
of the target person which was based on the expectation caused by the
stereotype. What began as a stereotype was confirmed in social reality.

Self-fulfilling prophecies tend to stabilize stereotypes and give them a
kernel of truth (see Chap. 3, "Sociocultural perspective"). Later in this chapter,
two areas in which expectation confirmation processes occur will be presented:
experimenter effects and pupil-teacher interaction.

Finally, one must remember the limits of exercising influence through self-
fulfilling prophecies. It may well be possible in an experimental situation or
within an institution (like a school) to influence a target person's self-concept
by false expectations (Fazio et al., 1981) or social comparisons (Morse &
Gergen, 1970). One must, however, add that outside the laboratory or the institution the target person's most important reference persons support and
stabilize the existing self-concept (see Swann, 1987). These additional influences encourage, inter alia, the tendency to self-verification and to
maintenance of the existing self-concept.

Vocal Communication: Nonverbal Cues and Social Perception

Verbal and nonverbal behavior contains many cues which can give the
"receiver" information about the personality of the "sender." Therefore, it
seems pertinent to ask what impressions about the personality of the sender
are created by particular cues. This general question will be limited in the
following to the importance of nonverbal cues for the attribution of personality characteristics (see Scherer, 1979; Scherer & Scherer, 1982).

Loudness, resonance, pitch, and warmth are aspects of the voice quality
which are perceived by listeners as cues which permit conclusions about the
speaker's personality. The attribution of personality characteristics can be
right or wrong in the sense that the target person's personality characteristics,
as measured by an objective questionnaire for example, may agree with the impression formed or not. Even if perceivers with a high interpersonal consensus
come to the conclusion that a particular cue is evidence of a particular personality characteristic, this conclusion can be a distortion of the objective personality structure or at least overemphasize the value of the signal in attributing a disposition.

In this context the "illusory correlation" phenomenon comes to mind, this
being based on implicit assumptions which are shared by a large number of
the population. Such illusory correlations involve popular misunderstandings
about the importance of particular cues. With the help of accuracy coefficients

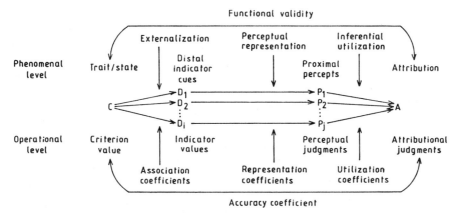

Figure 33. Externalization and inference in person perception. (After Scherer, 1978, p. 469. Reprinted by permission of John Wiley and Sons, Ltd.)

(see Figure 33) one can measure whether a sender's disposition is perceived adequately by the receivers.

In order to be able to analyze the process of attribution during communication better, it is sensible to take as a basis a model of the communication processes in which one can distinguish between externalizations of dispositions or psychological states by particular indicator cues (e.g., appearance and behavior) on the one hand and inferences about dispositions based on proximal percepts on the other hand. Such a model was developed by Scherer (1978), based on the lens model of Brunswik (1956; see Figure 33).

The question of whether personality characteristics of the sender are expressed in particular verbal or nonverbal features (externalization) can be answered with the help of association coefficients which show to what extent particular signals correlate with personality characteristics. A widely held assumption is, for example, that the voice pitch is a signal for emotional stability. But empirical results show that voice pitch does not vary systematically with the neuroticism of the speaker. Therefore, the indicator "pitch" is not a valid predictor of the criterion "emotional stability."

While externalization concerns the question of whether a particular expression is representative of a personality characteristic, inference is relevant to the question of what conclusions a perceiver can draw on the basis of particular proximal percepts. Distal indicator cues can be described as proximal percepts which determine the perceiver's impression formation. As for the relationship between attributions and dispositions (functional validity), it is possible to measure the degree of agreement with accuracy coefficients for the relationship between criterion values and attributional judgment.

As regards the compatibility between externalization and attribution, there is evidence that a medium voice pitch is an indicator of extroversion. In agreement with this, it was found that perceivers use a higher fundamental frequency of the voice as a signal for inferring extroversion. Similarly, the amount of participation in conversation appears to be a valid indicator of extroversion and dominance in the speaker (Scherer, 1979).

In general, it can be said that amongst people belonging to one cultural group there is a high consensus in the attributions made when they are presented with particular vocal proximal percepts (see Scherer, 1979). To this extent, one can talk about vocal stereotypes which are based on a high attribution consensus without necessarily having any functional validity. These stereotypes can be compared with ethnic stereotypes as measured by the attribution of characteristics (see Chap. 3, "Sociocultural perspective").

As already mentioned, some of these vocal stereotypes contain a kernel of truth. This statement must, however, be accompanied by the rider that during impression formation valid relationships are assumed to be more binding and systematic than they really are. In this respect one can talk about the usefulness of particular vocal percepts being overestimated in impression formation (Scherer, 1979). This overestimation of the closeness of the relationship between particular vocal percepts and the speaker's personality is an example of a general tendency in human judgment formation, as described by Campbell (1967). The rules of inference, as handed down in literary descriptions and the media, contribute to the occurrence of such overestimations of the correspondence between voice and personality (Scherer, 1979).

If there is a high consensus about vocal stereotypes, it seems feasible that, in addition to the influence of tradition, processes of self-fulfilling prophecies are at work and confer reality on such stereotypes (see Chap. 3, "Physical attractiveness and social interaction"; see also "Self-fulfilling prophecies and processes of expectation formation"). A speaker who uses a stereotyped style of speech could be induced by the expectations of other people to form a personality which corresponds to the stereotype (Scherer, 1979). False attributions by the "receivers," caused by vocal features, could lead to "falsified" interaction behavior, which only later elicits tendencies from the target person that at first were merely assumed (see Snyder, 1984). In this way the social environment can "force" through its expectations, which then appear valid in retrospect.

Another mechanism which contributes to vocal stereotypes being confirmed is the attempt by actors to assume particular social identities for themselves (Giles, 1979; Scherer, 1979). In order to make particular personality characteristics more probable, actors can use particular vocal stereotypes in their self-presentation. Certain features also have a functional value (e.g., length of speaking time with respect to dominance). Paralinguistic behavior is probably a function of internal processes and context (Scherer, Helfrich & Scherer, 1980).

Striving to signal a particular social identity is one reason for many ethnic vocal features (see Giles, 1979). In Chap. 3, the social identity theory (Tajfel & Turner, 1979), which is based on the hypothesis that people in general aspire to a positive ethnic identity, was described. One strategy for maintaining a positive ethnic identity is to maintain one's own linguistic distinctiveness, be it by use of one's own language or a specific dialect. In general, one can observe two different strategies which minorities without high prestige or groups with a low status can employ if they see their situation as illegitimate and unstable. On the one hand, they can try to make their speech become more like that of the majority of the group with high prestige (assimilation); on the other hand, it is possible to emphasize differences in accent, dialect, or mother tongue (accentuation).

Which strategy is employed depends not least on the "ethnolinguistic vitality" (Giles, 1979). This vitality is thought to be related positively to the status of the group (the more respected the language, the greater its vitality), to the number and territorial unity of the members of the speech community, and to the institutional support from schools, cultural organizations, and mass media. If the vitality is low, it should result in an "upward convergence" with the dominant language community. Conversely, high ethnolinguistic vitality should lead to a strategy of delimitation being followed which amounts to an accentuation of the existing linguistic differences (downwards divergence).

The tendency to a strategy of delimitation in verbal behavior should prevail particularly when a certain insecurity or permeability of the verbal barriers exists. It has been shown, for example, that Welsh people who were still learning the language rated their Welsh accent as stronger than those who already had a good command of the Welsh language (Bourhis, Giles & Tajfel, 1973). If the social identity appears to be threatened, ethnic signals will presumably be stressed in order to secure the distinction from other groups.

Verbal features often have a "surplus meaning" (Giles, Scherer & Taylor, 1979), which becomes clear in the style of speech of blacks in the United States, for example, and is seen in phonological differences as well as differences in grammar and choice of words. This surplus meaning serves as a cue in person perception which not only signals ethnic affiliation but can also show whether the sender wants to stress or cover up his/her personal verbal characteristics.

On the other hand, one must remember that stereotypes are not used for self-presentation but can be traps from which the targets of stereotypes want to free themselves (see Chap. 3, "Stereotype research — practical applications"). This is, for example, often true of age (see Helfrich, 1979) and sex (Smith, 1979). In the event of a vocal stereotype not being confirmed it is to be expected — as is the case generally for stereotypes — that there will be a tendency to maintain the stereotype (Giles et al., 1979; see Box T2). Illusory correlations, selectivity of recall, and retrospective errors protect many stereotypes against refutation for a long time. In this context it is also of interest that psychiatric patients often show unusual nonverbal behavior and speech patterns. The attribution of an improvement in their condition by experts correlates strongly with an accommodation of their paralinguistic speech behavior to the cultural norm (Wallbott & Scherer, 1980).

In addition, it should be mentioned that the surplus meaning of cues is not limited to paralinguistic features. An example of this is the distortion of the perceived size of coins (Holzkamp, 1965; Tajfel, 1957; Upmeyer, 1985). The positive valence of coins leads to an overestimation of their size. In one experiment (Holzkamp, 1965) the valences of objects were systematically varied. Circular tokens were used by teachers during school in recognition of good performance. The size of the tokens was assessed by the pupils before and after a 2-week conditioning phase. The pretest estimate was significantly smaller than the posttest estimate. In a control group in which tokens were not used as rewards there were no such differences.

In another experiment (Holzkamp, 1965) it was found that the size of a circular object (a shadow picture the size of a 5-Deutsche Mark coin) was estimated to be bigger when it was called a coin instead of a cardboard disk. The value of an object obviously influenced its perceived appearance. The pairing of value and size of coins led to a constant error (absolute accentuation).

Furthermore, it was established that the increase in the overestimation from small to large coins was greater than for corresponding paper disks (= relative accentuation). A number of social cues are probably linked to surplus meanings in the course of social learning so that perceivers use an acquired frame of reference to form an evaluative judgment. These judgment effects can be described as shifting the origin of the scale (absolute accentuation) and as stretching the scale (relative accentuation; Upmeyer, 1985).

Person Perception in Social Interaction: Practical Areas of Application

Experimenter Effects

The research on experimenter effects (see Rosenthal & Rosnow, 1969) represents one of the roots of research on expectation confirmation processes. The problems under discussion are not insoluble or proof that experiments should be abolished. With suitable precautions they can be eliminated or reduced to a minimum (see Carlsmith, Ellsworth & Aronson, 1976). The existence of experimenter effects contributes greatly to our substantial knowledge about social psychological processes.

As Holzkamp (1972) emphasized in his anthropological analysis of general psychology, experimenter and subject occupy unequal positions in the psychological experiment. While the experimenter determines the order of events and exercises control over the experiment, the subject is geared to reacting to set instructions and situations. This relationship can be seen as an asymmetrical interaction (Jones & Gerard, 1967). The experimenter follows his/her own plan and tells the subjects what to do, while the subject is limited in his/her behavior.

Such asymmetry is probably an important precondition for expectation confirmation effects which rely on questions and answers. In a conversation a superior person is more likely to determine the course of the conversation and apply a confirmatory questioning strategy than somebody of an equal status.

The asymmetry between experimenter and subject leads to the subject's being dependent on the experimenter's instructions, even to the point of carrying out quite inhuman instructions (Milgram, 1974). As a result of the experimental situation the subject often rates the experimenter's authority very highly. Under these conditions it is understandable that the experimenter's expectations can influence the reactions of the subjects through verbal and nonverbal behavior.

Experimenter expectation effects are well documented. Rosenthal (1976) analyzed 311 studies from eight fields of research (e.g., learning in animals, psychophysical judgments, person perception). A summary of all available results leaves no doubt that expectation effects can falsify experimental results (see Box I25 for an example).

Box I25. When experimenters make mistakes
In an experiment by Rosenthal and Fode (1963) the influence of experimenter expectations on the results of a study on person perception was demonstrated. The perceivers were shown ten photos of people. The task was to assess whether these people would be successful or not. The judgments were to be made on a scale with the end poles −10 (extremely unsuccessful) and +10 (extremely successful). Pretests showed that the series of photos elicited an average rating of 0. Each photo was seen as relatively neutral with respect to success and failure.

The experiment was then carried out by ten students who approached 206 subjects. The students were told that the aim was to replicate established experimental results. Five experimenters were told that the (neutral) photos were rated on average with +5. The other experimenters were informed that the average rating was −5. Although the experimenters were told to read the written instructions to the perceivers and not to make any further comments, the results showed that the previous information did influence the results. In the +condition an average of 0.40 was found while in the −condition the average rating was −0.08. Furthermore, each of the +experimenters had a higher average than each of the −experimenters. These results were replicated in two further studies (see Rosenthal, 1976).

In later studies experimenter expectation effects have been confirmed frequently. For example, the experimenter's expectations influenced the relative number of *man* and *animal* responses in the Rorschach test (Masling, 1965). If the experimenter believed that experienced testers would ascertain more *man* than *animal* responses, proportionally more *man* responses were given by the subjects than when it was conversely expected that experienced testers would find more *animal* than *man* responses.

In other studies, however, no statistically significant experimenter effects were found. The method of meta-analysis of independent empirical studies, as described by Hedges and Olkin (1984) and Rosenthal (1984), is well suited to establish trends in the results over a large number of independent studies. Such a meta-analysis shows that experimenter expectation effects occur when the hypotheses are known and it is also known how the subjects have been allocated to the experimental conditions (Rosenthal, 1976). In 109 studies there were expectation effects significant at the 5% level, while no significant effects were found in 202 studies (although the differences often tended in the expected direction). If one takes into account the actual differences in the mean responses of all 311 studies, one can conclude that nearly 50000 experiments with no effects would be necessary to bring the significance level over all studies to over 5%.

Experimenter expectation effects are among the best-documented results in social psychology. This has led to great care being exercised in social psychological studies in order to exclude experimenter expectation effects. If there is just the slightest doubt, the authors have to explain in great detail why it is definite that their results are not caused by experimenter influence (an example for this is Fazio et al., 1981).

One criticism of the studies on experimenter expectations concentrates on the question of whether one can use experiments to show that experimental results are distorted by expectation effects (Brandt, 1975). It is possible that experiments aimed at uncovering expectation effects are also subject to such expectation effects. Expectation effects can be just as effective in experiments critical of methodology as in other experiments. In the next section I will report on a study (Seaver, 1973) which demonstrates the difficulties involved in proving expectation effects in schools.

Teacher Expectation Effects

The question is now whether experimenter effects can be generalized for other areas. The issue on which most research has been done is that of teacher expectation effects. The pioneering study in this field was carried out by Rosenthal and Jacobson (1968), who observed over 20 months how the induction of positive expectations influenced pupils' intelligence, school performance, and assessed behavior. Teachers who had taken over new classes were given fictitious information indicating that approximately 20% of the pupils were expected to improve their performance considerably − so-called bloomers.

This information about the special capacity for intellectual development had an influence on the intelligence of children in the first and second grade as measured after 8 months. The study, which was performed in an elementary school in a lower class area of San Francisco, included 18 classes of grades 1 to 6. In each grade a low-track, a medium-track, and a high-track class were formed. While there was no substantial indication of an intellectual gain by the bloomers over the controls in grades 3, 4, 5, or 6, the increase in the intelligence of the bloomers in the first two grades was bigger than that of pupils not singled out. (The intelligence gain was calculated as the difference between a pretest which was given 4 months before the positive expectations were created and the main posttest which was given 12 months after the pretest and 8 months after the experimental manipulation.) In addition, in the first, second, and third grades the reading evaluation by the teachers of the bloomers increased more than the evaluation of the control pupils.

The higher grades (up to the sixth grade) did not show any expectation confirmation initially in the performance variables, although the intellectual curiosity of the bloomers in the sixth grade was assessed by the teachers as higher (which also applied to the bloomers in the first and second grades). However, after 20 months – when the final posttest was administered – this pattern changed: the pupils originally in the fifth grade proved to be particularly susceptible to the self-fulfilling prophecy, the pupils in this grade achieving a higher average intelligence score if they had been labeled as promising at the beginning of the field experiment. By comparison, among those originally in the first grade there was only a slight tendency towards fulfilling the expectation, while for those originally in the second and third grades a slight reversal was obtained, with the control pupils having improved their performance more than the bloomers.

This complex pattern of results – which is further complicated by sex and achievement level influences which partially interact with the expectation manipulation – cannot simply be reduced to one common denominator. The publication of the "Pygmalion study" provoked numerous criticisms, some of which tended to throw the baby out with the bath water (see Elashoff & Snow, 1971). In a rather complacent manner some authors tried to create the impression that expectancy effects in schools were a highly implausible assumption. The debate focused on alleged methodological flaws in the original Pygmalion study. I cannot go into great detail about the surrounding controversy here (see Elashoff & Snow, 1971; Rosenthal, 1976, 1985, 1987; Wineburg, 1987), but it is well worth reading if the reader is interested in the lively arguments which are presented in a classical dispute about conflicting results. The debate was not so much concerned with the question of whether expectancy effects occur or not – on the contrary, a general agreement has emerged that expectancy effects are widespread – but concentrated on the relationship between teacher expectancies and IQ. This emphasis was in part due to the fact that Rosenthal and Jacobson (1968) had used a little-known IQ test. In addition, success in an IQ test might depend on motivational influences, especially with young children.

Social psychologists have contributed in the meantime to clarifying the importance of self-fulfilling prophecies for performance, beliefs, and attitudes (see Darley & Fazio, 1980, Box T2; Snyder, 1984; see also Boxes I11, I12, I21, I23). The accumulation of many studies has also enabled the general trend in the data to become clearer (Harris & Rosenthal, 1985; Raudenbush, 1984).

In his meta-analysis, Raudenbush (1984) included 18 studies, which used IQ as a dependent variable and were conducted with normal children in grades

1 – 7. He demonstrated that the effects of expectation on IQ were related to the number of weeks of prior contact between teacher and pupils. A correlation analysis indicated that the size of teachers' expectation effects was strongly correlated with the number of weeks of prior contact ($r = -0.77$). While the size of the effect was moderate for studies without prior contact and somewhat smaller for studies with 1 week of prior contact, the eight studies with more than 2 weeks of prior contact between teacher and pupils found essentially no effect.

Raudenbush (1984) divided studies on teacher expectancy into two groups depending on the length of teacher-pupil acquaintance before an expectation was induced (2 weeks or less vs. more than 2 weeks). Note that the teachers in the Rosenthal and Jacobson study (1968) were new to the classes when the positive expectations were induced. A significant effect was only found for the low-contact studies. These results indicate that expectation effects are more pronounced for pupils who have been assigned recently to a new teacher. This pattern of results shows that the induction of expectations is more successful when no firm image of the pupil has been developed by the teacher. In this case the practical significance of the teacher expectation effect expressed as r^2 (variance explained) is 2.5% (for no prior contact) or 1.7% (for 1 week of prior contact). In contrast, the effects found in studies with 2 or more weeks of prior contact are practically zero. These results indicate that teacher expectancy effects are of moderate importance if they do not compete with the prior knowledge of the teacher. The amount of variance explained is rather small.

Raudenbush (1984) also solved another riddle which is contained in the results of the original Rosenthal and Jacobson study (1968). As mentioned before, expectation effects were only found for pupils in grades 1 and 2. Does this mean that older students can protect themselves against biased teacher expectations? Raudenbush included in his meta-analysis studies which were conducted with pupils in grade 7. Interestingly enough, grade 7 students showed a substantial expectation effect, as did students in grades 1 and 2 (but not those in grades 3 – 6).

In interpreting this result it is important to recognize that elementary school embraces grades 1 – 6 while grade 7 is the first year of junior high school. It is plausible to assume that expectations regarding pupils' achievement level are especially weak when the pupils start at a new school, while expectations are established in elementary school during the first years and are generally known to the pupils of a class and their teachers. In view of this established judgment, the attempt to induce new expectations by experimental manipulations might have been fruitless.

Another explanation for the grade-dependent pattern of results in the Rosenthal and Jacobson study can be derived from the assumption that teachers use more time for personal interaction with their pupils in the lower grades and generally prefer a whole-class lesson format in the higher grades of elementary school (Brophy, 1985). The likelihood of communicating expectancies successfully is obviously higher if the amount of personal teacher-pupil interaction is relatively large.

One criticism of studies of teacher expectations is that teachers were aware of the experimental hypothesis and were inclined to support the bloomers. This might lead to an artifact if the teachers themselves administered the IQ test, as occurred in the Rosenthal and Jacobson study. Seaver (1973) succeeded in measuring expectation effects nonreactively. His analysis used school documents out of the archives and was only carried out once the data had been "collected" (see Box 126).

Box 126. The first impression of brothers and sisters

Brothers and sisters often go to the same school. It is quite plausible that the impression which the oldest child leaves with the teacher influences what level of performance the teacher later expects from a younger brother or sister. Older brothers and sisters who only achieved a low level of performance should cause the teacher to expect the younger child to be not too capable. Older brothers or sisters who were high achievers should induce the expectation that the younger child will also do well.

To test this hypothesis an "experimental" group was formed consisting of children who had the same teacher in the first grade as an older brother or sister. The comparison group consisted of pupils who had an older brother or sister in the same school but did not have the same teacher. If the teacher forms positive expectations, the younger brother or sister should do better with the same teacher than with a new teacher. Conversely, with negative expectations a pupil in the "experimental" group should not perform as well as a pupil in the "control" group.

In order to test this hypothesis archive data from 79 sibling pairs were analyzed for the first school year. Besides the marks there was also information about the score in a school achievement test. In agreement with the theoretical analysis there was a statistically significant interaction between the test score of the older child (which was categorized as high or low) and the expectation variable (same teacher vs. new teacher) for different subtests. Similar trends were found in the marks, although the differences were not significant.

Although the empirical support for the expectation hypothesis does agree with the conjecture that teacher expectancies influence pupils' performance, the results can also be interpreted as a teacher quality effect (Reichardt, 1985). The good performance of the successful older brothers and sisters could be caused by their having a particularly good teacher who also taught their younger brothers and sisters. On the other hand, the poor performance of less successful older brothers and sisters could be because of poor teachers who then had a negative influence on the younger brothers and sisters. Therefore, one cannot exclude the possibility that the categorization of good and bad older brothers and sisters is not also a categorization of good and not so good teachers.

These critical thoughts show that no definite conclusions can be drawn from this quasi-experiment as regards expectation effects in schools. It is in fact quite possible that teacher quality and expectancy influenced the pattern of results in the same direction, but the possibility does remain that the results can be explained by effects of teacher quality alone.

The study by Seaver (1973) (see Box I26), where archive data were analyzed, was not based on a manipulated expectation arising from fictitious information but instead the expectation resulted "naturally" from the teacher's everyday school life. There is evidence to suggest that these natural expectancy effects have stronger and more persistent consequences than teacher expectations based on short-term manipulations (see Dusek & O'Connell, 1973; O'Connell, Dusek & Wheeler, 1974). Since expectations in everyday school life are normally "natural" in this sense, such naturally occurring expectations are important as regards the generalization and applicability of the Pygmalion results. These expectations are in many cases valid insomuch as pupils with a higher ability potential induce more positive teacher expectancies than pupils with a lower potential (Brophy, 1985). On the other hand, one must take into consideration that expectations about performance are also fed by information which is not directly relevant to ability such as the pupils' social class, sex, or race (Dusek & Joseph, 1985).

The question arises as to how teacher expectancy effects are produced. What are the mediating processes which can lead to expectation confirmation in school performance?

Rosenthal (1976) and Harris and Rosenthal (1985) considered four factors which are held to be responsible for the triggering of the Pygmalion effect:

1. *School climate:* The prediction was that teachers with positive expectations about performance tend to create a more friendly social and emotional atmosphere. They tend to display more positive attitudes towards the "good" students. For example, the meta-analysis indicated that teachers lean more towards good students, smile at them more, stand physically nearer to them and have more eye contact with them.
2. *Feedback:* The prediction was that positive performance expectations lead to praise and criticism which are more closely orientated to the actual achievements. The importance for teacher expectancy effects of mediating variables like inappropriate reinforcement, criticizing, and praising has been confirmed in many empirical studies (Brophy, 1985).
3. *Input:* A teacher with positive expectations makes an effort to teach the pupil difficult material.
4. *Output:* When the teacher's expectations are positive the pupils have more opportunity to speak and ask questions in class.

Harris and Rosenthal (1985) reported the results of a meta-analysis covering 135 empirical studies of interpersonal expectations, which were either performed in schools or were experimental simulations of learning processes. These studies showed that the factors climate, input, and output fostered interpersonal expectancy effects (Harris & Rosenthal, 1985). The feedback factor appears to be of little importance. Feedback in school seems on the whole to give information about the correctness of the answer and contains little "surplus" meaning.

The four-factor theory of the mediation of teacher expectancy effects rests on the assumption that self-fulfilling prophecies are transmitted via several communication channels. In fact, Harris and Rosenthal (1985) recorded 31 mediating variables, many of which appear to create expectancy effects. In the same spirit, Brophy (1985) listed 17 mechanisms for teacher expectancy effects.

The measured expectancy effect is assumed to be conveyed via several verbal and nonverbal channels of subprocesses. Another subprocess is added by Jamieson, Lydon, Stewart and Zanna (1987), who assumed that a highly motivated and competent teacher might enhance pupils' motivation and foster appropriate nonverbal and verbal behavior in the class.

Jamieson et al. (1987) managed to present a new teacher to two groups of eleventh graders as highly motivated and competent while no comparable comments were made in two control classes. The teacher taught the same material in her 3-week English unit in the four classes. As a result, pupils in the experimental classes displayed more appropriate nonverbal behavior. In addition, experimental subjects achieved better marks for a 3-week unit than control subjects. Ironically, the increase in performance in the experimental classes was smaller than the decrease in performance which occurred in the no-expectation classes, which might indicate that a negative contrast effect was induced because the teacher was confronted with two cooperative classes (who expected her to be competent) and two average classes (who had no special expectations). The number of classes was too small in this study to allow firm conclusions. Nevertheless, the possibility of pupil expectation effects is an interesting complement to the teacher expectation effect. It might well be that teachers who communicate positive expectations in their nonverbal and verbal behavior are perceived as better motivated and more competent by the bloomers.

A theoretical model which takes the influence of some of the mediating variables into account is based on the assumption that the teacher seeks control over his/her pupils and that the perceived control is greater when the pupils' performance is high (Cooper, 1979). Since the assumption that teachers prefer a higher level of perceived control is justified, the logical conclusion follows that they should turn first and foremost to those pupils from whom they expect high performance. Since pupils from whom poor results are expected receive little help and attention from the teacher, they may lose their faith in the idea that good performance pays.

Although it is certainly possible that biased teacher expectations influence school performance and pupils' IQs, studies of school teachers in general show that their perceptions of students are accurate and based on reality most of the time (Brophy, 1985). In addition, only a minority of teachers seem to develop rigid expectations which are not open to corrective feedback. Therefore, high teacher expectations usually reflect the good performance of high achievers and low teacher expectations are based on the not so good performance of low achievers.

While teachers in general seem to perceive students' performances relatively accurately, it is possible that a subgroup of teachers who develop rigid expectations which are resistant to change when contradictory evidence emerges are especially prone to exerting expectation effects on the performance of their pupils (Babad, Inbar & Rosenthal, 1982).

Another possibility which is suggested by Brophy (1985) is related to the differential treatment of whole classes. The practice of grouping students according to their performance in low-track and high-track classes means that teachers might be prone to facilitate the learning of pupils in high-track classes by their positive attitudes and expectations and to interfere with the learning of pupils in low-track classes because of their negative attitudes and low expectations. Segregation into separate classes of low-performing and high-performing students seems to activate corresponding expectation confirmation processes on the class level (Brophy, 1985). Differential treatment of whole classes as a consequence of different performance expectations seems to be of even greater importance in practice than differential treatment of individual pupils on the basis of individual performance expectations.

References

Abelson, R. P., & Kanouse, D. E. (1966). Subjective acceptance of verbal generalizations. In S. Feldman (Ed.), *Cognitive consistency. Motivational antecedents and behavioral consequents* (pp. 171–197). New York: Academic.

Abelson R. P., Leddo, J., & Gross, P. H. (1987). The strength of conjunctive explanations. *Personality and Social Psychology Bulletin, 13*, 141–155.

Abramson, L. Y., Seligman, M. E. P., & Teasdale, J. D. (1978). Learned helplessness in humans: Critique and reformulation. *Journal of Abnormal Psychology, 87*, 49–74.

Adams, G. R. (1982). Physical attractiveness. In A. G. Miller (Ed.), *In the eye of the beholder* (pp. 253–304). New York: Praeger.

Adorno, T. W., Frenkel-Brunswik, E., Levinson, D. F., & Sanford, R. N. (1950/1964). *The authoritarian personality*. New York: Wiley.

Ajzen, I. (1971). Attribution of dispositions to an actor: Effects of perceived decision freedom and behavioral utilities. *Journal of Personality and Social Psychology, 18*, 144–156.

Ajzen, I. (1977). Intuitive theories of events and the effects of base-rate information on prediction. *Journal of Personality and Social Psychology, 35*, 303–314.

Ajzen, I., & Fishbein, M. (1975). A Bayesian analysis of attribution processes. *Psychological Bulletin, 82*, 261–277.

Ajzen, I., & Fishbein, M. (1983). Relevance and availability in the attribution process. In J. Jaspars, F. D. Fincham, & M. Hewstone (Eds.), *Attribution theory and research: Conceptual, developmental and social dimensions* (pp. 63–89). London: Academic.

Ajzen, I., & Holmes, W. H. (1976). Uniqueness of behavioral effects in causal attribution. *Journal of Personality, 44*, 98–108.

Ajzen, I., Dalto, C. A., & Blyth, D. P. (1979). Consistency and bias in the attribution of attitudes. *Journal of Personality and Social Psychology, 37*, 1871–1876.

Allen, J. L., Walker, L. D., Schroeder, D. A., & Johnson, D. E. (1987). Attributions and attribution-behavior relations: The effect of level of cognitive development. *Journal of Personality and Social Psychology, 52*, 1099–1109.

Allgeier, E. R., & McCormick, N. B. (1983). *Changing boundaries. Gender roles and sexual behavior*. Palo Alto, CA: Mayfield.

Alloy, L. B. (1988). Expectations and situational information as cocontributors to covariation assessment: A reply to Goddard and Allan. *Psychological Review, 95*, 299–301.

Alloy, L. B., & Abramson L. Y. (1979). Judgment of contingency in depressed and nondepressed students: Sadder but wiser? *Journal of Experimental Psychology: General, 108*, 441−485.

Alloy, L. B., & Tabachnik, N. (1984). Assessment of covariation by humans and animals: The joint influence of prior expectations and current situational information. *Psychological Review, 91*, 112−149.

Alloy, L. B., Abramson, L. Y., Metalsky, G. I., & Hartlage, S. (1988). The hopelessness theory of depression: Attributional aspects. *British Journal of Clinical Psychology, 27*, 5−21.

Allport, G. W. (1954). *The nature of prejudice.* Cambridge, MA: Addison-Wesley.

Altemeyer, B. (1981). *Right-wing authoritarianism.* Manitoba: The University of Manitoba Press.

Amabile, T. M., DeJong, W., & Lepper, M. R. (1976). Effects of externally imposed deadlines on subsequent intrinsic motivation. *Journal of Personality and Social Psychology, 34*, 92−98.

Amir, Y. (1969). Contact hypothesis in ethnic relations. *Psychological Bulletin, 71*, 319−342.

Amir, Y. (1976). The role of intergroup contact in change of prejudice and ethnic relations. In P. A. Katz (Ed.), *Toward the elimination of racism* (pp. 245−308). New York: Pergamon.

Anderson, C. A. (1982). Inoculation and counterexplanation: Debiasing techniques in the perseverance of social theories. *Social Cognition, 1*, 126−139.

Anderson, C. A. (1983a). The causal structure of situations: The generation of plausible causal attributions as a function of type of event situation. *Journal of Experimental Social Psychology, 19*, 185−203.

Anderson, C. A. (1983b). Abstract and concrete data in the perseverance of social theories: When weak data lead to unshakeable beliefs. *Journal of Experimental Social Psychology, 19*, 93−108.

Anderson, C. A., & Sechler, E. S. (1986). Effects of explanation and counterexplanation on the development and use of social theories. *Journal of Personality and Social Psychology, 50*, 24−34.

Anderson, C. A., Lepper, M. R., & Ross, L. (1980). Perseverance of social theories: The role of explanation in the persistence of discredited information. *Journal of Personality and Social Psychology, 39*, 1037−1049.

Anderson, C. A., New, L., & Speer, J. R. (1985). Argument availability as a mediator of social theory perseverance. *Social Cognition, 3*, 235−249.

Anderson, N. H. (1965). Primacy effects in personality impression formation using a generalized order effect paradigm. *Journal of Personality and Social Psychology, 2*, 1−9.

Anderson, N. H. (1966). Component ratings in impression formation. *Psychonomic Science, 6*, 279−280.

Anderson, N. H. (1968). Application of a linear-serial model to a personality-impression task using serial presentation. *Journal of Personality and Social Psychology, 10*, 354−362.

Anderson, N. H. (1971). Two more tests against change of meaning in adjective combinations. *Journal of Verbal Learning and Verbal Behavior, 10*, 75−85.

Anderson, N. H. (1973). Serial position curves in impression formation. *Journal of Experimental Psychology, 97*, 8−12.

Anderson, N. H. (1974). Cognitive algebra: Integration theory applied to social attribution. In L. Berkowitz (Ed.), *Advances in experimental social psychology* (Vol. 7, pp. 1−101). New York: Academic.

Anderson, N. H. (1981). *Foundations of information integration theory.* New York: Academic.

Anderson, N. H., & Farkas, A. J. (1973). New light on order effects in attitude change. *Journal of Personality and Social Psychology, 28,* 88–93.

Anderson, N. H., & Hubert, S. (1963). Effects of concomitant verbal recall on order effects in personality impression formation. *Journal of Verbal Learning and Verbal Behavior, 2,* 379–391.

Arkin, R. M., & Baumgardner, A. H. (1985). Self-handicapping. In J. H. Harvey & G. Weary (Eds.), *Attribution: Basic issues and applications* (pp. 169–202). Orlando, FL: Academic.

Arkin, R. M., & Duval, S. (1975). Focus of attention and causal attributions of actors and observers. *Journal of Experimental Social Psychology, 11,* 427–438.

Aronson, E., Stephan, C., Sikes, J., Blaney, N., & Snapp, M. (1978). *The jigsaw classroom.* Beverly Hills, CA: Sage.

Asch, S. E. (1946). Forming impressions of personality. *Journal of Abnormal and Social Psychology, 41,* 258–290.

Asch, S. E., & Zukier, H. (1984). Thinking about persons. *Journal of Personality and Social Psychology, 46,* 1230–1240.

Ashmore, R. D. (1981). Sex stereotypes and implicit personality theory. In D. L. Hamilton (Ed.), *Cognitive processes in stereotyping and intergroup behavior* (pp. 37–81). Hillsdale, NJ: Erlbaum.

Ashmore, R. D., & DelBoca, F. K. (1981). Conceptual approaches to stereotypes and stereotyping. In D. L. Hamilton (Ed.), *Cognitive processes in stereotyping and intergroup behavior* (pp. 1–35). Hillsdale, NJ: Erlbaum.

Babad, E. Y., Inbar, J., & Rosenthal, R. (1982). Pygmalion, Galatea, and the Golem: Investigations of biased and unbiased teachers. *Journal of Educational Psychology, 74,* 459–474.

Balzer, H.-G., Schümer-Kohrs, A., & Schümer, R. (1974). Kontexteffekte bei der Eindrucksbildung [Context effects in impression formation]. *Zeitschrift für experimentelle und angewandte Psychologie, 21,* 25–38.

Bargh, J. A., & Pietromonaco, P. (1982). Automatic information processing and social perception: The influence of trait information presented outside of conscious awareness on impression formation. *Journal of Personality and Social Psychology, 43,* 437–449.

Bargh, J. A., & Thein, R. D. (1985). Individual construct accessibility, person memory, and the recall-judgment link: The case of information overload. *Journal of Personality and Social Psychology, 49,* 1129–1146.

Bargh, J. A., Bond, R. N., Lombardi, W. J., & Tota, M. E. (1986). The additive nature of chronic and temporary sources of construct accessibility. *Journal of Personality and Social Psychology, 50,* 869–878.

Bar-Hillel, M., & Fischhoff, B. (1981). When do base rates affect predictions? *Journal of Personality and Social Psychology, 41,* 671–680.

Barnes, R. D., Ickes, W., & Kidd, R. F. (1979). Effects of perceived intentionality and stability of another's dependency on helping behavior. *Personality and Social Psychology Bulletin, 5,* 367–372.

Bar-Tal, D. (1978). Attributional analysis of achievement-related behavior. *Review of Educational Research, 48,* 259–271.

Bartlett, F. C. (1932). *Remembering.* London: Cambridge University Press.

Bassok, M., & Trope, Y. (1983). People's strategies for testing hypotheses about another's personality: Confirmatory or diagnostic? *Social Cognition, 2,* 199–216.

Batson, C. D., Harris, A. C., McCaul, D., Davis, M., & Schmidt, T. (1979). Compassion or compliance: Alternative dispositional attributions for one's helping behavior. *Social Psychology, 42,* 405 – 409.

Becker, H. S. (1963). *Outsiders.* New York: Free Press.

Beckman, L. J. (1970). Effects of students' performance on teachers' and observers' attributions of causality. *Journal of Educational Psychology, 61,* 76 – 82.

Bellezza, F. S., & Bower, G. H. (1981). Person stereotypes and memory for people. *Journal of Personality and Social Psychology, 41,* 856 – 865.

Bem, D. J. (1967). Self perception: An alternative interpretation of cognitive dissonance phenomena. *Psychological Review, 74,* 183 – 200.

Bem, D. J. (1972). Self-perception theory. In L. Berkowitz (Ed.), *Advances in experimental social psychology* (Vol. 6, pp. 1 – 62). New York: Academic.

Ben-Ari, R., & Amir, Y. (1988). Intergroup contact, cultural information, and change in ethnic attitudes. In W. Stroebe, A. W. Kruglanski, D. Bar-Tal, & M. Hewstone (Eds.), *The social psychology of intergroup conflict* (pp. 151 – 165). Berlin: Springer.

Benesh, M., & Weiner, B. (1982). On emotion and motivation. *American Psychologist, 37,* 887 – 895.

Berger, J., Rosenholtz, S. J., & Zelditch, M. (1980). Status organizing processes. *Annual Review of Sociology, 6,* 479 – 508.

Bergius, R., Werbik, H., & Winter, G. (1970). Urteile deutscher Arbeitnehmer über Völker in Relation zur Zahl ihrer ausländischen Bekannten. I: Theorie, Methoden und kollektive Stereotype [Judgments of German workers about people of different nationalities in relationship to the number of their foreign aquaintances. I: Theory, method and collective stereotypes]. *Psychologische Beiträge, 12,* 241 – 310.

Berglas, S., & Jones, E. E. (1978). Drug choice as a self-handicapping strategy in response to noncontingent success. *Journal of Personality and Social Psychology, 36,* 405 – 417.

Bergler, R. (1976). *Vorurteile* [Prejudices]. Cologne: Deutscher Instituts-Verlag.

Berkowitz, L. (1969). Resistance to improper dependency relationships. *Journal of Experimental Social Psychology, 5,* 283 – 294.

Berscheid, E., & Graziano, W. (1979). The initiation of social relationships and interpersonal attraction. In R. L. Burgess & T. L. Huston (Eds.), *Social exchange in developing relationships* (pp. 31 – 60). New York: Academic.

Berscheid, E., Boye, D., & Darley, J. M. (1968). Effect of forced association upon voluntary choice to associate. *Journal of Personality and Social Psychology, 8,* 13 – 19.

Berscheid, E., Graziano, W., Monson, T., & Dermer, M. (1976). Outcome dependency: Attention, attribution, and attraction. *Journal of Personality and Social Psychology, 34,* 978 – 989.

Bierbrauer, G. (1979). Why did he do it? Attribution of obedience and the phenomenon of dispositional bias. *European Journal of Social Psychology, 9,* 67 – 84.

Bierhoff, H. W. (1980a). Naive psychologische Theorien und Eigenschaften als Funktion des Interaktionsmusters der Stimulusperson [Naive psychological theories and traits as a function of the interaction pattern of the stimulus person]. *Zeitschrift für Sozialpsychologie, 11,* 181 – 188.

Bierhoff, H. W. (1980b). *Hilfreiches Verhalten* [Altruistic behavior]. Darmstadt: Steinkopff.

Bierhoff, H. W. (1980c). *Einstellungen als soziale Kognitionen: Was folgt daraus?* [Attitudes as social cognitions: What does this imply?] Talk presented at the Annual Convention of Experimental Psychologists, Tübingen, FRG.

Bierhoff, H. W. (1988). *Sozialpsychologie* [Social psychology]. Stuttgart: Kohlhammer.

Bierhoff, H. W., & Bierhoff-Alfermann, D. (1976). The use of psychological theories by 'naive' judges: A study in implicit personality theory. *European Journal of Social Psychology, 6*, 429–445.

Bierhoff, H. W., & Bierhoff-Alfermann, D. (1977). Attribution impliziter Persönlichkeitstheorien in einer Interaktionssituation durch Beurteiler [Attribution of implicit personality theories in an interaction situation by perceivers]. *Zeitschrift für Sozialpsychologie, 8*, 50–66.

Bierhoff, H. W., & Bierhoff-Alfermann, D. (1983). Kognitive Prozesse im Motivationsgeschehen: Attributionen als Ursachenerklärungen von Handlungen [Cognitive processes and motivations: attributions as causal explanations of actions]. In H. Thomae (Ed.), *Theorien und Formen der Motivation* (pp. 93–226). Göttingen: Hogrefe.

Bierhoff, H. W., & Kramp, P. (1988). Bestätigende und widerlegende Informationen über Verläßlichkeit: Attributionseffekte [Confirmatory and disconfirmatory information about reliability: attribution effects]. Paper presented at the 30th Meeting of Experimental Psychologists, Marburg.

Bierhoff, H. W., & Schreiber, C. (1988). Erwartungsbestätigung durch verfälschte Eindrucksbildung in der sozialen Interaktion [Expectancy confirmation by biased impression formation in social interaction]. In B. Schäfer & F. Petermann (Eds.), *Vorurteile und Einstellungen* (pp. 251–280). Cologne: Deutscher Instituts-Verlag.

Bierhoff, H. W., Buck, E., & Klein, R. (1986a). Glaubwürdigkeit diagnostischer Kommunikationen: Urteilsbildung bei einer und bei zwei möglichen Ursachen [Credibility of diagnostic communications: Judgments based on one or two plausible causes]. *Diagnostica, 32*, 177–192.

Bierhoff, H. W., Buck, E., & Klein, R. (1986b). Social context and perceived justice. In H. W. Bierhoff, R. L. Cohen, & J. Greenberg (Eds.), *Justice in social relations* (pp. 165–185). New York: Plenum.

Bierhoff, H. W., Klein, R., & Kramp, P. (1987). *Hemmschwellen zur Hilfeleistung* [Inhibitions of altruism] (Final Research Report). Cologne: Federal Agency on Traffic.

Bierhoff-Alfermann D. (1977). *Psychologie der Geschlechtsunterschiede* [Psychology of sex differences]. Cologne: Kiepenheuer & Witsch.

Bierhoff-Alfermann, D. (1979). Interaktionsstil und Verhaltenserklärung durch Jungen und Mädchen [Interaction style and explanation of behavior by boys and girls]. *Psychologische Beiträge, 21*, 277–293.

Bierhoff-Alfermann, D., Bartels, M., Michels R., Pätzold, R., & Souren, R. (1980). Unerklärbarkeit des Mißerfolgs: Eine Variante defensiver Attribution [Unexplainability of failure: A variant of defensive attribution]. *Zeitschrift für Sozialpsychologie, 11*, 60–68.

Bilsky, W. (1988). Untersuchungen zur Rezeption prosozialer Dilemmata – Versuche angewandter Altruismusforschung [Studies in the reception of prosocial dilemmata – Attempts at applied altruism research]. In H. W. Bierhoff & L. Montada (Eds.), *Altruismus* (pp. 55–77). Göttingen: Hogrefe.

Bindra, D. (1976). *A theory of intelligent behavior.* New York: Wiley.

Block, J., & Funder, D. C. (1986). Social roles and social perception: Individual differences in attribution and error. *Journal of Personality and Social Psychology, 51*, 1200–1207.

Boggiano, A. K., & Main, D. S. (1986). Enhancing children's interest in activities used as rewards: The bonus effect. *Journal of Personality and Social Psychology, 51*, 1116–1126.

Boggiano, A. K., & Ruble, D. N. (1979). Competence and the overjustification effect: A developmental study. *Journal of Personality and Social Psychology, 37*, 1462–1468.

Boggiano, A. K., & Ruble, D. N. (1986). Children's responses to evaluative feedback. In R. Schwarzer (Ed.). *Self-related cognitions in anxiety and motivation* (pp. 195–227). Hillsdale, NJ: Erlbaum.

Borgida, E., & Brekke, N. (1981). The base rate fallacy in attribution and prediction. In J. H. Harvey, W. Ickes, & R. F. Kidd (Eds.), *New directions in attribution research* (Vol. 3, pp. 63–95). Hillsdale, NJ: Erlbaum.

Borgida E., & Nisbett, R. E. (1977). The differential impact of abstract vs. concrete information on decisions. *Journal of Applied Social Psychology, 7*, 258–271.

Bourhis, R. Y., Giles, H., & Tajfel, H. (1973). Language as a determinant of ethnic identity. *European Journal of Social Psychology, 3*, 447–460.

Bracken, H. von (1976). *Vorurteile gegen behinderte Kinder, ihre Familien und ihre Schulen* [Prejudices about handicapped children, their families, and their schools]. Berlin: Marhold.

Bradley, G. W. (1978). Self-serving biases in the attribution process: A reexamination of the fact or fiction question. *Journal of Personality and Social Psychology, 36*, 56–71.

Bramel, D. (1963). Selection of a target for defensive projection. *Journal of Abnormal and Social Psychology, 66*, 318–324.

Branco, K. J., & Williamson, J. B. (1982). Stereotyping and the life cycle: Views of aging and the aged. In A. G. Miller (Ed.), *In the eye of the beholder* (pp. 364–410). New York: Praeger.

Brandt, L. W. (1975). Experimenter-effect research. *Psychologische Beiträge, 17*, 133–140.

Brewer, M. B. (1977). An information-processing approach to attribution of responsibility. *Journal of Experimental Social Psychology, 13*, 58–69.

Brewer, M. B. (1979). The role of ethnocentrism in intergroup conflict. In W. G. Austin & S. Worchel (Eds.), *The social psychology of intergroup relations* (pp. 71–84). Monterey, CA: Brooks/Cole.

Brewer, M. B., & Miller, N. (1984). Beyond the contact hypothesis: Theoretical perspectives on desegregation. In N. Miller & M. B. Brewer (Eds.), *Groups in contact: The psychology of desegregation* (pp. 281–302). Orlando, FL: Academic.

Brewer, M. B., Dull, V., & Lui, L. (1981). Perceptions of the elderly: Stereotypes as prototypes. *Journal of Personality and Social Psychology, 41*, 656–670.

Brickman, P., Redfield, J., Harrison, A. A., & Crandall, R. (1972). Drive and predisposition as factors in the attitudinal effects of mere exposure. *Journal of Experimental Social Psychology, 8*, 31–44.

Brickman, P., Ryan, K., & Wortman, C. B. (1975). Causal chains: Attribution of responsibility as a function of immediate and prior causes. *Journal of Personality and Social Psychology, 32*, 1060–1067.

Brigham, J. C. (1971). Ethnic stereotypes. *Psychological Bulletin, 76*, 15–38.

Brophy, J. E. (1985). Teacher-student interaction. In J. B. Dusek (Ed.), *Teacher expectancies* (pp. 303–328). Hillsdale, NJ: Erlbaum.

Broverman, I. K., Vogel, S. R., Broverman, D. M., Clarkson, F. E., & Rosenkrantz, P. S. (1972). Sex-role stereotypes: A current appraisal. *Journal of Social Issues, 28*(2), 59–78.

Brown, R. (1965). *Social psychology.* New York: Free Press.

Bruner, J. S. (1957a). On perceptual readiness. *Psychological Review, 64*, 123–152.

Bruner, J. S. (1957b/1974). Going beyond the information given. In J. S. Bruner, *Beyond the information given* (pp. 218–238). London: Allen & Unwin.

Bruner, J. S., & Minturn, A. L. (1955). Perceptual identification and perceptual organization. *Journal of General Psychology, 53*, 21–28.

Bruner, J. S., & Postman, L. (1949). On the perception of incongruity: A paradigm. *Journal of Personality, 18,* 206–223.

Bruner, J. S., & Potter, M. C. (1964). Interference in visual recognition. *Science, 144,* 424–425.

Bruner, J. S., & Tagiuri, R. (1954). The perception of people. In G. Lindzey (Ed.), *Handbook of social psychology* (Vol. 2, pp. 634–654). Reading, MA: Addison-Wesley.

Bruner, J. S., Postman, L., & Rodrigues, J. (1951). Expectation and the perception of color. *American Journal of Psychology, 64,* 216–277.

Bruner, J. S., Goodnow, J. J., & Austin, G. A. (1956). *A study of thinking.* New York: Wiley.

Bruner, J. S., Shapiro, D., & Tagiuri, R. (1958). The meaning of traits in isolation and in combination. In R. Tagiuri & L. Petrullo (Eds.), *Person perception and interpersonal behavior* (pp. 277–288). Stanford, CA: Stanford University Press.

Brunswik, E. (1956). *Perception and the representative design of psychological experiments.* Berkeley, CA: University of California Press.

Burger, J. M., & Petty, R. E. (1981). The low-ball compliance technique: Task or person commitment? *Journal of Personality and Social Psychology, 40,* 492–500.

Buss, A. R. (1978). Causes and reasons in attribution theory: A conceptual critique. *Journal of Personality and Social Psychology, 36,* 1311–1321.

Byrne, D., London, O., & Reeves, K. (1968). The effects of physical attractiveness, sex, and attitude similarity on interpersonal attraction. *Journal of Personality, 36,* 259–271.

Byrne, D., Ervin, C. R., & Lamberth, J. (1970). Continuity between the experimental study of attraction and real-life computer dating. *Journal of Personality and Social Psychology, 16,* 157–165.

Calder, B. J., Ross, M., & Insko, C. A. (1973). Attitude change and attitude attribution: Effects of incentive, choice, and consequences. *Journal of Personality and Social Psychology, 25,* 84–99.

Campbell, D. T. (1963). Social attitudes and other acquired behavioral dispositions. In S. Koch (Ed.), *Psychology: A study of a science* (Vol. 6, pp. 94–172). New York: McGraw-Hill.

Campbell, D. T. (1967). Stereotypes and the perception of group differences. *American Psychologist, 22,* 817–829.

Cantor, N., & Mischel, W. (1977). Traits as prototypes: Effects on recognition memory. *Journal of Personality and Social Psychology, 35,* 38–48.

Cantor, N., & Mischel, W. (1979a). Prototypes in person perception. In L. Berkowitz (Ed.), *Advances in experimental social psychology* (Vol. 12, pp. 3–52). New York: Academic.

Cantor, N., & Mischel, W. (1979b). Prototypicality and personality: Effects on free recall and personality impressions. *Journal of Research in Personality, 13,* 187–205.

Cantor, N., Mischel, W., & Schwartz, J. C. (1982). A prototype analysis of psychological situations. *Cognitive Psychology, 14,* 45–77.

Cantor, N., Pittman, T. S., & Jones, E. E. (1982). Choice and attitude attributions: The influence of constraint information on attributions across levels of generality. *Social Cognition, 1,* 1–20.

Carlsmith, J. M., Ellsworth, P. C., & Aronson, E. (1976). *Methods of research in social psychology.* Reading, MA: Addison-Wesley.

Carroll, J. S. (1978). Causal attributions in expert parole decisions. *Journal of Personality and Social Psychology, 36,* 1501–1511.

Carroll, J. S., & Payne, J. W. (1976). The psychology of the parole decision process: A joint application of attribution theory and information-processing psychology. In J. S. Carroll & J. W. Payne (Eds.), *Cognition and social behavior* (pp. 13–32). Hillsdale, NJ: Erlbaum.

Carroll, J. S., & Payne, J. W. (1977). Crime seriousness, recidivism risk, and causal attributions in judgments of prison term by students and experts. *Journal of Applied Psychology, 62*, 595–602.

Carroll, J. S., & Siegler, R. S. (1977). Strategies for the use of base-rate information. *Organizational Behavior and Human Performance, 19*, 392–402.

Carroll, J. S., & Wiener, R. L. (1982). Cognitive social psychology in court and beyond. In A. H. Hastorf & A. M. Isen (Eds.), *Cognitive social psychology* (pp. 213–253). New York: Elsevier/North-Holland.

Carver, C. S., & Ganellen, R. J. (1983). Depression and components of depressive self-punitiveness: High standards, self-criticism, and overgeneralization. *Journal of Abnormal Psychology, 92*, 330–337.

Carver, C. S., Ganellen, R. J., & Behar-Mitrani, V. (1985). Depression and cognitive style: Comparisons between measures. *Journal of Personality and Social Psychology, 49*, 722–728.

Chaiken, S., & Baldwin, M. W. (1981). Affective-cognitive consistency and the effect of salient behavioral information on the self-perception of attitudes. *Journal of Personality and Social Psychology, 41*, 1–12.

Chaikin, A. L., & Cooper, J. (1973). Evaluation as a function of correspondence and hedonic relevance. *Journal of Experimental Social Psychology, 9*, 257–264.

Chaikin, A. L., & Darley, J. M. (1973). Victim or perpetrator? Defensive attribution of responsibility and the need for order and justice. *Journal of Personality and Social Psychology, 25*, 268–275.

Chaikin A. L., Siegler, E., & Derlega, V. J. (1974). Nonverbal mediators of teacher expectancy effects. *Journal of Personality and Social Psychology, 30*, 144–149.

Chapman, L. J., & Chapman, J. P. (1967). Genesis of popular but erroneous psychodiagnostic observations. *Journal of Abnormal Psychology, 72*, 193–204.

Chapman, L. J., & Chapman, J. P. (1969). Illusory correlation as an obstacle to the use of valid psychodiagnostic signs. *Journal of Abnormal Psychology, 74*, 271–280.

Cialdini, R. B., Cacioppo, J. T., Bassett, R., & Miller, J. A. (1978). Low-ball procedure for producing compliance: Commitment then cost. *Journal of Personality and Social Psychology, 36*, 463–476.

Clark, L. F., & Woll, S. B. (1981). Stereotype biases: A reconstructive analysis of their role in reconstructive memory. *Journal of Personality and Social Psychology, 41*, 1064–1072.

Clore, G. L., & Byrne, D. (1977). The process of personality interaction. In R. B. Cattell, & R. M. Dreger (Eds.), *Handbook of modern personality theory* (pp. 530–548). Washington, DC: Hemisphere.

Cohen, R., & Schümer, R. (1972). Kontexteffekte bei der Eindrucksbildung [Context effects in impression formation]. *Zeitschrift für Sozialpsychologie, 3*, 313–328.

Coke, J. S., Batson, C. D., & McDavis, K. (1978). Empathic mediation of helping: A two-stage model. *Journal of Personality and Social Psychology, 36*, 752–766.

Cook, T. D., & Campbell, D. T. (1979). *Quasi-experimentation. Design and analysis issues for field settings.* Chicago: Rand McNally.

Cooper, H. M. (1979). Pygmalion grows up: A model for teacher expectation communication and performance influence. *Review of Educational Research, 49*, 389–410.

Cooper, W. H. (1981). Ubiquitous halo. *Psychological Bulletin, 90*, 218–244.

Covington, M. V., & Omelich, C. L. (1979a). It's best to be able and virtuous too: Student and teacher evaluative responses to successful effort. *Journal of Educational Psychology, 71*, 688–700.

Covington M. V., & Omelich, C. L. (1979 b). Effort: The double-edged sword in school achievement. *Journal of Educational Psychology, 71*, 169–182.

Coyne, J. C., & Gotlib, I. H. (1983). The role of cognition in depression: A critical appraisal. *Psychological Bulletin, 94*, 472–505.

Crocker, J. (1981). Judgment of covariation by social perceivers. *Psychological Bulletin, 90*, 272–292.

Crocker, J. (1982). Biased questions in judgment of covariation studies. *Personality and Social Psychology Bulletin, 8*, 214–220.

Cronbach, L. J. (1955). Processes affecting scores on "understanding of others" and "assumed similarity". *Psychological Bulletin, 52*, 177–193.

Cunningham, J. D., & Kelley, H. H. (1975). Causal attributions for interpersonal events of varying magnitude. *Journal of Personality, 43*, 74–93.

Cunningham, M. R. (1986). Measuring the physical in physical attractiveness: Quasi-experiments on the sociobiology of female facial beauty. *Journal of Personality and Social Psychology, 50*, 925–935.

Dabbs, J. M., & Stokes, N. A. (1975). Beauty is power: The use of space on the sidewalk. *Sociometry, 38*, 551–557.

Dann, H. D., & Doise, W. (1974). Ein neuer methodologischer Ansatz zur experimentellen Erforschung von Intergruppen-Beziehungen [A new methodological approach to the experimental investigation of intergroup relationships]. *Zeitschrift für Sozialpsychologie, 5*, 2–15.

Dannenberg, U., & Winter, G. (1975). Urteile deutscher Arbeitnehmer über Völker in Relation zur Zahl ihrer ausländischen Bekannten. IV: Unterschiede zwischen verschiedenen Alters- und Schulbildungsgruppen [Judgments of German workers about people of different nationalities in relationship to the number of their foreign acquaintances. IV: Differences between groups varying in age and formal education]. *Psychologische Beiträge, 17*, 61–83.

Darley, J. M., & Fazio, R. H. (1980). Expectancy confirmation processes arising in the social interaction sequence. *American Psychologist, 35*, 867–881.

Darley, J. M., & Berscheid, E. (1967). Increased liking as a result of the anticipation of personal contact. *Human Relations, 20*, 29–40.

Darley, J. M., & Goethals, G. R. (1980). People's analyses of the causes of ability-linked performances. In L. Berkowitz (Ed.), *Advances in experimental social psychology* (Vol. 13, pp. 1–37). New York: Academic.

Darley, J. M., Fleming, J. H., Hilton, J. L., & Swann, W. B. (1988). Dispelling negative expectancies: The impact of interaction goals and target characteristics on the expectancy confirmation process. *Journal of Experimental Social Psychology, 24*, 19–36.

Davis, D., Rainey, H. G., & Brock, T. C. (1976). Interpersonal physical pleasuring: Effects of sex combinations, recipient attributes, and anticipated future interaction. *Journal of Personality and Social Psychology, 33*, 89–106.

Davis, K. E., & Jones, E. E. (1960). Changes in interpersonal perception as a means of reducing cognitive dissonance. *Journal of Abnormal and Social Psychology, 61*, 402–410.

Davis, M. H., & Stephan, W. G. (1980). Attributions for exam performance. *Journal of Applied Social Psychology, 10*, 235–248.

Deaux, K. (1985). Sex and gender. *Annual Review of Psychology, 36*, 49–81.

Deaux, K., & Lewis, L. L. (1984). Structure of gender stereotypes: Interrelationships among components and gender label. *Journal of Personality and Social Psychology, 46*, 991–1004.

Deaux, K., & Major, B. (1987). Putting gender into context: An interactive model of gender-related behavior. *Psychological Review, 94*, 369–389.

Deci, E. L. (1971). Effects of externally mediated rewards on intrinsic motivation. *Journal of Personality and Social Psychology, 18*, 105–115.

Deci, E. L. (1972). The effects of contingent and noncontingent rewards and controls on intrinsic motivation. *Organizational Behavior and Human Performance, 8*, 217–229.

Deci, E. L., & Ryan, R. M. (1980). The empirical exploration of intrinsic motivational processes. In L. Berkowitz (Ed.), *Advances in experimental social psychology* (Vol. 13, pp. 39–80). New York: Academic.

Dent, J., & Teasdale, J. D. (1988). Negative cognition and the persistence of depression. *Journal of Abnormal Psychology, 97*, 29–34.

Dermer, M., & Thiel, D. L. (1975). When beauty may fail. *Journal of Personality and Social Psychology, 31*, 1168–1176.

Deusinger, I. M. (1980). *Interpersonale Beurteilung* [Interpersonal judgment]. Göttingen: Hogrefe.

Dienstbier, R. A. (1972). A modified belief theory of prejudice emphasizing the mutual causality of racial prejudice and anticipated belief differences. *Psychological Review, 79*, 146–160.

Dion, K., Berscheid, E., & Walster, E. (1972). What is beautiful is good. *Journal of Personality and Social Psychology, 24*, 285–290.

DiVitto, B., & McArthur, L. Z. (1978). Developmental differences in the use of distinctiveness, consensus, and consistency information for making causal attributions. *Developmental Psychology, 14*, 474–482.

Dusek, J. B., & Joseph, G. (1985). The bases of teacher expectancies. In J. B. Dusek (Ed.), *Teacher expectancies* (pp. 227–250). Hillsdale, NJ: Erlbaum.

Dusek, J. B., & O'Connell, E. J. (1973). Teacher expectancy effects on the achievement test performance of elementary school children. *Journal of Educational Psychology, 65*, 371–377.

Duval, S., & Hensley, V. (1976). Extensions of objective self-awareness theory: The focus of attention-causal attribution hypothesis. In J. H. Harvey, W. J. Ickes, & R. F. Kidd (Eds.), *New directions in attribution research* (Vol. 1, pp. 165–198). Hillsdale, NJ: Erlbaum.

Duval, S., & Wicklund, R. A. (1972). *A theory of objective self-awareness.* New York: Academic.

Duval, S., & Wicklund, R. A. (1973). Effects of objective self-awareness on attribution of causality. *Journal of Experimental Social Psychology, 9*, 17–31.

Dweck, C. S., & Goetz, T. E. (1978). Attributions and learned helplessness. In J. H. Harvey, W. Ickes, & R. F. Kidd (Eds.), *New directions in attribution research* (Vol. 2, pp. 157–179). Hillsdale, NJ: Erlbaum.

Dweck, C. S., & Leggett, E. L. (1988). A social-cognitive approach to motivation and personality. *Psychological Bulletin, 95*, 256–273.

Eagly, A. H. (1987). *Sex differences in social behavior: A social-role interpretation.* Hillsdale, NJ: Erlbaum.

Eagly, A. H., & Kite, M. E. (1987). Are stereotypes of nationalities applied to both women and men? *Journal of Personality and Social Psychology, 53*, 451–462.

Eagly, A. H., & Steffen, V. J. (1984). Gender stereotypes stem from the distribution of women and men into social roles. *Journal of Personality and Social Psychology, 46*, 735–754.

Einhorn, H. J., & Hogarth, R. M. (1986). Judging probable cause. *Psychological Bulletin, 99*, 3–19.

Eisenberg, N. (Ed.) (1982). *The development of prosocial behavior.* New York: Academic.

Eisenberg, N. (1986). *Altruistic emotion, cognition, and behavior.* Hillsdale, NJ: Erlbaum.

Eiser, J. R. (1983). From attributions to behaviour. In M. Hewstone (Ed.), *Attribution theory. Social and functional extensions* (pp. 160–169). Oxford: Blackwell.

Eiser, J. R., & Stroebe, W. (1972). *Categorization and social judgment.* London: Academic.

Eiser, J. R., & Van der Pligt, I. (1984). Accentuation theory, polarisation, and the judgement of attitude statements. In J. R. Eiser (Ed.), *Attitudinal judgement* (pp. 43–63). Berlin: Springer.

Elashoff, J. D., & Snow, R. E. (1971). *Pygmalion reconsidered.* Worthington, OH: Jones.

Ellis, L. J., & Bentler, P. M. (1973). Traditional sex-determined role standards and sex stereotypes. *Journal of Personality and Social Psychology, 25*, 28–34.

Enzle, M. E., & Schopflocher, D. (1978). Instigation of attribution processes by attributional questions. *Personality and Social Psychology Bulletin, 4*, 595–599.

Enzle, M. E., Hansen, R. D., & Lowe, C. A. (1975). Causal attribution in the mixed-motive game: Effects of facilitory and inhibitory environmental forces. *Journal of Personality and Social Psychology, 31*, 50–54.

Erber, R., & Fiske, S. T. (1984). Outcome dependency and attention to inconsistent information. *Journal of Personality and Social Psychology, 47*, 709–726.

Fazio, R. H., & Zanna, M. P. (1981). Direct experience and attitude-behavior consistency. In L. Berkowitz (Ed.), *Advances in experimental social psychology* (Vol. 14, pp. 161–202). New York: Academic.

Fazio, R. H., Effrein, E. H., & Falender, U. J. (1981). Self-perceptions following social interaction. *Journal of Personality and Social Psychology, 41*, 232–242.

Feather, N. T., & Simon, J. G. (1971). Attribution of responsibility and valence of outcome in relation to initial confidence and success and failure of self and other. *Journal of Personality and Social Psychology, 18*, 173–188.

Feldman, N. S., Higgins, E. T., Karlovac, M., & Ruble, D. N. (1976). Use of consensus information in causal attributions as a function of temporal presentation and availability of direct information. *Journal of Personality and Social Psychology, 34*, 694–698.

Felson, R. B., & Bohrnstedt, G. W. (1980). Attributions of ability and motivation in a natural setting. *Journal of Personality and Social Psychology, 39*, 799–805.

Festinger, L., & Carlsmith, J. M. (1959). Cognitive consequences of forced compliance. *Journal of Abnormal and Social Psychology, 58*, 203–210.

Fiedler, K. (1980). Kognitive Verarbeitung statistischer Information: Der "vergebliche Konsensus-Effekt" [Cognitive processing of statistical information: the "futile consensus effect"]. *Zeitschrift für Sozialpsychologie, 11*, 25–37.

Fiedler, K. (1985). *Kognitive Strukturierung der sozialen Umwelt* [Cognitive structuring of the social environment]. Göttingen: Hogrefe.

Fiedler, K., & Semin, G. R. (1988). Actor-Observer-Attribution als Sprachphänomen [Actor-observer attribution as a linguistic phenomenon]. Paper presented at the 30th Meeting of Experimental Psychologists, Marburg.

Fiedler, K., Hemmeter, U., & Hofmann, C. (1984). On the origin of illusory correlations. *European Journal of Social Psychology, 14*, 191–201.

Fincham, F. D. (1985). Attributions in close relationships. In J. H. Harvey & G. Weary (Eds.), *Attribution: Basic issues and applications* (pp. 203–234). Orlando, FL: Academic.

Fincham, F. D., & Bradbury, T. N. (1987). The impact of attributions on marriage: A longitudinal analysis. *Journal of Personality and Social Psychology, 53*, 510–517.

Fincham, F. D., & Bradbury, T. N. (1988). The impact of attributions on marriage: Empirical and conceptual foundations. *British Journal of Clinical Psychology, 27*, 77–90.

Fincham, F. D., & Jaspars, J. M. (1979). Attribution of responsibility to the self and other in children and adults. *Journal of Personality and Social Psychology, 37,* 1589–1602.

Fincham, F. D., & Jaspars, J. M. (1980). Attribution of responsibility: From man the scientist to man as lawyer. In L. Berkowitz (Ed.), *Advances in experimental social psychology* (Vol. 13, pp. 81–138). New York: Academic.

Fincham, F. D., & Jaspars, J. M. (1983). A subjective probability approach in responsibility attribution. *British Journal of Social Psychology, 22,* 145–162.

Fincham, F. D., & Shultz, T. R. (1981). Intervening causation and the mitigation of responsibility for harm. *British Journal of Social Psychology, 20,* 113–120.

Fincham, F. D., Beach, S. R., & Baucom, D. H. (1987). Attribution processes in distressed and nondistressed couples: 4. Self-partner attribution differences. *Journal of Personality and Social Psychology, 52,* 739–748.

Finney, P., Merrifield, C., & Helm, B. (1976). The actor's behavioral history, his current role, and the divergence between actor and observer responsibility attributions. *Journal of Research in Personality, 10,* 358–368.

Fischhoff, B. (1975). Hindsight ≠ Foresight: The effect of outcome knowledge on judgment under uncertainty. *Journal of Experimental Psychology: Human Perception and Performance, 1,* 288–299.

Fischhoff, B. (1980). For those condemned to study the past: Reflections on historical judgment. In R. A. Shweder & D. W. Fiske (Eds.), *New directions for methodology of behavioral science: Fallible judgment in behavioral research.* San Francisco, CA: Jossey-Bass.

Fischhoff, B., & Beyth, R. (1975). "I knew it would happen". Remembered probabilities of once-future things. *Organizational Behavior and Human Performance, 13,* 1–16.

Fischhoff, B., & Lichtenstein, S. (1978). Don't attribute this to Reverend Bayes. *Psychological Bulletin, 85,* 239–242.

Fischhoff, B., Slovic, P., & Lichtenstein, S. (1979). Subjective sensitivity analysis. *Organizational Behavior and Human Performance, 23,* 339–359.

Fishbein, M., & Ajzen, I. (1973). Attribution of responsibility: A theoretical note. *Journal of Experimental Social Psychology, 9,* 148–153.

Fishbein, M., & Ajzen, I. (1975). *Belief, attitude, intention and behavior. An introduction to theory and research.* Reading, MA: Addison-Wesley.

Fiske, S. T. (1980). Attention and weight in person perception: The impact of extreme and negative behavior. *Journal of Personality and Social Psychology, 38,* 889–906.

Fiske, S. T., & Taylor, S. E. (1984). *Social cognition.* Reading, MA: Addison-Wesley.

Fiske, S. T., Kenny, D. A., & Taylor, S. E. (1982). Structural models for the mediation of salience effects on attribution. *Journal of Experimental Social Psychology, 18,* 105–127.

Fletcher, G. J. O., Fincham, F. D., Cramer, L., & Heron, N. (1987). The role of attributions in the development of dating relationships. *Journal of Personality and Social Psychology, 53,* 481–489.

Folger, R. (1986). Rethinking equity theory: A referent cognitions model. In H. W. Bierhoff, R. L. Cohen, & J. Greenberg (Eds.), *Justice in social relations* (pp. 145–162). New York: Plenum.

Folger, R., Rosenfield, D., & Hays, R. P. (1978). Equity and intrinsic motivation: The role of choice. *Journal of Personality and Social Psychology, 32,* 1021–1029.

Fong, G. T., & Markus, H. (1982). Self-schemas and judgment about others. *Social Cognition, 1,* 191–204.

Försterling, F., & Groeneveld, A. (1983). Ursachenzuschreibungen für ein Wahlergebnis [Causal attributions for an election result]. *Zeitschrift für Sozialpsychologie, 14,* 262–269.

Frankel, A., & Snyder, M.L. (1978). Poor performance following unsolvable problems: Learned helplessness or egotism. *Journal of Personality and Social Psychology, 36,* 1415–1423.

Freud, S. (1976). Introductory lectures on psychoanalysis. In J. Strachey (Ed. and Trans.), *The standard edition of the complete psychological works of Sigmund Freud* (Vols. 15 and 16). London: Hogarth. (Original work published 1916–1917)

Fromm, E. (1976). *To have or to be.* New York: Harper.

Funder, D.C. (1987). Errors and mistakes: Evaluating the accuracy of social judgment. *Psychological Bulletin, 101,* 75–90.

Gaelick, L., & Wyer, R.S. (1984). Freud's not-so-secret theories. In J.R. Royce & L.P. Mos (Eds.), *Annals of theoretical psychology* (Vol. 1, pp. 143–153). New York: Plenum.

Galper, R.E. (1976). Turning observers into actors: Differential causal attributions as a function of "empathy". *Journal of Research in Personality, 10,* 328–335.

Ganellen, R.J. (1988). Specificity of attributions and overgeneralization in depression and anxiety. *Journal of Abnormal Psychology, 97,* 83–86.

Gangestad, S., & Snyder, M. (1985). "To carve nature at its joints": On the existence of discrete classes of personality. *Psychological Review, 92,* 317–349.

Geer, J.H., Davison, G.C., & Gatchel, R.I. (1970). Reduction of stress in humans through nonveridical perceived control of aversive stimulation. *Journal of Personality and Social Psychology, 16,* 731–738.

Gerard, H.B., & Miller, N. (1975). *School desegregation.* New York: Plenum.

Gilbert, D.T., & Jones, E.E. (1986). Perceiver-induced constraint: Interpretations of self-generated reality. *Journal of Personality and Social Psychology, 50,* 269–280.

Gilbert, G.M. (1951). Stereotype persistence and change among college students. *Journal of Abnormal and Social Psychology, 46,* 245–254.

Giles, H. (1979). Ethnicity markers in speech. In K.R. Scherer & H. Giles (Eds.), *Social markers in speech* (pp. 251–289). Cambridge, England: Cambridge University Press.

Giles, H., Scherer, K.R., & Taylor, D.M. (1979). Speech markers in social interaction. In K.R. Scherer, & H. Giles (Eds.), *Social markers in speech* (pp. 343–381). Cambridge, England: Cambridge University Press.

Ginosar, Z., & Trope, Y. (1980). The effects of base rates and individuating information on judgments about another person. *Journal of Experimental Social Psychology, 16,* 228–242.

Goddard, M., & Allan, L. (1988). A critique of Alloy and Tabachnik's theoretical framework for understanding covariation assessment. *Psychological Review, 95,* 296–298.

Goffman, E. (1961). *Asylums.* Chicago: Aldine.

Goldberg, L.R. (1978). Differential attribution of trait descriptive terms to oneself as compared to well-liked, neutral, and disliked others: A psychometric analysis. *Journal of Personality and Social Psychology, 36,* 1012–1028.

Goldberg, L.R. (1981). Unconfounding situational attributions from uncertain, neutral, and ambiguous ones: A psychometric analysis of descriptions of oneself and various types of others. *Journal of Personality and Social Psychology, 41,* 517–552.

Gollwitzer, P.M., Earle, W.B., & Stephan, W.G. (1982). Affect as a determinant of egotism: Residual excitation and performance attributions. *Journal of Personality and Social Psychology, 43,* 702–709.

Goranson, R. E., & Berkowitz, L. (1966). Reciprocity and responsibility reactions to prior help. *Journal of Personality and Social Psychology, 3*, 227–232.

Graumann, C. F. (1960). Eigenschaften als Problem der Persönlichkeitsforschung [Traits as a problem of personality research]. In P. Lersch & H. Thomae (Eds.), *Persönlichkeitsforschung und Persönlichkeitstheorie* (pp. 87–154). Göttingen: Hogrefe.

Graumann, C. F. (1988). Der Kognitivismus in der Sozialpsychologie. Die Kehrseite der "Wende". [Cognitivism in social psychology. The other side of a turning-point]. *Psychologische Rundschau, 39*, 83–90.

Greenberg, J. (1985). Unattainable goal choice as a self-handicapping strategy. *Journal of Applied Social Psychology, 15*, 140–152.

Greenberg, J., Pyszczynski, T., & Solomon, S. (1982). The self-serving attributional bias: Beyond self-presentation. *Journal of Experimental Social Psychology, 18*, 56–67.

Greene, D., Sternberg, B., & Lepper, M. R. (1976). Overjustification in a token economy. *Journal of Personality and Social Psychology, 34*, 1219–1234.

Grusec, J. E., & Redler, E. (1980). Attribution, reinforcement, and altruism: A developmental analysis. *Developmental Psychology, 16*, 525–534.

Grusec, J. E., Kuczynski, L., Rushton, P., & Simutis, Z. M. (1978). Modeling, direct instruction, and attributions: Effects on altruism. *Developmental Psychology, 14*, 51–57.

Guilford, J. P. (1965). *Fundamental statistics in psychology and education* (4th ed.). New York: McGraw-Hill.

Gurwitz, S. B., & Dodge, K. A. (1977). Effects of confirmations and disconfirmations on stereotype-based attributions. *Journal of Personality and Social Psychology, 35*, 495–500.

Haber, R. N., & Hershenson, M. (1973). *The psychology of visual perception.* New York: Holt.

Hamill, R., Wilson, T. D., & Nisbett, R. E. (1980). Insensitivity to sample bias: Generalizing from atypical cases. *Journal of Personality and Social Psychology, 39*, 578–589.

Hamilton, D. L. (1981). Cognitive representations of persons. In E. T. Higgins, C. P. Herman, & M. P. Zanna (Eds.), *Social cognition. The Ontario Symposium* (Vol. 1, pp. 135–159). Hillsdale, NJ: Erlbaum.

Hamilton, D. L., & Bishop, G. D. (1976). Attitudinal and behavioral effects of initial integration of white suburban neighborhoods. *Journal of Social Issues, 32*(2), 47–67.

Hamilton, D. L., & Fallot, R. D. (1974). Information salience as a weighting factor in impression formation. *Journal of Personality and Social Psychology, 30*, 444–448.

Hamilton, D. L., & Gifford, R. K. (1976). Illusory correlation in interpersonal perception: A cognitive basis of stereotypic judgments. *Journal of Experimental Social Psychology, 12*, 392–407.

Hamilton, D. L., & Rose, T. L. (1980). Illusory correlation and the maintenance of stereotypic beliefs. *Journal of Personality and Social Psychology, 39*, 832–845.

Hamilton, D. L., & Sherman, S. J. (in press). Illusory correlations: Implications for stereotype theory and research. In D. Bar-Tal, C. F. Graumann, A. W. Kruglanski, & W. Stroebe (Eds.), *Stereotypes and prejudice: Changing conceptions.* New York: Springer.

Hamilton, D. L., & Zanna, M. P. (1974). Context effects in impression formation. *Journal of Personality and Social Psychology, 29*, 649–654.

Hamilton, D. L., Katz, L. B., & Leirer, V. O. (1980a). Organizational processes in impression formation. In R. Hastie, T. M. Ostrom, E. E. Ebbesen, R. S. Wyer, D. L. Hamilton, & D. E. Carlston (Eds.), *Person memory: The cognitive basis of social perception* (pp. 121–153). Hillsdale, NJ: Erlbaum.

Hamilton, D. L., Katz, L. B., & Leirer, V. O. (1980b). Cognitive representation of personality impression: Organizational processes in first impression formation. *Journal of Personality and Social Psychology, 39,* 1050–1063.

Hamilton, V. L. (1980). Intuitive psychologist or intuitive lawyer? Alternative models of the attribution process. *Journal of Personality and Social Psychology, 39,* 767–772.

Hamilton, V. L. (1986). Chains of command: Responsibility attribution in hierarchies. *Journal of Applied Social Psychology, 16,* 118–139.

Hansen, R. D. (1976). Actors rely on distinctiveness and observers rely on consensus: Two causal schemata. *Personality and Social Psychology Bulletin, 2,* 242–247.

Hansen, R. D. (1980). Commonsense attribution. *Journal of Personality and Social Psychology, 39,* 996–1009.

Hansen, R. D. (1985). Cognitive economy and commonsense attribution processing. In. J. H. Harvey & G. Weary (Eds.), *Attribution: Basic issues and applications* (pp. 65–85). Orlando, FL: Academic.

Hansen, R. D., & Donoghue, J. M. (1977). The power of consensus: Information derived from one's own and others' behavior. *Journal of Personality and Social Psychology, 35,* 294–302.

Hansen, R. D., & Hall, C. A. (1985). Discounting and augmenting facilitative and inhibitory forces: The winner takes almost all. *Journal of Personality and Social Psychology, 49,* 1482–1493.

Hansen, R. D., & Lowe, C. A. (1976). Distinctiveness and consensus: The influence of behavioral information on actors' and observers' attributions. *Journal of Personality and Social Psychology, 34,* 425–433.

Hansen, R. D., & Stonner, D. M. (1978). Attributes and attributions: Inferring stimulus properties, actors dispositions, and causes. *Journal of Personality and Social Psychology, 36,* 657–667.

Harris, M. J., & Rosenthal, R. (1985). Mediation of interpersonal expectancy effects: 31 meta-analyses. *Psychological Bulletin, 97,* 363–386.

Harris, M. B., Harris, R. J., & Bochner, S. (1982). Fat, four-eyed, and female: Stereotypes of obesity, glasses, and gender. *Journal of Applied Social Psychology, 12,* 503–516.

Harvey, J. H., & Weary, G. (1984). Current issues in attribution theory and research. *Annual Review of Psychology, 35,* 427–459.

Harvey, J. H., Town, J. P., & Yarkin, K. L. (1981). How fundamental is the "fundamental attribution error". *Journal of Personality and Social Psychology, 40,* 346–349.

Hastie, R., & Kumar, P. A. (1979). Person memory: Personality traits as organizing principles in memory for behavior. *Journal of Personality and Social Psychology, 37,* 25–38.

Hastie, R., Ostrom, T. M., Ebbesen, E. B., Wyer, R. S., Hamilton, D. L., & Carlston, D. E. (1980). *Person memory: The cognitive basis of social perception.* Hillsdale, NJ: Erlbaum.

Hastie, R., Park, B., & Weber, R. (1984). Social memory. In R. S. Wyer & T. K. Srull (Eds.), *Handbook of social cognition* (Vol. 2, pp. 151–212). Hillsdale, NJ: Erlbaum.

Hayden, D. C. (1987). Counselor and client responses to hypothesis-testing strategies. *Journal of Counseling Psychology, 34,* 149–156.

Hays, W. L. (1958). An approach to the study of trait implication and trait similarity. In R. Tagiuri & L. Petrullo (Eds.), *Person perception and interpersonal behavior* (pp. 289–299). Stanford, CA: Stanford University Press.

Hedges, L. V., & Olkin, I. (1985). *Statistical methods for meta-analysis.* Orlando, FL: Academic.

Heider, F. (1958). *The psychology of interpersonal relations.* New York: Wiley.

Heider, F. (in preparation). *The Notebooks* (6 Vols., edited by M. Benesh-Weiner). Munich, FRG: Psychologie Verlags Union.

Heider, F., & Simmel, M. (1944). An experimental study of apparent behavior. *American Journal of Psychology, 57*, 243–259.

Helfrich, H. (1979). Age markers in speech. In K. R. Scherer & H. Giles (Eds.), *Social markers in speech* (pp. 63–197). Cambridge, England: Cambridge University Press.

Hendrick, C., & Costantini, A. F. (1970). Effects of varying trait inconsistency and response requirements on the primacy effect in impression formation. *Journal of Personality and Social Psychology, 15*, 158–164.

Hendrick, C., Wallace, B., & Tappenbeck, J. (1968). Effect of cognitive set on color perception. *Journal of Personality and Social Psychology, 10*, 487–494.

Hepburn, C., & Locksley, A. (1983). Subjective awareness of stereotyping: Do we know when our judgments are prejudiced? *Social Psychology Quarterly, 46*, 311–318.

Herr, P. M. (1986). Consequences of priming: Judgment and behavior. *Journal of Personality and Social Psychology, 51*, 1106–1115.

Herr, P. M., Sherman, S. J., & Fazio, R. H. (1983). On the consequences of priming: Assimilation and contrast effects. *Journal of Experimental Social Psychology, 19*, 323–340.

Hewstone, M. (1983). The role of language in attribution processes. In J. Jaspars, F. D. Fincham, & M. Hewstone (Eds.), *Attribution theory and research: Conceptual, developmental and social dimensions* (pp. 241–259). London: Academic.

Hewstone, M., & Jaspars, J. (1983). A re-examination of the roles of consensus, consistency and distinctiveness: Kelley's cube revisited. *British Journal of Social Psychology, 22*, 41–50.

Hewstone, M., & Jaspars, J. (1987). Covariation and causal attributions: A logical model of the intuitive analysis of variance. *Journal of Personality and Social Psychology, 53*, 663–672.

Hewstone, M., & Jaspers, J. (1988). Implicit and explicit consensus as determinants of causal attribution: Two experimental investigations. *European Journal of Social Psychology, 18*, 93–98.

Hewstone, M., Benn, W., & Wilson, A. (1988). Bias in the use of base rates: Racial prejudice in decision-making. *European Journal of Social Psychology, 18*, 161–176.

Higgins, E. T., & Bargh, J. A. (1987). Social cognition and social perception. *Annual Review of Psychology, 38*, 369–425.

Higgins, E. T., Rholes, W. S., & Jones, C. R. (1977). Category accessibility and impression formation. *Journal of Experimental Social Psychology, 13*, 141–154.

Higgins, E. T., Herman, C. P., & Zanna, M. P. (1981). *Social cognition. The Ontario Symposium* (Vol. 1). Hillsdale, NJ: Erlbaum.

Higgins, E. T., King, G. A., & Mavin, G. H. (1982). Individual construct accessibility and subjective impressions and recall. *Journal of Personality and Social Psychology, 43*, 35–47.

Hilton, D. J., & Slugoski, B. R. (1986). Knowledge-based causal attribution: The abnormal conditions focus model. *Psychological Review, 93*, 75–88.

Hilton, J. L., & Darley, J. M. (1985). Constructing other persons: A limit on the effect. *Journal of Experimental Social Psychology, 21*, 1–18.

Himmelfarb, S., & Anderson, N. H. (1975). Integration theory applied to opinion attribution. *Journal of Personality and Social Psychology, 30*, 378–381.

Hirt, E. R., & Sherman, S. J. (1985). The role of prior knowledge in explaining hypothetical events. *Journal of Experimental Social Psychology, 21*, 519–543.

Hofstätter, P.R. (1966). *Einführung in die Sozialpsychologie* [Introduction to social psychology]. Stuttgart: Kröner.

Holzkamp, K. (1965). Das Problem der "Akzentuierung" in der sozialen Wahrnehmung [The problem of "accentuation" in social perception]. *Zeitschrift für experimentelle und angewandte Psychologie, 12*, 86–97.

Holzkamp, K. (1972). Verborgene anthropologische Voraussetzungen der allgemeinen Psychologie [Hidden anthropological preconditions in general psychology]. In K. Holzkamp, *Kritische Psychologie* (pp. 35–73). Frankfurt: Fischer.

Hormuth, S.E. (1986). Lack of effort as a result of self-focused attention: An attributional ambiguity analysis. *European Journal of Social Psychology, 16*, 181–192.

Hovland, C.I. (1952). A "communication analysis" of concept learning. *Psychological Review, 59*, 461–472.

Hovland, C.I. (1957). Summary and implications. In C.I. Hovland, W. Mandell, E.H. Campbell, T. Brock, A.S. Luchins, A.R. Cohen, W.J. McGuire, I.J. Janis, R.L. Feierabend, & N.H. Anderson (Eds.), *The order of presentation in persuasion* (pp. 129–157). New Haven, CT: Yale University Press.

Hovland, C.I., & Weiss, W. (1953). Transmission of information concerning concepts through positive and negative instances. *Journal of Experimental Psychology, 45*, 175–182.

Ickes, W.J., & Kidd, R.F. (1976). An attributional analysis of helping behavior. In J.H. Harvey, W.J. Ickes, & R.F. Kidd (Eds.), *New directions in attribution research* (Vol. 1, pp. 311–334). Hillsdale, NJ: Erlbaum.

Inhelder, B., & Piaget, J. (1958). *The growth of logical thinking from childhood to adolescence*. New York: Basic.

Irwin, M., Tripodi, T., & Bieri, J. (1967). Affective stimulus value and cognitive complexity. *Journal of Personality and Social Psychology, 5*, 444–448.

James, W. (1908). *Pragmatism*. New York: Longmans-Green.

Jamieson, D.W., Lydon, J.E., Stewart, G., & Zanna, M.P. (1987). Pygmalion revisited: New evidence for student expectancy effects in the classroom. *Journal of Educational Psychology, 79*, 461–466.

Janoff-Bulman, R., & Brickman, P. (1982). Expectations and what people learn from failure. In N.T. Feather (Ed.), *Expectations and actions: Expectancy-value models in psychology* (pp. 207–237). Hillsdale, NJ: Erlbaum.

Janoff-Bulman, R., & Timko, C. (1985). Cognitive biases in blaming the victim. *Journal of Experimental Social Psychology, 21*, 161–177.

Jaspars, J. (1983). The process of causal attribution in common sense. In M. Hewstone (Ed.), *Attribution theory. Social and functional extensions* (pp. 28–44). Oxford: Blackwell.

Jaspars, J., Hewstone, M., & Fincham, F.D. (1983). Attribution theory and research: The state of the art. In J. Jaspars, F.D. Fincham, & M. Hewstone (Eds.), *Attribution theory and research: Conceptual, developmental and social dimensions* (pp. 3–36). London: Academic.

Jellison, J.M., & Green, J. (1981). A self-presentation approach to the fundamental attribution error: The norm of internality. *Journal of Personality and Social Psychology, 40*, 643–649.

Jennings, D.L., Amabile, T.M., & Ross, L. (1982). Informal covariation assessment: Data-based versus theory-based judgments. In D. Kahneman, P. Slovic, & A. Tversky (Eds.), *Judgment under uncertainty: Heuristics and biases* (pp. 211–230). Cambridge, England: Cambridge University Press.

Johnson, D. W., Johnson, R., & Maruyama, G. (1984). Goal interdependence and interpersonal attraction in heterogeneous classrooms: A metanalysis. In N. Miller & M. B. Brewer (Eds.), *Groups in contact: The psychology of desegregation* (pp. 187−212). Orlando, FL: Academic.

Johnson, J. T., Jemmott, J. B., & Pettigrew, T. F. (1984). Causal attribution and dispositional inference: Evidence of inconsistent judgments. *Journal of Experimental Social Psychology, 20,* 567−585.

Johnson-Laird, P. N. (1975). Models of deduction. In R. J. Falmagne (Ed.), *Reasoning: Representation and process in children and adults* (pp. 175−199). Hillsdale, NJ: Erlbaum.

Jones, E. E. (1964). *Ingratiation. A social psychological analysis.* New York: Appleton-Century-Crofts.

Jones, E. E. (1976). How do people perceive the causes of behavior? *American Scientist, 64,* 300−305.

Jones, E. E. (1979). The rocky road from acts to dispositions. *American Psychologist, 34,* 107−117.

Jones, E. E. (1980). *Strategies in the shaping of competence attributions.* Paper presented at the Conference "Attributional approaches to human motivation", Bielefeld, FRG.

Jones, E. E. (1986). Interpreting interpersonal behavior: The effects of expectancies. *Science, 234,* 41−46.

Jones, E. E., & Davis, K. E. (1965). From acts to dispositions: The attribution process in person perception. In L. Berkowitz (Ed.), *Advances in experimental social psychology* (Vol. 2, pp. 219−266). New York: Academic.

Jones, E. E., & Gerard, H. B. (1967). *Foundations of social psychology.* New York: Wiley.

Jones, E. E., & Goethals, G. R. (1972). Order effects in impression formation: Attribution context and the nature of the entity. In E. E. Jones, D. E. Kanouse, H. H. Kelley, R. E. Nisbett, S. Valins, & B. Weiner (Eds.), *Attribution: Perceiving the causes of behavior* (pp. 27−46). Morristown, NJ: General Learning Press.

Jones, E. E., & Harris, V. A. (1967). The attribution of attitudes. *Journal of Experimental Social Psychology, 3,* 1−24.

Jones, E. E., & McGillis, D. (1976). Correspondent inferences and the attribution cube: A comparative reappraisal. In J. H. Harvey, W. J. Ickes, & R. F. Kidd (Eds.), *New directions in attribution research* (Vol. 1, pp. 389−420). Hillsdale, NJ: Erlbaum.

Jones, E. E., & Nisbett, R. E. (1972). The actor and the observer: Divergent perceptions of the causes of behavior. In E. E. Jones, D. E. Kanouse, H. H. Kelley, R. E. Nisbett, S. Valins, & B. Weiner (Eds.), *Attribution: Perceiving the causes of behavior* (pp. 79−94). Morristown, NJ: General Learning Press.

Jones, E. E., & Thibaut, J. W. (1958). Interaction goals as bases of inference in interpersonal perception. In R. Tagiuri & L. Petrullo (Eds.), *Person perception and interpersonal behavior* (pp. 151−178). Stanford, CA: Stanford University Press.

Jones, E. E., & Wortman, C. (1973). *Ingratiation: An attributional approach.* Morristown, NJ: General Learning Press.

Jones, E. E., Davis, K. E., & Gergen, K. J. (1961). Role playing variations and their informational value for person perception. *Journal of Abnormal and Social Psychology, 63,* 302−310.

Jones, E. E., Rock, L., Shaver, K. G., Goethals, G. R., & Ward, L. M. (1968). Pattern of performance and ability attribution: An unexpected primacy effect. *Journal of Personality and Social Psychology, 10,* 317−340.

Jones, E. E., Worchel, S., Goethals, G. R., & Grumet, J. F. (1971). Prior expectancy and behavioral extremity as determinants of attitude attribution. *Journal of Experimental Social Psychology, 7*, 59–80.

Jones, E. E., Goethals, G. R., Kennington, G. E., & Severance, L. J. (1972). Primacy and assimilation in the attribution process: The stable entity proposition. *Journal of Personality, 40*, 250–274.

Jones, E. E., Riggs, J. M., & Quattrone, G. (1979). Observer bias in the attitude attribution paradigm: Effect of time and information order. *Journal of Personality and Social Psychology, 37*, 1230–1238.

Jones, R. G., & Welsh, J. B. (1971). Ability attribution and impression formation in a strategic game: A limiting case of the primacy effect. *Journal of Personality and Social Psychology, 20*, 166–175.

Jones, S. C., & Panitch, D. (1971). The self-fulfilling prophecy and interpersonal attraction. *Journal of Experimental Social Psychology, 7*, 356–366.

Kahneman, D., Slovic, P., & Tversky, A. (Eds., 1982). *Judgment under uncertainty: Heuristics and biases.* Cambridge, England: Cambridge University Press.

Kammer, D. (1984). Die Kausaldimension Generalität: Vorauslaufende Bedingungen für das Zustandekommen globaler und spezifischer Attributionen [The causal dimension generality: Preceding conditions for the occurrence of global and specific attributions]. *Zeitschrift für experimentelle und angewandte Psychologie, 31*, 48–62.

Kanouse, D. E. (1972). Language, labeling, and attribution. In E. E. Jones, D. E. Kanouse, H. H. Kelley, R. E. Nisbett, S. Valins, & B. Weiner (Eds.), *Attribution: Perceiving the causes of behavior* (pp. 121–135). Morristown, NJ: General Learning Press.

Kaplan, M. F. (1971). Context effects in impression formation: The weighted average versus the meaning-change formulation. *Journal of Personality and Social Psychology, 19*, 92–99.

Kaplan, M. F. (1975). Evaluative judgments are based on evaluative information: Evidence against meaning change in evaluative context effects. *Memory & Cognition, 3*, 375–380.

Karlins, M., Coffman, T. L., & Walters, G. (1969). On the fading of social stereotypes: Studies in three generations of college students. *Journal of Personality and Social Psychology, 13*, 1–16.

Karniol, R., & Ross, M. (1976a). The development of causal attributions in social perception. *Journal of Personality and Social Psychology, 34*, 455–464.

Karniol, R., & Ross, M. (1976b). Children's attributions for rewarded behavior. Adding vs. discounting. Talk at the Annual Convention of the American Psychological Association, Washington, D. C.

Karniol, R., & Ross, M. (1979). Children's use of a causal attribution schema and the inference of manipulative intentions. *Child Development, 50*, 463–468.

Kassin, S. M. (1979). Consensus information, prediction, and causal attribution: A review of the literature and issues. *Journal of Personality and Social Psychology, 37*, 1966–1981.

Kassin, S. M. (1981). Distortions in estimating consensus from sequential events. *Personality and Social Psychology Bulletin, 7*, 542–546.

Kassin, S. M., & Lowe, C. A. (1979). On the development of the augmentation principle: A perceptual approach. *Child Development, 50*, 728–734.

Kassin, S. M., Lowe, C. A., & Gibbons, F. X. (1980). Children's use of the discounting principle: A perceptual approach. *Journal of Personality and Social Psychology, 39*, 719–728.

Katz, D., & Braly, K. W. (1933). Racial stereotypes of 100 college students. *Journal of Abnormal and Social Psychology, 28,* 280–290.

Katz, I. (1981). *Stigma: A social psychological analysis.* Hillsdale, NJ: Erlbaum.

Kelley, H. H. (1950). The warm-cold variable in first impression of persons. *Journal of Personality, 18,* 431–439.

Kelley, H. H. (1967). Attribution theory in social psychology. In D. Levine (Ed.), *Nebraska symposium on motivation* (Vol. 15, pp. 192–238). Lincoln, NE: University of Nebraska Press.

Kelley, H. H. (1972a). Attribution in social interaction. In E. E. Jones, D. E. Kanouse, H. H. Kelley, R. E. Nisbett, S. Valins, & B. Weiner (Eds.), *Attribution: Perceiving the causes of behavior* (pp. 1–26). Morristown, NJ: General Learning Press.

Kelley, H. H. (1972b). Causal schemata and the attribution process. In E. E. Jones, D. E. Kanouse, H. H. Kelley, R. E. Nisbett, S. Valins, & B. Weiner (Eds.), *Attribution: Perceiving the causes of behavior* (pp. 151–174). Morristown, NJ: General Learning Press.

Kelley, H. H. (1973). The processes of causal attribution. *American Psychologist, 28,* 107–128.

Kelley, H. H. (1979). *Personal relationships. Their structures and processes.* Hillsdale, NJ: Erlbaum.

Kelley, H. H., & Michela, J. L. (1980). Attribution theory and research. *Annual Review of Psychology, 31,* 457–501.

Kelley, H. H., & Stahelski, A. J. (1970). Social interaction basis of cooperators' and competitors' beliefs about others. *Journal of Personality and Social Psychology, 16,* 66–91.

Kelley, H. H., & Thibaut, J. W. (1978). *Interpersonal relations: A theory of interdependence.* New York: Wiley.

Kenny, D. A., & Albright, L. (1987). Accuracy in interpersonal perception: A social relations analysis. *Psychological Bulletin, 102,* 390–402.

Kenny, D. A., & Berman, J. S. (1980). Statistical approaches to the correction of correlational bias. *Psychological Bulletin, 88,* 288–295.

Kepka, E. J., & Brickman, P. (1971). Consistency versus discrepancy as clues in the attribution of intelligence and motivation. *Journal of Personality and Social Psychology, 20,* 223–229.

Kihlstrom, J. F., & Cantor, N. (1984). Mental representations of the self. In L. Berkowitz (Ed.), *Advances in experimental social psychology* (Vol. 17, pp. 1–47). Orlando, FL: Academic.

Klayman, J., & Ha, Y.-W. (1987). Confirmation, disconfirmation, and information in hypothesis testing. *Psychological Review, 94,* 211–228.

Knight, J. A., & Vallacher, R. R. (1981). Interpersonal engagement in social perception: The consequences of getting into the action. *Journal of Personality and Social Psychology, 40,* 990–999.

Köhler, W., & von Restorff, H. (1937). Zur Theorie der Reproduktion [The theory of reproduction]. *Psychologische Forschung, 21,* 56–112.

Kolditz, T. A., & Arkin, R. M. (1982). An impression management interpretation of the self-handicapping strategy. *Journal of Personality and Social Psychology, 43,* 492–502.

Kraut, R. E. (1973). Effects of social labeling on giving to charity. *Journal of Experimental Social Psychology, 9,* 551–561.

Kruglanski, A. W. (1970). Attributing trustworthiness in supervisor-worker relations. *Journal of Experimental Social Psychology, 6,* 214–232.

Kruglanski, A. W. (1980). Lay epistemo-logic – process and contents: Another look at attribution theory. *Psychological Review, 87,* 70–87.

Kruglanski, A. W., & Ajzen, I. (1983). Bias and error in human judgment. *European Journal of Social Psychology, 13*, 1–44.

Kruglanski, A. W., Hamel, J. Z., Maides, S. A., & Schwartz, J. M. (1978). Attribution theory as a special case of lay epistemology. In J. H. Harvey, W. Ickes, & R. F. Kidd (Eds.), *New directions in attribution research* (Vol. 2, pp. 299–333). Hillsdale, NJ: Erlbaum.

Kun, A. (1977). Development of the magnitude-covariation and compensation schemata in ability and effort attributions of performance. *Child Development, 48*, 862–873.

Kun, A., & Weiner, B. (1973). Necessary and sufficient causal schemata for success and failure. *Journal of Research in Personality, 7*, 197–207.

Landy, D., & Sigall, H. (1974). Beauty is talent: Task evaluation as a function of the performer's physical attractiveness. *Journal of Personality and Social Psychology, 29*, 299–304.

Landy, F. J., & Farr, J. L. (1980). Performance rating. *Psychological Bulletin, 87*, 72–107.

Langer, E. J., & Abelson, R. P. (1974). A patient by any other name...: Clinician group difference in labeling bias. *Journal of Consulting and Clinical Psychology, 42*, 4–9.

Langer, E. J., & Benevento, A. (1978). Self-induced dependence. *Journal of Personality and Social Psychology, 36*, 886–893.

Langer, E. J., & Newman, H. M. (1979). The role of mindlessness in a typical social psychological experiment. *Personality and Social Psychology Bulletin, 5*, 295–298.

Langer, E. J., & Roth, J. (1975). Heads I win, tails it's chance: The illusion of control as a function of the sequence of outcomes in a purely chance task. *Journal of Personality and Social Psychology, 32*, 951–955.

Langer, E. J., Taylor, S. E., Fiske, S. T., & Chanowitz, B. (1976). Stigma, staring, and discomfort: A novel stimulus hypothesis. *Journal of Experimental Social Psychology, 12*, 451–463.

Lassiter, G. D. (1986). Effect of superfluous deterrence on the perception of others. *Journal of Experimental Social Psychology, 22*, 163–175.

Latané, B., & Darley, J. M. (1976). *Help in a crisis: Bystander response to an emergency.* Morristown, NJ: General Learning Press.

Lau, R. R. (1984). Dynamics of the attribution process. *Journal of Personality and Social Psychology, 46*, 1017–1028.

Lau, R. R., & Russell, D. (1980). Attributions in the sports pages. *Journal of Personality and Social Psychology, 39*, 29–38.

Leddo, J., Abelson, R. P., & Gross, P. H. (1984). Conjunctive explanations: When two reasons are better than one. *Journal of Personality and Social Psychology, 47*, 933–943.

Lefcourt, H. (1976). *Locus of control.* Hillsdale, NJ: Erlbaum.

Lehr, U. (1980). Altersstereotypien und Altersnormen – Das Bild des alten Menschen in unserer Gesellschaft [Age stereotypes and age norms – The image of the old person in our society]. In K. D. Hartmann & K. F. Köppler (Eds.), *Fortschritte der Marktpsychologie* (Vol. 2, pp. 327–338). Frankfurt: Fachbuchhandlung für Psychologie.

Lepper, M. R., & Greene, D. (1975). Turning play into work: Effects of adult surveillance and extrinsic rewards on children's intrinsic motivation. *Journal of Personality and Social Psychology, 31*, 479–486.

Lepper, M. R., & Greene, D. (1978). Overjustification research and beyond: Toward a means-end analysis of intrinsic and extrinsic motivation. In M. R. Lepper & D. Greene (Eds.), *The hidden costs of reward: New perspectives on the psychology of human motivation* (pp. 109–148). Hillsdale, NJ: Erlbaum.

Lepper, M. R., Greene, D., & Nisbett, R. E. (1973). Undermining children's intrinsic interest with extrinsic reward: A test of the "overjustification" hypothesis. *Journal of Personality and Social Psychology, 28*, 129–137.

Lepper, M. R., Sagotsky, G., Dafoe, J. L., & Greene, D. (1982). Consequences of superfluous social constraints: Effects on young children's social inferences and subsequent intrinsic interest. *Journal of Personality and Social Psychology, 42*, 51–65.

Lerner, M. J. (1980). *The belief in a just world. A fundamental delusion.* New York: Plenum.

LeVine K. A., & Campbell, D. T. (1972). *Ethnocentrism: Theories of conflict, ethnic attitudes and group behavior.* New York: Wiley.

Lilli, W. (1982). *Grundlagen der Stereotypisierung* [The foundations of stereotyping]. Göttingen: Hogrefe.

Lindsay, P. H., & Norman, D. A. (1975). *Human information processing.* New York: Academic.

Lindskold, S. (1978). Trust development, the GRIT proposal, and the effects of conciliatory acts on conflict and cooperation. *Psychological Bulletin, 85*, 772–793.

Lippmann, W. (1922). *Public opinion.* New York: Harcourt Brace.

Locke, D., & Pennington, D. (1982). Reasons and other causes: Their role in attribution processes. *Journal of Personality and Social Psychology, 42*, 212–223.

Locksley, A., Borgida, E., Brekke, N., & Hepburn, C. (1980). Sex stereotypes and social judgment. *Journal of Personality and Social Psychology, 39*, 821–831.

Locksley, A., Hepburn, C., & Ortiz, V. (1982). Social stereotypes and judgments of individuals: An instance of the base-rate fallacy. *Journal of Experimental Social Psychology, 18*, 23–42.

Lopes, L. L. (1972). A unified integration model for "Prior expectancy and behavioral extremity as determinants of attitude attribution". *Journal of Experimental Social Psychology, 8*, 156–160.

Lord, C. G., Lepper, M. R., & Mackie, D. (1984). Attitude prototypes as determinants of attitude-behavior consistency. *Journal of Personality and Social Psychology, 46*, 1254–1266.

Lord, C. G., Lepper, M. R., & Preston, E. (1984). Considering the opposite: A corrective strategy for social judgment. *Journal of Personality and Social Psychology, 47*, 1231–1243.

Lord, C. G., Ross, L. & Lepper, M. R. (1979). Biased assimilation and attitude polarization: The effects of prior theories on subsequently considered evidence. *Journal of Personality and Social Psychology, 37*, 2098–2109.

Luchins, A. S. (1948). Forming impressions of personality. A critique. *Journal of Abnormal and Social Psychology, 43*, 318–325.

Luchins, A. S. (1957a). Primacy-recency in impression formation. In C. I. Hovland, W. Mandell, E. H. Campbell, T. Brock, A. S. Luchins, A. R. Cohen, W. J. McGuire, I. J. Janis, R. L. Feierabend, & N. H. Anderson (Eds.), *The order of presentation in persuasion* (pp. 33–61). New Haven, CT: Yale University Press.

Luchins, A. S. (1957b). Experimental attempts to minimize the impact of first impressions. In C. I. Hovland, W. Mandell, E. H. Campbell, T. Brock, A. S. Luchins, A. R. Cohen, W. J. McGuire, I. J. Janis, R. L. Feierabend, & N. H. Anderson (Eds.), *The order of presentation in persuasion* (pp. 62–75). New Haven, CT: Yale University Press.

Luhmann, N. (1973). *Vertrauen* [Trust]. Stuttgart: Enke.

Major, B. (1980). Information acquisition and attribution processes. *Journal of Personality and Social Psychology, 39*, 1010–1023.

Malinowski, B. (1948). *Magic, science and religion.* New York: Free Press.

Manis, M., & Armstrong, G. W. (1971). Contrast effects in verbal output. *Journal of Experimental Social Psychology, 7,* 381–388.

Manis, M., & Paskewitz, J. R. (1984a). Specificity in contrast effects: Judgments of psychopathology. *Journal of Experimental Social Psychology, 20,* 217–230.

Manis, M., & Paskewitz, J. R. (1984b). Judging psychopathology: Expectation and contrast. *Journal of Experimental Social Psychology, 20,* 363–381.

Manis, M., Dovalina, I., Avis, N. E., & Cardoze, S. (1980). Base rates can affect individual predictions. *Journal of Personality and Social Psychology, 38,* 231–248.

Manis, M., Avis, N. E., & Cardoze S. (1981). Reply to Bar-Hillel and Fischhoff. *Journal of Personality and Social Psychology, 41,* 681–683.

Manz, W. (1968). *Das Stereotyp* [The stereotype]. Meisenheim: Hain.

Manz, W., & Lück, H. E. (1968). Influence of wearing glasses on personality ratings: Crosscultural validation of an old experiment. *Perceptual and Motor Skills, 27,* 704.

Markus, H., & Zajonc, R. B. (1985). The cognitive perspective in social psychology. In G. Lindzey & E. Aronson (Eds.), *Handbook of social psychology* (Vol. 1, pp. 137–230). New York: Random House.

Maruyama, G., & Miller, N. (1980). Physical attractiveness, race, and essay quality. *Personality and Social Psychology Bulletin, 6,* 384–390.

Maruyama, G., & Miller, N. (1981). Physical attractiveness and personality. In B. H. Maher & W. B. Maher (Eds.), *Progress in experimental personality research* (Vol. 10, pp. 203–280). New York: Academic.

Masling, J. (1965). Differential indoctrination of examiners and Rorschach responses. *Journal of Consulting Psychology, 29,* 198–201.

Mayntz, R., Holm, K., & Hübner, P. (1969). *Einführung in die Methoden der empirischen Soziologie* [Introduction to the methods of empirical sociology]. Opladen: Westdeutscher Verlag.

McArthur, L. A. (1972). The how and what of why: Some determinants and consequences of causal attribution. *Journal of Personality and Social Psychology, 22,* 171–193.

McArthur, L. Z. (1976). The lesser influence of consensus than distinctiveness information on causal attributions: A test of the person-thing hypothesis. *Journal of Personality and Social Psychology, 33,* 733–742.

McArthur, L. Z. (1980). Illusory causation and illusory correlation: Two epistemological accounts. *Personality and Social Psychology Bulletin, 6,* 507–519.

McArthur, L. Z. (1981). What grabs you? The role of attention in impression formation and causal attribution. In E. T. Higgins, C. P. Herman, & M. P. Zanna (Eds.), *Social Cognition. The Ontario Symposium* (Vol. 1, pp. 201–246). Hillsdale, NJ: Erlbaum.

McArthur, L. Z. (1982). Judging a book by its cover: A cognitive analysis of the relationship between physical appearance and stereotyping. In A. H. Hastorf & A. M. Isen (Eds.), *Cognitive social psychology* (pp. 149–211). New York: Elsevier.

McArthur, L. Z., & Baron, R. M. (1983). Toward an ecological theory of social perception. *Psychological Review, 90,* 215–238.

McArthur, L. Z., & Friedman, S. A. (1980). Illusory correlation in impression formation: Variations in the shared distinctiveness effect as a function of the distinctive person's age, race, and sex. *Journal of Personality and Social Psychology, 39,* 615–624.

McArthur, L. Z., & Post, D. L. (1977). Figural emphasis and person perception. *Journal of Experimental Social Psychology, 13,* 520–535.

McCauley, C., & Stitt, C. L. (1978). An individual and quantitative measure of stereotypes. *Journal of Personality and Social Psychology, 36,* 929–940.

McCauley, C., Stitt, C. L., & Segal, M. (1980). Stereotyping: From prejudice to prediction. *Psychological Bulletin, 87*, 195–208.

McKee, J. P., & Sherriffs, A. C. (1957). The differential evaluation of males and females. *Journal of Personality, 25*, 356–371.

Meertens, R. W., Koomen, W., Delpeut, A. P., & Hager, G. A. (1984). Effects of hypothesis and assigned task on question selection strategies. *European Journal of Social Psychology, 14*, 369–378.

Mensh, I. M., & Wishner, J. (1947). Asch on "Forming impressions of personality": Further evidence. *Journal of Personality, 16*, 188–191.

Merton, R. K. (1968). *Social theory and social structure*. New York: Free Press.

Merz, F. (1962). Über die Beurteilung der persönlichen Eigenart unserer Mitmenschen [The judgment of personal characteristics in our fellow human beings]. *Archiv für Psychologie, 114*, 187–211.

Messé, L. A., Stollak, G. E., Larson, R. W., & Michaels, G. Y. (1979). Interpersonal consequences of person perception processes in two social contexts. *Journal of Personality and Social Psychology, 37*, 369–379.

Meyer, J. P., & Koelbl, S. L. M. (1982). Students' test performances: Dimensionality of causal attributions. *Personality and Social Psychology Bulletin, 8*, 31–36.

Meyer, J. P., & Mulherin, A. (1980). From attribution to helping: An analysis of the mediating effects of affect and expectancy. *Journal of Personality and Social Psychology, 39*, 201–210.

Meyer, W. U., & Schmalt, H. D. (1978). Die Attributionstheorie [The attribution theory]. In D. Frey (Ed.), *Kognitive Theorien der Sozialpsychologie* (pp. 98–136). Bern: Huber.

Michela, J. L., Peplau, L. A., & Weeks, D. G. (1982). Perceived dimensions of attributions for loneliness. *Journal of Personality and Social Psychology, 43*, 929–936.

Michotte, A. (1963). *The perception of causality*. London: Methuen.

Milgram, S. (1974). *Obedience to authority*. London: Tavistock.

Mill, J. S. (1846). *A system of logic*. New York: Harper.

Miller, A. G., Mayerson, N., Pogue, M., & Whitehouse, D. (1977). Perceivers' explanations of their attributions of attitude. *Personality and Social Psychology Bulletin, 3*, 111–114.

Miller, A. G., Jones, E. E., & Hinkle, S. (1981). A robust attribution error in the personality domain. *Journal of Experimental Social Psychology, 17*, 587–600.

Miller, A. G., Schmidt, D., Meyer, C., & Colella, A. (1984). The perceived value of constrained behavior: Pressures toward biased inference in the attitude attribution paradigm. *Social Psychology Quarterly, 47*, 160–171.

Miller, D. T. (1976). Ego involvement and attributions for success and failure. *Journal of Personality and Social Psychology, 34*, 901–906.

Miller, D. T., & Norman, S. A. (1975). Actor-observer differences in perceptions of effective control. *Journal of Personality and Social Psychology, 31*, 503–515.

Miller, D. T., & Porter, C. A. (1980). Effects of temporal perspective on the attribution process. *Journal of Personality and Social Psychology, 39*, 532–541.

Miller, D. T., & Ross, M. (1975). Self-serving biases in the attribution of causality: Fact or fiction? *Psychological Bulletin, 82*, 213–225.

Miller, D. T., & Turnbull, W. (1986). Expectancies and interpersonal processes. *Annual Review of Psychology, 37*, 233–256.

Miller, D. T., Norman, S. A., & Wright, E. (1978). Distortion in person perceptions as a consequence of the need for effective control. *Journal of Personality and Social Psychology, 36*, 598–607.

Miller, N., & Campbell, D. (1959). Recency and primacy in persuasion as a function of the timing of speeches and measurement. *Journal of Abnormal and Social Psychology, 59*, 1−9.

Miller, N., & Marks, G. (1982). Assumed similarity between self and other: Effect of expectation of future interaction with that other. *Social Psychology Quarterly, 45*, 100−105.

Miller, N., & Zabrack, M. L. (1975). IQ. In H. B. Gerard & N. Miller (Eds.), *School desegregation* (pp. 89−120). New York: Plenum.

Miller, R. L., Brickman, P., & Bolen, D. (1975). Attribution versus persuasion as a means for modifying behavior. *Journal of Personality and Social Psychology, 31*, 430−441.

Mills, J., & Jellison, J. M. (1967). Effect on opinion change of how desirable the communication is to the audience the communicator addressed. *Journal of Personality and Social Psychology, 6*, 98−101.

Monson, T. C. (1983). Implications of the traits v. situations controversy for differences in the attributions of actors and observers. In J. Jaspars, F. D. Fincham, & M. Hewstone (Eds.), *Attribution theory and research: Conceptual, developmental and social dimensions* (pp. 293−313). London: Academic.

Monson, T. C., & Snyder, M. (1977). Actors, observers, and the attribution process: Toward a reconceptualization. *Journal of Experimental Social Psychology, 13*, 89−111.

Montada, L. (1986). *Life stress, injustice, and the question "Who is responsible?"*. Reports from the Department of Psychology, University of Trier, Trier, FRG.

Morse, S., & Gergen, K. J. (1970). Social comparison, self-consistency, and the concept of self. *Journal of Personality and Social Psychology, 16*, 148−156.

Müller, G. F. (1980). Interpersonales Konfliktverhalten [Interpersonal conflict behavior]. *Zeitschrift für Sozialpsychologie, 11*, 168−180.

Mummendey, A. (1985). Verhalten zwischen sozialen Gruppen. Die Theorie der sozialen Identität [Behavior between social groups. The theory of social identity]. In D. Frey & M. Irle (Eds.), *Theorien der Sozialpsychologie* (Vol. 2, pp. 185−216). Bern: Huber.

Murdoch, B. B. (1962). The serial position effect of free recall. *Journal of Experimental Psychology, 64*, 482−488.

Murphy, K. R., & Reynolds, D. H. (1988). Does true halo affect observed halo? *Journal of Applied Psychology, 73*, 235−238.

Nagel, E. (1961). *The structure of science*. New York: Harcourt Brace.

Neuberg, S. L., & Fiske, S. T. (1987). Motivational influences on impression formation: Outcome dependency, accuracy-driven attention, and individuating processes. *Journal of Personality and Social Psychology, 53*, 431−444.

Newtson, D. (1976). Foundations of attribution: The perception of ongoing behavior. In J. H. Harvey, W. J. Ickes, & R. F. Kidd (Eds.), *New directions in attribution research* (Vol. 1, pp. 223−247). Hillsdale, NJ: Erlbaum.

Newtson, D., & Rindner, R. J. (1979). Variation in behavior perception and ability attribution. *Journal of Personality and Social Psychology, 37*, 1847−1858.

Nicholls, J. G. (1976). Effort is virtuous, but it's better to have ability: Evaluative responses to perceptions of effort and ability. *Journal of Research in Personality, 10*, 306−315.

Nisbett, R. E., & Borgida, E. (1975). Attribution and the psychology of prediction. *Journal of Personality and Social Psychology, 32*, 932−942.

Nisbett, R. E., & Ross, L. (1980). *Human inference: Strategies and shortcomings of social judgment*. Englewood Cliffs, NJ: Prentice-Hall.

Nisbett, R. E., & Schachter, S. (1966). Cognitive manipulation of pain. *Journal of Experimental Social Psychology, 2*, 227−236.

Nisbett, R. E., Caputo, C., Legant, P., & Marecek, J. (1973). Behavior as seen by the actor and as seen by the observer. *Journal of Personality and Social Psychology, 27*, 154–164.

Nisbett, R. E., Borgida, E., Crandall, R., & Reed, H. (1976). Popular induction: Information is not necessarily informative. In J. S. Carroll & J. W. Payne (Eds.), *Cognition and social behavior* (pp. 113–133). Hillsdale, NJ: Erlbaum.

Nisbett, R. E., Krantz, D. H., Jepson, C., & Fong, G. T. (1982). Improving inductive inference. In D. Kahneman, P. Slovic, & A. Tversky (Eds.), *Judgment under uncertainty: Heuristics and biases* (pp. 445–459). Cambridge, England: Cambridge University Press.

Nisbett, R. E., Krantz, D. H., Jepson, C., & Kunda, Z. (1983). The use of statistical heuristics in everyday inductive reasoning. *Psychological Review, 90*, 339–363.

O'Connell, E. J., Dusek, J. B., & Wheeler, R. J. (1974). A follow-up study of teacher expectancy effects. *Journal of Educational Psychology, 66*, 325–328.

Orvis, B. R., Cunningham, J. D., & Kelley, H. H. (1975). A closer examination of causal inference: The roles of consensus, distinctiveness, and consistency information. *Journal of Personality and Social Psychology, 32*, 605–616.

Orvis, B. R., Kelley, H. H., & Butler, D. (1976). Attributional conflict in young couples. In J. H. Harvey, W. J. Ickes, & R. F. Kidd (Eds.), *New directions in attribution research* (Vol. 1, pp. 353–386). Hillsdale, NJ: Erlbaum.

Ostrom, T. M. (1977). Between-theory and within-theory conflict in explaining context effects in impression formation. *Journal of Experimental Social Psychology, 13*, 492–503.

Passer, M. W., Kelley, H. H., & Michela, J. L. (1978). Multidimensional scaling of the causes for negative interpersonal behavior. *Journal of Personality and Social Psychology, 36*, 951–962.

Peabody, D. (1985). *National characteristics*. Cambridge, England: Cambridge University Press.

Pennington, C. C. (1987). Confirmatory hypothesis testing in face-to-face interaction: An empirical refutation. *British Journal of Social Psychology, 26*, 225–235.

Pepitone, A., & Hayden, R. G. (1955). Some evidence for conflict resolution in impression formation. *Journal of Abnormal and Social Psychology, 51*, 302–307.

Perlman, D., & Oskamp, S. (1971). The effects of picture content and exposure frequency on evaluations of negroes and whites. *Journal of Experimental Social Psychology, 7*, 503–514.

Peterson, C. (1980). Recognition of noncontingency. *Journal of Personality and Social Psychology, 38*, 727–734.

Peterson, C., & Seligman, M. E. P. (1984). Causal explanations as a risk factor for depression: Theory and evidence. *Psychological Review, 91*, 347–374.

Peterson, C., & Villanova, P. (1988). An expanded attributional style questionnaire. *Journal of Abnormal Psychology, 97*, 87–89.

Peterson, C., Semmel, A., von Baeyer, C., Abramson, L. Y., Metalsky, G. I., & Seligman, M. E. P. (1982). The Attributional Style Questionnaire. *Cognitive Therapy and Research, 6*, 287–299.

Peterson, C., Villanova, P., & Raps, C. S. (1985). Depression and attributions: Factors responsible for inconsistent results in the published literature. *Journal of Abnormal Psychology, 94*, 165–168.

Pettigrew, T. F. (1981). Extending the stereotype concept. In D. L. Hamilton (Ed.), *Cognitive processes in stereotyping and intergroup behavior* (pp. 303–331). Hillsdale, NJ: Erlbaum.

Piaget, J. (1932). *The moral judgment of the child*. New York: Harcourt Brace.

Piaget, J. (1952). *The origins of intelligence in children.* New York: International Universities Press.

Pittman, T. S., & D'Agostino, P. R. (1985). Motivation and attribution: The effects of control deprivation on subsequent information processing. In J. H. Harvey & G. Weary (Eds.), *Attribution: Basic issues and applications* (pp. 117–141). Orlando, FL: Academic.

Pittman, T. S., & Pittman, N. L. (1980). Deprivation of control and the attributional process. *Journal of Personality and Social Psychology, 39,* 377–389.

Pittman, T. S., Scherrer, F. W., & Wright, J. B. (1977). The effect of commitment on information utilization in the attribution process. *Personality and Social Psychology Bulletin, 3,* 276–279.

Postman, L., & Phillips, L. W. (1965). Short-term temporal changes in free recall. *Quarterly Journal of Experimental Psychology, 17,* 132–138.

Pruitt, D. J., & Insko, C. A. (1980). Extension of the Kelley attribution model: The role of comparison-object consensus, target-object consensus, distinctiveness, and consistency. *Journal of Personality and Social Psychology, 39,* 39–58.

Pyszczynski, T. A., & Greenberg, J. (1981). Role of disconfirmed expectancies in the instigation of attribution processing. *Journal of Personality and Social Psychology, 40,* 31–38.

Pyszczynski, T. A., & Greenberg, J. (1987). Self-regulatory perseveration and the depressive self-focusing style: A self-awareness theory of reactive depression. *Psychological Bulletin, 102,* 122–138.

Pyszczynski, T. A., Greenberg, J., & LaPrelle, J. (1985). Social comparison after success and failure: Biased search for information consistent with a self-serving conclusion. *Journal of Experimental Social Psychology, 21,* 195–211.

Quattrone, G. A. (1982). Overattribution and unit formation: When behavior engulfs the person. *Journal of Personality and Social Psychology, 42,* 593–607.

Quattrone, G. A., & Jones, E. E. (1978). Selective self-disclosure with and without correspondent performance. *Journal of Experimental Social Psychology, 14,* 511–526.

Raudenbush, S. W. (1984). Magnitude of teacher expectancy effects on pupil IQ as a function of the credibility of expectancy induction: A synthesis of findings from 18 experiments. *Journal of Educational Psychology, 76,* 85–97.

Raven, B. H., & Rubin, J. Z. (1976). *Social Psychology.* New York: Wiley.

Reeder, G. D. (1985). Implicit relations between dispositions and behaviors: Effects on dispositional attribution. In J. H. Harvey & G. Weary (Eds.), *Attribution: Basic issues and applications* (pp. 87–116). Orlando, FL: Academic.

Reeder, G. D., & Brewer, M. B. (1979). A schematic model of dispositional attribution in interpersonal perception. *Psychological Review, 86,* 61–79.

Reeder, G. D., & Fulks, J. L. (1980). When actions speak louder than words. Implicational schemata and the attribution of ability. *Journal of Experimental Social Psychology, 16,* 33–46.

Regan, D. T., & Fazio, R. (1977). On the consistency between attitudes and behavior: Look to the method of attitude formation. *Journal of Experimental Social Psychology, 13,* 28–45.

Regan, D. T., & Totten, J. (1975). Empathy and attribution: Turning observers into actors. *Journal of Personality and Social Psychology, 32,* 850–856.

Reichardt, C. S. (1985). Reinterpreting Seaver's (1973) study of teacher expectancies as a regression artifact. *Journal of Educational Psychology, 77,* 231–236.

Reisenzein, R. (1983). The Schachter theory of emotion: Two decades later. *Psychological Bulletin, 94,* 239–264.

Restorff, H. von (1933). Über die Wirkung von Bereichsbildungen im Spurenfeld [The effect of field formation on memory traces]. *Psychologische Forschung, 18*, 299–342.

Richardson, S. A., Goodman, N., Hastorf, A. H., & Dornbusch, S. M. (1961). Cultural uniformity in reactions to physical disabilities. *American Sociological Review, 26*, 241–247.

Riess, M., Rosenfeld, P., Melburg, V., & Tedeschi, J. T. (1981). Self-serving attributions: Biased private perceptions and distorted public descriptions. *Journal of Personality and Social Psychology, 41*, 224–231.

Riggs, J. M., Monach, E. M., Ogburn, T. A., & Pahides, S. (1983). Inducing self-perceptions: The role of social interaction. *Personality and Social Psychology Bulletin, 9*, 253–260.

Ring, K. (1964). Some determinants of interpersonal attraction in hierarchical relationships: A motivational analysis. *Journal of Personality, 32*, 651–665.

Riskey, D. R. (1979). Verbal memory processes in impression formation. *Journal of Experimental Psychology: Human Learning and Memory, 5*, 271–281.

Rodin, J., & Langer, E. (1980). The decline of control and the fall of self-esteem. *Journal of Social Issues, 36*(2), 12–29.

Rose, T. L. (1981). Cognitive and dyadic processes in intergroup contact. In D. L. Hamilton (Ed.), *Cognitive processes in stereotyping and intergroup behavior* (pp. 259–302). Hillsdale, NJ: Erlbaum.

Rosenberg, S., Nelson, C., & Vivekananthan, P. S. (1968). A multidimensional approach to the structure of personality impression. *Journal of Personality and Social Psychology, 9*, 283–294.

Rosenkrantz, P., Vogel, S., Bee, H., Broverman, J., & Broverman, D. M. (1968). Sex-role stereotypes and self-concepts in college students. *Journal of Consulting and Clinical Psychology, 32*, 287–295.

Rosenthal, R. (1976). *Experimenter effects in behavioral research*. New York: Wiley.

Rosenthal, R. (1984). *Meta-analytic procedures for social research*. Beverly Hills, CA: Sage.

Rosenthal, R. (1985). From unconscious experimenter bias to teacher expectancy effects. In J. B. Dusek (Ed.), *Teacher expectancies* (pp. 37–65). Hillsdale, NJ: Erlbaum.

Rosenthal, R. (1987). Pygmalion effects: Existence, magnitude, and social importance. *Educational Researcher, 16*(9), 37–41.

Rosenthal, R., & Fode, K. L. (1963). The effect of experimenter bias on the performance of the albino rat. *Behavioral Science, 8*, 183–189.

Rosenthal, R., & Jacobson, L. (1968). *Pygmalion in the classroom*. New York: Holt.

Rosenthal, R., & Rosnow, R. L. (1969). *Artifact in behavioral research*. New York: Academic.

Ross, L. (1977). The intuitive psychologist and his shortcomings: Distortions in the attribution process. In L. Berkowitz (Ed.), *Advances in experimental social psychology* (Vol. 10, pp. 173–220). New York: Academic.

Ross, L., & Anderson, C. A. (1982). Shortcomings in the attribution process: On the origins and maintenance of erroneous social assessments. In D. Kahneman, P. Slovic, & A. Tversky (Eds.), *Judgment under uncertainty: Heuristics and biases* (pp. 129–152). Cambridge, England: Cambridge University Press.

Ross L., Bierbrauer, G., & Polly, S. (1974). Attribution of educational outcomes by professional and nonprofessional instructors. *Journal of Personality and Social Psychology, 29*, 609–618.

Ross, L., Lepper, M. R., & Hubbard, M. (1975). Perseverance in self-perception and social perception: Biased attribution processes in the debriefing paradigm. *Journal of Personality and Social Psychology, 32*, 880–892.

Ross, L., Lepper, M. F., Strack, R., & Steinmetz, J. (1977). Social explanation and social expectation: Effects of real and hypothetical explanations on subjective likelihood. *Journal of Personality and Social Psychology, 35*, 817–829.

Ross, M. (1975). Salience of reward and intrinsic motivation. *Journal of Personality and Social Psychology, 32*, 245–254.

Ross, M., & Sicoly, F. (1979). Egocentric biases in availability and attribution. *Journal of Personality and Social Psychology, 37*, 322–336.

Ross, M., Karniol, R., & Rothstein, M. (1976). Reward contingency and intrinsic motivation in children: A test of the delay of gratification hypothesis. *Journal of Personality and Social Psychology, 33*, 442–447.

Ruble, D. N., & Feldman, N. S. (1976). Order of consensus, distinctiveness, and consistency information and causal attributions. *Journal of Personality and Social Psychology, 34*, 930–937.

Ruble, D. N., & Rholes, W. S. (1981). The development of children's perceptions and attributions about their social world. In J. H. Harvey, W. Ickes, & R. F. Kidd (Eds.), *New directions in attribution research* (Vol. 3, pp. 3–36). Hillsdale, NJ: Erlbaum.

Ruble, D. N., & Ruble, T. L. (1982). Sex stereotypes. In A. G. Miller (Ed.), *In the eye of the beholder* (pp. 188–252). New York: Praeger.

Rubovits, P. C., & Maehr, M. L. (1971). Pygmalion analyzed: Toward an explanation of the Rosenthal-Jacobson findings. *Journal of Personality and Social Psychology, 19*, 197–203.

Sackett, P. R. (1982). The interviewer as hypothesis tester: The effects of impressions of an applicant on interviewer questioning strategy. *Personnel Psychology, 35*, 789–804.

Sampson, E. E. (1971). *Social psychology and contemporary society.* New York: Wiley.

Schachter, S., & Singer, J. E. (1962). Cognitive, social and physiological determinants of emotional state. *Psychological Review, 69*, 379–399.

Schäfer, B. (1975). Das Eindrucksdifferential als Instrument zur Einstellungsmessung [The semantic differential as an instrument for measuring attitudes]. In R. Bergler (Ed.), *Das Eindrucksdifferential* (pp. 101–118). Bern: Huber.

Schäfer, B. (1983). Semantische Differential Technik [Semantic differential technique]. In H. Feger & J. Bredenkamp (Eds.), *Datenerhebung* (pp. 154–221). Göttingen: Hogrefe.

Schäfer, B. (1988). Entwicklungslinien der Stereotyp- und Vorurteilsforschung [Trends in research on stereotypes and prejudice]. In B. Schäfer & F. Petermann (Eds.), *Sozialpsychologische Beiträge zum Problem sozialer Orientierung* (pp. 11–65). Cologne: Deutscher Instituts-Verlag.

Schäfer, B., & Six, B. (1978). *Sozialpsychologie des Vorurteils* [Social psychology of prejudice]. Stuttgart: Kohlhammer.

Scheff, T. J. (1974). The labelling theory of mental illness. *American Sociological Review, 39*, 444–452.

Scherer, K. R. (1978). Personality inference from voice quality: The loud voice of extroversion. *European Journal of Social Psychology, 8*, 467–487.

Scherer, K. R. (1979). Personality markers in speech. In K. R. Scherer & H. Giles (Eds.), *Social markers in speech* (pp. 147–209). Cambridge, England: Cambridge University Press.

Scherer, K. R., & Scherer, U. (1982). Nonverbal behavior and impression formation in naturalistic situations. In H. Hiebsch, H. Brandstätter, & H. H. Kelley (Eds.), *Social psychology* (pp. 144–150). Amsterdam: North-Holland.

Scherer, U., Helfrich, H., & Scherer, K. R. (1980). Paralinguistic behavior: Internal push or external pull? In H. Giles, W. P. Robinson, & P. M. Smith (Eds.), *Language* (pp. 279–282). Oxford: Pergamon.

Schlenker, B. R. (1975). Self-presentation: Managing the impression of consistency when reality interferes with self-enhancement. *Journal of Personality and Social Psychology, 32*, 1030–1037.

Schlenker, B. R., & Leary, M. R. (1982). Social anxiety and self-presentation: A conceptualization and model. *Psychological Bulletin, 92*, 641–669.

Schmalt, H.-D. (1983). *Fear of failure motivation and causal attributions of success and failure.* Wuppertal: Wuppertaler Psychologische Berichte.

Schmalt, H.-D. (1986). *Motivationspsychologie* [Motivational psychology]. Stuttgart: Kohlhammer.

Schneider, D. J. (1976). *Social psychology.* Reading, MA: Addison-Wesley.

Schönbach, P., Gollwitzer, P., Stiepel, G., & Wagner, U. (1981). *Education and intergroup attitudes.* London: Academic.

Schwartz, S. H., & Ben David, A. (1976). Responsibility and helping in an emergency: Effects of blame, ability and denial of responsibility. *Sociometry, 39*, 406–415.

Schwartz, S. H., & Gottlieb, A. (1976). Bystander reactions to a violent theft: Crime in Jerusalem. *Journal of Personality and Social Psychology, 34*, 1188–1199.

Seaver, W. B. (1973). Effects of naturally induced teacher expectancies. *Journal of Personality and Social Psychology, 28*, 333–342.

Secord, P. F., & Backman, C. W. (1964). *Social psychology.* New York: McGraw-Hill.

Seligman, M. E. P. (1975). *Helplessness: On depression, development, and death.* San Francisco: Freeman.

Seligman, M. E. P., Abramson, L. Y., Semmel, A., & von Baeyer, C. (1979). Depressive attributional style. *Journal of Abnormal Psychology, 88*, 242–247.

Seligman, M. E. P., Peterson, C., Kaslow, N. J., Tannenbaum, R. L., Alloy, L. B., & Abramson, L. Y. (1984). Explanatory style and depressive symptoms among children. *Journal of Abnormal Psychology, 93*, 235–238.

Seligman, M. E. P., Castellon, C., Cacciola, J., Schulman, P., Luborsky, L., Ollove, M., & Downing, R. (1988). Explanatory style change during cognitive therapy for unipolar depression. *Journal of Abnormal Psychology, 97*, 13–18.

Semin, G. R., & Fiedler, K. (1988). The cognitive functions of linguistic categories in describing persons: Social cognition and language. *Journal of Personality and Social Psychology, 54*, 558–568.

Semin, G. R., & Strack, F. (1980). The plausibility of the implausible: A critique of Synder and Swann (1978). *European Journal of Social Psychology, 10*, 379–388.

Shaver, K. G. (1970). Defensive attribution: Effects of severity and relevance on the responsibility assigned for an accident. *Journal of Personality and Social Psychology, 14*, 101–113.

Shaver, K. G. (1985). *The attribution of blame: Causality, responsibility, and blameworthiness.* New York: Springer.

Shaver, K. G., & Drown, D. (1986). Causality, responsibility, and self-blame: A theoretical note. *Journal of Personality and Social Psychology, 50*, 697–702.

Sherif, M. (1979). Superordinate goals in the reduction of intergroup conflict: An experimental evaluation. In W. G. Austin & S. Worchel (Eds.), *The social psychology of intergroup relations* (pp. 257–261). Monterey, CA: Brooks/Cole.

Sherif, M., & Hovland, C. I. (1961). *Social judgment.* New Haven, CT: Yale University Press.

Sherif, M., Harvey, O. J., White, B. J., Hood, W. R., & Sherif, C. W. (1961). *Intergroup conflict and cooperation: The Robbers Cave Experiment.* Norman, OK: University of Oklahoma Book Exchange.

Sherman, S. J., & Corty, E. (1984). Cognitive heuristics. In R. S. Wyer & T. K. Srull (Eds.), *Handbook of social cognition* (Vol. 1, pp. 189–286). Hillsdale, NJ: Erlbaum.

Sherman, S. J., Ahlm, K., Berman, L., & Lynn, S. (1978). Contrast effects and their relationship to subsequent behavior. *Journal of Experimental Social Psychology, 14,* 340–350.

Sherman, S. J., Skov, R. B., Hervitz, E. F., & Stock, C. B. (1981). The effects of explaining hypothetical future events: From possibility to probability to actuality and beyond. *Journal of Experimental Social Psychology, 17,* 142–158.

Sherriffs, A. C., & McKee, J. P. (1957). Qualitative aspects of beliefs about men and women. *Journal of Personality, 25,* 451–464.

Shultz, T. R., Butkowsky, I., Pearce, J. W., & Shanfield, H. (1975). Development of schemas for the attribution of multiple psychological causes. *Developmental Psychology, 11,* 502–510.

Shweder, K. A. (1975). How relevant is an individual difference theory of personality? *Journal of Personality, 43,* 455–484.

Shweder, K. A. (1980). Factors and fiction in person perception: A reply to Lamiell, Foss, and Cavenee. *Journal of Personality, 48,* 74–81.

Sigall, H., & Landy, D. (1973). Radiating beauty: Effects of having a physically attractive partner on person perception. *Journal of Personality and Social Psychology, 28,* 218–224.

Sigall, H., & Page, R. (1971). Current stereotypes: A little fading, a little faking. *Journal of Personality and Social Psychology, 18,* 247–255.

Simon, J. G., & Feather, N. T. (1973). Causal attributions for success and failure at university examinations. *Journal of Educational Psychology, 64,* 46–56.

Simpson, D. D., & Ostrom, T. M. (1975). Effect of snap and thoughtful judgments on person impression. *European Journal of Social Psychology, 5,* 197–208.

Singer, J. L., & Kolligian, J. (1987). Personality: Developments in the study of private experience. *Annual Review of Psychology, 38,* 533–574.

Six, B., & Schäfer, B. (1985). Einstellungsänderung [Attitude change]. Stuttgart: Kohlhammer.

Sixtl, F. (1982). *Meßmethoden der Psychologie* [Measurement methods of psychology]. Weinheim: Beltz.

Skov, R. B., & Sherman, S. J. (1986). Information-gathering processes: Diagnosticity, hypothesis confirmatory strategies, and perceived hypothesis confirmation. *Journal of Experimental Social Psychology, 22,* 93–121.

Skrypnek, B. J., & Snyder, M. (1982). On the self-perpetuating nature of stereotypes about women and men. *Journal of Experimental Social Psychology, 18,* 277–291.

Slovic, P., Fischhoff, B., & Lichtenstein, S. (1977). Behavioral decision theory. *Annual Review of Psychology, 28,* 1–39.

Slovic, P., & Lichtenstein, S. (1971). Comparison of Bayesian and regression approaches to the study of information processing in judgment. *Organizational Behavior and Human Performance, 6,* 649–744.

Smedslund, J. (1963). The concept of correlation in adults. *Scandinavian Journal of Psychology, 4,* 165–173.

Smith, E. R., & Miller, F. D. (1979). Salience and the cognitive mediation of attribution. *Journal of Personality and Social Psychology, 37,* 2240–2252.

Smith, M. C. (1975). Children's use of the multiple sufficient cause schema in social perception. *Journal of Personality and Social Psychology, 32,* 737–747.

Smith, P. M. (1979). Sex markers in speech. In K. R. Scherer & H. Giles (Eds.), *Social markers in speech* (pp. 109–146). Cambridge, England: Cambridge University Press.

Smoke, K. L. (1933). Negative instances in concept learning. *Journal of Experimental Psychology, 16,* 583–588.

Snyder, M. (1974). Self-monitoring of expressive behavior. *Journal of Personality and Social Psychology, 30,* 526–537.

Snyder, M. (1981). On the self-perpetuating nature of social stereotypes. In D. L. Hamilton (Ed.), *Cognitive processes in stereotyping and intergroup behavior* (pp. 183–212). Hillsdale, NJ: Erlbaum.

Snyder, M. (1984). When belief creates reality. In L. Berkowitz (Ed.), *Advances in experimental social psychology* (Vol. 18, pp. 247–305). Orlando, FL: Academic.

Snyder, M. (1987). *Public appearances, private realities: The psychology of self-monitoring.* New York: Freeman.

Snyder, M., & Campbell, B. H. (1980). Testing hypotheses about other people: The role of the hypothesis. *Personality and Social Psychology Bulletin, 6,* 421–426.

Snyder, M., & Cantor, N. (1979). Testing hypotheses about other people: The use of historical knowledge. *Journal of Experimental Social Psychology, 15,* 330–342.

Snyder, M., & Gangestad, S. (1981). Hypothesis-testing processes. In J. H. Harvey, W. Ickes, & R. F. Kidd (Eds.), *New directions in attribution research* (Vol. 3, pp. 171–196). Hillsdale, NJ: Erlbaum.

Snyder, M., & Kendzierski, D. (1982). Acting on one's attitudes: Procedures for linking attitudes and behavior. *Journal of Experimental Social Psychology, 18,* 165–183.

Snyder, M., & Simpson, J. A. (1984). Self-monitoring and dating relationships. *Journal of Personality and Social Psychology, 47,* 1281–1291.

Snyder, M., & Skrypnek, B. J. (1981). Testing hypotheses about the self: Assessment of job suitability. *Journal of Personality, 49,* 193–211.

Snyder, M., & Swann, W. B. (1978 a). Behavioral confirmation in social interaction: From social perception to social reality. *Journal of Experimental Social Psychology, 14,* 148–162.

Snyder, M., & Swann, W. B. (1978 b). Hypothesis-testing processes in social interaction. *Journal of Personality and Social Psychology, 36,* 1202–1212.

Snyder, M., & Uranowitz, S. W. (1978). Reconstructing the past: Some cognitive consequences of person perception. *Journal of Personality and Social Psychology, 36,* 941–950.

Snyder, M., & White, P. (1981). Testing hypothesis about other people: Strategies of verification and falsification. *Personality and Social Psychology Bulletin, 7,* 39–43.

Snyder, M., Tanke, E. D., & Berscheid, E. (1977). Social perception and interpersonal behavior: On the self-fulfilling nature of social stereotypes. *Journal of Personality and Social Psychology, 35,* 656–666.

Snyder, M., Campbell, B. H., & Preston, E. (1982). Testing hypotheses about human nature: Assessing the accuracy of social stereotypes. *Social Cognition, 1,* 256–272.

Snyder, M., Berscheid, E., & Glick, P. (1985). Focusing on the exterior and the interior: Two investigations of the initiation of personal relationships. *Journal of Personality and Social Psychology, 48,* 1427–1439.

Synder, M. L., & Frankel, A. (1976). Observer bias: A stringent test of behavior engulfing the field. *Journal of Personality and Social Psychology, 34,* 857–864.

Snyder, M. L., & Jones, E. E. (1974). Attitude attribution when behavior is constrained. *Journal of Experimental Social Psychology, 10*, 585–600.

Snyder, M. L., Stephan, W. G., & Rosenfield, D. (1976). Egotism and attribution. *Journal of Personality and Social Psychology, 33*, 435–441.

Snyder, M. L., Stephan, W. G., & Rosenfield, D. (1978). Attributional egotism. In J. H. Harvey, W. J. Ickes, & R. F. Kidd (Eds.), *New directions in attribution research* (Vol. 2, pp. 91–117). Hillsdale, NJ: Erlbaum.

Snyder, M. L., & Wicklund, R. A. (1981). Attribute ambiguity. In J. H. Harvey, W. Ickes, & R. F. Kidd (Eds.), *New directions in attribution research* (Vol. 3, pp. 197–221). Hillsdale, NJ: Erlbaum.

Sodhi, K. S., & Bergius, R. (1953). *Nationale Vorurteile* [National prejudices]. Berlin: Duncker & Humblot.

Solomon, S. (1978). Measuring dispositional and situational attributions. *Personality and Social Psychology Bulletin, 4*, 589–594.

Spence, J. T., & Helmreich, R. L. (1978). *Masculinity & femininity: Their psychological dimensions, correlates, and antecedents.* Austin, TX: University of Texas Press.

Spence, J. T., Helmreich, R., & Stapp, J. (1975). Ratings of self and peers on sex role attributes and their relation to self-esteem and conceptions of masculinity and femininity. *Journal of Personality and Social Psychology, 32*, 29–39.

Srull, T. K. (1984). Methodological techniques for the study of person memory and social cognition. In R. S. Wyer & T. K. Srull (Eds.), *Handbook of social cognition* (Vol. 2, pp. 1–72). Hillsdale, NJ: Erlbaum.

Srull, T. K., & Wyer, R. S. (1979). The role of category accessibility in the interpretation of information about persons: Some determinants and implications. *Journal of Personality and Social Psychology, 37*, 1660–1672.

Srull, T. K., & Wyer, R. S. (1980). Category accessibility and social perception: Some implications for the study of person memory and interpersonal judgments. *Journal of Personality and Social Psychology, 38*, 841–856.

Stapf, K. H., Stroebe, W., & Jonas, K. (1986). *Amerikaner über Deutschland und die Deutschen. Urteile und Vorurteile* [American views of Germany and the Germans. Judgments and prejudices]. Opladen: Westdeutscher Verlag.

Staub, E. (1970). A child in distress: The effect of focusing responsibility on children on their attempts to help. *Developmental Psychology, 2*, 152–153.

Staub, E. (1978/1979). *Positive social behavior and morality* (2 Vols.). New York: Academic.

Staub, E., Bar-Tal, D., Karylowski, J., & Reykowski, J. (Eds., 1984). *Development and maintenance of prosocial behavior.* New York: Plenum.

Staudenmayer, H. (1975). Understanding conditional reasoning with meaningful propositions. In R. J. Falmagne (Ed.), *Reasoning: Representation and process* (pp. 55–79). Hillsdale, NJ: Erlbaum.

Stegmüller, W. (1969). *Probleme und Resultate der Wissenschaftstheorie und Analytischen Philosophie: Vol. 1. Wissenschaftliche Erklärung und Begründung* [Problems and results of the philosophy of science and analytical philosophy: Vol. 1. Scientific explanation and reasoning]. Berlin: Springer.

Stephan, C., Burnam, M. A., & Aronson, E. (1979). Attributions for success and failure after cooperation, competition, or team competition. *European Journal of Social Psychology, 9*, 109–114.

Stephan, W. G., & Feagin, J. R. (1979). *School desegregation.* New York: Plenum.

Stephan, W. G., & Stephan, C. W. (1984). The role of ignorance in intergroup relations. In N. Miller & M. B. Brewer (Eds.), *Groups in contact: The psychology of desegregation* (pp. 229–255). Orlando, FL: Academic.

Stevens, L., & Jones, E. E. (1976). Defensive attribution and the Kelley cube. *Journal of Personality and Social Psychology, 34*, 809–820.

Stewart, R. H. (1965). Effect of continuous responding on the order effect in personality impression formation. *Journal of Personality and Social Psychology, 1*, 161–165.

Storms, M. D. (1973). Videotape and the attribution process: Reversing actors' and observers' points of view. *Journal of Personality and Social Psychology, 27*, 165–175.

Strack, F. (1988). Social cognition: Sozialpsychologie innerhalb des Paradigmas der Informationsverarbeitung [Social cognition: Social psychology within the information processing paradigm]. *Psychologische Rundschau, 39*, 72–82.

Strack, F., Erber, R., & Wicklund, R. A. (1982). Effects of salience and time pressure on ratings of social causality. *Journal of Experimental Social Psychology, 18*, 581–594.

Strickland, L. H. (1958). Surveillance and trust. *Journal of Personality, 26*, 200–215.

Stroebe, W. (1980). *Grundlagen der Sozialpsychologie* [Fundamentals of social psychology]. Stuttgart: Klett.

Stroebe, W., & Insko, C. A. (in press). Stereotype, prejudice and discrimination. Changing conceptions in theory and research. In D. Bar-Tal, C. F. Grauman, A. W. Kruglanski, & W. Stroebe (Eds.), *Stereotypes and prejudice: Changing conceptions*. New York: Springer.

Stroebe, W., Lenkert, A., & Jonas, K. (1988). Familiarity may breed contempt: The impact of student exchange on national stereotypes and attitudes. In W. Stroebe, A. W. Kruglanski, D. Bar-Tal, & M. Hewstone (Eds.), *The social psychology of intergroup conflict* (pp. 167–187). Berlin: Springer.

Strohmer, D. C., & Chiodo, A. L. (1984). Counselor hypothesis testing strategies: The role of initial impressions and self-schema. *Journal of Counseling Psychology, 31*, 510–519.

Strohmer, D. C., & Newman, L. J. (1983). Counselor hypothesis-testing strategies. *Journal of Counseling Psychology, 30*, 557–565.

Suls, J., Witenberg, S., & Gutkin, D. (1981). Evaluating reciprocal and nonreciprocal prosocial behavior: Developmental changes. *Personality and Social Psychology Bulletin, 7*, 25–31.

Sumner, W. G. (1906). *Folkways*. New York: Ginn.

Swann, W. B. (1984). Quest for accuracy in person perception: A matter of pragmatics. *Psychological Review, 91*, 457–477.

Swann, W. B. (1987). Identity negotiation: Where two roads meet. *Journal of Personality and Social Psychology, 53*, 1038–1051.

Swann, W. B., & Ely, R. J. (1984). A battle of wills: Self-verification versus behavioral confirmation. *Journal of Personality and Social Psychology, 46*, 1287–1302.

Swann, W. B., & Hill, C. A. (1982). When our identities are mistaken: Reaffirming self-conceptions through social interaction. *Journal of Personality and Social Psychology, 43*, 59–66.

Swann, W. B., & Read, S. J. (1981). Self-verification processes: How we sustain our self-conceptions. *Journal of Experimental Social Psychology, 17*, 351–372.

Swann, W. B., Stephenson, B., & Pittman, T. S. (1981). Curiosity and control: On the determinants of the search for social knowledge. *Journal of Personality and Social Psychology, 40*, 977–989.

Sweeney, P. D., Anderson, K., & Bailey S. (1986). Attributional style in depression: A meta-analytic review. *Journal of Personality and Social Psychology, 50*, 974–991.

Tajfel, H. (1957). Value and the perceptual judgment of magnitude. *Psychological Review,* *64,* 192–204.

Tajfel, H. (1978). Social categorization, social identity and social comparison. In H. Tajfel (Ed.), *Differentiation between social groups: Studies in the social psychology of intergroup relations* (pp. 61–76). London: Academic.

Tajfel, H. (Ed., 1982). *Social identity and intergroup relations.* Cambridge, England: Cambridge University Press.

Tajfel, H., & Turner, J. (1979). An integrative theory of intergroup conflict. In W. G. Austin & S. Worchel (Eds.), *The social psychology of intergroup relations* (pp. 33–47). Monterey, CA: Brooks/Cole.

Tajfel, H., & Turner, J. (1986). The social-identity theory of intergroup conflict. In S. Worchel & W. G. Austin (Eds.), *Psychology of intergroup relations* (pp. 7–24). Chicago, IL: Nelson Hall.

Tajfel, H., & Wilkes, A. L. (1963). Classification and quantitative judgment. *British Journal of Psychology, 54,* 101–114.

Taylor, M. C., & Hall, J. A. (1982). Psychological androgyny: Theories, methods, and conclusions. *Psychological Bulletin, 92,* 347–366.

Taylor, S. E. (1981). A categorization approach to stereotyping. In D. L. Hamilton (Ed.), *Cognitive processes in stereotyping and intergroup behavior* (pp. 83–114). Hillsdale, NJ: Erlbaum.

Taylor, S. E., & Brown, J. D. (1988). Illusion and well-being: A social psychological perspective on mental health. *Psychological Bulletin, 103,* 193–210.

Taylor, S. E., & Crocker, J. (1981). Schematic basis of social information processing. In E. T. Higgins, C. P. Herman, & M. P. Zanna (Eds.), *Social cognition. The Ontario Symposium* (Vol. 1, pp. 89–134). Hillsdale, NJ: Erlbaum.

Taylor, S. E., & Fiske, S. T. (1975). Point of view and perceptions of causality. *Journal of Personality and Social Psychology, 32,* 439–445.

Taylor, S. E., & Fiske, S. T. (1978). Salience, attention, and attribution: Top of the head phenomena. In L. Berkowitz (Ed.), *Advances in experimental social psychology* (Vol. 11, pp. 249–288). New York: Academic.

Taylor, S. E., & Fiske, S. T. (1981). Getting inside the head: Methodologies for process analysis in attribution and social cognition. In J. H. Harvey, W. Ickes, & R. F. Kidd (Eds.). *New directions in attribution research* (Vol. 3, pp. 459–524). Hillsdale, NJ: Erlbaum.

Taylor, S. E., Fiske, S. T., Etcoff, N. L., & Ruderman, A. J. (1978). Categorical and contextual bases of person memory and stereotyping. *Journal of Personality and Social Psychology, 36,* 778–793.

Taylor, S. E., Crocker, J., Fiske, S. T., Sprinzen, M., & Winkler, J. D. (1979). The generalizability of salience effects. *Journal of Personality and Social Psychology, 37,* 357–368.

Ternus, J. (1926). Experimentelle Untersuchungen über phänomenale Identität [Experimental research on phenomenal identity]. *Psychologische Forschung, 7,* 81–136.

Tesser, A. (1980). Self-esteem maintenance in family dynamics. *Journal of Personality and Social Psychology, 39,* 77–91.

Tetlock, P. E. (1983). Accountability and the perseverance of first impressions. *Social Psychology Quarterly, 46,* 285–292.

Tetlock, P. E., & Levi, A. (1982). Attribution bias: On the inconclusiveness of the cognition-motivation debate. *Journal of Experimental Social Psychology, 18,* 68–88.

Tetlock, P. E., & Manstead, A. S. R. (1985). Impression management versus intrapsychic explanations in social psychology: A useful dichotomy? *Psychological Review, 92,* 59–77.

Thibaut, J. W., & Riecken, H. W. (1955). Some determinants and consequences of the perception of social causality. *Journal of Personality, 24,* 113–133.

Thomae, H. (1970). Theory of aging and cognitive theory of personality. *Human Development, 13,* 1–16.

Thompson, D. D. (1972). Attribution of ability from patterns of performance under competitive and cooperative conditions. *Journal of Personality and Social Psychology, 23,* 302–308.

Thompson, S. C., & Kelley, H. H. (1981). Judgments of responsibility for activities in close relationships. *Journal of Personality and Social Psychology, 41,* 469–477.

Thorndike, E. L. (1920). A constant error in psychological rating. *Journal of Applied Psychology, 4,* 25–29.

Thornton, B. (1984). Defensive attribution of responsibility: Evidence for an arousal-based motivational bias. *Journal of Personality and Social Psychology, 46,* 721–734.

Thornton, B., Hogate, L., Moirs, K., Pinette, M., & Presly, W. (1986). Physiological evidence of an arousal-based motivational bias in the defensive attribution of responsibility. *Journal of Experimental Social Psychology, 22,* 148–162.

Town, J. P., & Harvey, J. H. (1981). Self-disclosure, attribution, and social interaction. *Social Psychology Quarterly, 44,* 291–300.

Trope, Y., & Bassok, M. (1983). Information-gathering strategies in hypothesis-testing. *Journal of Experimental Social Psychology, 19,* 560–576.

Trope, Y., Bassok, M., & Alon, E. (1984). The questions lay interviewers ask. *Journal of Personality, 52,* 90–106.

Tulving, E. (1972). Episodic and semantic memory. In E. Tulving & W. Donaldson (Eds.), *Organization of memory* (pp. 381–403). New York: Academic.

Tulving, E., & Thomson, D. M. (1973). Encoding specificity and retrieval processes in episodic memory. *Psychological Review, 80,* 352–373.

Turner, J. C. (1984). Social identification and psychological group formation. In H. Tajfel (Ed.), *The social dimension: European developments in social psychology* (Vol. 2, pp. 518–538). Cambridge, England: Cambridge University Press.

Turner, J. C., & Oakes, P. J. (1986). The significance of the social identity concept for social psychology with reference to individualism, interactionism and social influence. *British Journal of Social Psychology, 25,* 237–252.

Tversky, A., & Kahneman, D. (1974). Judgment under uncertainty: Heuristics and biases. *Science, 185,* 1124–1131.

Tversky, A., & Kahneman, D. (1980). Causal schemas in judgments under uncertainty. In M. Fishbein (Ed.), *Progress in social psychology* (pp. 49–72). Hillsdale, NJ: Erlbaum.

Tyler, T. R. (1986). The psychology of leadership evaluation. In H. W. Bierhoff, R. L. Cohen, & J. Greenberg (Eds.), *Justice in social relations* (pp. 299–316). New York: Plenum.

Upmeyer, A. (1985). *Soziale Urteilsbildung* [Social judgment formation]. Stuttgart: Kohlhammer.

Vallacher, R. R., & Wegner, D. M. (1985). *A theory of action identification.* Hillsdale, NJ: Erlbaum.

Vallacher, R. R., & Wegner, D. M. (1987). What do people think they're doing? Action identification and human behavior. *Psychological Review, 94,* 3–15.

Vetter, H. (1961). Zur Lage der Frau an den westdeutschen Hochschulen [The situation of women in West German universities]. *Kölner Zeitschrift für Soziologie und Sozialpsychologie, 13,* 644–660.

Vinokur, A., & Ajzen, I. (1982). Relative importance of prior and immediate events: A causal primacy effect. *Journal of Personality and Social Psychology, 42,* 820–829.

Wallbott, H. G., & Scherer, K. R. (1980). Normal speech − normal people? Speculations on paralinguistic features, arousal and social competence attribution. In H. Giles, W. P. Robinson, & P. M. Smith (Eds.), *Language* (pp. 275−278). Oxford: Pergamon.

Walster, E., Berscheid, E., Abrahams, D., & Aronson, V. (1967). Effectiveness of debriefing following deception experiments. *Journal of Personality and Social Psychology, 6*, 371−380.

Wason, P. C., & Johnson-Laird, P. N. (1972). *Psychology of reasoning.* London: Batsford.

Watkins, M. J., & Peynircioğlu, Z. F. (1984). Determining perceived meaning during impression formation: Another look at the meaning change hypothesis. *Journal of Personality and Social Psychology, 46*, 1005−1016.

Watson, D. (1982). The actor and the observer: How are their perceptions of causality divergent? *Psychological Bulletin, 92*, 682−700.

Weary, G. (1980). Examination of affect and egotism as mediators of bias in causal attributions. *Journal of Personality and Social Psychology, 38*, 348−357.

Weary, G., & Arkin, R. M. (1981). Attributional self-presentation. In J. H. Harvey, W. Ickes, & R. F. Kidd (Eds.), *New directions in attribution research* (Vol. 3, pp. 223−246). Hillsdale, NJ: Erlbaum.

Weiner, B. (1972). *Theories of motivation: From mechanism to cognition.* Chicago: Rand McNally.

Weiner, B. (1974). Achievement motivation as conceptualized by an attribution theorist. In B. Weiner (Ed.), *Achievement motivation and attribution theory* (pp. 3−48). Morristown, NJ: General Learning Press.

Weiner, B. (1976). Motivation from the cognitive perspective. In W. K. Estes (Ed.), *Handbook of learning and cognitive processes* (Vol. 3, pp. 283−308). Hillsdale, NJ: Erlbaum.

Weiner, B. (1979). A theory of motivation for some classroom experiences. *Journal of Educational Psychology, 71*, 3−25.

Weiner, B. (1980a). May I borrow your classnotes? An attributional analysis of judgments of help-giving in an achievement-related context. *Journal of Educational Psychology, 72*, 676−681.

Weiner, B. (1980b). A cognitive (attribution)-emotion-action model of motivated behavior: An analysis of judgments of help-giving. *Journal of Personality and Social Psychology, 39*, 186−200.

Weiner, B. (1985a). "Spontaneous" causal thinking. *Psychological Bulletin, 97*, 74−84.

Weiner, B. (1985b). An attributional theory of achievement motivation and emotion. *Psychological Review, 92*, 548−573.

Weiner, B. (1986). *An attributional theory of motivation and emotion.* New York: Springer.

Weiner, B., Frieze, I., Kukla, A., Reed, L., Rest, S., & Rosenbaum, R. M. (1972). Perceiving the causes of success and failure. In E. E. Jones, D. E. Kanouse, H. H. Kelley, R. E. Nisbett, S. Valins, & B. Weiner (Eds.), *Attribution: Perceiving the causes of behavior* (pp. 95−120). Morristown, NJ: General Learning Press.

Weiner, B., Russell, D., & Lerman, D. (1978). Affective consequences of causal ascriptions. In J. H. Harvey, W. J. Ickes, & R. F. Kidd (Eds.), *New directions in attribution research* (Vol. 2, pp. 59−90). Hillsdale, NJ: Erlbaum.

Weiner, B., Russell, D., & Lerman, D. (1979). The cognition-emotion process in achievement-related contexts. *Journal of Personality and Social Psychology, 37*, 1211−1220.

Weiss, D. S. (1979). The effects of systematic variations in information on judges' descriptions of personality. *Journal of Personality and Social Psychology, 37*, 2121−2136.

Wells, G. L., & Harvey, J. H. (1977). Do people use consensus information in making causal attributions? *Journal of Personality and Social Psychology, 35*, 279−293.

West, S. G., & Brown, T. J. (1975). Physical attractiveness, the severity of the emergency and helping: A field experiment and interpersonal simulation. *Journal of Experimental Social Psychology, 11,* 531–538.

West, S. G., Gunn, S. P., & Chernicky, P. (1975). Ubiquitous Watergate: An attributional analysis. *Journal of Personality and Social Psychology, 32,* 55–65.

Wicklund, R. A. (1974). *Freedom and reactance.* Potomac, MD: Erlbaum.

Wicklund, R. A. (1982). Self-focused attention and the validity of self-reports. In M. P. Zanna, E. T. Higgins, & C. P. Herman (Eds.), *Consistency in social behavior. The Ontario Symposium* (Vol. 2, pp. 149–172). Hillsdale, NJ: Erlbaum.

Widiger, T. A., & Settle, S. A. (1987). Broverman et al. revisited: An artifactual sex bias. *Journal of Personality and Social Psychology, 53,* 463–469.

Widmeyer, W. N., & Loy, J. W. (1988). When you're hot, you're hot! Warm-cold effects in first impressions of persons and teaching effectiveness. *Journal of Educational Psychology, 80,* 118–121.

Wills, T. A. (1981). Downward comparison principles in social psychology. *Psychological Bulletin, 90,* 245–271.

Wilson, T. D., & Lassiter, G. D. (1982). Increasing intrinsic interest with superfluous extrinsic constraints. *Journal of Personality and Social Psychology, 42,* 811–819.

Wimer, S., & Kelley, H. H. (1982). An investigation of the dimensions of causal attributions. *Journal of Personality and Social Psychology, 43,* 1142–1162.

Wineburg, S. S. (1987). The self-fulfillment of the self-fulfilling prophecy. *Educational Researcher, 16*(9), 28–37.

Wishner, J. (1960). Reanalysis of "impressions of personality". *Psychological Review, 67,* 96–112.

Wolf, H. E. (1979). *Kritik der Vorurteilsforschung* [Criticism of research on prejudice]. Stuttgart: Enke.

Wolosin, R., Sherman, S. J., & Mynatt, C. R. (1972). Perceived social influence in a conformity situation. *Journal of Personality and Social Psychology, 23,* 184–191.

Wolosin, R. J., Sherman, S. J., & Till, A. (1973). Effects of cooperation and competition on responsibility attribution after success and failure. *Journal of Experimental Social Psychology, 9,* 220–235.

Word, C. O., Zanna, M. P., & Cooper, J. (1974). The nonverbal mediation of self-fulfilling prophecies in interracial interaction. *Journal of Experimental Social Psychology, 10,* 109–120.

Wortman, C. B. (1976). Causal attributions and personal control. In J. G. Harvey, W. J. Ickes, & R. F. Kidd (Eds.), *New directions in attribution research* (Vol. 1, pp. 23–52). Hillsdale, NJ: Erlbaum.

Wortman, C. B., Costanzo, P. R., & Witt, T. R. (1973). Effect of anticipated performance on the attributions of causality to self and others. *Journal of Personality and Social Psychology, 27,* 372–381.

Wrightsman, L. S. (1972). *Social psychology in the seventies.* Belmont, CA: Brooks/Cole.

Wyer, R. S. (1974). Changes in meaning and halo effects in impression formation. *Journal of Personality and Social Psychology, 29,* 829–835.

Wyer, R. S. (1976). An investigation of the relations among probability estimates. *Organizational Behavior and Human Performance, 15,* 1–18.

Wyer, R. S. (1977). The role of logical and nonlogical factors in making inferences about category membership. *Journal of Experimental Social Psychology, 13,* 577–595.

Wyer, R. S., & Carlston, D. E. (1979). *Social cognition, inference, and attribution.* Hillsdale, NJ: Erlbaum.

Wyer, R. S., & Dermer, M. (1968). Effects of context and instructional set upon evaluations of personality-trait adjectives. *Journal of Personality and Social Psychology, 9,* 7–14.

Wyer, R. S., & Gordon, S. E. (1982). The recall of information about persons and groups. *Journal of Experimental Social Psychology, 18,* 128–164.

Wyer, R. S., & Gordon, S. E. (1984). The cognitive representation of social information. In R. S. Wyer & T. K. Srull (Eds.), *Handbook of social cognition* (Vol. 2, pp. 73–150). Hillsdale, NJ: Erlbaum.

Wyer, R. S., & Srull, T. K. (1980). The processing of social stimulus information: A conceptual integration. In R. Hastie, T. M. Ostrom, E. B. Ebbesen, R. S. Wyer, D. L. Hamilton, & D. E. Carlston (Eds.), *Person memory: Cognitive basis for social perception* (pp. 227–300). Hillsdale, NJ: Erlbaum.

Wyer, R. S., & Srull, T. K. (1981). Category accessibility: Some theoretical and empirical issues concerning the processing of social stimulus information. In E. T. Higgins, C. P. Herman, & M. P. Zanna (Eds.), *Social cognition. The Ontario Symposium* (Vol. 1, pp. 161–197). Hillsdale, NJ: Erlbaum.

Wyer, R. S., & Srull, T. K. (Eds., 1984). *Handbook of social cognition* (3 Vols.). Hillsdale, NJ: Erlbaum.

Wyer, R. S., & Srull, T. K. (1986). Human cognition in its social context. *Psychological Review, 93,* 322–359.

Wyer, R. S., & Watson, S. F. (1969). Context effects in impression formation. *Journal of Personality and Social Psychology, 12,* 22–33.

Wyer, R. S., Bodenhausen, G. V., & Srull, T. K. (1984). The cognitive representation of persons and groups and its effect on recall and recognition memory. *Journal of Experimental Social Psychology, 20,* 445–469.

Wyer, R. S., Srull, T. K., & Gordon, S. (1984). The effects of predicting a person's behavior on subsequent trait judgments. *Journal of Experimental Social Psychology, 20,* 29–46.

Yarkin, K. L., Harvey, J. H., & Bloxom, B. M. (1981). Cognitive sets, attribution, and social interaction. *Journal of Personality and Social Psychology, 41,* 243–252.

Yarmey, A. D., & Johnson, J. (1982). Evidence for the self as an imaginal prototype. *Journal of Research in Personality, 16,* 238–246.

Zadney, J., & Gerard, H. B. (1974). Attributed intentions and informational selectivity. *Journal of Experimental Social Psychology, 10,* 34–52.

Zand, D. E. (1972). Trust and managerial problem solving. *Administrative Science Quarterly, 17,* 229–240.

Zanna, M. P., & Hamilton, D. L. (1972). Attribute dimensions and patterns of trait inferences. *Psychonomic Science, 27,* 353–354.

Zanna, M. P., & Hamilton, D. L. (1977). Further evidence for meaning change in impression formation. *Journal of Experimental Social Psychology, 13,* 224–238.

Zanna, M. P., Higgins, E. T., & Herman, C. P. (1982). *Consistency in social behavior. The Ontario Symposium* (Vol. 2). Hillsdale, NJ: Erlbaum.

Zillmann, D. (1971). Excitation transfer in communication-mediated aggressive behavior. *Journal of Experimental Social Psychology, 7,* 419–434.

Zillmann, D. (1978). Attribution and misattribution of excitatory reactions. In J. H. Harvey, W. J. Ickes, & R. F. Kidd (Eds.), *New directions in attribution research* (Vol. 2, pp. 335–368). Hillsdale, NJ: Erlbaum.

Zillmann, D. (1979). *Hostility and aggression.* Hillsdale, NJ: Erlbaum.

Zuckerman, M. (1978). Actions and occurrences in Kelley's cube. *Journal of Personality and Social Psychology, 36,* 647–656.

Zuckerman, M. (1979). Attribution of success and failure revisited, or: The motivational bias is alive and well in attribution theory. *Journal of Personality, 47,* 245–287.

Zuckerman, M., & Mann, R. W. (1979). The other way around: Effects of causal attributions on estimates of consensus, distinctiveness, and consistency. *Journal of Experimental Social Psychology, 15,* 582–597.

Zuckerman, M., Eghari, H., & Lambrecht, M. R. (1986). Attributions as inferences and explanations: Conjunctive effects. *Journal of Personality and Social Psychology, 51,* 1144–1153.

Author Index

Subject Index

Springer Series in Social Psychology

Springer Series in Social Psychology

Springer Series in Social Psychology